Sustainable Tourism:
A Global Perspective

Edited by
Rob Harris, Tony Griffin and Peter Williams

BUTTERWORTH
HEINEMANN

OXFORD AMSTERDAM BOSTON LONDON NEW YORK PARIS
SAN DIEGO SAN FRANCISCO SINGAPORE SYDNEY TOKYO

Butterworth-Heinemann
An imprint of Elsevier Science Limited
Linacre House, Jordan Hill, Oxford OX2 8DP
200 Wheeler Road, Burlington MA 01803

First published 2002

British Library Cataloguing in Publication Data
A catalogue record for this book is available from the British Library

Library of Congress Cataloguing in Publication Data
Sustainable tourism: a global perspective/edited by Rob Harris,
    Tony Griffin, and Peter Williams.
       p. cm.
    Includes bibliographical references.
    1. Ecotourism.   I. Harris, Rob, 1957–.   II. Griffin, Tony, 1954–.
    III. Williams, Peter, 1946 July 20–

    G156.5.E26 S87 2003   2002033207
    338.4'791 – dc21

ISBN 0 7506 89463

For information on all Butterworth-Heinemann publications visit
our website at www.bh.com

Composition by Genesis Typesetting, Rochester, Kent
Printed and bound in Great Britain by MPG Books Ltd, Bodmin

Sustainable Tourism: A Global Perspective

Contents

Acknowledgements

We would like to thank the contributors to this book, without whose passion for the area, and willingness to share their perspectives and insights, this book would not have progressed beyond 'the nice idea stage'. We also owe a debt of gratitude to our respective families for allowing us the time to complete this project, and to Sally North, Neil Coffey and Kathryn Grant at Butterworth-Heinemann for their support and encouragement.

List of contributors

André Brasser is PAN Parks Communications Manager, World Wide Fund for Nature – Netherlands (abrasser@wwfnet.org).

Terry DeLacey is Chief Executive, Cooperative Research Centre for Sustainable Tourism, Gold Coast, Australia. The CRC is a partnership between industry, universities and governments, to 'deliver innovation to enhance the environmental, economic and social sustainability of tourism'. It is part of the Australian government's Cooperative Research Centre's Programme which competitively establishes and seed-funds high quality, long-term, collaborative research centres with a strong focus on commercial outcomes. Previously, Dr DeLacey was foundation Dean of the Faculty of Land and Food Systems at the University of Queensland where he continues to hold a chair in environmental policy (T.DeLacy@mailbox.gu.edu.au).

Xavier Font is a Senior Lecturer in Tourism Management at Leeds Metropolitan University (UK), and member of the PAN Parks Advisory Board. His education is in tourism management and marketing, and his research focuses on marketing and management of ecolabels in tourism and hospitality. He has co-authored and co-edited three books in English (*Tourism ecolabelling: certification and promotion of sustainable management; Environmental management for rural tourism and recreation; Forest tourism and recreation*) and one in Spanish (*Marketing of tourist destinations: analysis and development*). Xavier has undertaken research and consultancy on ecolabels, sustainable development, and ecotourism for the EC, WWF, UNEP and WTO (X.Font@lmu.ac.uk).

Tony Griffin is a Senior Lecturer in the School of Leisure, Sport and Tourism, University of Technology, Sydney (UTS) and New South Wales node coordinator for the Cooperative Research Centre in Sustainable Tourism. Tony has worked in planning at local and federal government levels and, prior to joining the UTS in 1989, spent ten years teaching at the then Hawkesbury Agricultural College (now University of Western Sydney). He has published articles on hotel development and tourism environmental and educational issues, as well as being involved in consultancy projects dealing with resort/hotel feasibilities, tourism policy issues, environmental and social impacts of tourism, and tourism education and graduate career development. In recent years Tony has directed several major research projects dealing with visitor satisfaction in national parks, in association with the New South Wales National Parks Service.

Sam H. Ham is Director of the Center for International Training and Outreach and Professor of Environmental Communication and International Conservation at the University of Idaho's College of Natural Resources, Department of Resource Recreation and Tourism. He also holds courtesy appointments as Adjunct Professor in the Department of Management, Monash University, Australia, and as Affiliate Professor in the Department of Recreation Resources and Tourism at Colorado State University, USA. His research has focused on ecotourism guide training and obstacles to formal and non-formal environmental education in Latin America and the Caribbean, and more recently in Asia and the Pacific. He has authored more than 200 publications, including two widely acclaimed books on interpretive methods. In 1992 Sam was appointed to the Commission on Education and Communication by the World Conservation Union (IUCN) based in Switzerland (sham2@turbonet.com).

Rich Harrill is a Senior Business Associate with the Economic Development Institute, Tourism and Regional Assistance Centers (TRACS), at the Georgia Institute of Technology. He holds a master's degree in City and Regional Planning and a doctorate in Parks, Recreation, and Tourism Management from Clemson University (rich.harrill@edi.gatech.edu).

Rob Harris is a Senior Lecturer and Director of Continuing Professional Education in the School of Leisure, Sport and Tourism at the University of Technology, Sydney. Rob is the author/co-author or editor/co-editor of a number of books including *Sustainable Tourism: An Australian Perspective* (Butterworth-Heinemann). He has published in a variety of areas including sustainable tourism management, event management, education and training in the tourism and events fields and tourism services marketing. Rob is associate editor – Australia and the Pacific – for the *Environment Paper Series* (Glasgow Caledonian University) and is on the editorial board of the journal *Event Management*. Rob is a past president of the Australian Institute of Travel and Tourism and a recipient of an Australian Tourism Export Council award for his contribution to Australian tourism.

Colin Hunter's background training is in environmental science. However, following lectureship appointments at Leeds Metropolitan and Huddersfield Universities, his teaching and research interests broadened to encompass the broad themes of environmental planning and management. Colin is currently a Senior Lecturer in Environmental Geography in the Department of Geography and Environment at the University of Aberdeen. Particular research interests include the theory and practice of sustainable tourism development, urban environmental management, and water resources management. Colin is also currently the coordinator of the MSc programme in Sustainable Rural Development at Aberdeen University (c.j.hunter@abdn.ac.uk).

David Johnson is Head of the Maritime and Coastal Studies' Subject Group of Southampton Institute, UK. The Subject Group operates a portfolio of ten coastal and maritime degrees. A former Royal Navy officer, he has subsequently specialized in maritime environmental management. His doctorate is in coastal ecosystem restoration and his research interests include sustainable development and marine tourism. David is a professional member of the Institute for Leisure and Amenity Management, the Institute of Ecology and Environmental Management and the Chartered Institute of Water and Environmental Management. In 1996 he co-edited *Coastal Recreation Management* published by E&FN Spon, London. More recently he was a member of the panel that produced LA21 Roundtable Guidance on Sustainable Tourism for the UK Improvement and Development Agency (David.Johnson@solent.ac.uk).

Andrew Lepp is a doctoral student with the Department of Recreation, Parks and Tourism at the University of Florida. He received a master's degree in Natural Resource Management from the Oregon State University. His practical experience includes two years in Africa working with the Uganda Wildlife Authority (UWA). Most recently, as a consultant for UWA, he co-authored the tourism management plan for Bwindi Impenetrable National Park's Nkuringo gorillas. He has also worked for the US National Park Service. His research interests include tourism and rural development, nature tourism, and tourism and perceived risk (andylepp@ufl.edu).

Tanja Mihalič is Professor in Tourism, Economics and Management at University of Ljubljana, Faculty of Economics (Slovenia). Her qualifications are in economics, business administration and environmental policy. Tanja's research covers a wide range of economic and management issues related to tourism, including environmental policy measures in tourism. She has published numerous articles on environmental labelling in Slovene, German and English journals and is the author of the book *Environmental Economics in Tourism* (in Slovene and, with Claude Kaspar, in German). Tanja is responsible for bringing the Blue Flag Campaign to Slovenia, and is also the president of FEEE-S (Foundation for Environmental Education in Europe in Slovenia) – the Slovenian operator of the Blue Flag programme (tanja.mihalic@uni-lj.si).

Anita Pleumarom is a geographer and political scientist trained at the Free University of Berlin, Germany. She presently coordinates the Bangkok-based Tourism Investigation and Monitoring Team (tim-team) and is editor of *New Frontiers* – briefing on tourism, development and environment issues in the Mekong Subregion. She has also published in Thailand and internationally a number of articles on key issues in Third

World tourism, sustainable tourism development, ecotourism, and golf resort developments. Her organization, tim-team, is part of a wider network of non-governmental and grassroots organizations working for social and ecological justice and human rights in Southeast Asia and beyond (tim-team@access.inet.co.th).

Tom Potts is an Associate Professor with the Public Policy Program and a Cooperative Extension Specialist at the Strom Thurmond Institute of Government and Public Affairs at Clemson University. Dr Potts is also founder and director of the Developing Naturally Program at the Institute. He has extensive experience in community development efforts in America and Central Europe (Tpotts@clemson.edu).

Greg Ringer has held a number of academic positions including: Adjunct Assistant Professor, Planning, Public Policy and Management/International Studies Programs, University of Oregon, USA; Visiting Professor, Transnational Program, Waseda University, Japan; and Visiting Fulbright Professor of Tourism, Faculty of Forestry Makerere University, Uganda. His consulting activities have focused on the development of sustainable communities and protected area management. Currently he is involved in projects in the Caribbean, the Greater Mekong Subregion, and Thailand (gringer@OREGON.UOREGON.EDU).

Lesley Roberts is a researcher and lecturer in the Leisure and Tourism Management Department at the Scottish Agricultural College where she teaches on masters and first-degree courses in rural tourism and recreation. The focus of her research work is rural tourism development in both the UK and Eastern Europe. Lesley is particularly interested in exploring better ways of making academic research more available to the development and practitioner sectors. Her publications include a text attempting this, jointly authored with Derek Hall, entitled *Rural Tourism and Recreation: Principles to Practice*.

Esther Speck is a Research Associate at the Centre for Tourism Policy and Research, Simon Fraser University, Burnaby, British Columbia, Canada(c/-peterw@sfu.ca).

Christina Symko is a graduate of the School of Resource and Environmental Management at Simon Fraser University in Burnaby, British Columbia. Currently she is the projects coordinator of the Association of Whistler Area Residents for the Environment. Her work focuses on creating greater community awareness of the importance of natural areas in tourism regions as well as promoting more environmentally sustainable forms of community development (c/-peterw@sfu.ca)

David Weaver is a Professor in the Department of Health, Fitness and Recreation Resources at George Mason University, Virginia, USA. Prior to taking up this position he was a Senior Lecturer in the School of Tourism and Hotel Management at the Gold Coast campus of Griffith University,

Queensland. David earned his Ph.D. in the geography of tourism at the University of Western Ontario in 1986. He has authored or co-authored three tourism books: *Ecotourism in the less developed world* (CAB International); *Tourism management* (John Wiley & Sons); and *Ecotourism* (John Wiley & Sons), as well as twenty-seven refereed journal articles and eighteen book chapters. David sits on the editorial boards of four international refereed journals. His areas of research interest include: sustainable tourism, tourism management, ecotourism, resort cycle dynamics, tourism on small islands and other peripheral regions, resort timesharing, linkages between war and tourism, and the geopolitics of tourism (lnorden@gmu.edu).

David Waldron is a graduate of the School of Resource and Environmental Management at Simon Fraser University in Burnaby, British Columbia, Canada. He has worked as an engineer and environmental planner for the resort municipality of Whistler, and is currently coordinating the delivery of the natural step environmental management programme for that community (c/-peterw@sfu.ca).

Betty Weiler is Associate Professor of Tourism and Deputy Head, Department of Management, Monash University, Australia, where she teaches postgraduate and undergraduate courses on ecotourism, tour guiding and tourism planning and management. Betty has published over one hundred journal articles and book chapters, presented fifteen invited addresses and plenaries, and delivered dozens of symposia papers and workshops. In the past ten years, she has become a world leader in ecotour guide research and training as a means to sustainable tourism development (Betty.Weiler@buseco.monash.edu.au).

Peter Williams is a Professor and Director of the Centre for Tourism Policy and Research at Simon Fraser University, British Columbia, Canada. Peter's academic and professional work focuses on policy, planning, and management issues in tourism and outdoor recreation. Currently his research is concerned with the development of methods for assessing latent demand for natural and cultural resources; the establishment of sound environmental management strategies in tourism businesses; the creation of growth management strategies in tourism regions; and the use of Internet technologies for tourism research purposes. Peter is a former president of the Travel and Tourism Research Association, and serves on the editorial review boards of the *Journal of Travel Research*, *Journal of Sustainable Tourism*, *Tourism Recreation Research*, and *Event Management* (peterw@sfu.ca).

Preface

The challenge of the future is to choose a course that satisfies the market requirements for growth, maintains the natural balance that sustains our economies, and meets the needs and rights of global communities awakening to new dreams of health, prosperity, and peace

Jonathan Lash, *President, World Resources Institute*

Many of the issues and challenges associated with sustainable tourism development that were identified in the precursor to this book (Harris, R. and Leiper, N., 1995, *Sustainable Tourism: An Australian Perspective*, Butterworth-Heinemann, Sydney) are still very much in evidence today. These include: the difficulties associated with coordination and cooperation between the many stakeholders involved in bringing about sustainable tourism; the limitations inherent in the various tourism industry efforts (e.g., voluntary codes of practice) to drive the adoption of sustainable practices; and the resource and knowledge difficulties smallscale enterprises face in their efforts to make their operations 'greener'. While the tourism industry, policy makers and other stakeholders continue to grapple with these and other matters, it is nonetheless apparent that the shift towards a 'green paradigm' based on sustainable tourism development is occurring apace both within the tourism industry itself and in tourist destination regions. Fuelling this shift is the growing global consensus that, as the Secretary-General of the United Nations, Kofi Annan has noted that sustainable development is 'the new conventional wisdom'.

This 'new conventional wisdom' encourages businesses to move away from a sole focus on profit to a concern for what has become known as the 'triple bottom line'; that is, financial, social and environmental performance. For a business to be seen as sustainable it must therefore be one that:

> ... *excels on the traditional scorecard of return on financial assets and shareholder and customer value creation. It also embraces community and stakeholder success. It holds its natural and cultural environments to be as precious as its technology portfolio and its employees' skills.*
>
> (World Business Council for Sustainable Development, 2002, *Global Trends are Reshaping Business Strategy and Markets*)

Evidence that a growing number of tourism businesses are accepting the challenges posed by the triple bottom line approach can be found in a variety of sources. These include the ever-increasing number of publications dealing with the broad area of sustainable tourism development and the websites of various tourism industry, government and non-government organizations (NGOs). It is also evident from these same sources that a number of tourist destination areas, varying in scale from towns to countries and world regions (e.g., Europe), are taking significant steps towards creating a context in which sustainable tourism development can occur. Additionally, tourists themselves have been embraced by the push towards more sustainable tourism via such means as traveller codes of behaviour, education and interpretive programmes and laws, such as those associated with child sex tourism. Assisting in this general movement towards sustainable tourism are the various industry, NGO and government accreditation and education programmes that seek to guide businesses, communities and individuals in responding to the challenges sustainable tourism development poses.

This book, whilst providing examples of the previously noted efforts by the tourism industry, NGOs and governments to progress the goal of sustainable tourism, seeks to provide more than simply a 'best practice' perspective on sustainable tourism development, as its precursor did. Its approach is more holistic, dealing as it does with both the complexities associated with the concept of sustainable development itself and the challenges tourism businesses, governments, local communities and other stakeholders face as they pursue sustainable development outcomes in widely differing social, political, economic and physical environmental contexts. In this book these contexts from a geographical perspective, including those of Asia, Africa, the South Pacific, Australia, Europe, North America and the Caribbean; while from a political and economic perspective, they include developed and developing countries, democracies (both old and new), socialist regimes and military dictatorships.

In seeking to provide these perspectives we have employed a mix of case studies, regional overviews, and theoretical discussions. We hope that the overall 'balance' we have struck is appropriate for most readers and serves to enhance their appreciation of progress in the area, along with the various contextual complexities that surround such progress.

In order to structure material presented in this book we have used the following section headings:

- Issues and Perspectives;
- Accreditation, Education and Interpretation;
- Tourist Destination Areas; and
- Tourism Enterprises and Attractions.

Additionally, we have included a section entitled *Selected Organizations and Programmes*. This section contains summary details regarding the general nature and activities of selected organizations involved in sustainable tourism development, as well as brief descriptions of programmes that have been designed for this purpose.

Rob Harris
Tony Griffin
Peter Williams

April 2002

Part 1

Issues and Perspectives

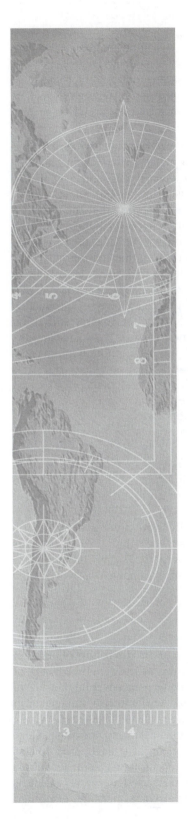

CHAPTER 1

Aspects of the sustainable tourism debate from a natural resources perspective

Colin Hunter

Introduction

As with other industrial sectors and fields of academic study, tourism research has also responded to the popularization of the concept of sustainable development in the wake of the World Commission on Environment and Development's Report, *Our Common Future* (WCED, 1987). Hence, a growing proportion of the academic and policy orientated tourism literature is now devoted to examining the theory and practice of 'sustainable tourism' (ST). Indeed, 1993 saw the first edition of a journal entirely devoted to the topic: the *Journal of Sustainable Tourism*. Although not ignoring the importance of theoretical developments in ST, it is interesting to note the emphasis placed on practical implementation in the editorial which introduced this new journal:

> *It is easy to discuss sustainability. Implementation is the problem . . . The time has now come 'to walk the talk'.* (Bramwell and Lane, 1993: 4)

However, this chapter is based on the belief that tourism researchers have, in general, not discussed theoretical aspects of ST enough (even allowing for developments in the subject area since 1993); a view shared by some other tourism researchers such as Milne (1998) and Sharpley (2000). Admittedly, it is easy to tire of sustainability rhetoric, but this should not discourage in-depth analyses of the theoretical underpinnings of the concept of ST. It is argued here that too many studies appear to lack a clear vision of ST, and that without such clarity rather too many 'walks' (continuing with Bramwell and Lane's analogy) may meander aimlessly for too long, or even head in the wrong direction altogether. A key theme of this chapter is that much ST research is open to a charge of intellectual introversion, and that the clarity required to better understand interpretations of ST, and mechanisms of implementation, is to be found in the wider sustainable development (SD) and environmental management literature. Detailed discussion of sustainability is not easy, but it is necessary in order to better understand the different perceptions of ST that are now emerging, and to make more informed choices about the future development of tourism at destination areas.

The chapter begins with a section which argues for the need to look outwards in formulating perceptions of ST, beyond the immediate concerns of tourism and the restrictive confines of much current tourism research. This is followed by the formulation of two broad, and simplified, variants of ST, as informed by an overview of different interpretations of the general concept of SD. Where possible, studies from the academic tourism literature are used to illustrate divergent opinion on the meaning of ST. The reader should also note that throughout this chapter sustainability is examined from a natural environment perspective. I, therefore, acknowledge that a comprehensive overview of the SD/ST debate is not provided.

Sectoral parochialism

It would appear that every conceivable sector or discipline or interest grouping has now attempted to translate aspects of the general concept of SD to its own, more familiar, disciplinary or intellectual frame of reference. For example, I have come across works addressing sustainability in the context of architecture, agriculture, business, cities, economy, forestry, heritage, industry, land use, planning, rural development, society, and water resources. A sceptic might suggest that all this endeavour has more to do with academics recognizing a publication's 'gift horse' than with the altruistic pursuit of knowledge. However, let us assume that genuine intellectual curiosity is at work, perhaps combined with what Wilbanks (1994) describes as the power of the phrase 'sustainable development' to capture a widespread sense of impending global eco-disaster and the need for change in the way societies utilize natural resources. Also, given the current dominance of the western, scientific-reductionist approach to understanding the world (e.g., Carley and Christie, 1992), it is not surprising that so much effort has been expended on interpreting SD in a piecemeal, highly focused and sector-specific manner.

Clearly, sector-specific analyses of SD are required. Academics and practitioners from different backgrounds must bring their own expertise to the issues involved, focusing on those of most immediate relevance. However, this does not mean that they need necessarily lose sight of the implications of their own work for other sectors or disciplines, or that they become detached from the ongoing debate on the meaning and implications of SD. One must at least be aware of the limitations and potential difficulties inherent in sector-specific approaches to under-standing and implementing SD. This may be particularly true of tourism which, by its very nature, is a nebulous industry characterized by many direct and indirect connections with other sectors, interests and activities (e.g., Cater, 1995). Recently, for example, the UK suffered a major outbreak of 'foot-and-mouth' disease, a highly contagious viral infection affecting cloven-hoofed animals including cattle, pigs and sheep. In an attempt to control the spread of this disease millions of farm animals were destroyed, and restrictions placed upon access to the countryside in both infected and non-infected areas. The latter course of action greatly reduced tourist activity throughout rural areas of the UK, bringing hardship to many tourism businesses. Nothing could more clearly illustrate the linkages that exist between tourism activity and the health, or otherwise, of other sectors.

In all the discussion and debate about aspects of SD, such as inter- and intragenerational equity, the issue of sectoral fragmentation would appear to have been largely forgotten. A reminder of the World Commission's view (WCED, 1987: 63) is timely:

> *Intersectoral connections create patterns of economic and ecological interdependence rarely reflected in the ways in which policy is made. Sectoral organizations tend to pursue sectoral objectives and to treat their impacts on other sectors as side effects, taken into account only if compelled to do so . . . Many of the environment and development problems that confront us have their roots in this sectoral fragmentation of responsibility. Sustainable development requires that such fragmentation be overcome.*

Very often it is the sectoral organizations referred to above that are responsible for policy formulation and implementation, and they may take their lead from, or at least be informed by, the views of academic researchers. Unfortunately, tourism researchers would appear to be as prone to intellectual introversion as colleagues in other fields of study.

Despite the surely incontrovertible truth that the magnitude and nature of tourism development in almost any area will be affected by a wide range of other existing and planned development types, e.g., housing, transport, retailing, health service provision, light industry, nature conservation and agriculture, the tourism literature brims with plans, strategies, models and frameworks constructed solely, or almost exclusively, from a tourism perspective. Yet, many of these have been published under the banner of sustainability and some even claim to be holistic, based upon attempts to integrate only two concerns: tourism development and nature conservation (Hunter, 1995). It is disappointing to find that even otherwise excellent recent studies, which seek to harmonize tourism activities with regional resource characteristics, apparently see no need to explore, or even summarize, how the proposed tourism development planning frameworks might link in with the characteristics of, and development plans for, other sectors (e.g., Priskin, 2001; Ahn *et al.*, 2002).

Worse still, while many 'sustainable' tourism studies simply ignore other sectors, some studies have a distinctly confrontational tone, where the potential for competition between tourism and other sectors for access to natural resources is highlighted. If one perceives ST as the 'need' to constantly maintain and extend the tourism resource base and tourism activity in all areas (i.e., exclusive self-interest), then it becomes possible to see (sustainable) tourism as under threat from SD policies (e.g., McKercher, 1993a); surely a rather bizarre twist of logic. However, accepting that exclusive sectoral self-interest is not in keeping with the spirit of SD more broadly, then the integration of activities and interests becomes a key task. As McKercher (1993b: 14) also argues:

For sustainable tourism to occur, it must be closely integrated with all other activities that occur in the host region.

This attitude exemplifies a more realistic, mature and holistic strand of thought on the nature of ST that correctly challenges the understandable tendency towards sectoral parochialism in sustainable tourism research. Thus, McKercher's view is echoed by Wall (1993) who criticizes single-sector tourism development planning in Bali, and Aravot (1992) who concludes that tourism planning should be part of general development planning to allow better coordination of effort and the 'interweaving of mutual influences' (p. 17). Relatedly, Lane (1994) warns of the over-reliance of rural areas on tourism, promoting policies which work towards a balanced, diverse rural economy and one, therefore, which is more resilient (sustainable) in the face of change. More recently, Collins (1999), in asking the question, 'deck chairs or ploughshares?', takes issue with the parochial attitude evident amongst many tourism researchers who fail to recognize a role for other sectors in the sustainable development of an area.

If a parochial or 'precious' (Hunter, 1995) view of tourism is apparent amongst some tourism researchers, then it is not surprising to find this attitude even more evident amongst tourism policymakers and trade organizations. In a report on tourism's economic impact, the World Travel and Tourism Council (WTTC, 1999), for example, describes as 'top performers' those countries with the greatest reliance on travel and tourism. Some twenty countries are described as 'leading the way' with regard to the proportion of employment dependent upon travel and tourism, with the 'top' four countries (Anguilla, British Virgin Islands, Bahamas and Saint Lucia) having more than 50 per cent of employment in the travel and tourism trade. For many with more of an eye on the implications of general sustainable development, such a heavy reliance on any single sector would be seen as very worrying, perhaps particularly so if the sector in question is as fickle as the international tourism market. At best, the attitude of the WTTC is irresponsible. It is, however, apparently echoed by the World Tourism Organization (WTO) as the following observation by Lanfant and Graburn (1992: 112) illustrates:

> *At Zakopane in August 1989, the members of the Academy (International Academy for the Study of Tourism) considered Alternative Tourism as a means to contribute to the 'sustainable development' of a society, whereas by October at the WTO meeting in Tamanrasset, Alternative Tourism had become co-opted as a way to ensure the sustainable development of tourism itself. That should give us something to think about.*

Surely, this sleight of hand by the WTO will eventually come to be seen (at least by the great majority of 'objective' academics) as indicative of an industry 'walking' in the wrong direction. Alternative tourism must also be sustainable tourism and, in the sense of retaining any philosophical link with its parental concept of SD, the notion of ST only really makes sense if it is used as shorthand for tourism's contribution to SD (e.g., Hunter, 1995; Collins, 1999), irrespective of the type (mass, alternative, eco-, nature-based, green, soft, hard, etc., etc.) of tourism being considered.

Thus, at the most fundamental level, there is a dichotomy in ST thinking: should ST be concerned with attempting to create the conditions whereby tourism flourishes as an end in itself, or should ST thinking be directed at finding a role for tourism as part of a more holistic strategy encompassing the more general aims of SD? In his 'state-of-the-art' review of ST, Butler (1999) recognizes this dichotomy, not for the first time, by distinguishing between 'sustainable tourism' (as a descriptor of the former position) and 'development of tourism on the principles of sustainable development' (as a descriptor of the latter position). Butler, rightly, regards ambiguity in the use of the term 'sustainable tourism' as a major issue:

> *The key problem, in my mind, is the current inability to define to the satisfaction of all, or even most, of the stakeholders in tourism, exactly what is meant by 'sustainable tourism'.* (Butler, 1999: 19)

Unfortunately, it is not clear, at least to me, which of the interpretations of ST Butler prefers. Any suggestion that the term 'sustainable tourism' be reserved solely as a descriptor of the former position above is unlikely to be widely adopted given its historical use as shorthand for either position. The existence of these two fundamentally different inter-pretations of ST highlights the importance of providing clear theoretical guidance for tourism researchers and policymakers, hopefully encourag-ing better explanation of the particular position adopted. Although it is true to say that many of the lists of principles of ST that have been derived over recent years are very similar in character to the key concerns of SD (Sharpley, 2000), this does not necessarily mean that ST policy and practice will follow what has been described as an 'extra-parochial' paradigm (Hunter, 1995) where the primary goal is for tourism to contribute to the wider goals of SD.

Ambiguity in the use of the term 'sustainable tourism' may also arise because SD is a contested concept. Despite claiming to examine the meaning of SD in the context of tourism, Butler (1999), as with many other authors, fails to provide any real detail of the SD debate: for example, the desired degree of substitution between natural capital (resources) and human-made capital, or the meaning of human needs and wants. Enhanced understanding of the concept of ST cannot await the (impossible) dream of a unifying definition, but rather must emerge through the more clearly articulated description of alternatives, and with an ongoing debate amongst those willing to defend alternative positions. I believe in a vision of ST dedicated to tourism's wider contribution to SD. Logically, adherence to this alternative requires ST researchers (followed, hopefully, by policymakers) to engage with the debate on the meaning of SD, and to address key aspects of the arguments that have emerged since the publication of the World Commission's report (WCED, 1987). The following section provides a very brief overview of key aspects of the SD debate. Fuller accounts can be found in the ST literature (e.g., Hunter, 1997; Holden, 1999), with the most detailed of these (from a natural resources perspective) provided by Collins (1999).

Interpretations of sustainable development

It is now widely accepted that any quest for a universally applicable definition of sustainable development (SD) is not likely to be successful, and in recent years sustainability theory has advanced through the articulation of a range of possible interpretations of SD and their applicability under a variety of circumstances (e.g., Mitlin, 1992; Turner *et al.*, 1994; Wilbanks, 1994; Hanley, 2000). In exploring the details of the concept of SD, many issues have emerged as points of controversy and departure for adherents to different visions of environmentalism and the meaning of 'development'; Sharpley (2000) provides a useful analysis of development theory in the context of ST. Debate has revolved around such inter-related issues as: the role of economic growth in promoting human well-being; the substitutability of natural resource capital with human-made capital created through economic growth and technological innovation; the criticality of various components of the natural resource base and the potential for substitution; the ability of technologies and environmental management methods to decouple economic growth and environmental degradation; the meaning of the value attributed to the natural world and the rights of non-human species; and the degree to which a systems perspective should be adopted entailing a primary concern for maintaining the functional integrity of ecosystems.

These issues have become interwoven in a complex debate on how best to achieve, or strive to achieve, equity in the nature of opportunities to access natural resources which create human well-being, and in the distribution of the costs and benefits (social, economic and environmental) that ensue from the utilization of resources (e.g., Fox, 1994). Equity implies attempting to meet *all* basic human needs and, perhaps, the satisfaction of human wants, both now (intragenerational equity) and in the future (intergenerational equity). That is, the avoidance of development and the concomitant utilization of natural resources which maintains, creates or widens spatial or temporal differences in human well-being. Of course, interpretations of human needs and wants vary, and the use of these terms constitutes an important part of the SD debate. Furthermore, under some interpretations of SD, equity also applies across species barriers, in particular the inherent right of non-humans to exist above and beyond any utilitarian value imposed by humans (Williams, 1994). Hughes (2001) provides an interesting account of how an animal rights perspective brought about a structural change in tourism provision in the UK with reference to the viewing of dolphins.

Thus, the concept of SD can be shaped to fit a spectrum of world views, encompassing different ethical stances and management strategies (Owens, 1994). Interpretations of sustainable development can be classified as ranging from 'very strong' to 'very weak' (Turner *et al.*, 1994). Rather than detail here all the characteristics of different visions of SD, the reader is referred to Table 1.1 which summarizes four major SD positions. Frequently, the very weak (traditional resource exploitative) and very strong (extreme resource preservationist) interpretations of sustainability are disregarded by many commentators as being rather too extreme. For example, the former lacks an environmental stewardship ethic and concern for the intragenerational distribution of development costs and benefits, while the anti-growth ethos of the latter may also contravene the intragenerational principle by denying the poorest people enhanced quality of life through economic growth. Most debate, therefore, has focused on the distinction between weak and strong interpretations (Collins, 1999; Table 1.1).

There can be little doubt that weak interpretations dominate the thinking behind the great majority of governmental and other policy statements on SD; for example, the 'need' for continued economic growth is never apparently questioned. Certainly, the World Commission (WCED, 1987) recognized the importance of economic growth in poverty-stricken areas of the Third World in order to meet basic needs, and there was no preclusion to continued economic growth in developed countries. However, amongst academic commentators the question of whether or

Sustainability position	Defining characteristics
Very weak	anthropocentric and utilitarian; growth orientated and resource exploitative; natural resources utilized at economically optimal rates through unfettered free markets operating to satisfy individual consumer choice; infinite substitution possible between natural and human-made capital; continued well-being assured through economic growth and technical innovation.
Weak	anthropocentric and utilitarian; resource conservationist; growth is managed and modified; concern for distribution of development costs and benefits through intra- and intergenerational equity; rejection of infinite substitution between natural and human-made capital with recognition of some aspects of the natural world as critical capital (e.g., ozone layer, some natural ecosystems); human-made plus natural capital constant or rising through time; decoupling of negative environmental impacts from economic growth.
Strong	(eco)systems perspective; resource preservationist; recognizes primary value of maintaining the functional integrity of ecosystems over and above secondary value through resource utilization; interests of the collective given more weight than those of the individual consumer; adherence to intra- and intergenerational equity; decoupling important but alongside a belief in a steady state economy as a consequence of following the constant natural assets rule; zero economic and human population growth.
Very strong	bioethical and eco-centric; resource preservationist to the point where utilization of natural resources is minimized; nature's rights or intrinsic value in nature encompassing non-human living organisms and even abiotic elements under a literal interpretation of Gaianism; anti-economic growth and for reduced human population.

Source: Hunter (1997), adapted from Turner *et al.* (1994).

Table 1.1
A simplified description of the sustainable development spectrum

not continued economic growth can be justified in developed countries where basic needs are already met and greater well-being largely equates to the satisfaction of wants (e.g., more vacation opportunities), has become a contentious one.

Frequently, however, visions of SD (and ST) are merely couched in the language of 'balance', i.e., finding the right balance between the need for development and the need for environmental protection (the *degree* of protection is usually not made clear). Apart from the likelihood that one person's balance is another's imbalance, the language of balance can be misleading, being used to mask the reality that economic growth is generally the primary concern (Healey and Shaw, 1994). As pointed out by Cater (1995), with specific reference to ST, economic growth via tourism development will often conflict with environmental protection. What Cater describes as 'win/win' situations (where tourism development results in both wealth creation and environmental betterment) are, in my view, relatively rare, although examples, such as that of the Cape Byron Headland Reserve in Australia (Brown and Essex, 1997), do appear to exist. Usually, therefore, difficult trade-off decisions under 'win/lose' conditions have to be made. Tosun (2001), based upon an analysis of ST in Turkey, argues that the complex socio-economic and environmental trade-off decisions that have to be made may be particularly difficult in developing countries. Although economic concerns may dominate in most situations, the outcome of the decision-making process will vary according to the background and training of decision makers and to the specific circumstances surrounding the development proposal.

Logically, if it is accepted that alternative interpretations of SD are inevitable and that ST should be about trying to contribute to the wider goals of SD, then it must surely be recognized that ST cannot be seen as a rigid code. Rather, ST should be seen as a flexible or adaptive paradigm, whereby different tourism development pathways may be appropriate according to local conditions (Hunter, 1997). Of course, this leaves one open to a charge of:

> *neatly side-stepping the need for a concise definition.* (Sharpley, 2000: 1)

Some recent work, however, suggests that it may be useful to examine particular types of tourism development using an adaptive conceptual framework for ST: see, for example, Holden's (1999) analysis of downhill skiing in the Cairngorms area of the Scottish Highlands. Also, there may be a link between an adaptive view of ST developed from a natural resources perspective and the recent construction of a dynamic notion of sustainability in cultural tourism put forward by Tucker (2001). Additionally, and as argued earlier, it is unreasonable to expect a universally acceptable and concise definition of ST to emerge, at least in the near future. A very widely accepted definition of ST would almost certainly need to be rather vague and couched in the language of balance, and thus 'side-step' the reality of difficult trade-off decisions. A concise (and precise) definition would need to recognize the primary importance of one of the key aspects of ST; e.g., environmental protection, or economic growth, a parallel process to choosing between weak or strong versions of SD. As I hope to demonstrate below, the prospect of all, or even a large majority, of commentators agreeing on either a weak or strong model for ST appears rather remote. The work of Miller (2001) will serve for the moment in illustrating how far we appear to be away from agreement as to the meaning of ST. In trying to develop indicators for ST, Miller conducted a Delphi survey of academic experts who had recently published relevant journal papers. Miller found considerable disagreement over the meaning of sustainability and where the 'borders of the concept exist' (quoted from the paper's abstract). Certainly, without much more informed debate on its conceptual underpinnings, a widely accepted and detailed model of ST will never emerge.

For the time being, a clear, detailed and frank account of why a particular pathway or sustainability interpretation has been chosen, and one which certainly avoids the banal rhetoric of balance, is more important than the search for a theoretical construct suitable as a vehicle for policy formulation under all circumstances. Unfortunately, many studies in the tourism literature that incorporate an attempt to define ST do not venture beyond the rhetoric of balance and the underlying rationale for policy formulation, and action therefore remains obscured (Hunter, 1997). Of course, obscurity may be a deliberate ploy where those with vested interests want the primacy of, say, economic growth to remain hidden, but most academic commentators should not have this excuse. The inevitability of trade-offs in development decision-making cannot, however, be obscured. Thus, even where tourism studies published under the banner of sustainability fail to address its meaning, or limit discussion to talk of balance, individual preferences and sympathies frequently appear as the description of a particular 'sustainable' tourism development unfolds. By default, therefore, different ST pathways are already being described, but only in relatively few studies does this appear to be a self-conscious process.

The remainder of this chapter is devoted to an analysis of two interpretations of ST: a model building exercise using material from the tourism literature, and simplified constructs based loosely on weak and strong perceptions of SD. However rudimentary these may be, perhaps attempts like this will find some utility and encourage studies of ST to preface the 'walk' part with a short 'talk' explaining, or even justifying, the planned route.

Meanings of sustainable tourism

The categorization of interpretations means using labels, and labels are frequently long-winded (consider 'extreme resource preservationist', for example). For the sake of convenience, shortened descriptors/personifications are used below: 'light green' (LG) and 'dark green' (DG). Table 1.2 is an attempt to bring together a range of attitudinal tendencies with respect to tourism and the environment, thereby providing a summary of the two variants of ST. In general, these variants are scale-independent and could apply at different levels, from the individual business up to a national tourism development plan or policy statement. The following paragraphs consider some aspects of Table 1.2 in slightly more detail, and with reference to specific studies in the academic tourism literature, where possible.

Light green tendencies	Dark green tendencies
advocate and strongly pro-adaptancy	cautionary and knowledge-based
benefits of tourism assumed	benefits of tourism must be demonstrated
precious view of tourism as a sector and sectoral self-interest dominates	tourism need not necessarily be a component of sustainable development in an area and sectoral integration required
maintain tourism activity in existing destinations and expand into new ones	widen economic base if high dependency on tourism and engage in full proactive assessment of new tourism development
tourism products must be maintained and evolve according to market need (nature is a commodity)	natural resources must be maintained and impacts reduced (preferably minimized) where possible with products tailored accordingly (nature has existence value)
environmental action only when required and beneficial (i.e., legal obligation, to tackle specific problem, marketing benefit and cost saving)	environmental impacts always considered as a matter of routine
narrow scope and geographical scale of environmental concern	wide range of potential and actual impacts considered beyond immediate geographical setting (e.g., hotel, complex, destination area)
disperse and dilute activity (spread)	focus and concentrate activity (confine)
industry self-regulation as dominant management approach	wide range of management approaches and instruments required
introspective focus on tourism research and management literature	(more likely to reinvent the wheel)
most likely to have a direct involvement in the industry	most likely to have training in an environment-type academic discipline

Table 1.2
Simplified descriptions of light green and dark green variants of sustainable tourism

Perhaps with training in tourism (or one of the social sciences dominated by economic aspects of development) and/or with a direct professional interest in tourism, LG is a tourism enthusiast, most likely to be found speaking from Jafari's (1989) 'advocacy' platform. For LG, tourism is intrinsically good and has an inherent right to expand. After all, people evolved through natural processes, are part of nature and, therefore, anything they do is 'natural'. If people want the world to be a playground, then this is nothing more than natural selection, with the selection process driven by the need to meet the desires of tourists in terms of destination area characteristics. Growth is good and the key issue is how to maintain it in existing enclaves and foster it where tourism is as yet absent, or 'underdeveloped'. Hence, satisfying demand (as expressed by the preferences of individual tourists or tourist types) through correctly tailored products is the fundamental task. LG may also be found speaking from Jafari's (1989) 'adaptancy' platform, in so far as ST is primarily about finding new strategies for tourism to maintain and increase measures of its economic activity (e.g., visitor numbers and expenditure).

Typically, LG's environmental concern is limited to the maintenance of sufficient environmental quality at the destination (probably largely through industry self-regulation) to ensure the continued survival of existing tourism products and the development of new products at existing and new locations. Where LG does make explicit reference to environmental issues these will tend to be very product-linked, greatly limiting scope and scale to those aspects of direct, immediate and tangible relevance to the survival and promotion of the product; for example, landscape and visual amenity, local ecosystem attributes, and elements of townscape. This amounts to little more than beautifying the environment for tourism (clean streets and palm trees), rather than a radical appraisal of the environmental functioning of a destination area, resort centre, enclave or even individual hotel complex.

This highly product-focused, anthropocentric view often leads to relatively little attention being paid to natural resource demands, with the environmental side-effects of growth only tackled retrospectively if possible and/or economically viable (House, 1997; Stabler, 1997). Both Hughes (1996) and MacLellan (1998), for example, are critical of Scottish tourism policy for its over-riding focus on economic growth targets; with the banner of sustainability being used, it is argued, principally as a means of providing new opportunities to market nature-based tourism products, such as wildlife tourism. Relatedly, Klemm (1992), in a review of the sustainability of the tourism product offered by the French region of Languedoc-Roussillon, barely touches upon the environmental implications of tourism development, so acute is the focus on changes made to the product in order to maintain its appeal to tourists.

Another exemplar of LG thinking is provided by Owen *et al.* (1993:470) in their description of 'Project Conwy' in Wales, put forward as a practical example of successful sustainable tourism development:

Major efforts of investment have taken place in Conwy in order to transform the town from what was once a down-market beach resort holiday destination for the 'candy-floss-brigade' to an up-market, walled heritage town.

Going up-market in Conwy in order to improve and sustain its appeal involved a number of actions. These included: construction of a town bypass (in the form of an estuarine tunnel) and the first phase of a marina; the instigation of a four year town lighting plan covering street lighting; the lighting of key buildings and decorative lighting; the search for a private developer to establish a 'quality' caravan park close to the town; and the further extension of out of town parking facilities. Unfortunately, we are not told of the natural resource implications (energy use, habitat loss, water supply issues, etc.) of these 'sustainable' tourism practices. Thus, environmental concern is narrowly scoped, being primarily focused on visual amenity, and geographically very limited.

At its most extreme, the LG position may become so 'pale' as to represent little more than the traditional, resource-exploitative and economic-growth-driven paradigm of SD. Butcher (1997: 31), for example, provides a scathing attack on the whole concept of sustainability, arguing that:

The denigration of human progress embodied in the sustainability paradigm is likely to hold back humanity from facing up to and solving the problems of poverty and underdevelopment. It is hence a far bigger problem than some of the troublesome by-products of unplanned tourism development.

This assertion is not one that would be met with much sympathy by many engaged in the SD/ST debate. Nonetheless, Butcher's position is clear and he does not shirk from engaging with the broader sustainability debate. This is surely preferable to misconceptions that the meaning and implications of 'sustainability' are somehow already widely understood and agreed; an issue highlighted by Butler (1999) in his ST review.

In contrast to LG thinking, those who adhere to the DG variant of ST are, it is suggested, much more likely to have background training in disciplines such as ecology, geography and the environmental sciences, and are most likely to express views from cautionary or knowledge-based perspectives (Jafari, 1989). Advocates of DG thinking typically espouse the importance of the precautionary principle, the need for proactive or anticipatory tourism development planning (perhaps in a multi-sectoral sense), and the systematic monitoring of changes to the natural environment/capital stock of natural resources using a variety of environmental management techniques. Broadly speaking, the emphasis is on the protection of natural resources that support tourism, rather than the promotion of tourism-related economic growth for its own sake or as an end in itself. Goodall and Stabler (1997: 291), for example, argue that:

In the face of uncertainty, irreproducibility of natural resources and the possible irreversibility of decisions, it should be assumed that a tourist activity or development might damage the environment. Unless there is clear scientific evidence to the contrary, decision-making should err on the side of caution where uncertainty exists as to the long-term consequences of current tourism resource use.

Likewise, Stabler (1997: 16) suggests that environmental appraisal should be a prelude to development actions, and that tourism's reliance on the natural environment as its primary resource base 'must compel it to move in the direction of ecocentrism'. Similarly, Collins (1999) clearly argues the case for strong forms of sustainability conditions in the context of tourism development as being the most appropriate for preserving biodiversity. He equates a strong sustainability position with a non-declining stock of natural capital over time. At a practical level, this strong sustainability philosophy is embodied in the, albeit local, 'constant natural capital rule' (see also Table 1.2) adopted in the definition of ST derived for two World Heritage Areas in Australia by Driml and Common (1996). Although dating from the mid-1990s, the paper by Driml and Common is still, in my view, the best yet available at linking ST theory and practice: following a review of alternative potential interpretations of sustainability, a clear theoretical stance is adopted according to local conditions/ requirements, and then implementation mechanisms are described. This is an excellent example of practice following theory, and is exactly what is needed as a matter of routine in ST research (Collins, 2001).

DG is also much more likely than LG to believe in concentrating and limiting tourist activity rather than spreading and 'diluting' it. For example, contrast the aim of the Scottish Tourist Board (STB) to spread tourist activity away from the centres of Edinburgh and Glasgow (STB, 1994), with the view of Wheeller (1993: 128):

How can we argue that spreading the tourist load spatially is solving the problem when one of the problems is the spatial spread of tourism?

Wherever tourism occurs the DG variant of ST is likely to entail a more widely scoped, geographically extensive and stronger degree of environmental concern and action than the LG variant. It is suggested (Table 1.2) that DG will tend to consider impacts upon a wider range of resources and throughout a wider geographical area, recognizing that it is important to understand impacts beyond the immediate tourist setting. By way of illustration, Gill and Williams (1994) stress the importance of regional planning to the successful management of tourism development at individual resort centres and beyond, arguing that too narrow a geographical focus for management initiatives may simply transfer problems from individual centres to surrounding areas. This attitude might be taken as illustrating the less parochial conceptualization of ST typical of the DG variant. The importance of sub-national, regional planning is relatively frequently recognized in the tourism literature (e.g., Dowling, 1993; Wall, 1993; Hall and Wouters, 1994; Priskin, 2001; Ahn *et al.*, 2002), perhaps particularly where access to some sites within a region is strictly controlled or prohibited on the grounds of exceptional ecological value.

It is also likely that DG will argue for systematic environmental monitoring as a matter of course as part of tourism development appraisal (e.g., Butler, 1999) even if this has significant cost implications, whereas LG will tend to think and act on environmental issues only when required or there is some direct advantage involved. For example, a requirement to act might come in the form of a legal obligation, or where an environmental problem, such as sewage pollution of beaches, sufficient to affect the satisfaction of tourists emerges. Direct advantage might manifest itself in several ways, the most attractive being some form of direct financial saving. Environmental guidelines for those managing tourism businesses, for example, frequently stress the potential savings available by 'going green', through reduced energy costs and other actions (e.g., English Tourist Board *et al.*, 1992). Similarly, Stabler and Goodall (1997) recently highlighted the much greater likelihood of tourism businesses incorporating environmental objectives and practices if these brought lower costs and/or higher revenues, with reference to the hospitality sector in Guernsey. Another form of direct advantage might be where limited environmental betterment is linked to a new marketing strategy designed to kickstart a flagging (hence 'unsustainable') local industry. This approach is described by Morgan (1991) for Majorca in Spain.

Perhaps more controversially, other discriminators might be advanced to distinguish between LG and DG variants. In Table 1.2, mention is made of the willingness to learn from other academic disciplines and the broader environmental management literature. A number of studies in the tourism literature have stressed the importance of measuring the general environmental performance of tourism operations, or aspects thereof, and encouraging the use of waste-free and low-waste technologies (e.g., Buckley, 1996; Lukashina *et al.*, 1996; Buckley and Araujo, 1997; Tabatchnaia-Tamirisa *et al.*, 1997). Furthermore, there are also studies where a detailed examination of the meaning, and tensions, of ST clearly benefits from an appreciation of the wider sustainable development literature (e.g., Henry and Jackson, 1996), and also where the range of environmental management policy approaches and implementation techniques is examined in the context of tourism (e.g., Hjalager, 1996). More recently, Ko (2001) stresses the importance of utilizing and applying contributions from other disciplines in aiding the assessment of ST. Perhaps these efforts, of themselves, may be seen as heralding a recent move towards DG sustainable tourism thinking, as an ability to engage with the concepts to be found in the wider environmental management literature can be seen as a cornerstone of the DG variant, because, potentially, this encourages the use of a wider range of methods and tools in the analysis and management of tourism's impacts.

This type of engagement also lessens the chance of tourism researchers and practitioners 'reinventing the wheel'. In the comparison of a number of tools for the management of tourism and recreation conducted by Wight (1998), for example, one is struck by the similarities (rather than the differences) between Visitor Impact Management (VIM) and Visitor Experience and Resource Protection (VERP) systems, and the more widely known (and used) approach of Environmental Impact Assessment, and its variant Strategic Environmental Assessment (see, for example, Hunter and Green, 1995). Likewise, when Wight calls for systems such as VIM and VERP to be employed as ongoing, iterative management tools, the similarity with Environmental Auditing and Environmental Management Systems is all too evident (the reader is referred to Goodall, 1995, and Todd and Williams, 1996, for examples of the use of these techniques in a tourism context).

Conclusions

The idea of SD appears to have caught the imagination of many tourism researchers and policymakers. Enthusiasm generates a real desire for change, and a rush to operationalize principles of ST. However, these principles are frequently little more than very general statements of intent, and often raise more questions than they answer. Many studies of ST fail to provide an in-depth analysis of precisely how the term is being used or interpreted. Obviously, any kind of improvement in the environmental functioning of tourism operations can be seen as beneficial, but environmental betterment comes in many forms and does not necessarily mean long-term sustainability.

Well over a decade after the publication of the World Commission's report, *Our Common Future* (WCED, 1987), there is still a need to clarify the theoretical underpinnings of ST, but relatively few studies in the literature have set about this task, particularly in the context of the ongoing SD debate. It is clear, however, that neither SD or ST are value-free concepts (Butler, 1999). Whereas debate on the meaning and implications of SD has been intense (Hanley, 2000), resulting in relatively clearly defined alternative interpretations, this has generally not permeated the ST literature to the same extent. Nonetheless, because use of the term 'sustainable tourism' brings with it the preconceptions and values of the user, distinctive variants of ST have emerged over the last decade or so, although usually not in a self-conscious manner. If we accept that, as with general SD, a unifying definition or conceptualization of ST is unlikely to emerge, then the study of ST must advance through enhanced awareness of, and debate around, more clearly articulated alternatives. If these alternatives become better understood, then it should ease the operationalization of ST as the 'ground rules', or key questions, for decision-making become more apparent, irrespective of the particular label attached to the tourism product.

There have recently been signs of a more detailed consideration of theoretical aspects of ST. Some commentators have shown willingness to espouse and defend alternative interpretations, based upon issues raised in the broader SD literature. Unfortunately, the multidisciplinary nature of (sustainable) tourism research can mitigate against the proper understanding of arguments put forward. This would appear to be the case with, for example, Velikova's (2001) commentary on Collins (1999) (see also Collins, 2001, for the rejoinder). It is even the case that a theoretical examination of SD and ST can lead to the conclusion that, 'the concept of sustainable tourism development is . . . a red herring' (Sharpley, 2000:14). Sharpley reaches this conclusion based partly upon the idea that ST should, but effectively cannot contribute to the broader goals of SD (see below). Most commentators would, I suggest, disagree with Sharpley's conclusion, particularly as his work does not really examine the different meanings of SD. Nonetheless, it is important to question the basic assumptions underlying the concept of ST.

This said, and without wishing to sound glib, ST is a notion that if we did not have, then we would have to invent, and so in this chapter an attempt has been made to organize a range of views on key issues into two broad ST variants: 'light green' (LG) and 'dark green' (DG) (Table 1.2). Perhaps the most fundamental choice facing tourism researchers and policymakers lies in deciding upon the basic purpose of ST thinking: should this (indeed, can this) be directed at the tourism sector in isolation, or should ST thinking be more holistic (multisectoral) and directed primarily at attempting to meet the more general goals of SD? These interpretations can be seen as indicative of LG and DG thinking, respectively, and the case for the DG alternative here is surely the stronger one, although strategic, coordinated and spatially extensive planning is a difficult task (Collins, 1999). Other discriminators between LG and DG variants can best be derived from the ongoing SD debate; for example, the degree of protection afforded to the natural environment, the extent to which the precautionary principle is employed, and the nature of environmental management mechanisms used. Without a systematic analysis of the ST literature, it is very difficult to discern a trend towards either LG or DG thinking (at least as far as the academic literature is concerned), although a strong strand of DG opinion is evident, and it would appear that more researchers are engaging with the broader environmental management literature in the search for appropriate means of identifying and controlling the impacts of tourism.

Whether one tends towards LG or DG thinking, in whole or in part, it is important that tourism researchers and policymakers are aware of alternative interpretations of ST, including the different development pathways that these signal, and that they also make the effort to provide clear reasoning for the stance adopted. With a final apology to Bramwell and Lane (1993) for again referring to their quote given at the start of this chapter, we need to be able to 'talk' to other disciplines engaged in sustainability research and practice, and ensure that we 'walk' on clearly marked paths. Both of these require a more proactive engagement with the general SD debate and literature.

Acknowledgements

This chapter is based upon an earlier paper: Hunter, C. (2001) Sustainable tourism theory: an overview from a natural resources perspective. *Environment Papers Series* **4**(2), 42–52.

References

Ahn, B., Lee, B. and Shafer, C.S. (2002) Operationalizing sustainability in regional tourism planning: an application of the limits of acceptable change framework. *Tourism Management* **23**, 1–15.

Aravot, I. (1992) Local tourism in Misgav region – a different model? *Proceedings of an International Seminar on Architecture of Soft Tourism*, pp. 11–18. Istanbul: Yildiz University Faculty of Architecture Press.

Bramwell, B. and Lane, B. (1993) Sustainable tourism: an evolving global approach. *Journal of Sustainable Tourism* **1**(1), 1–5.

Brown, G. and Essex, S. (1997) Sustainable tourism management: lessons from the edge of Australia. *Journal of Sustainable Tourism* **5**(4), 294–305.

Buckley, R. (1996) Sustainable tourism: technical issues and information needs. *Annals of Tourism Research* **23**(4), 925–8.

Buckley, R. and Araujo, G. (1997) Environmental management performance in tourism accommodation. *Annals of Tourism Research* **24**(2), 465–9.

Butcher, J. (1997) Sustainable development or development? In M. Stabler (ed.) *Tourism and Sustainability: Principles to Practice*, pp. 27–38. Wallingford: CAB International.

Butler, R.W. (1999) Sustainable tourism: a state-of-the-art review. *Tourism Geographies* **1**(1), 7–25.

Carley, M. and Christie, I. (1992) *Managing Sustainable Development*. London: Earthscan.

Cater, E. (1995) Environmental contradictions in sustainable tourism. *The Geographical Journal* **161**(1), 21–8.

Collins, A. (1999) Tourism development and natural capital. *Annals of Tourism Research* **26**(1), 98–109.

Collins, A. (2001) Thinking economically about sustainable tourism. *Annals of Tourism Research* **28**(3), 809–11.

Dowling, R. (1993) An environmentally-based planning model for regional tourism development. *Journal of Sustainable Tourism* **1**(1), 17–36.

Driml, S. and Common, M. (1996) Ecological economics criteria for sustainable tourism: applications to the Great Barrier Reef and Wet Tropics World Heritage Areas, Australia. *Journal of Sustainable Tourism* **4**, 3–16.

English Tourist Board, Countryside Commission and Rural Development Commission (1992) *The Green Light: A Guide to Sustainable Tourism*. London: English Tourist Board.

Fox, W. (1994) Ecophilosophy and science. *The Environmentalist* **14**, 207–13.

Gill, A. and Williams, P. (1994) Managing growth in mountain tourism communities. *Tourism Management* **15**(3), 212–20.

Goodall, B. (1995) Environmental auditing: a tool for assessing the environmental performance of tourism firms. *The Geographical Journal* **161**(1), 29–37.

Goodall, B. and Stabler, M. (1997) Principles influencing the determination of environmental standards for sustainable tourism. In M. Stabler (ed.) *Tourism and Sustainability: Principles to Practice*, pp. 279–304. Wallingford: CAB International.

Hall, M. and Wouters, M. (1994) Nature tourism in the sub-Antarctic. *Annals of Tourism Research* **21**, 355–74.

Hanley, N. (2000) The concept of sustainable development: an economic perspective. *Progress in Environmental Science* **2**(3), 181–203.

Healey, P. and Shaw, T. (1994) Changing meanings of 'environment' in the British planning system. *Transactions of the Institute of British Geographers* **19**, 425–38.

Henry, I. and Jackson, G. (1996) Sustainability of management processes and tourism products and contexts. *Journal of Sustainable Tourism* **4**(1), 17–28.

Hjalager, A. (1996) Tourism and the environment: the innovation connection. *Journal of Sustainable Tourism* **4**(4), 201–16.

Holden, A. (1999) High impact tourism: a suitable component of sustainable policy? The case of downhill skiing development at Cairngorm, Scotland. *Journal of Sustainable Tourism* **7**(2), 97–107.

House, J. (1997) Redefining sustainability: a structural approach to sustainable tourism. In M. Stabler (ed.) *Tourism and Sustainability: Principles to Practice*, pp. 89–104. Wallingford: CAB International.

Hughes, J. (1996) Tourism and the environment: a sustainable partnership? *Scottish Geographical Magazine* **112**(2), 107–13.

Hughes, P. (2001) Animals, values and tourism: structural shifts in UK dolphin tourism provision. *Tourism Management* **22**, 321–9.

Hunter, C. (1995) On the need to re-conceptualise sustainable tourism development. *Journal of Sustainable Tourism* **3**, 155–65.

Hunter, C. (1997) Sustainable tourism as an adaptive paradigm. *Annals of Tourism Research* **24**(4), 850–67.

Hunter, C. and Green, H. (1995) *Tourism and the Environment: A Sustainable Relationship?* London: Routledge.

Jafari, J. (1989) An English language literature review. In J. Bystrzanowski (ed.) *Tourism as a Factor of Change: A Socio-Cultural Study*, pp. 17–60. Vienna: Center for Research and Documentation in Social Sciences.

Ko, J. (2001) Assessing progress of tourism sustainability. *Annals of Tourism Research* **28**(3), 817–20.

Klemm, M. (1992) Sustainable tourism development: Languedoc-Roussillon thirty years on. *Tourism Management* June, 169–80.

Lane, B. (1994) Sustainable rural tourism strategies: a tool for development and conservation. *Journal of Sustainable Tourism* **2**(1&2), 102–11.

Lanfant, M.F. and Graburn, N.H. (1992) International tourism reconsidered: the principle of the alternative. In V. Smith and W. Eadington (eds) *Tourism Alternative*, pp. 88–112. Philadelphia: University of Pennsylvania Press.

Lukashina, N., Amirkhanov, M., Anisimov, V. and Trunev, A. (1996) Tourism and environmental degradation in Sochi, Russia. *Annals of Tourism Research* **23**, 654–65.

MacLellan, R. (1998) Tourism and the Scottish environment. In R. MacLellan and R. Smith (eds) *Tourism in Scotland*, pp. 112–34. London: International Thomson Business Press.

McKercher, B. (1993a) The unrecognized threat to tourism: can tourism survive 'sustainability'? *Tourism Management* April, 131–6.

McKercher, B. (1993b) Some fundamental truths about tourism: understanding tourism's social and environmental impacts. *Journal of Sustainable Tourism* **1**(1), 6–16.

Miller, G. (2001) The development of indicators for sustainable tourism: results of a Delphi survey of tourism researchers. *Tourism Management* **22**, 351–62.

Milne, S. (1998) Tourism and sustainable development: the global-local nexus. In M. Hall and A. Lew (eds) *Sustainable Tourism: A Geographical Perspective*, pp. 35–48. London: Longman.

Mitlin, D. (1992) Sustainable development: a guide to the literature. *Environment and Urbanization* **4**, 111–24.

Morgan, M. (1991) Dressing up to survive: marketing Majorca anew. *Tourism Management* **12**, 15–20.

Owen, R.E., Witt, S. and Gammon, S. (1993) Sustainable tourism development in Wales: from theory to practice. *Tourism Management* **14**, 463–74.

Owens, S. (1994) Land, limits and sustainability: a conceptual framework and some dilemmas for the planning system. *Transactions of the Institute of British Geography* **19**(4), 439–56.

Priskin, J. (2001) Assessment of natural resources for nature-based tourism: the case of the Central Coast Region of Western Australia. *Tourism Management* **22**, 637–48.

STB (1994) *Scottish Tourism Strategic Plan*. Edinburgh: Scottish Tourist Board.

Sharpley, R. (2000) Tourism and sustainable development: exploring the theoretical divide. *Journal of Sustainable Tourism* **8**(1), 1–19.

Stabler, M. (1997) An overview of the sustainable tourism debate. In M. Stabler (ed.) *Tourism and Sustainability: Principles to Practice*, pp. 1–22. Wallingford: CAB International.

Stabler, M. and Goodall, B. (1997) Environmental awareness, action and performance in the Guernsey hospitality sector. *Tourism Management* **18**(1), 19–33.

Tabatchnaia-Tamirisa, N., Loke, M., Leung, P. and Tucker, K. (1997) Energy and tourism in Hawaii. *Annals of Tourism Research* **24**(2), 390–401.

Todd, S. and Williams, P. (1996) From white to green: a proposed environmental management system framework for ski areas. *Journal of Sustainable Tourism* **4**(3), 147–73.

Tosun, C. (2001) Challenges of sustainable tourism development in the developing world: the case of Turkey. *Tourism Management* **22**, 289–303.

Tucker, H. (2001) Tourists and Troglodytes: negotiating for sustainability. *Annals of Tourism Research* **28**(4), 868–91.

Turner, R.K., Pearce, D. and Bateman, I. (1994) *Environmental Economics: An Elementary Introduction*. Hemel Hempstead: Harvester Wheatsheaf.

Velikova, M. (2001) How sustainable is sustainable tourism? *Annals of Tourism Research* **28**(2), 496–9.

Wall, G. (1993) International collaboration in the search for sustainable tourism in Bali, Indonesia. *Journal of Sustainable Tourism* **1**(1), 38–47.

Wheeller, B. (1993) Sustaining the ego. *Journal of Sustainable Tourism* **1**, 121–9.

Wight, P. (1998) Tools for sustainability in planning and managing tourism and recreation. In M. Hall and A. Lew (eds) *Sustainable Tourism: A Geographical Perspective*, pp. 75–91. London: Longman.

Wilbanks, T. (1994) 'Sustainable development' in geographic perspective. *Annals of the Association of American Geographers* **84**, 541–56.

Williams, C. (1994) From red to green: towards a new antithesis to capitalism. In G. Haughton and C. Williams (eds) *Perspectives Towards Sustainable Environmental Development*, pp. 165–80. Aldershot: Avebury.

World Commission on Environment and Development (WCED) (1987) *Our Common Future*. Oxford: Oxford University Press.

World Travel and Tourism Council (WTTC) (1999) *Travel and Tourism's Economic Impact*. London: World Travel and Tourism Council.

CHAPTER 2

An optimistic perspective on tourism's sustainability

Tony Griffin

Introduction

One does not have to be an optimist to believe that tourism will grow substantially over the next century. Apparently, however, one does have to be an optimist to regard this as a positive development. As tourism has burgeoned in the latter half of the twentieth century it has been accused of being many things: a despoiler of pristine natural environments, a destroyer of valued lifestyles and age-old cultures, and an exploiter of poor nations. Tourism, it is claimed, ultimately degrades the attractive natural and cultural features of a place and thus can neither sustain the basic resources on which it relies, nor rely on itself as an industry in the long term. If these charges are valid then tourism either should be severely restrained or will eventually burn itself out, but not before causing a great deal of damage. When looking into the future this scenario gives little cause for optimism about the long-term sustainability of tourism.

It is possible, however, to regard tourism's future growth as not only assured but also highly desirable. That is not to suggest that tourism has not and will not cause problems, but these are not insurmountable and are potentially outweighed by the opportunities for improving the human condition. Tourism as a mass international phenomenon is in its infancy, barely fifty years old, and it is possible to learn from past mistakes. The existence of this book, a vast body of literature on tourism's impact, and numerous prescriptive tomes on sustainability, demonstrate a willingness and ability to learn. The optimistic view could be taken that tourism will continue to grow, that the challenges consequently presented can be met, and that the ultimate outcome will be positive, depending on how well both the tourism industry and governments respond to those challenges.

Tourism's growth: patterns and prospects

A glance into the recent past reveals a remarkable increase in international tourist arrivals from 25 million in 1950 to 664 million in 1999, an average annual growth rate of 7 per cent (WTO, 2001a). By the year 2020 international arrivals are predicted to reach 1.18 billion, representing an average annual growth rate of 4.1 per cent. Long-haul travel is predicted to grow even faster (WTO, 2001b). Such forecasts seem reasonable given the likelihood that most of the forces driving past growth will continue for the foreseeable future: faster, larger aircraft leading to lower real travel costs; more widespread affluence in a greater number of countries; reduction of barriers to travel imposed by nations on their own citizens and visitors; and the globalization of media raising people's awareness of the world outside their own domains and tweaking their interest in experiencing other places. The only significant uncertainty revolves around the long-term consequences of the attacks on the World Trade Centre on September 11, 2001. The maintenance of the relatively peaceful global conditions which had been experienced for the previous fifty years are certainly threatened by these events, compounded by fears about the security of air travel. However, there are signs that international travel is recovering from those traumatic events and the ongoing effects are likely to be regional rather than global (WTO, 2002). The most likely outcome is that travel plans may be delayed, or destinations and modes of travel that are perceived to be safer will be substituted. From a sustainability perspective the result may be that more pressure is placed on domestic and shorthaul destinations for major markets.

Provided the current conflicts can be resolved or at least contained, it is highly likely that over the next few decades vastly more people will travel more often and to a wider range of international destinations. The trends are already apparent. In 1950 the top fifteen receiving countries accounted for 97 per cent of all international arrivals, a share that had declined to 62 per cent by 1999 (WTO, 2001c). Over the next twenty years arrivals are predicted to grow fastest in the emerging destinations of the East Asia-Pacific region, followed by Africa, the Middle East and South Asia, albeit in some cases from fairly low bases (WTO, 2001b). Casting some doubt on the accuracy of some of these predictions is the prospect that the events and consequences of September 11 are likely to have their most profound impact on travel to the Middle East and parts of South Asia. However, other destinations further from the conflict, such as Latin America and southern and eastern Africa, may benefit and grow more rapidly than predicted.

From 1985 to 1998 outbound travel growth from the rapidly developing countries of East Asia-Pacific averaged 8.5 per cent per year compared to the global average of 5.3 per cent (WTO, 2001d). Rising, and more widely distributed, affluence reduced the economic barriers to travel for citizens of those countries, and this was often accompanied by the extension of rights to paid holidays and the reduction of economically motivated political barriers to travel. Based on this experience, a clear consequence of economic prosperity is a realization of the desire to travel, and as this extends to other regions throughout the twenty-first century a continual supply of new travellers is assured. With time, increasing affluence should enable international travel to change from being an aspiration to an expectation for many more people, as has occurred in the economically developed world in the latter half of the twentieth century.

Concerns and doubts over tourism's growth

The events of September 11 aside, there are other reasons to believe that this future will not, or even should not, be realized. One of the greatest uncertainties lies in at least maintaining the current historically low cost of international travel. With plans well advanced for the introduction of larger and more fuel-efficient aircraft the medium-term outlook is promising, but looking further into the future there must be concerns about the increasing scarcity of oil. Maintaining low travel costs may be contingent on developing alternative power sources and continually improving technology. Given the scale of the international travel industry, however, an optimistic view would be that there is a substantial incentive to anticipate and counteract this problem.

Developments in computer and information technology, such as the Internet and virtual reality may, it has been suggested, reduce the need or desire to travel. This notion can be summarily dismissed by considering the nature of the tourism experience and what motivates it. Tourism, in essence, is sensual, emotive and driven by a desire to experience a different place in more than two dimensions. The sights, sounds, smells, tastes, ambience and people are integral to the experience, as is the actual presence of the tourist within this milieu. Vicarious experiences can simulate some aspects but not the totality. Moreover, they cannot provide the surprise discoveries, sense of adventure and chance encounters that actual travel affords. It is more likely that the greater awareness of other places engendered by information technology will stimulate a desire to authenticate by direct experience. In this regard the developments in information technology could be seen as an extension of the globalization of media, a factor that has contributed to the growth in tourism over recent decades.

Far more difficult to challenge is the claim that tourism is ultimately unsustainable because of its impacts on environments and cultures that then make destinations less appealing. Large-scale tourism, both international and domestic, is often portrayed as a juggernaut, consuming one destination after another and then rolling on. Tourism could become self-limiting in that accommodating the anticipated growth over the next twenty years may create the conditions for a subsequent decline. Signs are emerging, however, that the tourism industry has learnt some valuable lessons on the downside of its 'success' and has taken steps to secure its own future. Codes of environmental ethics and accreditation schemes have burgeoned and environmental management initiatives have been developed in key industry sectors. While some of these efforts may be viewed as cynical exercises, designed to improve tourism's public image, they have, arguably, served to raise awareness that tourism can do potential harm, and placed sustainability firmly on the tourism agenda. The greatest risk is that such standards may only be selectively applied to situations where there may be some political or commercial advantage in doing so, or where high environmental standards are already evident within regulatory frameworks and the standards do little more than confirm compliance. With regard to achieving sustainability, there are differential challenges for destinations in the developed as opposed to the less developed world, and the following sections of this chapter will highlight these challenges.

Challenges for developed nations

While ostensibly the problems of coping with tourism's growth may appear to be most profound in less developed nations, given the projections discussed above, developed nations will experience the greatest increase in tourist numbers over the next twenty years. Their growth rates in tourist visitation may be lower but these are occurring from a much larger initial base. The projections also do not include domestic tourism, which in many developed nations involves far greater numbers than international tourism. If the events of September 11 are prolonged, destinations within developed nations may be placed under even more pressure because there is likely to be a shift from international to domestic travel. A number of significant challenges emerge from this scenario.

The first is to determine whether the best way to cope with this growth is to allow further development of existing destinations, or to open up new destinations for tourism. The problem with the first option is that many destinations will have reached the point where they have lost their appeal for substantial portions of the tourist market and may, in fact, be in absolute decline. The second option involves an expansion of the tourism frontier and intensification in existing low-key destinations. The danger of this strategy is that it could entrench an ongoing process of invasion and succession, as the tourists with a preference for the more low-key destinations, and the industry that caters for their needs, continually move on in search of new experiences and opportunities. As this process occurs it is likely to create a situation where tourism increasingly threatens other values such as biodiversity and habitat protection. In the light of these probabilities, there would seem to be a strong case for focusing considerable attention on the revitalization of existing destinations. Rather than accepting that such destinations have reached or exceeded their capacities, effort may need to be put into enhancing their capacity as a way of taking pressure off hitherto less developed places.

The second challenge is for developed nations to make more effective use of the tools for achieving sustainable tourism development that they have at their disposal. Developed nations are generally well equipped to handle the anticipated growth in tourism over the next few decades in ways that do not compromise sustainable development objectives. With respect to controlling the impacts of tourism, which is at the heart of sustainable tourism development, there is a substantial and growing knowledge base, particularly in relation to ecological impacts. Moreover, there is the technical know-how to deal effectively with many such impacts. Most importantly, though, is the fact that there are long-standing legislative frameworks that enable many negative consequences of tourism to be controlled or prevented.

Virtually all developed nations have environmental or land use-planning systems in place, which incorporate both forward planning and environmental impact assessment procedures and requirements. All development, tourism included, is controlled through such mechanisms, with the regulations and laws associated with providing a means of effective enforcement. The precise details and mechanisms differ from system to system, but the fact remains that such regulations and laws exist and are a well-accepted part of the development scene in their respective nations. However, the problem in using these laws to enhance the sustainability of tourism often lies in their practical application and in the complexity of the concept of sustainability itself. Most environmental planning systems involve some degree of judgement and discretion on the part of political decision-makers. Trade-offs are often made involving the acceptance of some costs; for example, environmental or social, in return for, say, economic benefits. It can be argued that such a trade-off is not inconsistent with sustainable development principles given that the concept is multidimensional and it is open to interpretation with regard to what is in the best long-term interests of a particular community. When faced with a choice decision-makers may, moreover, opt for the alternative that is geared to viewing the 'long term' as ending at the next election. Thus the problem becomes one of lacking not the means but rather the political will to appropriately enforce the means.

Challenges for less developed nations

The emerging destinations of the less developed world are less likely to have their long-term interests protected as tourism develops. Less developed nations are particularly vulnerable for a number of reasons. They possess environmental and cultural features that tourists from the developed world wish to experience, given the right health, safety and security conditions. Given their existing low material standards of living, they also possess a powerful economic incentive to develop tourism rapidly and with as few constraints as possible. If sustainable development is open to interpretation and is a multidimensional concept incorporating economic, sociocultural and ecological considerations, then less developed nations are understandably likely to place higher priority on the economic dimension. I recently had the experience of teaching a course on environmental management for tourism in Cambodia. It was difficult to talk persuasively about culturally sensitive architecture and the need for travel and tourism businesses to reduce greenhouse gas emissions in a country where there is no ready access to clean drinking water and in which the basic infrastructure has been dismantled and ravaged by decades of war. Understandably, the perceived need for economic development was paramount. It becomes even more difficult when the United States, the wealthiest and arguably the greatest contributor to a number of environmental problems, fails to demonstrate its willingness to make sacrifices in return for enhanced global sustainability by refusing to ratify the Kyoto Protocol on greenhouse gas emissions. If the United States is unwilling to compromise its material well-being, why should Cambodia?

The irony is that to achieve economic development through tourism, many less developed countries have felt it necessary to take steps that may reduce the long-term benefits they receive. Less developed nations lack capital to initiate tourism and provide the necessary supporting infrastructure. Consequently, they have frequently ceded control of tourism development to foreign interests. To attract capital they have offered a variety of concessions, such as tax breaks, liberal access to land and low environmental standards that may reduce establishment and operating costs. The result can be a failure to capture much of the income stream generated from tourism. There is no easy solution to this dilemma, but ironically it may lie in the growth of tourism itself. The combination of a growing market, increasing diversification in types of experiences and destinations sought, and rising levels of experience amongst tourists will likely lead to the industry constantly seeking out new destinations. Bargaining power under such a scenario, for so long in the hands of the multinational corporations, would shift in favour of destinations, although this is certainly not an immediate prospect and relying on this solution may require some patience.

In the interim, less developed nations must either rely on the genuine good intentions of the international tourism industry to act beyond the regulatory requirements that might be imposed upon them, or take some fairly limited steps to partially reduce the deleterious effects of tourism without deterring foreign investment. The former is likely to depend on the industry perceiving commercial advantage, either through cost savings or greater appeal to customers, in being more mindful of its impacts. The latter may rely on adopting measures that do not produce the reverse effects for potential investors in terms of costs and consumer demand. Providing some degree of local participation in, and control over, tourism planning and development decisions is one potential method that could be adopted. It is, after all, a fairly standard feature of regulatory frameworks in developed countries and in principle allows 'acceptable' tourism to be negotiated between development interests and the host community. However, achieving this in practice may be far more problematic in that few less developed nations have political structures that have effectively devolved power to local community levels. Implementing this strategy may require funda-mental political change in many less developed countries before it is practicable on a large scale.

It is far more difficult to be optimistic about the prospects of tourism developing sustainably in less developed nations than in developed ones. The need for economic development is far more urgent, and the political and legal means for controlling tourism and its impacts far less evident. It may be that we in the developed world have to allow those nations more latitude with their interpretation of sustainability. The transfer of knowledge concerning the potential long-term consequences of tourism is important, however, as it allows those nations to make informed choices. It can only be hoped that the sometimes less-than-democratic regimes that govern such countries will make those choices based on the best interests of their current and future generations. Just as has occurred with tourism in the developed world as well, less developed nations must, perhaps, be given the opportunity to learn from their own experiences, which may reveal to them the value of focusing on the long term and the means of developing tourism sustainably.

Quality or quantity?

The discussion thus far has been based on the premise that the growth of tourism is inevitable and that countries, and destinations within them, will have to learn to cope with that growth and/or make more effective use of the means at their disposal. In this regard developed nations are in a better position. A general alternative, however, for all nations where the lifestyle, culture and natural environment are felt to be under threat, may be to focus on quality rather than quantity. This oft-promoted solution aims to reduce tourism's harmful effects without sacrificing economic benefits. The approach typically advocated is to provide high quality facilities and services and thereby attract high spending tourists, selective restraint operating through price. If adopted broadly it could constrain the growth of tourism below predicted levels, but will it be effective in achieving its aims, and is it socially desirable? In relation to the first question there must be doubts. High expenditure does not mean high yield, given that there are greater costs associated with providing higher quality. Given the greater capital commitment required this might also exacerbate less developed nations' reliance on foreign capital. Its desirability depends on how the social benefits of travelling are perceived. The mere fact that tourism has grown so rapidly and that new countries have emerged as major markets as soon as their citizens have the economic means and freedom to travel implies that individuals perceive great benefits. In the twenty-first century do we wish to reverse a significant trend of the twentieth century and revert to the conditions of the nineteenth century when only the most privileged could travel internationally?

If the answer to this question is in the negative then other solutions must be sought to more directly mitigate the impacts of tourism without unduly constraining growth. As discussed in relation to developed nations, there is a substantial, growing knowledge base about most of tourism's impacts, plus the technical means and legislative models to achieve this. A significant problem, however, remains in relation to one area of impact, that is, on culture.

The vexed question of cultural sustainability

The issues in relation to cultural sustainability are far more complex than in relation to, say, biophysical impacts. A pessimistic view on tourism would suggest that its continued growth could dramatically transform cultures and create a homogenized world. Arguably, threats to cultures are more profound and seriously viewed in relation to less developed nations. This is so as the more developed nations provide, and will continue to generate, the vast bulk of tourists, and because they are likely, through the investment process, to maintain control over much of the tourism development in poorer nations. An optimist, however, could retort that cultural change is inevitable and not necessarily undesirable; and moreover, that tourism could counteract other change agents and actually help maintain cultures, thus contributing to, rather than threatening, sociocultural sustainability. Understanding this viewpoint, however, requires an examination of the nature of both culture and international tourism, and the relationship between them.

Simply conceived, culture represents a certain group of people's way of life, beliefs and values. Cultures evolve as mechanisms for survival, maintaining social cohesion and making sense of the world. Specific cultures are products of the environments where they are formed and are limited by knowledge, including that of other cultures. International tourism can change cultures in a variety of ways: it brings people from different cultures into direct contact thereby making them aware of different ways of life, beliefs and values; it commodifies components of culture for tourist consumption thereby changing their meaning; and it can lead to host cultures adopting aspects of the tourists' culture in order to accommodate them. Given the likely growth in tourism the potential for cultural transformation over the next few decades is profound.

Should we resist or embrace such change? The answer is probably mixed but can perhaps be best answered by posing a less equivocal question: should we deny people, both hosts and tourists, the opportunity to expand their horizons by experiencing other ways of life and of viewing the world? Cultures have evolved over the centuries through just such processes and the next century will be no different. Tourism will be one of many change agents, along with economic globalization, improved communication technology, migration and more widespread access to international media. If anything, international tourism could slow the pace of cultural change, trading as it does on cultural differences. It thereby provides an economic incentive for destinations to maintain their culture as a means of attracting tourists. The mere fact that tourists wish to experience a culture may create a sense of pride and reinforce a belief in its intrinsic worth. The real danger from tourism may be that it serves to preserve examples of picturesque poverty when a certain degree of cultural change is both desired and desirable. It is hard to argue, for example, that the black township of Soweto should be preserved, and the way of life of its inhabitants maintained, so that the tour operator businesses based on this 'attraction' can be sustained. Quite clearly there are instances where maintaining a current way of life is not desirable. The concept of cultural sustainability must necessarily embrace a degree of change if future generations are to have a better life, which is a fundamental objective of sustainable development.

Conclusion

The ultimate optimistic perspective is that as we progress through the current century the world will become a closer, more harmonious place, partly because many more of its inhabitants will have experienced it more broadly through tourism. Both tourists and hosts can benefit from this process. Tourism represents an acknowledgement of the value of differences and the desire to experience them. The resulting social contact offers not only the potential to understand and ultimately respect those differences, but also to learn from them. If cultures consequently become more similar it may in fact engender a sense that the things that unite us as human beings are more profound than those that divide us. Restraining tourism may only serve the interests of elites who have been complaining about other tourists since Thomas Cook first escorted his 'hordes' to 'their' beauty spots. While the growth of tourism will inevitably present challenges over the next century, particularly in less developed nations, on balance there is little reason not to be reservedly optimistic about its ultimate sustainability.

References

World Tourism Organization (2001a) 'Historical trend international tourist arrivals'. Available: http://www.world-tourism.org/market_research/data/historical_arrivals.html.

World Tourism Organization (2001b) 'WTO Long-term forecast tourism 2020 vision'. Available: http://www.world-tourism.org/market_research/data/forecast.html.

World Tourism Organization (2001c) 'Diversification of tourism'. Available: http://www.world-tourism.org/market_research/data/diversification.html.

World Tourism Organization (2001d) 'Outbound tourism'. Available: http://www.world-tourism.org/market_research/data/outbound.html.

World Tourism Organization (2002) 'Tourism Recovery Already Underway'. Available: http://www.world-tourism.org/newsroom/Releases/more_releases/march2002/berlin.html.

Part 2

Accreditation, Education and Interpretation

Interpretation as the centrepiece of sustainable wildlife tourism

Sam H. Ham and Betty Weiler

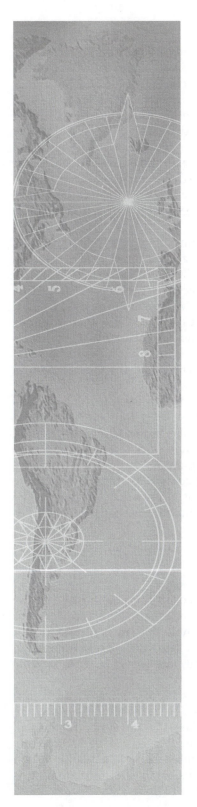

Introduction

For the most part, tourism operators see interpretation as a means of adding value to wildlife tourism; while managers of protected areas appreciate its value in both managing on-site visitor behaviour and contributing to long-term wildlife conservation. Tourists, the primary target of interpretation, have a different perspective again on interpretation, seeing interpretative services as part of the overall experience that they have purchased. Whether delivered in the form of self-guided media (such as web sites, field guides, exhibits, brochures and audiovisual programmes) or face-to-face services (such as guided tours, overland excursions, talks, and demonstrations), such services have the potential to contribute both intellectual and emotional elements to a tourist's wildlife experience. It is the various roles that interpretation performs from the perspective of these three groups, and the link that such roles have to economic and ecological sustainability of wildlife tourism, that is the focus of this chapter. It begins by defining what we mean by *interpretation* and by *sustainability*. We then go on to outline how interpretation contributes to sustainability via four primary pathways.

Interpretation

What is meant by 'interpretation'? Originally defined by Tilden (1957), interpretation is an educational activity aimed at revealing meanings and relationships to people about the places they visit and the things they see and do there. As we have argued elsewhere (Weiler and Ham, 2000; Ham and Weiler, 2002), interpretation lies at the heart and soul of what any good tour guide can and should be doing, whether guiding visitors on land or on water; whether on foot, using non-motorized forms of travel (e.g., canoe, raft, mountain bike or horseback), or vehicle-based tours (e.g., bus, four-wheel drive, riverboat or sea-going vessels); and whether the company or tour is labelled as ecotourism or is part of an adventure, cultural, or heritage product, attraction or resort programme.

While interpretive tour guiding is very important, interpretation is not just about face-to-face communication on guided tours. It also includes non-personal or 'static' interpretation such as printed materials, signs, exhibits, self-guided walks, and various electronic media (see Trapp *et al.*, 1991; Ham, 1992; Van Gameren, in press). Interpretation is used by tour operators as well as by resorts, lodges, attractions, theme parks, museums, parks, zoos, visitor centres, and so on. Many of these use interpretive media in an effort to enhance visitors' understanding and appreciation of the environments being visited and the various natural and cultural phenomena experienced.

Moscardo *et al.*'s (2000) literature review on wildlife tourism as well as Muloin *et al.*'s (2001) study of indigenous wildlife tourism in Australia identified guides as the interpretive service most frequently used in wildlife settings. Other popular media for wildlife tourism include interpretive signs, brochures, guidebooks, animal shows and displays, audiovisual presentations and interactive computers. In our view, these media are more than just ways to transmit information to visitors. The premise of this chapter is that they constitute informational pathways to sustainable tourism.

Sustainability

The concept of sustainability first appeared on the public scene in the report put out by the World Commission on Environment and Development (better known as the Brundtland Commission) in 1987. The idea of sustainable development is that economic growth and environmental conservation are not only compatible, they are *necessary partners*. One cannot exist without the other.

Sustainable tourism is tourism that is developed and maintained in a manner, and at such a scale, that it remains economically viable over an indefinite period and does not undermine the physical and human environment that sustains and nurtures it. It needs to be *economically* sustainable, because if tourism is not profitable then it is a moot question to ask whether it is environmentally sustainable – tourism that is unprofitable and unviable will simply cease to exist.

So, while debate continues over the esoteric definition of sustainability (see, for example, Robinson and Bennett, 2000) for our purposes here it includes both ecologically and economically desirable outcomes. The remainder of this chapter looks at these two dimensions of sustainability, and how interpretation is central to each.

How does interpretation contribute to economic sustainability?

Interpretation can facilitate *economic sustainability* in two main ways: first, by satisfying customer demand, and second, by creating local employment.

To what extent do *visitors demand* interpretation? According to the recent report by Fredline and Faulkner (2001), one out of every five international visitors surveyed by the Australian Bureau of Tourism Research in 2000 said that their decision to visit Australia was influenced by the opportunity to 'experience wildlife'. A key question here is what do visitors mean by '*experiencing* wildlife'? For example, to what extent are learning and information seeking important motivations for tourists?

We know that learning and information seeking are important motivations for many nature-based tourists, including wildlife tourists (e.g., Ballantyne *et al.*, 1998; Moscardo *et al.*, 1998; Ham and Weiler, 2001; Armstrong and Weiler, 2002). What goes on inside a tourist's head strongly influences the on-site experience. There is evidence that visitors want accurate, timely and relevant information during their experience. In fact, visitors seek information about the places they visit not only while they are *on-site*, but also *before* and *after* their visit. Indeed, they *expect* it, and they *demand* it as part of the experience for which they have paid.

In other words, wildlife tourists want to get the right information, in the right way, at the right time, and to the extent that they do this, their experience is more satisfying. Successful tourism businesses know this, and they concentrate as much on developing and delivering interpretive services as they do other aspects of their business. Wildlife tourism operators who provide interpretive services offer more than a physical experience: they offer an intellectual and emotional experience. It is this combination that creates satisfied customers, because of the connection that interpretation creates between people and the places they go to experience wildlife. To the extent that guided and self-guided interpretation helps wildlife tourists establish an intellectual and emotional connection with a place, the quality of their experiences will be enhanced. Providing quality interpretation is a primary means by which such links are established.

The 'connection' idea is important. Interpreting a place is not just a process of filling wildlife tourists' heads with endless facts and figures about animals and habitat. Something else must happen. We know from our own research on tourists' perceptions of quality guiding in Galapagos and Alaska that the best wildlife interpretation engages the visitor both intellectually and emotionally, and that it is personal, relevant and meaningful for them. Although visitors often mention the guide's factual 'knowledge' as being important to their experience, our research (Ham and Weiler, 2002) reveals that when visitors are asked to comment on the guide's personal contribution to their satisfaction, virtually none of them mention the sheer volume of facts given by their guides. They do, however, repeatedly allude to ways in which the guide's commentaries helped them to relate, connect, and care about the place and the wildlife that live there.

Enhancing visitor experiences through interpretation, whether guided or self-guided, makes business sense for the operator whose daily concern is economic sustainability. According to Conservation International, a Washington, DC-based environmental organization, high quality interpretation 'can also improve business by increasing the quality of guests' experience, increasing repeat visitation and occupancy rates, providing unique marketing opportunities and allowing hotels to charge higher rates' (Sweeting et al., 1999: 27).

Researchers are finding increasing evidence that nature-based tourists expect not just raw factual information, but interpretation, as part of their experiences, and that, for many, high quality interpretation is a major contributor to their satisfaction (e.g., Pearce and Moscardo, 1998). In another study, Ham and Weiler (2000) found that guided and self-guided interpretive services contributed more to the satisfaction of nature-based tourists in Panama than did their use of most types of recreation facilities such as swimming and fishing areas, campgrounds, restrooms, and trails.

Is interpretation an integral part of all wildlife tourism? There is mounting evidence that interpretation enhances many wildlife tourism experiences, and that like most nature-based tourists, even very educated, well-travelled and highly experienced wildlife tourists seek out and appreciate quality interpretation. However, research is needed about how different market segments respond to interpretive options, whether interpretation affects visitors' choice of tours, and the extent to which tourists' satisfaction varies with the type of interpretive offering. In general, though, the evidence to date certainly suggests that interpretation contributes to visitor satisfaction, and research on other forms of tourism has found that satisfied customers create positive word-of-mouth advertising and repeat visitation, all of which contribute to economic sustainability.

Interpretation facilitates economic sustainability not only by satisfying customers, but also by *creating jobs*. A conclusion of Muloin et al.'s (2001) study of indigenous wildlife tourism in Australia was that involvement of indigenous people as guides and interpreters adds an authentic element to a wildlife tourism experience that is valued by many tourists and adds depth to visitors' understanding of wildlife.

People with local knowledge, and with a passion for the place in which they have grown up and come to love, have the two essential ingredients that make the best interpretive guides: they are knowledgeable and they are passionate. Training and employing local people as guides and interpreters represents an important sustainable development strategy because it produces a type of employment that is based on, and even demands, an unspoiled environment (Weiler and Ham, 2001). For those employed in the industry, the economic value of protecting their very livelihoods is compelling. So training and employing locals as interpretive guides not only provides satisfied customers, it also provides satisfied locals who become important allies in the protection of both the natural and the cultural environments that form the basis of the wildlife tourism industry (Weiler and Ham, 2002).

How does interpretation facilitate ecological sustainability?

In wildlife tourism, interpretation acts, firstly, as an on-site regulator of visitor behaviour – it is a key strategy for managing environmental impacts. Secondly, interpretation influences not only what people know and do on-site, but potentially what visitors believe about conservation generally. Interpretation can thus play a key role in long-term conservation.

What is the role of interpretation in *influencing and regulating visitor behaviour*? In attempting to develop a conceptual framework for wildlife tourism, Reynolds and Braithwaite (2001) discuss several strategies for controlling visitors, particularly in the context of tourist interactions with wildlife. Beyond the physical strategies (such as regulating group size and access) that have dominated management to date, they invoke the idea of 'intellectual control', which they describe as the use of a tour guide and other interpretive mechanisms to transmit knowledge and at the same time influence on-site visitor behaviour.

Interpretation has, of course, been employed for decades by agencies such as the Canadian Parks Service and several land management agencies in the US, for precisely this purpose. More recently, the US National Park Service (Kohen and Sikoryak, 1999) has implemented a sophisticated interpretive planning process aimed at informing decisions such as which audiences will be targeted with which strategic messages (themes), with the specific purpose of influencing visitor experiences and often behaviour. In Australia, Parks Victoria is embarking on a very similar planning process.

These strategic interpretive planning strategies are underpinned by two related theories of human behaviour: the theory of reasoned action (Fishbein and Ajzen, 1975) and the theory of planned behaviour (Ajzen, 1991). Twenty-five years of research based on these related theories have confirmed that much human behaviour, or at least behavioural intent, is *consistent with* our attitudes, and that these attitudes are consistent with our *beliefs*. Although relationships between beliefs, attitudes, behavioural intent and behaviours are more complex than this, the main implication is that if you want to influence how a person feels and acts toward a thing, you need to influence what they *believe* about it. As Ham and Krumpe (1996) have explained in detail, when interpretation is designed and delivered to influence a tourist's beliefs about an animal, an animal's habitat, or a concept such as 'respecting' or 'protecting' that animal or its habitat, it can potentially have profound impacts.

This is a different strategy than, say, just filling an allotted time period with facts and details about wildlife. It is more strategic and more purposeful, in the sense that it is aimed at a known desired outcome. This is thematic interpretation: the idea of communicating beliefs in an effort to strategically influence attitudes and ultimately behaviours. According to Ham and Krumpe (1996), a theme expresses a belief about something. So whether it is a guide's commentary, an exhibit text, or a web site that is communicating to a visitor, the intent of thematic interpretation is to plant a seed that can become the foundation of a new belief related to a desired behavioural outcome. Of course, it must be done in a fun and entertaining way in order to be satisfying, but it is more strategic than just entertaining for entertainment's sake.

Around the world, protected area managers have put considerable resources into using interpretation as a way of influencing and regulating visitor behaviour, all in the interests of minimising negative impacts and facilitating sustainability (Ham 1992; Roggenbuck, 1992; Alder, 1996; Lackey and Ham, 2001; Lackey et al., 2002). The involvement of the commercial sector in controlling visitor behaviour has been more recent and much less strategic. However, park management agencies are well aware that interpretation has been largely taken out of their hands by government cut-backs and privatization, and are increasingly keen to 'use' the commercial sector for communicating minimal impact messages, managing visitor behaviour and role modelling appropriate practices at least while visiting protected areas.

Research by Armstrong and Weiler (2002), in cooperation with Parks Victoria in Australia, found that licensed tour operators in national parks could be doing much more in the way of delivering interpretive messages that act as a park management tool. Participant-observation and audiorecording of guide commentary on twenty guided tours found that seventeen of the guides delivered 107 messages related to Parks Victoria's goals. In relation to the length of the tours (many were full-day tours) and the amount of commentary, this is a very small number. The most frequently delivered messages were about minimizing impacts while on tour. Few messages imparted by the guides touched on the importance or difficulty of protected area management. The responsibility largely rests with the managers of protected areas being proactive in identifying and even requiring particular messages to be communicated by licensed tour operators, as a way of influencing on-site behaviour.

In addition to influencing what people know and do on-site, interpretation can play a role in *long-term conservation* by influencing what visitors come to believe about the area, about the importance of the resources being protected and about the strategies being used to protect them. Through the well-documented 'sleeper effect' process, it can be argued that a day spent observing or thinking about wildlife, whether free-roaming or captive, can theoretically turn into something much bigger in the form of new beliefs implanted in a tourist's psyche (see, for example, Hovland et al., 1953; Gruder et al., 1978; Lariscy and Tinkham, 1999). As we will see shortly, that, of course, depends on the themes the tourist leaves with and the kind of reinforcement she or he experiences in the coming days and weeks, but it *can* happen.

However, evaluating the extent to which interpretation does this involves much more than just recording visitors' recall of ecological facts. The Parks Victoria study previously noted identified the kinds of messages delivered by operators and recalled by visitors, but did not go further in measuring whether these messages get translated into environmental attitudes, behavioural intentions and ultimately conservation behaviours. Longitudinal research of this type is difficult but necessary to determine how interpretation impacts on long-term conservation. Likewise, Lackey and Ham (2001) reported that Yosemite National Park (USA) visitors could remember some of the messages aimed at them regarding appropriate food storage behaviour in black bear country, yet improper food storage persists as a problem in the park. Guided by the theories outlined earlier, researchers believe that messages need to be redirected to target visitors' specific beliefs about storing food properly.

Direct evidence exists that high-quality thematic interpretation con- tributes to tourists' attitudes and behaviour in support of wildlife conservation. A theme-driven communication campaign developed for Lindblad Expeditions passengers in the Galapagos Islands (see Ham and O'Brien, 1998; Ham, 2001) directly resulted in significant increases in passenger donations to the Galapagos Conservation Fund (GCF). Guided by the theories of reasoned action and planned behaviour, the GCF campaign consisted primarily of strategically developed messages that were developed and delivered to passengers via onboard interpretive panels, guide commentaries at various islands, in evening debriefings, and in pre-visit information sent to passengers prior to their departure. According to Solutions Site Case Study (2001):

> The development of an organized communications strategy unques- tionably resulted in consistent responses from our guests. This has translated into an average of about $4000 per week in steady support for Galapagos conservation.
> (http://www.solutions-site.org/cat1_sol116.htm)

Although demonstration of interpretation's success in achieving the ultimate goal of long-term conservation awaits further study, such results do suggest that thematic interpretation can indeed contribute in positive ways to how wildlife tourists think, feel, and behave with respect to wildlife conservation in a place like Galapagos.

Conclusion

Much remains to be learned about interpretation's role in sustainable wildlife tourism. However, the evidence presented in this chapter suggests that interpretation, strategically packaged and creatively delivered, can contribute to sustainable wildlife tourism by: (1) satisfying customer demand, (2) creating opportunities for local employment, (3) influencing on-site visitor behaviour, and (4) promoting a conservation ethic in tourists that may extend well beyond their on-site experience. These are both the premise and promise of interpretation in sustainable wildlife tourism: done well, it enhances the wildlife experience of tourists, acts as a mechanism for job creation, serves as an on-site management tool, and acts as a strategic communication medium for long-term conservation.

References

Ajzen, I. (1991) The Theory of Planned Behavior. *Organizational Behavior and Human Decision Processes* **50**: 179–211.

Alder, J. (1996) Costs and Effectiveness of Education and Enforcement, Cairns Section of the Great Barrier Reef Marine Park. *Environmental Management* **20**(4), 541–51.

Armstrong, K. and Weiler, B. (2002) 'They said what to who?!' – Messages delivered on guided tours in Victorian protected areas. Presented to *Tour Guiding and Heritage Interpretation: Seminar on Research for the 21st Century*. Melbourne.

Ballantyne, R., Packer, J. and Beckmann, E. (1998) Targeted interpretation: Exploring relationships among visitors' motivations, activities, information needs and preferences. *Journal of Tourism Studies* **9**(2): 14–25.

Brundtland, H.-G. (1987) *Our Common Future: Report of the World Commission on Environment and Development*. UNESCO.

Fishbein, M. and Ajzen, I. (1975) *Belief, Attitude, Intention and Behavior: An Introduction to Theory and Research*. Reading: Addison-Wesley.

Fredline, E. and Faulkner, W. (2001) *International Market Analysis of Wildlife Tourism*. Wildlife Tourism Research Report Series, Gold Coast, CRC for Sustainable Tourism.

Gruder, C., Cook, T., Hennigan, K., Flay, B., Alessis, C. and Halama, J. (1978) Empirical tests of the absolute sleeper effect predicted from the discounting cue hypothesis. *Journal of Personality and Social Psychology* **36**: 1061–74.

Ham, S. (1992) *Environmental Interpretation: A Practical Guide for People with Big Ideas and Small Budgets*. Golden, CO, USA: Fulcrum/North American Press.

Ham, S. (2001) A Theory-based Approach to Campaign Planning for Traveler's Philanthropy. Invited address to Traveler's Philanthropy Summit, hosted by Business Enterprises for Sustainable Tourism (BEST), Punta Cana Resort, Dominican Republic, Nov. 9–11.

Ham, S. and Krumpe, E. (1996) Identifying Audiences and Messages for Nonformal Environmental Education: A Theoretical Framework for Interpreters. *Journal of Interpretation Research* **1**(1): 11–23.

Ham, S. and O'Brien, T. (1998) *The Galapagos Conservation Fund: A Case Study in Developing an Organized Communication Strategy for Conservation Fundraising*. New York: Lindblad Expeditions, Inc.

Ham, S. and Weiler, B. (2001) 100,000 Beating Bird Hearts: Tourism, Wildlife and Interpretation. Keynote presentation at the First National Conference on Wildlife Tourism in Australia. Hobart, Tasmania, Australia, October 28–30 (www.crctourism.com.au).

Ham, S. and Weiler, B. (2002) Toward a Theory of Quality in Cruise-based Nature Guiding. *Journal of Interpretation Research* **6**(1), in press.

Hovland, C., Janis, I. and Kelley, H. (1953) *Communication and Persuasion*. Yale University Press.

Kohen, R. and Sikoryak, K. (1999) Comprehensive Interpretive Planning. *Legacy* **10**(4): 25–30.

Lackey, B. and Ham, S. (2001) Human-Bear Interaction Assessment, Yosemite National Park, California. Interim Research Report submitted to the National Park Service and the Yosemite Fund, November.

Lackey, B., Ham, S. and Quigley, H. (2002) *Message Catalog: Human-Bear Messages in Yosemite Valley*. Center for International Training and Outreach, Department of Resource Recreation and Tourism, University of Idaho.

Lariscy, R. and Tinkham, S. (1999) The sleeper effect and negative political advertising. *Journal of Advertising* **28**(4): 13–30.

Moscardo, G., Pearce, P.L. and Haxton, P. (1998) Understanding rainforest tourist expectations and experiences. *1998 Australian Tourism and Hospitality Research Conference*. Bureau of Tourism Research, 295–308.

Moscardo, G., Woods, B. and Greenwood, T. (2000) *Understanding Visitor Perspectives on Wildlife Tourism*. Wildlife Tourism Research Report Series: No. 2, Gold Coast, CRC for Sustainable Tourism.

Muloin, S., Zeppel, H. and Higginbottom, K. (2001) *Indigenous Wildlife Tourism in Australia*. Wildlife Tourism Research Report Series: No. 15, Gold Coast, CRC for Sustainable Tourism.

Pearce, P.L. and Moscardo, G. (1998) The role of interpretation in influencing visitor satisfaction: A rainforest case study. *1998 Australian Tourism and Hospitality Research Conference*. Bureau of Tourism Research, pp. 309–19.

Reynolds, P. and Braithwaite, D. (2001) Towards a conceptual framework for wildlife tourism. *Tourism Management* **22**: 31–42.

Robinson, J. and Bennett, E. (2000) *Hunting for Sustainability in Tropical Forests*. New York: Columbia University Press.

Roggenbuck, J. (1992) Use of Persuasion to Reduce Resource Impacts and Visitor Conflicts. Chapter 7, in Manfred, M. (ed.), *Influencing Human Behavior: Theory and Applications in Recreation, Tourism, and Natural Resources Management*. Champaign, Illinois, USA: Sagamore Publishing, pp. 149–208.

Solutions Site Case Study (2001) The Galapagos Conservation Fund (GCF). In Section V of web site: http://www.solutions-site.org/cat1_sol116.htm.

Sweeting, J.E.N., Bruner, A.G. and Rosenfeld, A.B. (1999) *The Green Host Effect: An Integrated Approach to Sustainable Tourism and Resort Development*. Conservation International Policy Paper. Washington, DC: Conservation International.

Tilden, F. (1957) *Interpreting Our Heritage*. Chapel Hill, NC, USA: University of North Carolina Press.

Trapp, S., Gross, M. and Zimmerman, R. (1991) *Signs, Trails and Wayside Exhibits: Connecting People and Places*. Stevens Point, WI, USA: University of Wisconsin, Stevens Point Press, Inc.

Van Gameren, M. (in press) Strengths and Weaknesses of Different Interpretive Devices. Section 2.7.1 in *Information, Interpretation and Education Manual*. Melbourne: Parks Victoria.

Weiler, B. and Ham, S.H. (2000) Tour Guides and Interpretation in Ecotourism. Chapter 35, in Weaver, D. (ed.), *The Encyclopedia of Ecotourism*. Wallingford, UK: CABI Publishing, pp. 549–64.

Weiler, B. and Ham, S.H. (2001) Tour Guide Training: Lessons for Malaysia about What Works and What's Needed. Chapter 10 in Nyland, C., Smith, W., Smyth, R. and Vicziany, M. (eds), *Malaysia Business in the New Era*. Cheltenham, UK: Edward Elgar, pp. 149–61.

Weiler, B. and Ham, S. (2002) Tour Guide Training: A Model for Sustainable Capacity Building in Developing Countries. *Journal of Sustainable Tourism* **10**(1), 25–69.

Travel ecology and developing naturally: making theory–practice connections

Thomas D. Potts and Rich Harrill

Introduction

As development theories evolve, approaches to the use of tourism as a development tool need to be revisited to reflect these changes. A careful balance must be struck between new ideas and successful existing practices. This chapter presents a case study concerning how an innovative conceptual framework was integrated into a community tourism programme at Clemson University, USA. Over the last twenty years, the 'Developing Naturally' programme at Clemson has grown from serving local clients on a case-by-case basis to facilitating community development in eighty-eight countries. While the efficacy of the programme has yet to be fully measured, the 150 000 (electronic) requests for information that have been received, resulting international partnerships, and field experiences to date indicate that it has been well received. As the programme has evolved from being local to international in scope, its basic framework has changed from one based on resource conservation, to one employing a sustainable development paradigm. In more recent times, a further development has occurred with a post-sustainable ethic termed 'travel ecology' being employed as the conceptual foundation for the Developing Naturally programme. This chapter overviews the development of this framework, placing emphasis on the coevolution of theory and practice.

Programme evolution

In the early 1980s, the tourism extension programme at Clemson University focused on the development of nature-based tourism in relation to recreational fisheries along the Southeastern US coast. Using resource conservation as a conceptual framework, this programme included the identification of natural resources (e.g., fishery location and mapping), inventory of associated infrastructure (e.g., guide services, charter captains, and marinas), resource marketing including cooperative efforts in promotion and advertising (e.g., printed guides, brochures, magazine ads, and trade shows), conservation education and other university supported public service programmes (e.g., charter captain workshops, special tournaments, television programmes, and newspaper articles).

While the fisheries programme was successful in increasing economic return for the recreational fisheries industry at the local level, and in the development of a conservation ethic within the recreational fisheries industry, the research team did not simultaneously address social, economic, and environmental concerns as called for in today's sustainable development programmes. The emphasis of the programme was essentially on industry development and conserving a natural resource for the benefit of specific local communities. Indeed, as with many similar programmes implemented at this time, the focus was very much on the development of tourism instead of developing communities for tourism, although these efforts were still called 'community tourism development'.

By the late 1980s, the tourism extension programme began receiving requests for development assistance in Central Europe, a region struggling with severe economic development problems resulting from a disintegrating Soviet Bloc. Our first overseas tourism development project was undertaken under the auspices of Volunteers in Overseas Cooperative Assistance (VOCA) and involved working within their Polish Agricultural Extension programme. The Polish experience provided unique insights into issues related to tourism and community development as this region underwent a radical social and economic transition from communism to democracy. The initial emphasis of the programme was to create new economic opportunities in the tourism area for farmers who had lost their traditional sources of income in the Soviet farm products market. The tourism infrastructure in these communities was, however, virtually non-existent. Villagers were striving to survive and had little faith in any plan for the future no matter how promising. During a local town meeting conducted by a Clemson University researcher concerning tourism development, a small farmer expressed his frustration and pessimism toward the future. When the researcher stated that tourism would offer some hope for bringing additional income to the community, the farmer responded by shouting, 'Hope! Hope! Hope is the Angel of Despair!'

In recognition of the context in which the programme was to operate, it was decided to focus on stimulating local entrepreneurship, within the context of sustainable agritourism, which included the development of Bed and Breakfast (B and B) enterprises. At the time, sustainable development was thought to be an appropriate paradigm for this type of tourism because it provided an alternative to mass tourism models. Smallscale bed and breakfast development was considered ideal for this situation, as it required little additional economic expenditures for the farm family, while at the same time bringing new income into the community. In 1995, a paper developed at Clemson University, *Beginning a Bed and Breakfast in South Carolina: Guidelines for Development* (www.strom.clemson.edu/publications/Potts/bb/bb1–3.pdf), was adapted and translated into Polish so it could be used as a resource for the programme. Over thirty bed and breakfast workshops were held in the country's rural communities. This effort resulted in the creation of several tourism associations and numerous farm-based bed and breakfast operations in Poland, hosting visitors from across Europe.

In one area with numerous small organic farms, the concept of a healthy bed and breakfast venue was developed, targeting the health-conscious German tourist. Meetings and workshops were also held with mayors and village officials featuring tourism development, based on a 'home town discovery' process (see later discussion) for community development tourism. However, while working in an area that lacked infrastructure and social capital, researchers began to realize that sustainable development had limitations in such contexts. Many of the case studies used in sustainable development programmes came from developed or semi-developed settings, and as such addressed few of the problems associated with 'starting from scratch'.

Conceptual background

Up until the time that researchers began to question the efficacy of sustainable development in certain contexts, tourism extension pro-grammes at Clemson closely reflected overall trends in the tourism research field. For example, the marine fisheries project outlined earlier was influenced by environmental planning and policy dating back to Ian McHarg's *Design with nature* (1969), in that it utilized predetermined spatial attributes to locate fisheries in environmentally and commercially advantageous positions. The programme was also influenced by Gunn's *Vacationscape: defining tourism regions* (1972) in that it was expressly concerned with identifying and making use of regional tourism resour-ces. Although these technical approaches fostered a new awareness of tourism as a development issue, they placed little emphasis on resident attitudes or citizen participation.

By 1979, Gunn, in *Tourism planning: basics, concepts, and cases*, called for a much broader approach to tourism development and importantly, more local participation throughout the planning process. Seekings (1980, p. 253) echoed this sentiment, stating, 'Tourism has become too important to be left to the experts.' Throughout the 1980s and 1990s, community-driven planning efforts were investigated by numerous researchers (Murphy, 1983, 1988, 1993; Blank, 1989; Keogh, 1990; Prentice, 1993; Jamal and Getz, 1995). In 1995, researchers at Clemson University published *Hometown Discovery: a development process for tourism* (Amos and Potts, 1992). This publication was influenced by the books *An approach to assessing community tourism potential* (Harris *et al.*, 1989) and *Small town tourism development* (Howell, 1987). The purpose of *Hometown Discovery* was to allow residents to 'discover' their hometown regarding tourism potential and plans for appropriate tourism development. This process would later be used as the basis for the Developing Naturally programme.

The *Hometown Discovery* publication provided residents with the opportunity to develop a customized tourism development plan for their area. Key headings in this book were:

- Is tourism for us?
- What will we need? (Maps, documents, etc.)
- What are our human resources? (Natural, built, etc.)
- Service and infrastructure
- Financing
- Market conditions
- Targeting customers
- Benchmarks (making a calendar)
- Communications inventory
- Visitation trends
- Competition analysis
- Comprehensive overview (putting in all together)
- Implementation (action steps).

The use of *Hometown Discovery* by communities involved the creation of a planning team. This team would act to rank and map resources, identify community assets and deficiencies, and develop a strategy for tourism development in their area. The *Hometown Discovery* publication was initially utilized by various communities throughout South Carolina. In more recent times, it has been translated by Polish and Russian organizations with an interest in community tourism development in their respective countries.

During the 1990s, sustainable development began to be incorporated into the tourism field and featured in Inskeep's *Tourism planning: an integrated and sustainable approach* (1991) and Gunn's 1994 edition of *Tourism planning*. By 1994, work began on a revision of the Hometown Discovery programme and the next year *Developing naturally: an exploratory process for nature-based community tourism* (Potts and Marsinko, 1995) was published. This publication built on the Hometown Discovery process with the addition of an analysis chapter dedicated to maintaining resource quality and a section on identifying potential nature visitors. At the time, the researchers identified nature-based tourism with sustainable development, only to the extent that they both shared a common environmental ideal. As a result of the researchers' Polish experience, they came to identify nature-based tourism with much larger issues embraced within the concept of sustainable development, such as politics and culture. As a result, the document *Developing Naturally* eventually became the centrepiece of a more comprehensive programme sponsored by Clemson University's Strom Thurmond Institute. The programme is today called 'Developing Naturally: enhancing communities' and is downloadable from the World Wide Web.

A travel ecology approach

In 1996, we undertook a comprehensive review of the literature in the areas of sustainability, tourism, and community development. This effort was part of an overall plan to explain the barriers and associated social attitudes toward development we found in our Eastern European experience as well as trying to locate our experiences in the constellation of ideas that fall under the rubric 'sustainable tourism'. This review led to a presentation entitled *In search of a travel ecology paradigm* (Potts and Harrill, 1997) at the Travel and Tourism Research Association national conference. This paper detailed the evolution of conservation, carrying capacity, eco-development, and sustainability, culminating in a travel ecology paradigm that challenged professionals to think beyond sustainability or 'sustaining tourism'. With a close affinity to the fields of cultural and political ecology, *travel ecology* implies that tourism planning and policy should help create communities that become resilient enough to survive in a highly volatile political and economic environment and think beyond mere 'sustaining' tourism or some specific aspect of tourism development. Thus, we consider 'travel ecology' as theoretical shorthand for 'sustainable community tourism development', although in some respects improving on 'tourism sustainability' as a conceptual foundation by emphasizing a more holistic approach to community development and ecological enhancement. A subsequent presentation in 1998, *Developing Naturally: toward a travel ecology approach* (Potts and Harrill, 1998a), at the National Tourism Extension Conference, was used as an opportunity to engage in substantial dialogue regarding what we perceived as limitations relating to current approaches to sustainable tourism development and to further refine the 'travel ecology' concept. We felt that tourism planners and professionals, including ourselves, had, in general, historically focused narrowly on developing tourism. Although tourism professionals had engaged with the concept of sustainability, they had not appreciated the potential that tourism offered for long-term enhancement of communities and associated environments. Subsequently, the opportunity through tourism to build environments where individuals could reach their potential had not been fully appreciated.

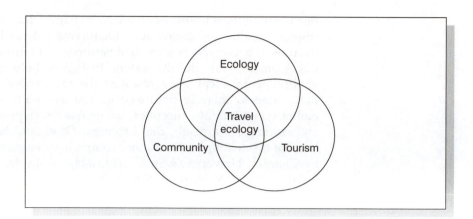

Figure 4.1
Travel ecology
model. *Travel
ecology* differs
from ecotourism,
nature based and/
or 'sustainable'
tourism models
due to its emphasis
on enhancement
and focus on
community

Today, the Developing Naturally programme, based on the conceptual foundation of travel ecology, calls for a restructuring of research and planning programmes in a direction that moves beyond sustainability and toward an investigation of how the relationships between community, ecology, and travel can be used not only to sustain, but enhance human communities (Figure 4.1). The travel ecology approach is based on six principles with broad applicability to many types of 'communities', including local, regional, national, and international communities (Potts and Harrill, 1998b). We view these principles as contributing to tourism theory, rather than constituting a definitive model or process (Getz, 1986).

Discovery

The initial planning phase of 'discovery' is based upon the participation of all relevant stakeholders within a development area, for example citizens in a local village. A key to successful planning is the development of self-awareness within the community that occurs when residents inventory their own social, economic, and environmental resources. This inventory process allows the resident to discover 'sense of place'; that combination of built and natural environment, history, and local culture that make a place unique. Through public discourse about the importance and value of these discovered resources individuals can address fears about potential changes and expectations for improvement. The original impetus behind Hometown Discovery and Developing Naturally was to design a process allowing residents to perceive their community's tourism resources from the perspective of an outsider – to 'discover' the community's tourism potential through collaborative, democratic forums. The process of discovery can at times be a turbulent phase in the tourism planning process, as conflicts in interest group values are gradually uncovered. The sustainable tourism literature places little emphasis on the potential conflicts arising over resource distribution and use. Conversely, the travel ecology approach recognizes that open public conflict and democratic decision-making are necessary conditions for the creation of resilient communities, and that open dialogue is an excellent method of social learning. During this discovery phase a tourism planner should mediate and lead negotiations between community groups with conflicting interests regarding tourism.

Mutuality

During the discovery phase visions for the communities' future are gradually uncovered. One should expect that consensus can be reached on some issues, and residents will find that they have common ground from which they can move toward an agreed goal of a better quality of life for community members. Mutuality means that citizens engage in a common language emphasizing shared values, ideas, and concerns while respecting one another's opinions. Healthy communities have a sense of mutuality that goes beyond the coordination of limited benefits, segmented goals or roles (Selznick, 1996: 198). The absence of mutuality that occurs during political transitions such as from communism to democracy can make tourism planning extremely difficult. Resource scarcity, political distrust, and the lack of social organization make tourism planning, much less sustainable tourism, extremely difficult to achieve in these contexts. Although infrequently emphasized, sustainable development is about relationship building: between generations, between social groups and institutions, and between individuals sharing nature's wealth on a local basis.

Locality

We are often asked to 'think globally' when we need to think and act locally. The travel ecology approach emphasizes 'backyard activism' or the 'geography of everywhere': the recognition that all landscapes, no matter how mundane, contribute to the community tourism product. With tourism development in Central Europe, the researchers were pleased to find that residents had a very detailed 'cognitive map' of local places, a perspective rarely found in the homogenized West. Locality begins with the notion that environmental awareness toward environments such as rainforests or savannas begins with an awareness of commonplace environments. This is not to advocate an abandonment of 'endangered' environments, only that awareness of locality is critical to the development of 'sense of place' – often mentioned (Berry, 1993) as a component of community. The travel ecology approach is based upon the belief that the community is both a socially constructed and ecologically grounded place. Social networks and natural and built environments in which such networks evolve are mutually reinforcing elements of community. Environments may dictate both quality of life and economic resources opportunities. Individuals who recognize their relationship to the local environment more fully understand their neighbours and their common foundations.

Historicity

Historical knowledge is indispensable to the tourism planning process, despite the postmodern contention that 'history is dead' (Ritzer, 1993). As sustainable tourism models often emphasize 'best practices' management grounded in the present, a community's historical patterns of land and resource use are often neglected in sustainable development plans and policies. Tourism planners should become thoroughly familiar with oral and written traditions if they are to fully appreciate how residents interact with one another and their environment. In the Central European experience, it was found that there was some historical 'amnesia' due to Soviet efforts at cultural assimilation, while other traditions, particularly religious and folk, remained strong in the hearts of the people. The researchers realized that an awareness and appreciation of local history and culture on the part of the residents was important to developing an authentic and viable local tourism product. More importantly, however, this re-emphasis of their own history and culture resulted in a stronger sense of identity and self-esteem, which proved as valuable to long-term economic development as the recovery of some forgotten art form or cultural practice. Perhaps the greatest negative impact of long-term occupation was the loss of historical values relating to freedom. People had forgotten how to freely express themselves in public without fear of recrimination. They had lost the ability to govern themselves from the bottom up. This loss necessitates the development of discovery programmes and projects that teach listening, sharing, and public entrepreneurship.

Potentiality

Whereas sustainable tourism tends to emphasize the integration of social, economic, and ecological concerns (Inskeep, 1991), the travel ecology approach emphasizes notions of growth and maturation along with integration. Thus, travel ecology is an integrative and developmental approach, whereas sustainable tourism is often conceived as simply integrative. It is not enough to consider disparate community character-istics holistically; it is also important to consider these elements as they longitudinally change and transform the character and complexion of a community. This developmental perspective becomes critical in under-developed settings such as Central Europe in the same way that the first years of a child are considered critical to the development of a healthy, functional adult. A major tenet of Bookchin's (1996) philosophy of *social ecology* is that the relationships between society and nature are co-evolutionary and developmental, rather than only the sum of integrated parts. For example, a sustainable community may be seen as one that is whole, that has reached its potential in maintaining a high quality of life for all residents.

Enhancement

Sustainable tourism as we have practised it, stresses the alleviation of negative impacts while obtaining maximum sustainable yield for the industry. For example, quantitative carrying capacity is generally thought of as a tool for determining the number of visitors a resource can sustain without unacceptable degradation. We believe that carrying capacity can be enhanced through democratic dialogue and participation. How is carrying capacity related to a political idea like democracy? The management of the global commons is intrinsically a political problem. Hardin (1968) in his famous essay *Tragedy of the commons* suggested that centralized authority would be necessary to prevent an ecological overshoot of the commons. Interestingly, under centralized Soviet rule many areas of Central Europe experienced severe negative impacts. Absentee owners are certainly not an essential component of wise stewardship. In reality, the local inhabitants of an area, due to their proximity to the resource base, their dependency, and their sense of place, have greater potential for making 'wise' choices. Sustainable development and local enhancement is possible through an active and democratic society that allocates scarce resources through participatory deliberation at home. The impetus for sustainability should become stronger if liberties and freedoms are nurtured. The Developing Naturally projects in Slovakia and Poland provided the basis for an understanding of the necessity of mutuality and locality, that public buy-in and free expression is essential. Perhaps the project's greatest success was the facilitation of these attributes through the programme planning processes. It became evident that teaching tourism development through discovery actually taught citizens how to take charge and enhance their communities. In this respect, the need to establish tourism and democracy in Central Europe and other regions is related and is not treated as a separate issue under the travel ecology approach.

Operational strategies

As previously discussed the principles of Discovery, Mutuality, Locality, Historicity, Potentiality, and Enhancement are the key components of travel ecology concept, which is the supporting foundation for the Developing Naturally programme. The overall goal of Developing Naturally is to enhance communities around the globe by developing and providing resource materials and workshops based upon these principles. Our experiences and the influences of significant contributions of others in the field of tourism and community development suggest that the programme needed to be broader in scope than previous conservation and sustainable development approaches. In response to this call the following strategies guide the Developing Naturally programme:

- Enhancing communities' quality of life on a long-term basis
- Improving destinations, rather than only 'developing' destinations
- Creating community environments that nurture human potential
- Building linkages between individual homes and neighbourhoods to national and international organizations

- Facilitating public discovery processes that promote democratic principles through participation and self-reliance
- Addressing ecological change within the local community context
- Preserving community culture and heritage, inclusive of all groups and histories.

Programme management

Although the Developing Naturally programme has the ambitious goal of enhancing communities throughout the world by developing and providing resource materials and workshops, the reality is that it is a physically small programme located at Clemson University's Strom Thurmond Institute of Government and Public Affairs. Due to recent technological advancements in computer capabilities and Internet access, in 1998 Developing Naturally began to provide resource material available at no charge to the recipient on the World Wide Web. Resource manuals are developed and adapted for Internet distribution and made available on the web at http://www.developingnaturally.com/. One permanent director staffs the programme and a high value is placed on the creation of, and long-term use of, informal partnerships. It is the programme's philosophy that materials should be adapted for local communities and therefore international volunteer partnerships are used to identify programme needs, translate publications, and facilitate workshops in their prospective regions. Current international partners include: VOKA (VOCA)-Vidiecka Organizacia pre Komunitne Aktivity, Mateja Bela University in Slovakia, Rivne State Technical University, Ukraine, and Universidad de Ciencias Comerciales, Nicaragua. Programme activities have also been supported by the US Peace Corp, ACDI/VOCA, and the Fulbright Commission.

Products presently available include materials for community tourism planning, home-based business development, development of eco-tourism enterprises, and recycling. In 2001, government, educational, private sector, and individuals in over eighty-eight countries downloaded over 40 000 of our documents.

Overall, the goal of the programme is to develop at least two partners on each continent in the near future. Marketing will be broadened through additional participation in international conferences. Fundraising will be undertaken to support an additional staff member with multiple language skills and to hold annual partnership meetings. New product development will be focused on guidelines for increasing public participation (listening projects), home-based business development (crafts), and enhancing community environments (urban forestry, small parks).

Conclusion

Social scientists often use worldviews or paradigms to frame their research efforts. These frameworks help researchers make sense of evidence, allow for continuity between research programmes, and contribute to disciplinary cohesion. Blindly following the lead of the top researcher in the dominant paradigm may advance an academic career, while challenging the popular paradigm is often an unwise career move. Practitioners often quote the dominant perspective or paradigm to make their efforts seem innovative although their actual practice may have changed very little. However, researchers and practitioners alike must be aware of the constant evolution of concepts and ideas. The concept of sustainable development evolved from such precursors as conservation, preservation, carrying capacity, and eco-development, and continues to evolve. For the Developing Naturally programme, the researchers took a critical look at sustainable development from a paradigmatic perspective instead of attaching the term to their final product. We actively looked for differences between the practice and the theory to improve both. In the end, we found enough differences to develop our own framework, 'travel ecology'. We encourage other researchers to help us develop this framework in an era of rapid global political, economic, and technological change.

It is our belief that tourism professionals are at an exciting crossroads in history in which they can make a positive difference in the quality of life around the world. By adopting a travel ecology type of approach, we believe the tourism industry can be proactive regarding the future and advance beyond sustainability, providing a form of tourism development that will encourage a more holistic form of community development. For the first time, through such tools as the Internet, we have the opportunity to build partnerships and educate on a global basis at an extremely low cost.

Since the Industrial Revolution, we have been saddled with a narrow ideology of development: development for economic sake alone, beginning with conventional or industrial development and now through a relatively narrow perspective toward 'sustainable' development. Through the evolution of concepts such as travel ecology, we are now provided with the opportunity to abandon the narrow traditional development paradigm altogether. The focus of the tourism researcher, planner, developer, etc., should transcend that of sustaining environments for future generations. The focus of tourism planners should be more than tourism projects that produce a maximum sustainable yield for that industry alone. The industry has the potential to improve the world, not just sustain itself. Properly planned tourism can enhance human communities on a scale compatible with their resources and infrastructure. By emphasizing the principles of discovery, mutuality, locality, historicity, potential, and enhancement, we think we can conceive a model for tourism that can help millions of individuals reach their potential in a global society.

References

Amos, C.J. and Potts, T.D. (1992) *Hometown discovery: A development process for tourism.* Clemson, SC: Clemson University Cooperative Extension Service.

Berry, W. (1993) *Sex, economy, freedom and community.* New York. Cambridge University Press.

Blank, U. (1989) *The community tourism industry imperative: The necessity, the opportunity, and its potential.* State College, PA: Venture Publishing.

Bookchin, M. (1996) *The philosophy of social ecology.* New York: Black Rose Books.

Getz, D. (1986) Models in tourism planning: Towards integration of theory and practice. *Tourism Management* **7**(2), 21–32.

Getz, D. and Jamal, T.B. (1994) The environmental-community symbiosis: A case for collaborative tourism planning. *Journal of Sustainable Tourism* **2**(3), 152–73.

Gunn, C.A. (1972) *Vacationscape: Designing tourism regions.* New York: Van Nostrand Reinhold.

Gunn, C.A. (1979) *Tourism planning: Basics, concepts, and cases.* New York: Crane, Russak.

Gunn, C.A. (1994) *Tourism planning: Basics, concepts, and cases.* 3rd edn. New York: Taylor and Francis.

Hardin, G. (1968) The tragedy of the commons. *Science* **162**, 1243–8.

Harris, C.C., Timko, S.E. and McLaughlin, W.J. (1989) *An approach to assessing community tourism potential.* Moscow, ID: Department of Wildland Recreation Management, College of Forestry, Wildlife and Range Sciences.

Howell, R.L. (1987) *Small town tourism development.* Clemson, SC: Department of Parks, Recreation, and Tourism Management, College of Forest and Recreation Resources.

Inskeep, E. (1991) *Tourism planning: An integrated and sustainable approach.* New York: Van Nostrand Reinhold.

Jamal, T.B. and Getz, D. (1995) Collaboration theory and community tourism planning. *Annals of Tourism Research* **22**(1), 186–204.

Keogh, B. (1990) Public participation in community tourism planning. *Annals of Tourism Research* **17**(3), 449–65.

McHarg, I.L. (1969) *Design with Nature.* Garden City, NY: Doubleday Press.

Murphy, P.E. (1983) Tourism as a community industry: An ecological model of tourism development. *Tourism Management* **4**(3), 180–93.

Murphy, P.E. (1988) Community driven tourism planning. *Tourism Management,* **9**(2), 96–104.

Murphy, P.E. (1993) Community-driven tourism planning and residents' preferences. *Tourism Management* **14**(3), 218–27.

Potts, T.D. and Harrill, R. (1997) *In search of a travel ecology paradigm.* Presentation at the Travel and Tourism Research Association, Norfolk, VA.

Potts, T.D. and Harrill, R. (1998a) *Developing naturally: Toward a travel ecology approach.* Presentation at the National Tourism Extension Conference, Hershey, PA.

Potts, T.D. and Harrill, R. (1998b) Enhancing communities for sustainability: A travel ecology approach. *Tourism Analysis* **3**(3,4), 133–42.

Potts, T.D. and Marsinko, A. (1995) *Developing naturally: An exploratory process for nature-based community tourism.* Clemson, SC: Strom Thurmond Institute, Clemson University Cooperative Extension Service.

Prentice, R. (1993) Community-driven tourism planning and residents' preferences. *Tourism Management* **14**(3), 218–27.

Ritzer, G. (1993) *The mcdonaldization of society.* Thousand Oaks, CA: Pine Tree Press.

Seekings, J. (1980) Pro bono publico: The case for a systematic system, in D.W. Hawking, Shafer, E.L. and Rovelstad, J.M. (eds), *Tourism planning and development issues,* pp. 251–7). Washington, DC: George Washington University.

Selznick, P. (1996) In search of community, in Vitek, W. and Jackson, W. (eds), *Rooted in the land: Essays on community and place,* pp. 195–203. New York: John Wiley and Sons.

CHAPTER 5

Green Globe: sustainability accreditation for tourism

Tony Griffin and Terry DeLacey*

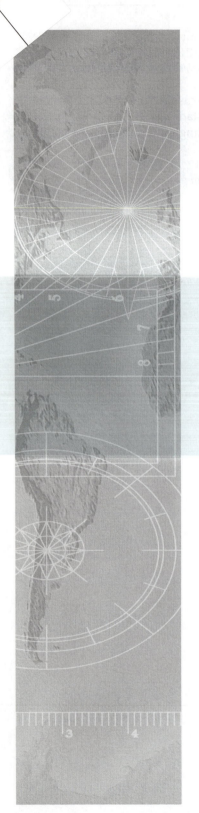

Introduction

Making tourism more sustainable requires action on a number of fronts. Regulation by government can, for example, establish minimum standards of performance with regard to the generation of certain environmental impacts. Strategic environmental planning of tourism, supported by laws relating to land use and environmental impact assessment, can anticipate a range of potential problems and establish protective measures to prevent them arising, or at least mitigate them to some extent. The degree and scope of government regulation required, however, may be determined by the tourism industry's willingness and ability to adopt sustainable environmental practices. At the same time there may be some matters that are difficult to regulate, or, where regulations are imposed, difficult to enforce

*In the interests of transparency the authors wish to indicate a degree of personal involvement with Green Globe. Terry DeLacey works for CRC Tourism, the organization responsible for the Green Globe programme in Australia, while Tony Griffin is engaged in research projects for the same organization.

effectively. Industry self-regulation may thus have a role in extending the scope of performance improvements with respect to sustainability.

At least three issues have a bearing on whether tourism enterprises will adopt self-regulatory sustainable practices: (1) knowledge of appropriate practices and technologies to adopt in a certain context; (2) the perception that some benefits will arise as a result of adopting such practices; and (3) the existence of effective sanctions to ensure that an appropriate level of environmental performance is maintained. Industry accreditation schemes are one form of self-regulation that have attempted to address these issues. They are generally based on operators achieving certain performance standards, in return for which the operator receives the right to use an identifiable logo or brand, which demonstrates their environmental credentials to other industry operators and customers. The scheme is often supported by advisory services that provide knowledge on the benefits of improving environmental performance and how best to achieve the standards. The sanction is typically the withdrawal of the right to use the logo and the consequent loss of any advantage that it confers, should the standards not be maintained.

One of the more comprehensive environmental accreditation schemes which has been developed in the last decade is Green Globe. Its scope is geographically global, it is designed to cover all sectors of the tourism industry, and it encompasses the accreditation of not only operators but also tourist destinations. It is supported by a research capacity and set of advisory services, and arguably has gone further than most such schemes in terms of ensuring the credibility of its assessment of candidates and their ongoing adherence to the standards. Moreover, it is a multifaceted programme which seeks to encourage improvements in the environmental performance of the tourism industry in ways other than the formal accreditation process. This chapter describes the evolution of Green Globe and the programmes that it operates, with particular emphasis on the accreditation scheme. It reviews and discusses the effectiveness of the programme and the contribution it can potentially make to enhancing the sustainability of tourism.

An overview of Green Globe

History

Green Globe was established by the World Travel and Tourism Council (WTTC) with the aim of implementing the Agenda 21 principles defined at the 1992 Rio Earth Summit (Green Globe, 1997a). The WTTC executive approved its establishment in March 1994 and it became operational in July of that year (Dain Simpson & Associates and Calkin & Associates, 1997). Originally it was a wholly owned subsidiary of the WTTC, with its chief executive also being president of WTTC. Since 1999, however, it has operated as an independent company limited by guarantee and overseen by an international advisory council, which comprises representatives from the tourism industry, non-government organizations and environmental consultancies around the world (Green Globe 21, 1999). This reorganization was accompanied by a renaming, to 'Green Globe 21', and a change in focus, from primarily an environmental education and awareness programme to a formal accreditation scheme, which had been initiated prior to the reorganization. It operates from a head office in the United Kingdom, which is also responsible for Europe and the Middle East. Regional offices have been established in Australia, covering the Asia/Pacific region, Puerto Rico, responsible for the Americas, and most recently an Africa office in South Africa. The regional offices operate through joint ventures with other organizations. In Australia, the programme is operated by the Cooperative Research Centre for Sustainable Tourism (CRC Tourism), while the Caribbean Alliance for Sustainable Tourism (CAST) and Green Seal operate the programme in the Americas.

Initially, membership of Green Globe was open to any travel and tourism business or destination organization willing to make a commitment to improving their environmental performance. To become a member, a company or organization was required to specify certain annual performance targets, related to Green Globe's priority action areas, to which it then became committed. This commitment had to be made at Chief Executive Officer level. To maintain membership the company then had to report annually on its success in achieving its targets. Green Globe undertook no formal monitoring process but simply reviewed its members' annual performance reports (Sisman, personal communication, 30 January 1998). Prior to the reorganization the vast majority of members, approximately 85 per cent, were relatively small businesses, with turnovers of less than US$1 million. Large organizations with turnovers in excess of US$30 million comprised only about 5 per cent of the membership (Sisman, personal communication, 30 January 1998). An annual turnover-based fee was payable, in return for which the members received a variety of advisory publications, access to professional environmental expertise and training opportunities, the right to use the Green Globe logo, access to a range of promotional benefits, and automatic entry into the Green Globe annual awards that recognized members' achievements (Green Globe, 1997a).

Membership

Membership grew from less than 100 at the end of 1994 to 547 in 103 different countries in 1998. At that time, while there were members in all continents, there was far from an even global distribution. Western Europe contributed the largest proportion of members, over 40 per cent, although its share had progressively declined as membership increased in other parts of the world. In March 1997 Western Europe had accounted for about 55 per cent of members (see Table 5.1). The greatest growth occurred in the Caribbean where membership increased more than tenfold in 1997, largely due to a strategic alliance being formed between Green Globe and the Caribbean Hotel Association and the subsequent establishment of the Caribbean Alliance for Sustainable Tourism (Green Globe, 1997b). Membership also more than doubled in South Asia and China in 1997, although the numbers here were still relatively small. In

Region	Members (March 1997)	Members (February 1998)	Percentage increase
Africa	28	36	28.6
Australia/New Zealand/Japan	18	18	0.0
Caribbean	7	76	985.7
Eastern Europe	17	21	23.5
Latin and South America	38	36	−5.3
Middle East	27	32	18.5
North America	42	36	−14.3
Other East Asia	17	23	35.3
Pacific	3	2	−33.3
South Asia and China	12	33	175.0
Western Europe	256	234	−8.6
Total	465	547	17.6

Source: Green Globe Annual Review 1996/97 and Membership List, February 1998.

Table 5.1
Green Globe membership by geographic region, 1997/1998

most other regions membership continued to increase steadily until 1998, although declines were experienced in Latin and South America, North America and the Pacific. In 1998 the countries with the greatest number of members were the United Kingdom with seventy members, Germany with fifty-seven and the USA with twenty-seven. Few countries outside these three contributed more than a dozen members each.

From 1994 to 1998 there was an average annual resignation rate of about 10 per cent. The reasons for resignation varied but most commonly it was due to business failure or changes in management (Sisman, personal communication, 30 January 1998). Given the small scale of most members this was to be expected. Green Globe reserved the right not to renew a company's membership if it failed to maintain its active commitment or implementation of its agreed programme. According to the managing director at the time, however, this was never invoked and all resignations were voluntary (Sisman, personal communication, 30 January 1998).

In 1998, approximately three-quarters of members were accommodation establishments, ranging from international hotels and resorts to camps and youth hostels, although the Hotel Inter-Continental chain alone accounted for nearly 10 per cent of membership. Tour operators were the second largest group, comprising a further 15 per cent. The remainder of members covered a wide range of organizations, including carriers, regional and national tourist organizations, tourism consultants, development and investment companies, local government bodies, museum authorities and even one educational establishment (Sisman, personal communication, 30 January 1998).

Region	Number of members	Percentage of total members
Africa	22	3.4
Australia/New Zealand/Japan	145	22.2
Caribbean	184	28.3
Eastern Europe	2	0.3
Latin and South America	20	3.7
Middle East	31	4.7
North America	13	2.0
Other East Asia	7	1.1
Pacific	1	0.2
South Asia and China	25	3.8
Western Europe	200	30.8
Total	651	100.0

Source: Green Globe Membership List, December 2001. Available: http://greenglobe21.com and http://ggasiapacific.com.au.

Table 5.2
Green Globe members by geographic region, 2001

Since 1999, 'membership' has been based on a three-tiered accreditation programme, which is described further later in this chapter. At the end of 2001 there were 516 companies or organizations that were members of Green Globe, with the vast majority having 'affiliate' status, the lowest level in the accreditation process. The geographic spread, although still involving all continents, had narrowed somewhat, with a total of seventy-three countries represented (see Table 5.2). The greatest proportion of members still came from Western Europe, even though the numbers declined after the reorganization. Membership in the Caribbean continued to grow to the point where it challenged Western Europe as the most prominent region. Together these two regions accounted for nearly three-quarters of all members. For all other regions membership numbers declined, particularly in Asia, North America and Eastern Europe.

Industry partners

Green Globe also has industry links through its affiliation with a variety of what are termed 'industry partners'. At the time of writing Green Globe had the support of twenty-six such partners (see Table 5.3). These generally comprise national industry peak organizations, such as the New Zealand Tourism Industry Association, Africa Travel Association and the Hungarian Society of Tourism, broadly based international associations, such as Pacific Asia Travel Association, or sector-specific national and international associations, such as Airports Council International, European Tour Operators Association and the International

ACI	Airports Council International
AITO	Association of Independent Tour Operators
ATA	Africa Travel Association
ASATA	Association of South African Travel Agents
ATS	Adventure Travel Society
BITOA	British Incoming Tour Operators Association
EFCT	European Federation of Conference Towns
ETOA	European Tour Operators Association
HCIMA	Hotel and Catering International Management Association
IACVB	International Association of Convention and Visitors Bureaus
IATA	International Air Transport Association
IFWTO	International Federation of Women's Travel Organizations
IH&RA	International Hotel & Restaurant Association
IHEI	International Hotels Environment Initiative
IIPT	International Institute for Peace through Tourism
MATUR	Hungarian Society of Tourism
NZTIA	New Zealand Tourism Industry Association
PATA	Pacific Asia Travel Association
RSA	Receptive Services Association
SATH	Society of the Advancement of Travellers with Handicaps
SITE	Society of Incentive Travel Executives
SPARC	South Pembrokeshire Programme for Action with Rural Communities
TIA	Travel Industry Association of America
TIANS	Travel Industry Association of Nova Scotia
TS	The Tourism Society
WATA	World Association of Travel Agencies

Source: Green Globe 21 (2001) *Green Globe 21 – Company Information – Industry Partners.* Available: http://www.greenglobe21.com.

Table 5.3
Green Globe Industry Partners, December 2001

Hotels Environmental Initiative. The partners work with Green Globe to promote membership of the programme amongst their members.

Goals

Green Globe's original primary objective was 'to provide low-cost, practical means for all Travel and Tourism companies to undertake improvements in environmental practice' (Green Globe, 1997b: 1). Its more specific goals were to:

- increase environmental responsiveness throughout the Travel and Tourism industry – including suppliers and customers;
- encourage global participation from tourism destinations and companies of all sizes and sectors;
- ensure that the beneficial links between good environmental practice and good business practice are understood;

- demonstrate, through the GREEN GLOBE logo, the commitment of the Travel and Tourism industry to improving environmental practices; and
- highlight leading examples of best practice and outstanding progress through Achievement Awards.

In its initial manifestation its prime *modus operandi* involved providing various services and information packages to its members, based on the following set of priority action areas derived from Agenda 21:

- waste minimization, reuse and recycling;
- energy efficiency, conservation and management;
- management of fresh water resources;
- waste water management;
- control of hazardous substances;
- company transport and the environment;
- land-use planning and management;
- involvement of staff, customers and communities in environmental issues;
- design for sustainability;
- partnerships for sustainable development;
- noise control; and
- environmentally sensitive purchasing policy (Green Globe, 1998a: 2).

While maintaining its focus on the abovementioned priority areas, in its current form the goals have been simplified to reflect its emphasis on the accreditation programme. The stated goals are to:

- encourage companies and communities off all sizes to join Green Globe 21 to show their commitment to sound environmental practice;
- promote the simple fact that adopting good environmental practice makes good long-term business sense;
- explain examples of industry best practice to Businesses and to Governments; and
- sustain the quality of our holidays for our children – and our children's children (Green Globe 21, 2001a: 1).

Programmes

The main programme which Green Globe 21 operates in order to pursue its goals is an accreditation programme, or 'certification' as it is called. The programme applies to both tourism organizations and destinations. Both aspects of this programme were introduced prior to the reorganization but have been substantially developed since that time. Green Globe also operates a number of other, less significant programmes, including:

- annual awards;
- projects, incorporating training and advisory services; and
- consumer awareness activities.

Each of these minor programme areas will be described briefly, before a more complete review of the certification programme is provided.

Annual Awards

Green Globe has been conducting its annual achievement awards programme since 1996. The stated aims of the programme are to: 'recognise outstanding achievement within the Green Globe programme; encourage further progress; serve as an example for other companies to follow; and demonstrate leadership of the Travel and Tourism industry on key environmental issues' (Green Globe, 1997c: 1). The awards are

---

Distinction Awards

Turtle Island, Fiji
La Cabana All Suite Beach Resort, Aruba
Strattons Hotel, UK
Victoria Falls Safari Lodge, Zimbabwe

Commendation Awards

Avis Europe, UK
Avis Rent a Car System Inc., USA
Bali Inter-Continental Resort, Indonesia
Boardmans, UK
Borneo Eco Tours, Malaysia
Explore Worldwide, UK
Hotel Inter-Continental, Singapore
Hotel Mocking Bird Hill, Jamaica
Inter-Continental Budapest, Hungary
Jeddah Conference Palace, Saudi Arabia
Jetwing Hotels, Sri Lanka
Maho Bay Camps, Virgin Islands
Melia Bali Hotel, Indonesia
Presidente Inter-Continental Cancun, Mexico
Quetta Serena Hotel, Pakistan
Table Mountain Aerial Cableway, South Africa
Zomerlust Gastehuis, South Africa

Recognition Awards

The Orchid, India
Landsker Countryside Holidays, UK

Source: Green Globe 21 (2001) *International Award Programme*. Available: http://www.greenglobe21.com.

Table 5.4
Green Globe Award Winners, 2000

open to all Green Globe members and judging is based primarily on the annual reports submitted by members on their own performance over the preceding year. Each company is assessed on its performance in relation to the priority action areas, defined earlier in this chapter. Based on these criteria, awards are made at two levels: Distinction Awards for demonstrating outstanding achievement across all action areas, and Commendation Awards for demonstrating significant improvements in environmental performance (Green Globe, 1998a). In 2001 the programme was tied to the benchmarking and certification process and drew on outside advice in determining award winners (Green Globe 21, 2001b).

A new category, Recognition Awards, was added in 1997 to acknowledge achievements outside Green Globe membership. These are based on nominations of companies by individual Green Globe industry partners which, in the partner's view, have made the most significant environmental improvements over the preceding year (Green Globe, 1997d). Table 5.4 lists the 2000 award winners in each category. The award winners are fairly well spread geographically and to a lesser extent across industry sectors, with the predominance of hotels and resorts reflective of the composition of Green Globe membership.

Projects

Green Globe offers a range of services to both members and non-members for assistance on specific projects. Areas of project support include:

- the raising of environmental awareness in the local tourism industry;
- training and education;
- organization of conferences and seminars; and
- specific consultancy support for environmental projects (Green Globe 21, 2001a).

One such project involved working with three French ski operators and an industry partner, the Association of Independent Tour Operators, on developing a scheme that would generate money from visitors for local environmental protection and conservation works. This was part of a larger Visitor Payback Project funded by the European Union (Green Globe, 1997e). Other projects have included conducting an international training conference on risk assessment and crisis management, and undertaking an environmental review of the UK Marriott Hotel chain, with a view to implementing an environmental management system (Green Globe 21, 2001a).

Consumer awareness

There are two levels on which consumer awareness is relevant to Green Globe's operations: one is making tourists aware of their potential impacts and how they can contribute to more environmentally sustainable tourism; the other is awareness of the Green Globe 'brand' and what it might mean in terms of environmental management practices, which might in turn affect their destination and product choices. As regards the first level, Green Globe in its early days produced a leaflet entitled 'Tips for Travellers' which provided essentially behavioural advice for tourists on what to do before, during and after a trip. Included in the advice was to 'try to travel with companies which are making a positive environmental statement by being members of GREEN GLOBE' (Green Flag International Ltd, 1995: 1). Green Globe estimated that it distributed about 50 000 of these leaflets annually through its member companies (Green Globe, 1997b). More recently, Green Globe has introduced the concept of the 'Green Globe 21 Traveller', whereby consumers can register as 'supporters of sustainable tourism' and thereby receive information through the Internet, including special deals from members, join discussion forums and have access to travel planning advice (Green Globe 21, 2001c).

On the second level Green Globe clearly appreciates the significance of consumer recognition of the brand, stating in an early annual report that:

> In recent years brand images have become ever more important in marketing and product development and the world's public have come to expect differing levels of quality from different brands. GREEN GLOBE members have to be confident in the GREEN GLOBE brand before they will use it. (Green Globe, 1997b: 7)

Indeed, since Green Globe's inception it has stressed the right to use the brand and the commercial benefits that will flow from it as a way of encouraging new membership (Green Globe, 1997a). However, until the introduction of the Green Globe Traveller concept little had been done to raise consumers' awareness of Green Globe, and limited research has been conducted on the current level of awareness. Limited consumer testing of the brand by some hotel members took place in the late 1990s (Sisman, personal communication, 30 January 1998). In its early days, Green Globe had no consumer advertising budget (Dain Simpson & Associates and Calkin & Associates, 1997) and effectively relied on the World Travel and Tourism Council for its general marketing (Sisman, personal communication, 30 January 1998). The introduction of the Traveller concept and the information flow this provides goes some way towards redressing this deficiency.

The certification programme

Overview

Green Globe's formal certification process was launched in November 1997. The general purpose of the programme is to provide members with an avenue for independent verification that they are meeting certain standards with respect to environmental performance. It thus represents a level of environmental accreditation beyond the commitment to the cause and largely self-administered performance evaluation embodied in the original membership scheme. The certification process is based on the 'Green Globe 21 Standard'. This document sets out the requirements needed to meet a level of environmental and socio-economic management performance which meets environmentally sustainable development outcomes sought by *Agenda 21*, incorporating the triple bottom line principles of economic, sociocultural and ecological sustainability. The original standards were those relating to Environmental Management Systems as defined by the International Organisation for Standardisation (ISO) (Green Globe, 1997e). These are currently being adapted to reflect the World Tourism Organization (WTO), Global Code of Ethics and regional/national variants. Verification and subsequent certification are carried out by a number of contracted, independent companies, including *Societe Generale de Surveillance SA* (SGS), the world's largest testing, inspection and verification organization. Some degree of flexibility is allowed, with a company being required to reach a level deemed appropriate to its size, type and location (Green Globe, 1998b).

The certification programme is open to all travel and tourism industry sectors, and all sizes and types of operations, including companies, communities and protected areas, referred to collectively as 'operations'. The incorporation of 'communities' into the process is an extension of an earlier programme that was designed to afford tourist destinations the opportunity to improve upon, and receive Green Globe acknowledgement for, their environmental management practices and performance. The destination programme pre-dated the introduction of the certification programme, with Jersey being the first destination to be awarded Green Globe status in November 1997, the same time that the certification programme was launched. 'Communities', in Green Globe terminology, are equivalent to destinations.

There are three levels of status within the programme: Affiliate, Benchmarked, and Certified (see Figure 5.1). Affiliate status is typically the entry level and is roughly equivalent to the original membership status in that it reflects a commitment to the cause of sustainable tourism without any formal verification of environmental performance. It may serve as a one-year trial period before progressing to the next stage and confers the right to use the Green Globe Affiliate stamp, but not the logo. Benchmarked status involves the preparation of an environmental performance report and confers wider benefits on the operation, including the right to use the Green Globe logo and additional support from the Green Globe organization. Operations may choose to enter the programme at the Benchmarked level, or indeed the final Certified level,

Figure 5.1
Green Globe stamps and logos (Source: Green Globe 21, 2001c)

thereby foreshortening the process. Achieving Certified status requires submitting to a full, independent verification of environmental performance. Certified operations are then able to use the Green Globe logo with an added tick. The logo may only be used after the successful completion of the process. At this time a certificate is issued which has a unique serial number, is year dated and has an expiry date.

The Standard

The Green Globe 21 Standard has evolved and improved through research, analysis and experience with its application over time. Initially it was based on an ISO style approach involving an environmental policy and a 'tick the box' checklist. This process-based system has been improved dramatically by adding performance outcomes. A process system alone can easily mean that a company might achieve all requirements of the Standard, but could still be failing to achieve sustainability outcomes. A more sophisticated but workable Standard has been developed. The latest Standard, introduced in April 2001, drives quantification of actual environmental performance through benchmarking.

The Standard is based on required performance criteria, organized into the following five sections:

- Environment and Social Sustainability Policy;
- Regulatory Framework;
- Environmental and Social Sustainability Performance;
- Environmental Management System; and
- Stakeholder Consultation and Communication.

Each section of the Standard is briefly described below.

Environment and Social Sustainability Policy • • •

This section is prescriptive and requires that applicant operations have a written Environment and Social Sustainability Policy that:

- is adopted and promoted at the highest managerial level in the operation;
- commits to year-on-year improvements in relevant sustainability performance indicators;
- commits to compliance with relevant environmental legislation and regulations;
- establishes a framework for regularly recording and measuring performance indicators, analysing performance and setting targets;
- commits to give special consideration to employment of local persons and use of local products and services;
- is actively communicated to employees, customers and suppliers, and made available to all stakeholders;
- is reviewed annually; and
- demonstrates an understanding of the WTO Global Code of Ethics for Tourism and regional/national variants.

Regulatory Framework • • •

This section reinforces the importance of a regulatory framework to the attainment of sustainability objectives by requiring operations to:

- maintain an up-to-date register of relevant legislation, regulations and other requirements and comply with all;
- maintain records of compliance and where compliance was not maintained, records of remedial action taken; and
- comply with any special guide developed by Green Globe for a particular geographical location.

Environmental and Social Sustainability Performance • • •

This section establishes the framework for benchmarking an operation's environmental and social performance by specifying that an operation shall:

- assess the significance of the positive and negative impacts of its activities, products and services in each of the key performance areas;
- annually benchmark environmental and socio-economic performance (in the key performance areas) against Green Globe Benchmarking Indicators and achieve a Green Globe Benchmarking Report above Green Globe Baseline performance for all indicators;
- establish targets to reduce negative/improve positive impacts in key performance areas;
- develop an improvement programme to implement performance objectives and targets; and
- monitor progress to ensure year-on-year improvement.

Environmental Management System • • •

An environmental management system (EMS) is an integral part of the Green Globe Standard, hence this section requires an operation to:

- develop, implement and maintain a documented EMS, or in the case of communities or protected areas, an environmental management framework (EMF);
- nominate a senior executive officer of the operation to be responsible for the implementation, ongoing performance and outcomes of the EMS;
- provide, where necessary, training for all staff with key responsibilities for actions within the EMS;
- take steps to correct situations not conforming with the Sustainability Policy and prevent their re-occurrence;
- using the Green Globe Benchmarking Report, ensure that a minimum significant improvement is achieved in the relevant performance area(s);

- retain records demonstrating conformance with requirements of the standard, and records of monitoring activity;
- assess possible environmental impacts of planned, accidental and emergency situations and develop and implement minimization and mitigation plans; and
- regularly undertake review of the EMS or EMF and the Sustainability Policy in fulfilling the requirements of the Standard.

Stakeholder Consultation and Communication • • •

This section states that operations shall:

- regularly communicate their environmental and social performance resulting from participation in the programme to customers and stakeholders;
- determine the significance of its impacts through consultation with stakeholders;
- encourage and respond to feedback on the Sustainability Policy and targets;
- encourage customers and suppliers to engage in their environmental and socio-economic programmes; and
- inform customers about sensitive local customs, ways of life, natural areas, environmental issues and how best to contribute to the local economy.

Participating in Green Globe: Affiliates

Affiliate status is the introductory stage, where organizations are learning about sustainable tourism and the Green Globe path. Affiliates pay a fee, fixed for companies but variable for communities, in return for which they receive such benefits as listing on the Green Globe website; use of the Affiliate Stamp for marketing purposes; and web-based access to information on Benchmarking, Certification, the Standard, sector guides and performance indicators. They also have access to the list of Green Globe registered Environmental Management support consultants. Operations are encouraged to enrol in the Benchmarking or Certification process and to take practical steps towards improving their sustainability performance. As at the end of 2001, over 80 per cent of participants in Green Globe were at the Affiliate stage.

Participating in Green Globe: Benchmarking

Benchmarking was added to the programme in April 2001. Its very recent inclusion accounts for the very low numbers of participants, ten, which had achieved Benchmarked status by the end of 2001. However, it represents a significant development in sustainability accreditation for tourism by focusing on the measurement of real environmental and socio-economic performance of tourism operations. The process is applicable to operations worldwide and hence provides an internationally comparable performance standard. Benchmarking can either be undertaken as an end in itself, or as an essential part of the Certification process. A variable fee, depending on the characteristics and size of the company or community, is paid for undergoing benchmarking. There is no compulsion for a Benchmarked operation to proceed to full certification.

Benchmarking targets major environmental concerns by measuring the environmental performance of companies and destinations in the following nine Key Performance Areas:

- greenhouse gas emissions;
- energy conservation and management;
- fresh water resource use;
- ambient air quality protection;
- waste water management;
- waste minimization, reuse, recycling (including hazardous substances)
- ecosystem conservation and management (including biodiversity impact, particularly on habitats);
- environmental and land use planning, particularly in areas of high social and environmental value; and
- local social, cultural and economic impact, in particular, respecting local culture and generating maximum local employment.

The benchmarking process involves operations collecting measures of indicators for Key Performance Areas on an annual basis, and the subsequent preparation of a Benchmarking Assessment Report. It is similar in logic to the generation of an annual financial performance report. Green Globe has researched and selected both the performance criteria, called Benchmarking Indicators, and their measures in order to ensure they are practical, easily measured and provide an accurate picture of an operation's performance. Green Globe will work with operations to choose the best measures for their situation. For example, the measurement of the overall energy consumption for a hotel uses the annual electricity, gas, diesel and other fuel bills as its source of information. The benchmarking process employs a common unit of measurement, e.g., megajoules for energy, and assists with the conversion of the collected information to this unit. A compact disc is supplied to Benchmarking operations and, when energy bill data is entered, the CD automatically calculates the energy consumption in megajoules. This information is then converted to a ratio. When the energy usage is combined with the hotel's total annual number of guest nights, the result is a ratio of the hotel's fossil energy use per guest night. Such ratios provide a basis for comparison, and allow for differences in the scale of operations and for growth or contraction of operations over time. For a tourist railway or airline, a similar calculation could produce an energy figure per passenger kilometre.

The information collected by an operation is dispatched to Green Globe, which evaluates the performance in each key area and calculates an aggregated Reporting Index. A Benchmarking Report is then produced for the operation, which indicates its current standing and provides advice as to where appropriate and worthwhile improvements may be made. Green Globe has established Baseline and Best Practice levels of performance in order to illustrate where an operation is placed within its sector of the industry. It allows comparison with industry best practice, and for improvements in performance to be tracked annually. The Baseline level also takes into account variation between countries. Figure 5.2 illustrates the Baseline and Best Practice concept.

To receive a Green Globe Benchmarked Certificate, the measures in all Key Performance Areas must be above the Baseline level, and the operation must have a sustainability policy. Operations are subject to annual review and this level of performance must be maintained in order for an operation to retain its Benchmarked status. If an indicator's measure is above the Baseline, but below Best Practice, the operation is encouraged to make annual improvements for that indicator. Once Best Practice is achieved for all Key Performance Areas, operations are encouraged to maintain this level of performance and to select supplementary performance indicators to facilitate continuous improvement.

Whilst a key issue in defining sustainability performance benchmarks is that they must be credible by reflecting best practice, they must also be achievable by reflecting local conditions and the type of activity being certified (Figure 5.2). The intention of Green Globe is not to discourage the industry by setting standards that only a few can achieve, but rather to encourage, through its services and support, widespread adoption of the principle of continuous improvement towards achieving sustainable tourism. The baseline level reflects performance indicators developed at the global, regional, national and even local levels, where applicable, and will evolve over time.

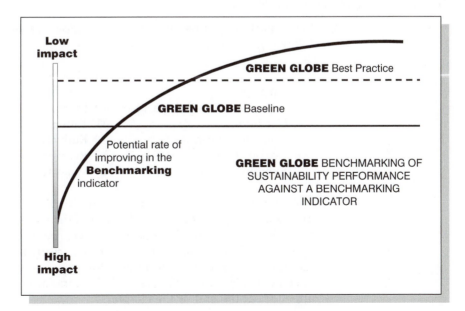

Figure 5.2
Benchmarking of environmental performance

A focus on greenhouse gases • • •

The greenhouse gas issue, intimately linked to energy, encompasses both fixed and mobile assets, and transcends local and international boundaries. It provides the most high profile international sustainability performance currency by which to gauge and benchmark performance. The issue has particular relevance to the tourism industry, given that it consumes significant amounts of fossil fuels. Green Globe has consequently asked its participants to concentrate on this area for improvement, with the major focus being reduced energy use per customer, although the sequestration side of the equation is also taken into account. Thus greenhouse gas emission reductions can be measured collectively through reductions in energy use for all purposes and the primary consumption of raw materials, as well as the sequestration of carbon through habitat conservation. Green Globe provides a means by which its participants can monitor and enhance their performance, primarily through energy savings, which translate directly into significant economic and environmental benefits. The Green Globe database of benchmarking and performance criteria also enables operations to benchmark their performance, not just locally, but internationally.

A key long-term function of Green Globe is to stimulate initiatives for tackling non-compliance in meeting emissions targets. There is a particular focus on capacity building in developing countries, such as the transfer of climate-friendly technologies, and establishing the Kyoto protocol's market-based mechanisms – emissions trading, carbon trading, joint implementation and a clean development mechanism.

Benchmarking for companies • • •

Benchmarking guides have been developed to assist operations in the following fourteen travel and tourism sectors:

1 Airlines	8 Golf courses
2 Airports	9 Hotels
3 Campsites/caravan parks	10 Marinas
4 Car hire	11 Tour operators
5 Convention centres	12 Railways
6 Cruise ships	13 Restaurants
7 Exhibition halls	14 Vineyards

At the time of writing, further guides were being developed. The guides assist operations to work through the steps to achieve Benchmarking. They recognize the key differences between travel and tourism operations through the inclusion of Key Performance Area indicators and measures specifically determined for each sector. An example of the Green Globe Sector Performance Indicators for Hotels is provided in the appendix at the end of the chapter.

Benchmarking for communities (destinations) • • •

Green Globe's destination accreditation programme actually pre-dates the introduction of certification. The stated aim of the programme, when initiated, was to provide 'a framework to guide tourist locations towards sustainable development based on the principles of Agenda 21' (Green Globe, 1998c: 2). To be considered, destinations first had to demonstrate that there were strong environmental issues or opportunities to be dealt with, that the local tourism industry would have a role in the process, and that there was strong support from all stakeholders (Sisman, personal communication, 30 January 1998). Destinations are an appropriate scale for considering sustainable tourism management, planning and development. Effective planning generally occurs at the destination level, usually through local government, and a new tourism product would be developed within a destination image and brand.

In November 1997 Jersey was the first destination to be awarded Green Globe status after an evaluation and accreditation process that took two years. Its involvement in the programme was seen to be a natural progression from a previous environmental review that had been conducted. Since that time another two destinations have been certified: Vilamoura in the Algarve region of Portugal and Cumbria in the United Kingdom. A number of other destinations are currently going through the process. The range of applicants varies in scale from small resort towns, such as Aviemore in Scotland, to local government areas, regions and cities, and extends up to a national level. One case, the Holy Trail, even transcends national boundaries. Table 5.5 presents a list of some of the current applicants.

Community	Country
Algarve	Portugal
Aviemore	United Kingdom
Bournemouth	United Kingdom
Camiguin Island	Philippines
Capetown	South Africa
Dominica	n/a
Douglas Shire	Australia
Geneva	Switzerland
Holy Trail	Jordan, Egypt and Israel
Ifuago Rice Terraces	Philippines
Koh Samui	Thailand
Redlands Shire	Australia
Scottish Borders	United Kingdom
Sri Lanka	n/a
Ulugan Bay	Philippines
Victoria Falls	Zimbabwe

Source: Green Globe 21 (2001) *Community – Current Participants.* Available: http://www.greenglobe21.com.

Table 5.5
Examples of communities working towards Green Globe certification, 2001

The accreditation process for communities is designed to be flexible enough to deal with a number of different scales of destination and may involve working with a variety of destination-based organizations to initiate and drive the process, from both the public and private sectors. In Jersey, the Philippines and Dominica the programme was initiated and supported by government at the highest level, whereas in Vilamoura the initiator was a private resort developer and operator, Lusotur SA.

In keeping with the fundamental Green Globe principles, a destination is required to demonstrate environmental performance according to the principles of *Agenda 21*. Subsequent to certification, it must demonstrate continuous improvement. Beyond this, a destination must encourage cooperation between the tourism industry, governments, non-government organizations and communities at a local level. Local political, cultural and social conditions are considered in order to create a realistic, achievable programme of action that is flexible to suit a location's various attributes. A key intended result of destination certification is the increased involvement of the private sector in environmental action, which will create synergies through the application of a common framework and in turn provide the opportunity to heighten community and consumer awareness through the Green Globe destination brand. The implementation of a Green Globe destination programme also requires the presence of a lead organization that can deliver on both sustainable tourism development and environmental regulation.

The accreditation of Green Globe destinations requires detailed research on developing clear indicators, benchmarks and targets. Certification of community performance will also require new approaches from third party auditing companies. The Green Globe destination concept is a complex one, but it has enormous potential to harness market forces to drive the environmental sustainability of Communities and Protected Areas. At the time of writing pilot studies were being undertaken in Douglas and Redlands Shires in Queensland, Australia and Kaikoura in the South Island of New Zealand. Given the complexity of communities, the pilot studies were focusing especially on expanding the Benchmark criteria and developing Benchmarking Indicators. In a similar vein a pilot resort project had commenced in Bournemouth (UK).

Green Globe is currently re-evaluating its approach to certifying entire communities as well as protected areas as sustainable tourism destinations, with a view to having an upgraded Certification programme for both Communities and Protected Areas in place by the end of 2001. This upgrading process reflects the desire by a number of Communities and Protected Areas for both acknowledgement of their environmental performance and a desire to improve such performance via a benchmarking process.

Participating in Green Globe: Certification

To achieve the Green Globe brand with distinctive tick, all operations are required to undergo independent third-party assessment against the Green Globe 21 Standard. Accredited companies and assessors undertake such certification assessments. Certified operations must undergo an annual review to maintain their certified status. Operations registering for certification automatically receive the same benefits as those registering for Benchmarking. Benchmarking is a necessary step before certification and, once they have been successfully benchmarked, an applicant is able to use the Green Globe logo without a tick. By the end of 2001, forty-one participants had been Certified.

As with benchmarking, an operation pays a variable fee for the certification process. Various advisory services and resources are available to assist applicants with the process. The operation initiates work on the requirements of the Green Globe 21 Standard in preparation for Certification Assessment. Environmental management professionals may provide guidance on the EMS as well as customizing performance criteria, and assessor companies may participate in a pre-assessment of environmental performance. The operation then undertakes a self-assessment against the Green Globe Checklist. Once it considers that it is ready, the operation requests Green Globe to organize a Certification Assessment. Green Globe then assigns the task to an accredited certification organization, which is provided with the Benchmarking Report. An assessment checklist is completed, on the basis of which Green Globe determines whether to approve Certification. Successful applicants are subject to annual Benchmarking and Certification Assessment to ensure continued compliance with performance standards.

An evaluation of Green Globe

Green Globe is a relatively young organization with a rather ambitious set of objectives, and it may consequently be a little too early to fully evaluate its success. At the time of writing it had been operating for eight years, but only three in its current from. Its main programme, the certification scheme, had been operating for less than five years, with one of the main components, the benchmarking process, operational for only a year. What is probably its most ambitious programme, relating to the accreditation of destinations, has been going a little longer than most other programmes, but the sheer complexity of the task means that this takes a long period to implement and even longer to bear fruit. In principle, however, Green Globe represents possibly the most global, cross-sectoral approach to industry self-regulation thus far attempted.

There are at least two basic concerns with industry accreditation programmes such as Green Globe. The first is whether a significant proportion of the industry will embrace it. In the short term this depends very much on the perceived benefits of participating, and in the longer term on whether it can be demonstrated that those benefits have been realized. The second concern is whether such certification and ecolabel schemes achieve real environmental improvements. Amongst other things, this would depend on the criteria on which the accreditation is based, the quality and objectivity of the assessment process, ongoing monitoring and enforcement procedures, and the effectiveness of sanctions that might be imposed for non-adherence to the required standards. The two concerns are interrelated, as whether a scheme achieves real improvement will influence its credibility and hence adoption by the industry, while the realization of benefits to participants will impact on the effectiveness of the strongest possible sanction, i.e., the withdrawal of accreditation. The credibility of the scheme also impacts on the value placed on it by consumers, which affects the potential of the scheme to confer marketing advantage on the accredited operator. How effectively Green Globe has addressed these concerns is discussed below.

Will the industry participate?

Initially this depends on the perceived benefits. Green Globe promotes itself as: (1) offering a number of benefits to participants, including cost savings, (2) assisting in compliance with environmental legislation, (3) widening market appeal, and (4) improving the quality of the customer experience. The first two are relatively easy to demonstrate; the second two are more problematic and contentious.

Benchmarking and certification can directly contribute to improvements in the efficiency of operations through the use of fewer resources. Savings can be achieved through reduced energy consumption, reduced waste generation, reduced use of potable water and enhanced efficiency arising from treating such issues in an integrated, systematic manner. Such savings quickly become apparent and can be clearly articulated to prospective applicants. Being part of the accreditation process can also have considerable human resource benefits, including improved staff commitment and greater productivity linked to clear sustainability policies and programmes, and improved knowledge and awareness of sustainability issues through targeted environmental training and on-the-job implementation.

The Green Globe 21 Standard includes requirements relating to the regulatory framework and thereby encourages an understanding of and compliance with it. Inherent in many environmental planning regulatory frameworks, however, are discretionary elements relating to broad matters of public interest and a host community's feelings about tourism in general or specific tourism developments. Hence improving the relations between tourism operations and their local communities can smooth the path for acceptance by regulators. Again, through the standard, operations are actively encouraged to work with local communities through transparent and participatory consultation and communication activities, as well as incorporation of 'buy local' and 'employ local' strategies where feasible and appropriate. Multi-stakeholder consultation is a requirement of the process and Green Globe provides a tried and tested system.

The extent to which a marketing advantage is conferred on an operation is debatable. There is a widely held perception, at least, that the tourist market is becoming increasingly conscious of environmental issues and will prefer operators who can clearly demonstrate that they are behaving in an environmentally benign way. Certainly there is ample evidence of tourists being well intentioned in this regard. Various recent studies (Mori, 1995; Travel Industry of America, 1997; Mori, 1998; Tearfund, 2000) have shown that a majority of travellers express a preference for environmentally and socially responsible companies and a willingness to pay more for their services. Some doubts have been raised, however, about whether such good intentions actually translate into purchasing behaviour (Blamey, 1995; Blamey *et al.*, 1999).

Of course none of this debate about tourists' purchasing preferences means anything unless they are aware of what an environmental logo infers about the behaviour of the operator. Without this awareness the logo has no credibility. Hence for participants to realize this benefit there must be some effort put into increasing consumer awareness of the programme so that informed choices can be made. The introduction of the concept of the Green Globe Traveller goes some way towards addressing this issue, although there is no clear evidence about the effectiveness of this, or indeed the general level of consumer awareness about Green Globe at this stage. This may be only a temporary limitation, a function of the youth of Green Globe and in particular its benchmarking and certification programme, and could be resolved with time as membership increases and the use of the logo becomes more commonplace. Realistically, though, if Green Globe is to get significant participation from the millions of businesses involved in the tourism industry it will require a major marketing effort directed at the world's consumers. This effort will require a commitment of considerable financial resources by Green Globe and/or its partners and members.

In terms of actually attracting numbers of participants, Green Globe could be labelled as a moderate success. On the surface, achieving a membership of a little over 650 in eight years is hardly awe-inspiring in an industry the size of tourism, particularly as numbers have been static for the past four years. However, the fact that Green Globe has experienced a major reorientation in that period and is still in the process of fully developing its programmes provides a partial explanation for this. A strength of the organization, too, is that it has at least gained a foothold in a large number of countries, the global impact of which is somewhat lessened by its heavy concentration in two regions: Western Europe and the Caribbean. The Caribbean and New Zealand experiences, however, show what can be achieved with effective promotion of the scheme to industry by a strategic partner. In regions where it has managed to gain a significant foothold, and is able to demonstrate achievement, it may well eventually prove to be influential, particularly if it can deliver the promised commercial benefits to its members. The incorporation of destinations into the certification programme also has the potential to strengthen the organization's regional presence and membership numbers by creating greater awareness. The number of destinations currently involved in the process is encouraging, as is the fact that some are at a national level.

Will it achieve real environmental improvements?

Green Globe was originally conceived as a membership-based programme whereby companies joined and implemented sustainable tourism practices based on *Agenda 21* principles. It achieved some degree of profile within the industry, and through its training and advisory services, heightened awareness of environmental and sustainability principles and practices. In its original form, Green Globe was very simple. It required a company to pay an annual fee and develop an environmental policy and checklist. In return, the company received advisory materials on environmental impacts and means to minimize them, and the right to use the Green Globe logo. The logo represented a statement of intent to undertake improvement.

In the late 1990s Green Globe moved into certification. The key to this was the introduction of independent verification of the achievements of an operation, thereby legitimizing its credentials for certification. A two-logo process was established, whereby the operation could use the logo without a tick during its path towards certification, which had to be undertaken within two years, and the logo with a tick once certified. Without certification Green Globe membership involved little more than a commitment to a voluntary code of practice which was rather informally enforced, although membership was at least likely to raise a company's awareness of certain environmental issues and how best to deal with them.

A report on tourism certification schemes published in 2000 criticized tourism ecolabel schemes as a 'greenwash' that allowed less-than-green companies to falsely market their products (WWF-UK, 2000). Although the report generally recognized Green Globe as the most serious approach of any global programme it was nevertheless argued that Green Globe had shortcomings. Companies joining Green Globe and paying the entrance fee could use the logo without any requirement that their claims of environmental and social responsibility be assessed and rated by independent experts. Concern was also expressed that the programme was focused on process rather than on the achievement of tangible improvements and outcomes. In addition, the programme was criticized for not taking into consideration the variations in tourism operations in terms of scale, nature, capital, location and sector.

In response to these criticisms Green Globe initiated improvements. In February 2000, Green Globe began to develop a new framework, focusing on measurable outcomes as well as process. The decision was taken to introduce the concept of benchmarking sustainability performance, and thereby enable the measurement of real improvements. The key steps included the introduction of the educational Affiliate concept, and the strengthening of the Standard to include baseline benchmarking and quantification of environmental and socio-economic performance. The result was an improved certification system that married process with performance and gave scope for systematic progress towards fully verified accreditation. The use of the logo was subsequently limited to those operations which had been successfully benchmarked above a baseline level of performance in all Key Performance Areas, and Benchmarking was made a compulsory step in the certification process. The process now possesses rigour in the breadth and depth of assessment, precision in the measurement of sustainability performance, an appropriate focus on outcomes, independent verification by experts, and practical means of supporting operations in getting through it.

The programme also includes practical means of maintaining compliance with the performance standards, including an effective sanction for non-compliance and an apparent willingness to use it. In committing to maintaining the integrity of the brand, Green Globe has withdrawn the right to use the brand for matters of non-compliance, or where the use of the brand has been abused. A dispute process has been instituted, based on ISO Certification guides and involving independent assessment of the dispute. In the event of an incident of non-compliance, Green Globe requires rectification, which may involve both immediate and longer-term corrective action before certification is restored.

Green Globe has also taken a number of steps to ensure that it maintains the quality of its assessment processes. The organization's sales and marketing functions have been separated from its research and development activities. Ongoing research and development, now conducted by the Cooperative Research Centre for Sustainable Tourism in Australia, is vital to maintaining the quality and appropriateness of the Standard and the Sector Performance Indicators. Supplementing this, the International Advisory Council provides crucial peer review of both the Standard and the Sector Performance Indicators. Experience gained through implementing the scheme, including feedback from customers and consumers, and feedback from the community, contributes to Green Globe's system of continuous improvement. Finally, there is a clear separation of functions between the certification assessors and the environmental management advisors/consultants who may assist operations to prepare for benchmarking and certification. This helps to maintain the impartiality and integrity of the process.

Conclusion

Certainly in principle, Green Globe stands up well to scrutiny. It has all the essential elements of a credible accreditation and certification programme and has responded well to past constructive criticism of its operations. It clearly has the potential to deliver improvements in the sustainability performance of tourism firms and destinations. However, the true measure of its success, in delivering meaningful improvements, will be the scale and level on which it operates; that is, its ability to attract participants from the tourism industry who are willing to pursue benchmarking and certification. At this early stage, very few companies or communities have pursued this path. If the bulk of participants remain at the Affiliate stage, its efficacy must be open to question. If there is a progression by most only to the Benchmarked stage some credibility questions might still remain, given that there is no independent verification of performance required. If, on the other hand, Green Globe can encourage a large number of tourism companies and destinations to achieve and maintain full Certification it is likely to make a substantial contribution to the cause of sustainability. This is a challenging task, given the time and expense for those involved in following this path, and to do so will require them to be convinced of the benefits that will arise. In the long term Green Globe will need to be able to demonstrate those benefits and to take steps, such as raising consumer awareness, to increase the prospects of the promised benefits being realized. For tourism businesses, even those with the best of ethical intentions, the emphasis is nonetheless likely to be on the commercial benefits of participation, such as cost savings and increased levels of demand.

The destination component of the certification programme is perhaps the one with the greatest potential to produce significant results. It expands the programme beyond reliance on commercial motivations, and has the ability to reach a large number of operators and stakeholders and encourage cooperative action. By generally incorporating governments as well as industry and by focusing on broad environmental protection and conservation, land use planning and infrastructure development, this component has the potential to improve environmental management practices beyond those sometimes marginal measures which an individual enterprise might employ simply to produce costs savings or gain a marketing advantage. Arguably it is in this realm of collective action that the greatest gains are likely to be made with respect to sustainable tourism development.

Acknowledgement

We wish to thank Mr Dick Sisman, former Managing Director Green Globe.

References

Blamey, R. (1995) *The Nature of Ecotourism*. Bureau of Tourism Research, Canberra.

Blamey, R., Bennett, J., Louviere, J. and Morrison, M. (1999) *Validation of a Choice Model Involving Green Product Choice*. Choice Modelling Research Report No. 10, University of New South Wales, Canberra.

Dain Simpson & Associates and Calkin & Associates (1997) *A Review of Green Globe*. Unpublished report prepared for Tourism Council Australia's Environment Committee.

Green Flag International Ltd (1995) *Tips for Travellers*, prepared for Green Globe. Available: http://www.wttc.org.

Green Globe (1997a) *What is Green Globe?* Available: http://www.wttc.org.

Green Globe (1997b) *Annual Review 1996/97*. Available: http://www.wttc.org.

Green Globe (1997c) *Green Globe Achievement Awards 1997*. Available: http://www.wttc.org.

Green Globe (1997d) *Green Globe Rewards Environmental Excellence*, news release, 10 March. Available: http://www.wttc.org.

Green Globe (1997e) *New Environmental Standard Demonstrates Compliance with Agenda 21*, news release, 19 November. Available: http://www.wttc.org.

Green Globe (1997f) *Green Globe Newsletter*, Issue 6, January. Available: http://www.wttc.org.

Green Globe (1997g) *Green Globe Training Programmes*. Available: http://www.wttc.org.

Green Globe (1998a) *Green Globe Members List by Country – February 1998*. Available: http://www.wttc.org.

Green Globe (1998b) *Green Globe Certification*. Available: http://www.wttc.org.

Green Globe (1998c) *Green Globe Destinations*. Available: http://www.wttc.org.

Green Globe (1998d) *Green Globe Industry Associates – February 1998*. Available: http://www.wttc.org.

Green Globe 21 (1999) *New International Advisory Council for Green Globe 21*, news release, 17 November. Available: http://www.greenglobe21.com.

Green Globe 21 (2001a) *Company Information – Current Projects*. Available: http://www.greenglobe21.com.

Green Globe 21 (2001b) *International Award Program*. Available: http://www.greenglobe21.com.

Green Globe 21 (2001c) *Traveller Status*. Available: http://www.greenglobe21.com.

MORI (1995) *Business and the Environment*. MORI, London.

MORI (1998) *Public Views on Travel and the Environment*. MORI, London.

Tearfund (2000) *Tourism – An Ethical Issue. Market Research Report*, produced by IPSOS-RSL for Tearfund, Middlesex.

WWF-UK (2000). *Tourism Certification: An Analysis of Green Globe 21 and Other Tourism Certification Programmes*, a report by Synergy for WWF-UK, London.

Appendix

Benchmarking for hotels: an example of Green Globe Sector Performance Indicators (May 2001)

The indicators include the requirement for an environmental and socio-economic policy and measures against the key environmental and social policy and measures against the key environmental performance areas. The text of the Hotel Sector Performance Indicators is reproduced here.

HOTELS: Sustainability Policy

Objective: Produce a clear and straightforward written policy that addresses key sustainability issues raised in the GREEN GLOBE 21 STANDARD.

The Sustainability Policy is an operation's statement with respect to its assessment, control and where appropriate, continual improvement, of environmental and local socio-economic impacts. The areas that need to be covered are included in the GREEN GLOBE 21 STANDARD and will reflect the Global Code of Tourism Ethics.

Indicator measure: A Sustainability Policy has been produced, endorsed by the operation's executive officer responsible for the GREEN GLOBE programme.

HOTELS: Energy consumption

Objective: Minimize overall energy consumption.

Significant levels of energy can be consumed by infrastructure (for example, buildings, recreational facilities) and transport facilities (including customer transfer, maintenance and on-site vehicles). An overall reduction in energy consumed will have a positive impact on operational costs and can have major environmental benefits, primarily through conservation of natural resources and lowering associated greenhouse gas emissions.

Energy can be consumed from a variety of sources (e.g., grid electricity, natural gas, gasoline, diesel) and total usage is assessed on a standard energy unit basis (megajoules, MJ). Electricity consumption is often quoted in kilowatt-hours (kWh) and in the case of other sources, such as diesel, petroleum, liquefied propane gas (LPG) and natural gas, by volume. All can be readily converted to joules using GREEN GLOBE supplied conversion factors.

Indicator measure: Total energy consumption (MJ) pa/Guest nights pa *or* Area under roof (m²).

Greenhouse gas reductions: Reduction in emissions from energy production and distribution.

Note (1) *GREEN GLOBE recognizes that many Travel and Tourism operations are already very energy efficient and/or further significant reductions in energy from non-renewable fossil fuel sources may, for operational and commercial reasons, not be feasible. Therefore, an optional indicator demonstrating the level of involvement in carbon sequestration to offset greenhouse gas emissions is recognized.*

Note (2) *GREEN GLOBE also acknowledges that many operations are making significant efforts to utilize energy from renewable sources (e.g., wind, solar, hydro), conserving both resources and minimizing greenhouse gas emissions. This can be recognized through adoption of an optional indicator that highlights the percentage of renewable energy consumed pa.*

HOTELS: Potable water management

Objective: Minimize consumption of potable water.

The operation may be a significant consumer of potable water supplies, not only for human consumption, but also for other activities such as washing, recreational facilities, gardens and surface cleaning, etc. Many Travel and Tourism operations are located in regions where fresh water is a concern, such that positive action leading to an overall reduction (from lowering demand and increasing reuse and recycle) will be a significant contribution to the local environment and the long-term sustainability of the operation.

The indicator monitors the overall efficiency of potable water usage with a view to promoting reduction without compromising the operation.

Indicator measure: Water consumed (kL) pa/Guest nights pa *or* Area under roof (m^2).

Greenhouse gas reductions: Reduction in emissions from energy required for potable water treatment, distribution and disposal.

HOTELS: Solid waste reduction

Objective: Reduce the amount of solid wastes.

Used or waste materials sent to landfills represent a loss of resources, and their replacement will increase greenhouse gases from production and transport of their replacements. The first step for the operation should be to look to reduce quantities of materials consumed (including packaging), to then consider reuse, or if not possible, recycle.

As part of the Sustainability Policy, consideration should be given to the options that have the best local environmental impact. For example, recycling may not always be feasible (e.g., no local facility) and on-site waste to energy systems may be a better route, obtaining both energy and a reduction in the volume of waste disposed (measured either as uncompacted, or mechanically compacted, material).

Indicator measure: Volume of waste landfilled (m^3) pa/Guest nights pa *or* Area under roof (m^2).

Greenhouse gas reductions: Reduction in emissions from energy required for material production, and subsequent waste transposition and disposal.

HOTELS: Social commitment

Objective: Develop and maintain positive, productive and sustainable contributions to the local community.

A key issue in achieving sustainability is to consider the social as well as environmental impact of the operation with local communities. Respecting, where appropriate, local traditions and customs, and purchasing, where possible, local goods and services are positive contributions that can be made, and should be incorporated into the operation's Sustainability Policy. Other considerations should include active participation in local committees and organizations.

The indicator to monitor is the number of owners, managers and/or employees that have a primary address close to the operation (for remote operations, such as on small non-populated islands, the nearest permanent township can be used instead of the operation). This encourages local employment and minimizes environmental impacts due to personnel transportation.

Indicator measure: Employees with their primary address within 20 km of the operation/total employees.

Greenhouse gas reductions: Reduction in emissions from transport energy consumption.

HOTELS: Resource conservation

Objective: Reduce consumption of natural resources and the impact on ecosystem biodiversity.

An active policy of purchasing supplies of materials from sources using environmentally sound ingredients and processes can be a major contribution to resource conservation and biodiversity (i.e., through less impact on the balance of the local ecosystem).

The type of paper used by the operation (e.g., for promotional material, stationery, toilets) is a high profile example where significant worthwhile reductions in environmental impacts can be achieved. A strategy of internal reuse and recycle where possible, coupled with the use of products proven to be environmentally friendly (such as those carrying credible ecolabels) should be adopted.

For paper, ecolabels are likely to signify avoidance of chlorine-based bleaches, use of biodegradable inks and dyes, and use of wood from sustainable plantations.

Indicator measure: Ecolabel paper purchased pa/Total paper purchased per annum.

Greenhouse gas reductions: Reduction in emissions associated with virgin raw material consumption.

HOTELS: Cleaning chemicals

Objective: Reduce chemicals discharged into the environment.

The active (non-water) chemical ingredients of cleaning products (e.g., soaps, shampoos, laundry detergents, dishwashing detergents, floor and carpet cleaners) can end up in both wastewater (from toilets, washbasins, kitchens, etc.) and stormwater systems (from roofs, car parks, etc.). These are potential sources of contamination of natural water bodies in terms of toxicity and disturbance of the natural balance of ecosystems (e.g., phosphates from detergents are known to contribute to eutrophication).

Along with an overall reduction in the gross amount of chemicals consumed per annum, increased use of ecolabelled biodegradable cleaning products would be a significant step towards overall reduction in chemical contamination of the environment. Active chemical usage is based on the weight of non-biodegradable chemicals in all solids and solutions used for cleaning.

Indicator measure: Non-biodegradable cleaning chemical use (kg) pa/ Guest nights pa *or* Area under roof (m^2).

Greenhouse gas reductions: Reduction in emissions from energy required for chemical production and water contamination treatment.

Optional indicators for hotels

Carbon sequestration • • •

Objective: Commitment to offset greenhouse gas production.

The long-term solution to reducing greenhouse gas production by Travel and Tourism is to tackle it at source by introducing more efficient, less non-renewable energy intensive equipment and procedures.

However, application of this 'cleaner production' or 'ecoefficiency' approach will take time. Additionally, many operations in the industry are already energy efficient and/or further significant reductions in energy from fossil fuel sources may for operational and commercial reasons not be feasible.

CARBON SEQUESTRATION

Growing forests naturally remove carbon dioxide (CO_2) from the atmosphere and convert the carbon into new tree biomass (CO_2), resulting in carbon storage (sequestration) in both wood and soils.

Sequestration can be an acceptable mechanism to offset net carbon emissions under the Kyoto Protocol, although restrictions do apply. In particular carbon sequestration will be credited only for trees planted after January 1, 1990.

There may be a case, therefore, for looking for alternative strategies to help offset the production of greenhouse gases. One potential solution is involvement in carbon sequestration as an immediate move towards making the operation carbon neutral.

The issue is to evaluate the total amount of carbon dioxide (CO_2) generated through all the operation's activities and to offset as much as possible through uptake by natural tree growth. Involvement in carbon sequestration can be through large-scale national and international programmes, as well as by direct actions in promoting local tree planting schemes.

Indicator measure: CO_2 sequested (tonnes) pa/Total CO_2 generated (tonnes) per annum.

Greenhouse gas reductions: Reduction in the impact of CO_2 emissions on global warming.

HOTELS: Operation selected indicator

Objective: Positive commitment to the local environment, society and economy.

The operation is encouraged to nominate at least one other indicator that they consider particularly relevant to its operation and its environmental impact, and worthy of promotion. This may be operation or locality specific, and will reflect its commitment to improving local issues (e.g., water quality, endangered species, habitat preservation, cultural heritage, community development).

Examples of possible indicators that can be used are listed below, but a more comprehensive list is included on the GREEN GLOBE web sites and reflecting the full spectrum of the Global Code of Tourism Ethics.

Examples of operation selected indicator measures

- Renewable energy consumption pa/Total energy consumption per annum;
- Number of environmentally accredited operators and suppliers dealt with pa/Total number of operators and suppliers dealt with per annum;
- Monetary contributions made to sponsor conservation projects pa/Net turnover of operation per annum;
- Area used for habitat conservation (ha)/Total property area (ha);
- Value of consumable products purchased produced locally (within country) pa/Total value of consumable products purchased per annum;
- Monetary contributions made to sponsor local community activities pa/Net turnover of operation per annum; and
- Use of GREEN GLOBE sponsored Entrepreneurship Handbook with local community.

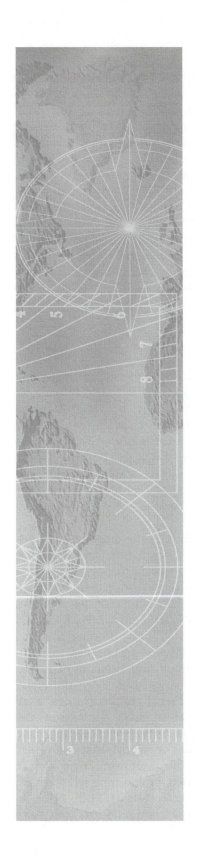

CHAPTER 6

The European Blue Flag campaign for beaches in Slovenia: a programme for raising environmental awareness

Tanja Mihalic

Introduction

Over the last decade a number of schemes have been developed to raise environmental awareness and standards of behaviour in relation to tourism. This case study provides an overview of how one such scheme, the Blue Flag campaign for beaches in Slovenia, operates. The process of creating environmental awareness through this scheme is discussed, and the key elements of a successful Blue Flag campaign are identified with the aid of an environmental responsibility model. Attention is also paid to the link between the Blue Flag campaign and the growth of environmental awareness in Slovenia's tourism industry, where the campaign is seen as both a tool for improving environmental quality and a means of promoting safe beaches. However, as the Blue Flag criteria become more demanding, a development welcomed by those concerned with integrated coastal management, there is potential for conflict with tourism industry interests, an issue discussed in the conclusion to this case study.

Development of the Blue Flag campaign

The environmental quality of a destination is a key factor in making travel-related decisions (Pizam, 1991: 79; Inskeep, 1991: 339; Mieczkowski, 1995: 11; Middleton, 1997: 136; Font, 2001: 2). There is some evidence that a growing segment of visitors turn away from what they consider to be polluted destinations, with tourists not willing to trade lower environmental quality for a lower price (OECD, 1992: 8). This is especially true where health risks from air or water pollution are perceived as a problem (Middleton, 1997: 138), as illustrated by the decline in western Mediterranean tourism in the early 1990s (Mieczkowski, 1995: 210).

The Blue Flag logo, a white circle with a bottle floating on three wave crests, is a symbol used to denote a beach or marina that has met specific environmental criteria, and as such is meant to convey a message of personal health and safety to those using them. It originated in a pollution-tracking campaign of the Foundation for Environmental Education in Europe (FEEE). This campaign involved the use of bottles containing messages that requested those finding them to contact FEEE, and was designed to track the spread of solid waste at sea (FEEE, 1990). The Blue Flag programme was first launched in France in 1985, and was, at that time, concerned only with the water quality of beaches. In that year, eleven French municipalities were awarded the Blue Flag for their bathing water quality and wastewater treatment. By 1986 that number had risen to forty-three. The following year the campaign broadened to encompass a further nine countries, as well as marinas, as an activity of the European Year of the Environment. Co-ordination of this expanded programme fell to FEEE and the Commission of the European Communities (FEEE, 1990). In subsequent years the Blue Flag campaign continued to grow (see

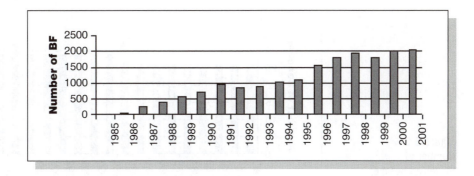

Figure 6.1
Numbers of Blue
Flag beaches in
Europe, 1985–2001

Figure 6.1), under the umbrella of FEEE, and with the help of its national branches in each participating country. In 2001, Blue Flags were awarded to 2041 sea and inland water beaches and 713 marinas in twenty-one European countries:

Belgium	Finland	Italy	Slovenia
Bulgaria	France	Latvia	Spain
Croatia	Germany	The Netherlands	Sweden
Cyprus	Greece	Norway	Turkey
Denmark	Ireland	Portugal	United Kingdom
Estonia			

In 2001, for the first time, the campaign will travel beyond Europe to South Africa and the Caribbean (FEEE, 2001a). With the spreading of the campaign to non-European countries FEEE has now been renamed FEE (Foundation for Environmental Education), with the words 'in Europe' removed from its name.

The Blue Flag campaign in Slovenia

Slovenia is a new transitional country that was established in 1991 when it separated from the former Yugoslavia. Geographically, it lies in the north-east corner of the Adriatic Sea, between the Italian and Croatian seasides, and has a 46-kilometre-long coastline with thirty-one public beaches. Tourism along this coastline is highly developed, with 1.6 million tourist nights being spent in its resort towns. This figure represents more than 25 per cent of total tourist nights in Slovenia (SORS, 2000).

In socialist Slovenia environmental issues were not high on the political agenda. Arguably, the first time concerns were raised concerning the environmental effects of tourism was at the Tourism Forum, a component of the Alpe Adria tourism fair in the capital Ljubljana in 1992 (Mihalič, 1992). At this time, however, there appeared to be little desire on behalf of the tourism industry to address environmental

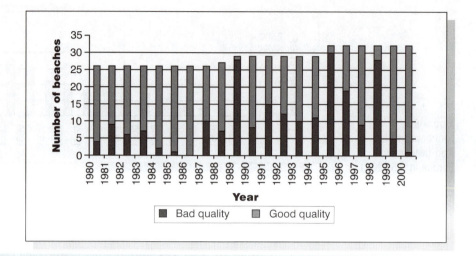

Figure 6.2
Number of Slovenian beaches by bathing water quality (according to national legislation), 1994–2000

quality issues. Indeed, some Forum participants were concerned that to do so could damage the image of Slovenia's coastal tourism product. Given that at the year prior to the Forum, 52 per cent of Slovenian beaches, according to government tests, did not meet national standards for bathing water quality (see Figure 6.2), such a view is perhaps understandable.

After 1991 environmental awareness in Slovenia started to develop rapidly due to the increased flow of information from beyond the state's now open borders. Additionally, many foreign consultants from different fields were hired by the new democratically elected government, to advise it on various matters, including environmental management. It was in this atmosphere of change and the reappraisal of old practices and ideas, that the concept of sustainability became integrated into the national tourism development strategy (Sirše *et al.*, 1993). External pressures were also serving at this time to push beach tourism operators in the direction of being more environmentally aware. For example, international tour operators, especially the German tour operator Turistic Union International (TUI), checked the environmental performance of its partners and identified Blue Flag beaches and marinas in its catalogues.

In 1993 the Ministry for Industry, then responsible for tourism, spurred on, in part, by a group comprising enlightened members of the tourism industry, institutions involved in tourism research, and several journalists with an interest in the environment, asked the Faculty of Economics at the University of Ljubljana to establish contact with the international Blue Flag authorities and initiate efforts to obtain the European 'environmental mark' for Slovenian marina and beach tourism. Contact with FEEE was successfully achieved and an attempt was made to house the Blue Flag campaign within the existing National Tourism Association. FEEE foresaw the possibility of a conflict of

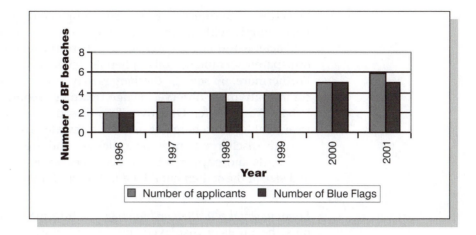

Figure 6.3
Numbers of
applicant and
awarded Blue Flag
beaches in
Slovenia,
1996–2001

interest with this arrangement and suggested the creation of a new non-governmental organization with a clear general aim to increase environmental awareness through the activities of FEEE. Accordingly, the above-mentioned group of enthusiasts joined with representatives from health institutions, environmental organizations and government to set up the Foundation for Environmental Education in Europe-Slovenia (FEEE-S). This body became a member of FEEE in 1994. In the role of 'a godparent', the Italian national FEEE operator worked closely with the Slovenian organization to help implement the Blue Flag campaign in Slovenia.

In Slovenia the marina Blue Flag campaign started in 1995 and the beach campaign in 1996. In 1996 two beach applicants met all the standards and were awarded the blue logo; by 2001 this number had climbed to six (Figure 6.3). Over this same period (see Figure 6.3), a number of beaches were also rejected. Indeed, in 1997 and 1999 when no Slovenian beach was successful in gaining a Blue Flag award, media and public debate on water quality and broader issues relating to tourism and environmental quality increased dramatically.

Blue Flag Award criteria

Criteria for being awarded a Blue Flag are pre-defined by the FEEE Blue Flag campaign and are merely implemented by each national operator. For the 2001 bathing season there were twenty-seven criteria for beaches that related to four key aspects (FEEE, 2001b). Some of the criteria relating to each of these four areas are given here for illustrative purposes.

- *Water quality.* The criteria here state that there must be compliance with requirements and standards such as those of the EU's Bathing Water

Directive. This directive prescribes the percentage of test results that must comply with guideline and imperative values for total and faecal colibacteria and faecal streptococci. There are also standards on colour, transparency, mineral oils, phenols content and other substances. Furthermore, no sewage discharges may affect the beach area, and the community must observe sewage treatment requirements of the EU's Urban Waste Water Directive. This directive sets exact standards for treatment and discharge of urban wastewater and requires that all the sewage discharged must be collected and treated. It sets different standards and implementation deadlines according to the type of area and size of the settlement (Hellenic Society for the Protection of Nature, 2001: 9).

- *Environmental education and information.* Information on flora and fauna must be publicly displayed, including advice on how to behave, to minimize impacts on these. Data on bathing water quality also needs to be displayed on the beach in the form of a table or figure that can be easily understood.

- *Environmental management and facilities.* Example criteria are: rubbish bins in adequate numbers that are properly secured and regularly maintained and emptied; safe access paths to the beach; facilities for receiving recyclable materials; the presence of local land-use and development plans for the coastal zone; and the active promotion of sustainable transport to and along the beach area (i.e., bicycling, walking or public transport).

- *Safety and services.* Requirements relate to such matters as: the presence of beach guards; first aid services; provision of drinking water; access and facilities for people with disabilities; and general maintenance of buildings and equipment.

Some Blue Flag criteria are imperatives, like the water quality criteria or litter bins in adequate numbers, while others are merely guidelines, such as recycling waste materials. A beach that does not comply with one or more of the imperative criteria cannot be awarded a Blue Flag. Each year a number of guideline criteria become imperative and new criteria may be added. The same criteria apply for candidates from all states. Where national legislation is stricter on a particular issue, this must be complied with rather than the Blue Flag criterion. For example, the Slovenian national standards on bathing water quality are stricter than those of the EU, which form the basis of the Blue Flag standards.

At the moment the Blue Flag beach campaign only relates to operated urban beaches. The beach operator (who is licensed by local government) can act directly to fulfil some criteria (e.g., provision of beach access for people with disabilities), whereas the fulfilment of others (e.g., the new EU Urban Waste Water Directive), may call for the engagement of the local community and other partners, even the national government.

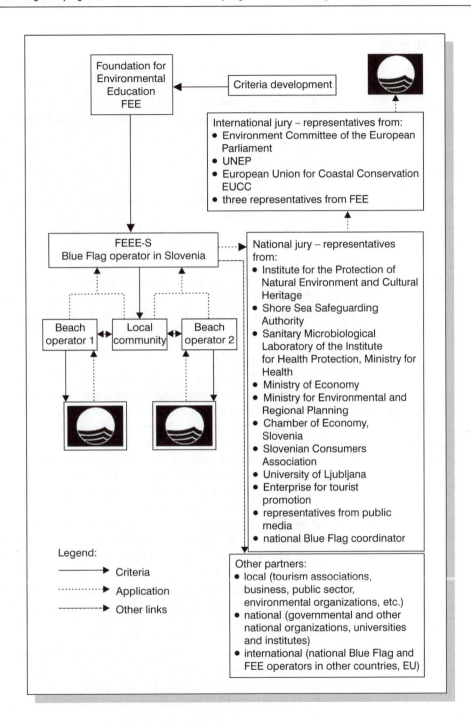

Figure 6.4
Organizational chart
of the Slovenian
Blue Flag
campaign:
participants and
application
procedures

Partners in the Blue Flag campaign

The Blue Flag campaign works at three levels: local, national and international (see Figure 6.4).

Local level

At the local level, the Slovenian campaign involves direct and indirect partners. According to the application procedure, direct partners are the beach operator and the local government. The beach operator makes the initial decision to apply for a Blue Flag, and application is then made on its behalf by the local government (in Figure 6.4 the local community) to the Slovenian national Blue Flag organization (FEEE-S). The involvement of local authorities is necessary since they have many responsibilities regarding the Blue Flag criteria. These include waste-water treatment, organizing the collection of rubbish, ensuring visitor safety on beaches and incorporating environmental considerations into local planning. Additionally, the local community must have a land-use and development plan for its coastal zone. This plan, and the current activities of the community in the coastal zone, must be in compliance with planning regulations and coastal zone protection regulations. Although such criteria are of no direct value to beach visitors, they generally push tourism development in the local community in a more environmentally friendly direction. Directly they do not communicate the message on environmental quality, but in the long run they contribute to it.

The beach operator in Slovenia works with the Blue Flag co-ordinator from the national organization in order to ensure that all criteria that are the responsibility of the beach operator are met. Amongst others, the authorized beach operator or beach owner is responsible for drinking water sources on the beach, toilets, rubbish collection, displaying the relevant criteria, informing beach visitors on environmental matters concerning their use of the area, and obtaining and displaying regular water quality results in a form that can be easily understood.

At the local level, many other indirect participants are involved in the Blue Flag campaign. Organizations, such as local associations, local businesses and tourist associations have an interest in obtaining the Blue Flag for a local beach. They may also have interests that are in line with the aims of the campaign and therefore they might act to co-operate in Blue Flag activities within their local community or with the national organization itself. As regards this last point, the Slovenian Blue Flag campaign has relationships with the Sanitary Microbiological Laboratory, conservation organizations, environmental organizations, the Institute for Protection of the Natural Environment and Cultural Heritage, as well as with other partners in the coastal community, as shown in Figure 6.4. Also, the local population has a vested interest in the success of the campaign, and it is therefore in their interests to support it in whatever ways they can.

National level

The Blue Flag campaign within Slovenia is coordinated at the national level by the FEEE-S (Foundation for Environmental Education of Europe in Slovenia). This body is a voluntary, independent, non-profit, and non-governmental association. Its main aim is to raise environmental awareness in Slovenia. It acts to inform the public regarding matters associated with environmental protection; it organizes and manages various activities of the international organization FEE, of which it is a full member, and also represents Slovenia within this organization.

The FEEE-S, as the national Blue Flag co-ordinator, works with local communities and other parties interested in applying for Blue Flags. At the same time, it represents the Blue Flag campaign's interests vis-à-vis national authorities such as the Ministry for the Environment and Regional Planning, and Health Ministry and Ministry for Sport, Science and Education.

The Slovenian international jury (see Figure 6.4) meets once a year and selects applicants who are then sent before the International Jury of FEE.

International level

As of 2001 the Blue Flag scheme involved twenty-one European and one non-European country (South Africa), which work under the international umbrella organization known as FEE (Foundation for Environmental Education).

FEE's primary role is to promote environmental education, and in doing this it offers its members four general environmental-awareness raising projects: Eco Schools, Young Reporters for the Environment, Learning about Forests and the Blue Flag Campaign (FEE, 2001: 1). These programmes are delivered/conducted through a network of national operators under common standards and criteria. FEE's headquarters are presently in England, and decisions regarding its activities and policies, etc., are made by its annual general assembly.

The Blue Flag, as one of the FEE's campaigns, is run through the European Blue Flag secretariat in Copenhagen. Its activities include: organizing meetings for national operators to discuss common problems and future changes to Blue Flag criteria; facilitating the exchange of information and expertise among countries; the production of common European information and promotional materials; and the running of the European Jury (UNEP, 1996: 10).

Contribution to environmental responsibility

The Blue Flag campaign for environmentally responsible beaches and marinas started out as a way of encouraging local authorities to provide clean and safe beaches and marinas for tourists and local residents. But the campaign has been increasingly conducted within the much wider context of environmental management of the coastal area, and the criteria used in the campaign have been progressively broadened. The cam-

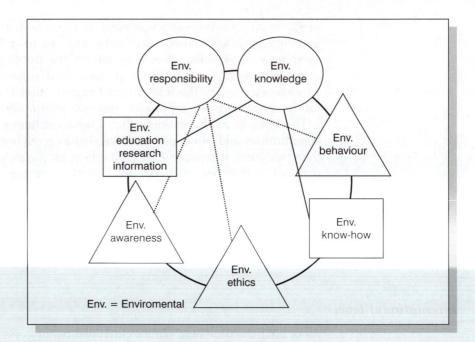

Figure 6.5
Know-how as an essential element of the environmental responsibility– knowledge model

paign's long-term objectives are to improve environmental awareness of the coastal environment and promote environmental behaviour, thereby developing environmental responsibility.

Environmental responsibility and *environmental knowledge* are two main foundation elements that help to explain how an environmental campaign works. In the model presented in Figure 6.5 they are presented as the overriding essential elements. In this model *environmental responsibility* is connected to environmental awareness, ethics and behaviour. Environmental responsibility requires both an awareness of environmental problems and behaviour that complies with environmental ethics. Thus, environmental behaviour is only possible if environmental awareness and ethics exist.

Environmental damage arising from, for example, improper behaviour may also be due to human ignorance (Frey, 1985: 39). Human ignorance is often caused through insufficient education, research, and information. Since environmental disasters may develop over a long period, a direct link with concrete human actions may not be visible; therefore a lack of understanding and information is often the real reason why such disasters arise. If humans had sufficient information about the consequences of their actions, such disasters may not happen. This is illustrated by the second foundation element in the model, *environmental knowledge*. This model element consists of two parts: environmental education, research and available information on the one hand and environmental know-how on the other. The latter refers to knowledge on appropriate criteria and the means of technical, financial, managerial and organizational implementation of environmental action, such as how to carry out water testing, and how to construct purifying plants in order to meet defined standards.

The Blue Flag campaign offers pre-defined criteria for the environmentally appropriate management of beaches and local communities. In Figure 6.5, the environmental know-how of the Blue Flag campaign is placed between environmental ethics (what is right and what is wrong) and environmental behaviour, and is seen as a connecting element (how to do it properly). Environmental education, research and information are presented as important elements in the creation of environmental awareness, which is the main aim of the Blue Flag campaign. For Slovenia, Blue Flag's environmental information potential is especially important. Amongst other things, the Blue Flag campaign informs the public about environmental quality and, at the same time, the Slovenian FEEE-S is pushing for public availability of all environmental quality data in order to promote and speed up environmental problem-solving through public pressure.

The effectiveness of the Blue Flag campaign can be partially judged by how well it addresses the elements of this model. In that regard, Kernel (1997) examined the environmental education, awareness and behaviour outcomes of Blue Flag from the perspectives of national tourism organizations, national Blue Flag juries, FEE member organizations and national environmental organizations in fourteen European countries. According to that survey 80 per cent of tourism organizations, 81 per cent of national FEE branch organizations and 60 per cent of environmental organizations believed that the campaign had raised environmental awareness. The results also showed that there was still a gap between awareness and environmental behaviour, with less than 30 per cent of respondents believing that the Blue Flag campaign actually changed the behaviour of visitors (Kernel, 1997: 5).

Conclusion

Tourism can provide an incentive for 'cleaning up' the overall environment through control of water, littering, and for improving environmental aesthetics through landscaping programmes, urban planning and better buildings maintenance (Inskeep, 1991: 343). In the Mediterranean region there is much justifiable concern being expressed about marine pollution, and hence there is a significant role for a campaign like Blue Flag. The campaign has now reached a stage where it is sufficiently established in Europe for the possession of a Blue Flag to mean something to visitors, or at least to tourism businesses. The previously mentioned survey by Kernel (1997: 5) revealed that 24 per cent of tourism organizations believed that visitors preferred Blue Flag beaches over others. Having a Blue Flag signifies a safe and clean beach with good water quality, while not having, or losing one, may raise questions about water quality in the public media (Frank, 2001; Henderson, 2001; Mansfield, 2001).

The number of Slovenian Blue Flag beaches is still relatively low: five Blue Flag sea beaches out of a potential thirty-two, representing only 15 per cent of the total. On the other hand, all three Slovenian marinas were awarded the Blue Flag logo in 2000 and 2001. The low number of applications from Slovenian beaches is due to the very complex criteria that have to be fulfilled by the beach operator, although more are preparing to apply in the near future. Nevertheless, the Blue Flag campaign in Slovenia can be regarded as a successful tool for addressing environmental problems and implementing internationally recognized standards.

Finally, it has to be emphasized that environmental impacts are not always controllable by the beach operator or tourism business. The Blue Flag is awarded on the basis of the water quality of the beach; yet the organization responsible may not be able to control sources of pollution whose origination, for example, might be located some distance away, being carried by wind and currents. Hence the need to link the management of resources in a given area through a broader coastal management plan, and to engage communities in the decision-making processes associated with such plans. In this regard, FEEE-S is now being challenged to change Blue Flag's image so that it comes to be seen as a tool for progressing integrated sustainable development in coastal areas that is beneficial not only to the tourism industry, but also to local communities. According to Kernel (1997), such an aim is in line with how environmental organizations in European countries primarily consider the Blue Flag campaign. Forty-two per cent of those organizations, as opposed to less than 10 per cent of national tourism organizations expected Blue Flag to promote integrated coastal area management and control.

References

FEE (2001) *Statutes*. Foundation for Environmental Education, European secretariat, Norwich.

FEEE (1990) *The Blue Flag Campaign*. Foundation for Environmental Education in Europe, European office, Copenhagen.

FEEE (2001a) *The Blue Flag Campaign 2001*. http:www.blueflag.org. (Retrieved 14.06.2001.)

FEEE (2001b) *Untitled Document*. http://www.blueflag.org/criteria/beachc.htm. (Retrieved 28.05.2001.)

FEEE-S (2001) Internal databank. Foundation for Environmental Education in Europe – Slovenia, Portorož.

Font, X. (2001) Regulating the Green Message: The Players in Ecolabelling. In *Tourism Ecolabelling. Certification and Promotion of Sustainable Management*. Edited by Font, X., Buckley, R.C., Wallingford: CAB International, pp. 1–17.

Frank, B. (2001) Taking the waters in the UK. *Sunday Times*, March 24, 2001, London http:/wwwproquest.umi.com. (Retrieved 14.07.2001.)

Frey, B.S. (1985) *Umweltökonomie*. V&R, Goettingen.

Hellenic Society for the Protection of Nature (2001) *The Blue Flag. Guidance Notes to the Blue Flag Criteria for Beaches*. Hellenic Society for the Protection of Nature, Athens.

Henderson, M. (2001) Clean beaches. *The Times*, June 6, 2001, London. http:/wwwproquest.umi.com (Retrieved 14.07.2001.)

Inskeep, E. (1991) *Tourism Planning: an Integrated and Sustainable Development Approach*. New York: Van Nostrand Reinhold.

Kernel, P. (1997) *Survey of opinions among national interests about the Blue Flag Campaign*. FEEE, Copenhagen.

Lübbert, C. (1998) Umweltkennzeichnungen für touristische Angebote: Einstellungen deutscher Urlauber – Ergebnisse eine Pilotstudie. Fachtagung 'Umweltkennzeichningen im Tourismus' am 29. Oktober 1998 an der Ludwig-Maximilians-Universität München (LMU). Deutsches Wirtschaftswissenschaftliches Institut für Fremdenverkehr e.V. an der Universität München, München, pp. 22–31.

Mansfield, P. (2001) Postcard from Brighton. *Evening Standard*, June 27, 2001, London. http:/wwwproquest.umi.com. (Retrieved 14.07.2001.)

Middleton, V.T.C. (1997) Sustainable Tourism: A Marketing Perspective, in M.J. Stabler: *Tourism Sustainability. Principles to Practice*. Wallingford: CAB International, pp. 129–42.

Mieczkowski, Z. (1995) *Environmental Issues of Tourism and Recreation*. London: University Press of America.

Mihalič, T. (1992) Definitions, kinds and possibilities of environmental tourism forms (in Slovene). Paper presented at the *Alpe Adria Tourism Forum*, March 1992, Ljubljana.

Mihalič T. (1996) Ecological Labelling in Tourism. In *Sustainable Tourism in Islands and Small States. Issues and Policies*. Edited by Briguglio, L., Archer, B., Jafari, J. and Wall, G. Cassell, London, pp. 57–70.

Mihalič, T. (2000) Environmental management of a tourist destination. A factor of tourism competitiveness. *Tourism Management 21*, Special Issue, pp. 65–78.

Mihalič, T. (2001) Environmental Behavior Implications for Tourist Destinations and Ecolables. In *Tourism Ecolabelling. Certification and Promotion of Sustainable Management*. Edited by Font, X. and Buckley, R.C., Wallingford: CAB International, pp. 57–70.

OECD (1992) *Tourism policy and international tourism in OECD member countries*. OECD (Organization for Economic Cooperation and Development), Paris.

Pizam, A. (1991) The management of Quality Destination. *Proceedings of the Association Internationale d'Experts Scientifiques du Tourisme* (AIEST): Vol. 33. Quality Tourism – Concept of Sustainable Tourism Development, Harmonizing Economical, Social and Ecological Interests, pp. 79–88. St Gallen: Niedermann Druck.

Sirše, J., Stroj-Vrtačnik, I. and Pobega, N. (1993) *Slovenian Tourism Development Strategy* (in Slovene). IER (Institute for Economic Research), Ljubljana.

SORS (2000) Statistical Yearbook. Republic of Slovenia. SURS (Statistical Office of the Republic of Slovenia), Ljubljana.

UNEP (1996) *Awards for Improving the Coastal Environment. The Example of the Blue Flag.* UNEP (United Nations Environmental Programme), Paris.

Župan, J. (2001) *Sanitary quality of bathing water on the Slovenian coast for the years 1974–2000* (in Slovene). Institute for Health Protection, Koper.

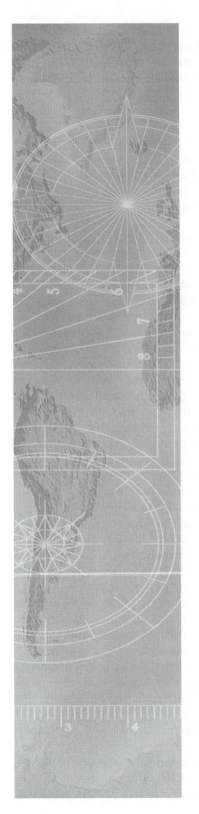

CHAPTER 7

PAN Parks: WWF's sustainable tourism certification programme in Europe's national parks

Xavier Font and André Brasser

The context and nature of PAN Parks

Tourism is one of the largest industries in Europe, and has the potential to become a key contributor to the preservation of rural European landscapes and social structures through the regeneration of economically depleted areas. Although coastal and city tourism are still the highest in terms of visitor numbers, it is rural and mountain tourism that is showing particularly strong growth in the European context, and this is mostly around protected areas. The IUCN (1994; in Blangy and Vautier, 2001) lists four reasons why the 1990s have offered increased opportunities for protected areas, all of which apply to Europe:

1. human populations are relatively stable and affluent;
2. there are declining pressures on land in many areas because of agricultural surpluses and reduced military activity;
3. there is a high level of public support for conservation; and
4. there is a climate of international cooperation.

Given these trends, the threat to protected areas in Europe has diminished, particularly from such activities as resource extraction and agriculture (WWF, 2000). Nonetheless, land use pressures remain evident due to limited land availability, with tourism and recreation being amongst the greatest contributors to such pressure in the context of Europe's national parks (FNNPE, 1993). It is also the case that the increasing use of natural areas for these purposes has generated a stronger commitment by governments and the broader community to their preservation (Font and Tribe, 2000).

There are between 10 000 and 20 000 protected areas in Europe; although the number is high, many are generally smallholdings containing pockets of biodiversity and few are large enough to allow for the free roaming of large mammals. It is also evident that the level of protection, the presence of multiple use objectives, level of funding, and state intervention/permissiveness vary significantly between these areas. In response to these, and other issues, the European Commission developed Natura 2000 as their strategy for environmental conservation. As part of this strategy, two tourism-related projects have been identified as being particularly relevant to the implementation of this strategy (European Commission, 2000a, 2000b). The first one of these is the European Charter for Sustainable Tourism in Protected Areas, headed by the Parcs Naturels Régionaux de France under the auspices of the Europarc Federation, and supported by the IUCN. The Charter developed by this project has been tested in ten European national parks, and these have been acknowledged as well-managed protected areas that have made continuous efforts towards making tourism and conservation compatible. The second, and the focus of this case study, is the PAN Parks network of protected areas. PAN Parks is the result of a partnership established in 1997 between the World Wide Fund for Nature-Netherlands and the Dutch Molecaten Group, a leisure and tourism-based corporation with assets of 45 million euros and an annual turnover of 13.5 million euros, which develops holiday villages in Europe.

The concept behind PAN Parks is one of creating 'a network of natural areas with an international reputation for outstanding access to wildlife and excellent tourist facilities, combined with effective habitat protection and the minimal environmental impact possible' (WWF, 1998: 1). Given this goal, PAN Parks has sought to develop:

- a recognizable network of well-managed, protected natural areas which welcome visitors and avoid potentially conflicting activities;
- a partnership between the authorities of protected areas, the local population, and commercial and nature conservation organizations;
- a way to promote well managed natural areas to create a balance between nature conservation, local development, tourism and recreation; and
- an organization to increase the number of well-supervised natural areas in Europe. (WWF, undated: 3).

In essence, the PAN Parks project is trying to create a network of 'Yellowstone Parks' in Europe. The intention being one of identifying protected areas holding wilderness characteristics and tourist attractiveness, not only of national but also of pan-European importance, encouraging the sustainable environmental and tourism management of these areas, and promoting visitation to them. The concept of reproducing the success of American parks in tourism is an ambitious challenge for Europe. There are no more than 100 parks that would qualify on size alone. Most of these are located in Eastern Europe, where problems such as overstretched budgets, little tourism infrastructure, limited visitor management experience and where local use of parks for poaching and illegal harvesting exist. Yet the preservation of these areas in the medium term, and the link via corridors between the remaining pieces of wilderness in Europe in the long term, could have an invaluable impact on the preservation of the regions' wildlife.

PAN Parks and the European Charter are working jointly to benefit from synergies between their projects. Cees Lager, CEO of the Molecaten Group, sees the benefits in tourism development that are linked to nature conservation, and views the inclusion of non-financial returns on investment, such as nature conservation, as a key value in this project. At the same time, however, Lager notes that for the project to be successful, acceptable financial returns must be forthcoming to those that invest in it. PAN Parks Accommodation BV is the limited liability company made up of investing partners, and initially managed by Molecaten, that will seek investors to provide 'appropriate accommodation (to be called PAN Villages) at approved PAN Parks, to generate income for its shareholders and to provide financial support for the PAN Parks Foundation' (Pan Parks Foundation, undated: 7). Molecaten and other investors will 'help protect and develop many of Europe's most beautiful wilderness areas while enjoying a sound return on their investment' (Pan Parks Foundation, undated: 1). It is unclear at this early stage what percentage of profits will be distributed to shareholders, used for reinvestment purposes or allocated to the Foundation.

This case study discusses the process of engaging a core group of European parks in the development and implementation of habitat, visitor, tourism and business management strategies in their process of application for the PAN Parks quality trademark, and ultimately to ensure a more sustainable use of the parks' resources. The first section reviews the applicants to PAN Parks and the benefits from application as presented by the PAN Parks Foundation and perceived by the applicants. This is followed by a review of the key principles of the process of compliance assessment (Font, 2002; Font and Tribe, 2001) and how PAN Parks is following this process of setting up criteria, ensuring the criteria are assessable, verifying standards of applicants, certification of results and ensuring recognition and acceptance by the target audiences. Since PAN Parks is still in its early years, this case study focuses on the outcomes from the first stage and critically assesses the main challenges to be faced if the programme is to contribute to sustainable tourism.

The PAN Parks candidates

For parks to qualify for inclusion in the PAN Park network they need to be large (usually over 25 000 hectares), with evidence of outstanding environmental quality and management. The candidates listed in Table 7.1 were present at the first Candidate PAN Parks Conference, held in Holland in June 2001. PAN Parks aims to appoint another six out of a preliminary list of ten other parks as prospective candidates in the near future.

The parks that have so far been selected as official candidates for inclusion in the PAN Park network represent some of the richest natural resources of Europe. They are home to large mammals and predators such as wolf, chamois, bears, lynx, moose and eagle. As examples, there are 200 rare animal species in Bieszczady, 100 Marsican Brown Bears and sixty Appenine wolves in Abbruzzo, and 6300 chamois in Mercantour. Besides their animal wealth, these parks are also sites of high concentration of species. Triglav has combined 5500 species of flora and fauna within its boundaries. Abruzzo has one third of the higher order plants of Italy, and Oulanka has 500 species of vascular plants, which is unusual given its northern location. Mercantour is home to 2000 species of plants, including sixty species of orchids, 200 rare and 300 endemic species, due to landscapes ranging from Mediterranean (20 kilometres away from the sea) to Alpine (3000 metre high mountains with glaciers). Slovensky raj has more than 2100 species of butterflies due to its high concentration of gorges and caves.

Many of the candidate parks have a wide range of facilities: Abruzzo has fifteen visitor centres and ten mountain refuges, Oulanka has thirty-six cooking and camp fires, thirty-two campsites and eight unlocked cabins for recreational use, and Triglav has thirty-two alpine houses and huts. Land use in these parks varies, and although they all have core conservation areas, poaching and illegal hunting are still common. Some parks, such as Triglav which generates 40 per cent of its funds from tourism and recreation, are already benefiting from visitation; however, such parks tend to be the exception rather than the rule. In general, most parks rely on governmental funds, with tourism benefits being captured by nearby communities. Oulanka typifies this situation, with its manage-

Name of area	Country	Area (ha)	Visitors per year	Strengths	Weaknesses
Abbruzo National Park	Italy	43 950	2 000 000	1600 small-scale businesses in operation. Local people represented on board of directors.	No distinct management plan document.
Bieszczady National Park	Poland	29 200	250 000	Trilateral Man and Biosphere Reserve. 70 per cent of park is strictly protected.	Park is perceived as limiting to local development.
Fulufjallets Nature Reserve	Sweden	35 000	100 000	Local people are interested in PAN Parks.	Traditional use of resources.
Mercantour National Park	France	68 500	550 000	Partnership with Gites Panda. Twinned with Italian park.	Conflicts with shepherds on wolf issue. Local people have just started to realize importance of tourism.
Oulanka National Park	Finland	27 500	150 000	Park can raise income for itself. Local people are active in park management issues.	There is no co-operation with local companies. Park does not communicate with local communities.
Slovensky raj National Park	Slovak Rep.	32 774	500 000	Comparative advantage in Slovakia, well-known park. Close working relationships with PAN Parks office.	Pressure on environment from high level of visitation. Land use problems due to contradictions in zoning.
Triglav National Park	Slovenia	83 807	720 000	History of co-operation with local communities. No hunting on 25 000 hectares.	Pressure on environment from high levels of visitation. Limited co-operation between groups associated with tourism in the park.

Source: adapted from PAN Parks Courier, 2001.

Table 7.1
Candidate PAN Parks

ment noting that it gains no revenue from its 120 000 visitors, yet it is estimated that 30 per cent of the income from the neighbouring towns is attributable to tourists visiting the park.

Short- and long-term benefits to the parks

The current candidates for inclusion in PAN Parks are acting to pilot the processes and materials that have been developed for the project. Each candidate park must demonstrate that it is performing at a high level in at least one area covered by the scheme, and parks are encouraged to share information in order to reach acceptable benchmarks as they seek to move from 'candidate' status to become a verified member of it.

Parks can benefit from WWF support in training and resources to meet the scheme's criteria, and once they qualify certified parks can use the PAN Parks logo for marketing purposes. Table 7.2 shows a list of benefits categorized according to whether a park has been verified and certified, is a candidate park aiming for verification, or has made prospective enquiries but not yet entered the process as a candidate. The benefits of working towards the PAN Parks standards are not clear to every park, and in the last three years many parks have shown interest for a short period of time, after which they have decided not to go forward. Out of the current parks working towards certification (seven), the two in France and Italy, with longer experience in tourism management, have been most critical of the benefits that can be gained from the process, whereas parks with lower tourist numbers have shown more interest.

The benefits that PAN Parks lists in Table 7.2 generally coincide with park managers' expectations of the outcomes from this process. In general, park managers view PAN Parks as a quality trademark; however, what each park seeks from the scheme is dependent on their specific circumstances (PAN Parks Courier, 2001). The anticipated benefits for each park include opportunities for increased, mainly international, tourism business (Fulufjället, Mercantour, Triglav, Oulanka), networking and research opportunities (Abruzzo, Bieszczady, Mercantour, Slovensky raj, Triglav), and closer co-operation with local populations and stake-holders (Oulanka, Slovensky raj).

As regards tourism benefits, when Cees Lager, from the Molecaten group, introduced the first Candidate PAN Parks conference in 1999 he did so by highlighting the market demand for ecotourism that can be experienced in relative comfort. While the desire to service this market niche was central amongst his group's decision to support the PAN Park concept, there is no obligation on the part of participating parks to allow PAN Villages to be developed within their boundaries. At the commencement of 2002, only two candidate parks, Bieszczady and Fulufjället, had decided to proceed with proposals to develop PAN Villages (PAN Parks Supervisory Board, 2000). Fulufjället PAN Village, for example, is intending to include forty self-catering chalets with planning permission for a total of sixty-two; the construction of infrastructure will be completed by summer 2002 and the chalets by 2003, with the Village to be opened on 1 July 2004 (PAN Parks Foundation, undated).

Benefits	Verified park	Candidate park	Prospective park
Introduction of a PAN Park Village	(✓)		
PAN Parks Foundation support	✓		
Access to loans	✓		
Access to EU subsidies	✓		
Access to on-site conservation projects	✓	✓	
Training material and opportunities	✓	✓	
Inclusion in PAN Parks brochures	✓	✓	
Communication package	✓	✓	
Local partner website	✓	✓	
Benefits from PAN Parks research	✓	✓	✓
Access to the PAN Parks intranet	✓	✓	✓
Promotion at the PAN Parks website	✓	✓	✓
PAN Parks Courier (magazine)	✓	✓	✓

Source: PAN Parks internal information not published.
(✓) PAN Park Villages will be introduced on a longer-term basis.

Table 7.2
PAN Parks benefits to verified, candidate and prospective candidate parks

Most candidate parks have stated that PAN Parks has given them a medium-term goal and a short-term pathway to put into practice a variety of actions that have been on the 'back burner' for some time. Community consultation and the development of visitor and tourism management strategies are the short-term benefits mentioned most often. Besides these general considerations, two examples can be given of the benefits of PAN Parks to prospective candidate parks to date. Firstly, PAN Parks is helping promote tourism to the Bialowieza National Park (Poland), a prospective candidate park (see http://www.poland.pan-parks.org). Secondly, Fulufjället Nature Reserve has submitted a proposal to the European Union to be reclassified as a National Park, which has been accepted and will become operational in 2002 in part due to the support of PAN Parks. To assess the possible long-term benefits of PAN Parks it is necessary to review the process that applicants will have to follow in their efforts to achieve certification.

Standards

A standard is a document approved by a recognized body that provides for common and repeated use of a prescribed set of rules, conditions, or requirements (Toth, 2000). Setting standards is one of the hardest elements of a project of this type, since varying geographical and other site specific conditions mean what is appropriate for one park may not be acceptable elsewhere. For example, slash and burn is a traditional practice in Finland that has been lost over the years, and in the Koli National Park (Finland) this practice has been reintroduced as a mean of rescuing traditions, yet forest fire is a major threat to national parks in the Mediterranean (Font and Tribe, 2000). Another major difficulty arises from differences in national legislation, practices and objectives. Ideally, standards should not be below any national legislative requirements, but if a standard reflects the highest level of current law and practice this might be too demanding for some countries. For these reasons the standards PAN Parks has developed tend to be a mixture of environmental performance and environmental management (Font, 2002).

PAN Parks is developing its standards in the form of criteria, grouped under five principles (Anon, 2001). A manual of good practice for parks needing support to meet the requirements of these principles will be developed, which will include case studies from pilot sites (see the Discussion section later).

Principles and criteria

PAN Parks has laid out five principles for assessment of each member park's performance and management (see Table 7.3). The first three principles are under the control of the park's management unit, whereas the fourth and fifth principles are more challenging, since they recognize the dependence between the park and its surroundings, and the need for the park to engage with a variety of stakeholders in determining limits of acceptable change from tourism.

The first principle relates to a park's natural heritage, and acts as a 'filter' to ensure that a park is worthy of inclusion in the Pan Parks project. The second principle concerns the degree of management effectiveness exhibited in the protection of the natural environment. The third principle relates to the park's visitor management strategy and plan, including the provision of education and interpretation to visitors. These first three principles could be seen as somewhat predictable given the objectives of the project, and it is therefore not surprising that they were the first agreed to. The two subsequent principles are more innovative and therefore have received more attention here.

The fourth principle pertains to the sustainable tourism development strategy of the park and its zone of influence, ensuring that development around the park is in keeping with the values of the area, taking into account visitor needs as well as environmental, socio-economic and cultural constraints. This is a challenging principle since the park's management has limited influence over what takes place outside its boundaries. Nonetheless, park authorities need to see beyond their physical boundaries since the activities taking place in neighbouring towns and villages rely in many ways on the park, and also affect the use of the park's resources.

The fifth principle is linked to the quality of the park's business partners. It extends principle 4 by requiring the park to set up agreements with individual companies that commit themselves to being assessed against a set of criteria, which includes demonstrating how they can support the park's objectives and contribute to their implementation. This implies that parks will have to identify and communicate potential benefits to those businesses aiming to become partners. Organizations with which partnerships may be established extend beyond those

Principles	Criteria
Principle 1: Natural values. PAN Parks are large protected areas, representative of Europe's natural heritage and of international importance for wildlife and ecosystems.	• The area is adequately protected by means of an enforced act or decree. • The protected area is of Europe-wide importance for the conservation of biological diversity and contains the best existing representatives of original natural ecosystems in the region. • The minimum size of the protected area is 25 000 hectares.
Principle 2: Habitat management. Design and management of the PAN Park aims to maintain and, if necessary, restore the area's natural ecological processes and its biodiversity.	• Design of the protected area aims to maintain natural ecological values. • Regulations protecting the area are adequately enforced. • The protected area has an integrated management plan that is actively implemented. Regular monitoring and assessment of the plan are carried out and there is provision for updating and monitoring the plan in light of the results of this. • Management of the protected area makes use of zoning or some other system that ensures protection of the area's nature conservation values while allowing for human activities compatible with this. • If the protected area is zoned, there is an unfragmented core zone of at least 10 000 hectares where no extractive use is permitted and where the only management interventions are those aimed at restoring natural ecological processes. • If the protected area is not zoned, management of the whole area aims to maintain and, if necessary, restore key natural ecological processes. • The protected area's management system pays particular attention to threatened and endemic species. • In the case of a protected area adjacent to a national border, transborder co-operation in management is actively sought after.

Table 7.3
Summary of principles and associated criteria

Principles	Criteria
Principle 3: Visitor management. Visitor management safeguards the natural values of the PAN Park and aims to provide visitors with a high-quality experience based on the appreciation of nature.	• The protected area has a visitor management plan that is actively implemented. Regular monitoring and assessment of the plan are carried out and there is provision for updating and modifying the plan in light of the results of this. • Visitor management safeguards the natural values of the protected area. • Under the visitor management plan visitors are offered a wide range of high-quality activities based on the appreciation of nature. • Visitor management creates understanding of and support for the conservation goals of the protected area. • The protected area has a visitor centre, for which clear goals and a policy are set out in the visitor management plan. • The visitor management plan includes training programmes for staff and others involved in the provision of services to visitors.
Principle 4: Sustainable Tourism Development Strategy. Protected Area Authority and its relevant partners in the PAN Parks region aim at achieving a synergy between nature conservation and sustainable tourism by developing a Sustainable Tourism Development Strategy (STDS), committing to it and jointly taking responsibility in its implementation.	• The protected area and its region have sufficient tourism potential and carrying capacity for sustainable tourism. • The present tourism activities do not harm the protected area in order to implement its nature conservation goals. • Protected Area Authority and local stakeholders have the opportunity to co-operate within the framework of an official forum that aims at developing a Sustainable Tourism Development Strategy (hereafter STDS). • An Executive PAN Park Organization (hereafter EPPMO) or an existing forum for co-operation, which could assume responsibility for implementing PAN Parks, has been established in which all relevant stakeholders have formally confirmed their support and commitment to the conservation goals of the protected area and PAN Parks Organization. The EPPMO (or similar) formulates, implements and monitors an STDS for the protected area and its surrounding region.

Table 7.3
(Continued)

Principles	Criteria
	• Tourism development and existing tourism activities, which are under the control of EPPMO, are based on sustainable use of the ecological resources of the region. • Tourism development and tourism activities are based on sustainable use of the socio-economic resources of the region, including minority and if necessary indigenous people issues. • Tourism development and tourism activities are based on sustainable use of the cultural resources of the region. • The STDS's communications and marketing strategy aims at informing all target groups.
Principle 5: Business partners. PAN Parks' business partners as legal enterprises are committed to the goals of the protected area in their region and the PAN Parks Organization, and actively cooperate with other stakeholders to effectively implement the region's Sustainable Tourism Development Strategy as developed by the local EPPMO (see principle 4).	• PAN Parks business partners follow all national legislation related to their business. • Business partners support the protected area and its management goals. • PAN Parks business partners are committed to the PAN Parks Organization and its goals. • Business partners actively participate in the implementation of Sustainable Tourism Development Strategy as developed by EPPMO and verified by PAN Parks Organization.

Table 7.3
Continued

involved in the tourism industry to encompass any business or association that can prove it has a vested interest in, or influence on, a park. It is also noteworthy that any international organization wishing to use a park will be encouraged to be certified by a relevant body (for example, Green Globe 21) or to be involved in recognizable programmes (such as the Tour Operators Initiative for Sustainable Tourism Development). Partner bodies will also be encouraged to be part of a forum involved in the sustainable tourism development strategy (principle 4). However, their involvement in decision-making will depend on their relationship to the area. For example, hotels, inbound tour operators and shops trading directly with tourists will have a greater say than outbound tour operators from overseas, since the former have made a long-term investment in the destination and rely on the long-term sustainable use of the park's resources, whereas the latter can easily move their business away from the area.

The principles and associated criteria noted previously were field tested in 1999. Once a basic 'shell' was agreed, indicators were introduced to verify the criteria. These were tested in a second round of consultations that involved the self-assessment of seventeen national parks from fourteen countries. After this consultation phase was complete the principles and criteria were further evolved with the assistance of: the Société Générale de Surveillance (SGS) Hungary (principles 1 to 3); Europarc (principle four); and an independent consultant (principle 5). Flowing from this process was the present (September 2000) set of principles and criteria (Kun, 2001).

Assessment, verification and certification

The process associated with assessment, verification and standardization involves the following steps:

1. the park's management unit submits an assessment, which is made on the basis of the checklist (principles 1–3). Any area will be able to download the application form from the PAN Parks web page (www.panparks.org);
2. the assessment is evaluated by PAN Parks and a decision is made whether it seems to be worth verifying it;
3. the park, with expert support from PAN Parks, will devise a plan to meet the requirements of the criteria, and collect evidence for each one of the indicators, by a negotiated date;
4. the verifiers travel to the area to review evidence;
5. verifiers submit their recommendation to the PAN Parks Foundation; and
6. certification is awarded and/or recommendations for improvements needed to meet the standards are provided to the management of the park.

The assessment process (step 2) will be guided by the use of indicators that will serve to determine a park's performance against a specific principle and its associated criteria. In Table 7.4 an example of indicators has been given. If a park moves on to step 3 it is given the status of candidate and provided with training resources and other benefits. Candidature periods are negotiated individually with parks depending on their current position, demonstrating the open and flexible approach

Criterion	Indicators
The protected area has a visitor management plan that is actively implemented. Regular monitoring and assessment of the plan are carried out and there is provision for updating and modifying the plan in light of the results of this.	• Provide the visitor management plan (an English summary and a copy (if available)). • Provide information of the plan's long- and short-term goals. • Provide information on the resources available for the implementation of the visitor management plan. • Describe how the effects of the visitor management plan's actions are being monitored. • Indicate how the plan can be revised accordingly.

Table 7.4
Assessment indicators linked to criteria (from principle 3, criterion 3.1)

taken by PAN Parks in encouraging applicants to set their own agendas. At the end of the candidature period the park will submit a report detailing their progress in meeting the five principles and their associated criteria. To assist parks in working their way through the candidature process, PAN Parks conducts workshops at which parks develop their initial draft strategies. The first of these was conducted in Holland in June 2001 and was attended by all the current (seven) candidate parks.

Once a candidature period is over, and the park concerned has submitted a report, a verification process takes place. This involves a site visit and a review of desk evidence such as plans, minutes of meetings, procedures, surveys, assessments and so on. PAN Parks has opted for third party verification, involving the contracting of independent individuals (Kun, 2001). Other approaches to the verification process were considered, but they were found to have limitations. PAN Parks staff, for example, could have been used for this purpose, but it was felt that a conflict of interest might arise from having the same staff that provided support throughout the process being asked to do the assessment. Another option was to contract an external company to undertake all verifications; however, the small scale of PAN Parks does not make this feasible. PAN Parks plans to have eight parks verified by 2006.

During a workshop held in Zwolle, the Netherlands, on 11 April 2000, participants agreed that the PAN Parks Foundation must develop its own verification manual, which can be provided to a third party verifier in order to undertake the required field verification. With this goal in mind, Société Générale de Surveillance (SGS) Hungary was appointed to develop a verification manual including general guidelines and check-lists. SGS is one of the world leaders in verification, testing and certification and has collaborated closely with Green Globe 21. Once developed, the manual will be tested and finalized through field trials in pilot areas. The manual will then be available to independent experts contracted as verifiers. The process of developing the manual and finalizing the principles and criteria system, including measurable and objective indicators, was due for completion in October 2001.

Exact fees for involvement in the programme, and the associated use of the PAN Parks logo, have yet to be set. Nonetheless, fees will be subsidized by 50 per cent for European Union countries and up to 75 per cent for EU Accession countries, including Eastern Europe, where most applicants are based. The fees will be used for third-party verification and for providing other services, such as consultants or training programmes. The cost of operating PAN Parks is much higher than the fees paid by members, and the operations of the secretariat function of the PAN Parks Foundation, membership services, and publications will require external funding. Such funding will be provided by the Molecaten group in the short to medium term; with its longer-term capacity/willingness to do so likely to be linked to its success in establishing PAN Villages in, or adjacent to, participating parks. A complicating factor here is that once a park is certified and a village built (optional under the scheme), if the park concerned later comes into question there is the potential for a conflict of interest to emerge between the accommodation and the certification arms. This is an issue that PAN Parks Foundation is aware of but has not yet determined how to resolve.

Recognition and acceptance

Recognition and acceptance of the PAN Parks trademark will be driven by a communications campaign conducted directly by the PAN Parks organization, the parks themselves and the distributors of tourism products. This process will be costly, and as such it is one of the major drawbacks of certification systems of this kind. At present, PAN Parks are communicating with four groups: pilot PAN Parks and self-assessment participants, WWF-offices, (potential) investors and (potential) partners, all with different information needs (van Ladesteijn, 2000).

Assessing the success of PAN Parks

PAN Parks started as a concept in 1997, and for the ensuing years has been in the development and piloting stage, mainly involving the organization of internal structures, development of systems for compliance assessment, and establishment of links with potential candidates. It would appear that the experience to date of candidate parks has been positive for those in need of expertise in natural area and tourism management, which are mainly located in the more remote parts of Northern Europe, or in Eastern Europe. Those in wealthier areas, and with more experience in these areas, however, appear to be questioning the benefits of their involvement. Indeed, one potential fate of PAN Parks is for it to become a programme that engenders a more proactive approach to park management in the less developed parts of Europe.

Whether individual parks involved in the scheme become more sustainable than they otherwise would have been without input from PAN Parks is difficult to assess. It can be said, however, that principles 4 and 5 of the scheme that concern the engagement of local communities and organizations, along with businesses, in the development of national areas are in line with the more progressive attitudes evident amongst some park managers (Blangy and Vautier, 2001). They also reflect the perceptions on conservation embodied in Natura 2000 (European Commission, 2000a, 2000b). Only once PAN Parks has progressed to the point where it has certified a number of parks, can the question of how successful or otherwise it has been in enhancing standards of natural area conservation, while at the same time facilitating tourism development of such areas, be answered. This question would make the subject of a worthwhile future study.

References

Anon (2001) PAN Parks principles and criteria, principles 1–5, April 2001, draft for consultation.

Blangy, S. and Vautier, S. (2001) Europe, in Weaver, D. (ed.) *The Encyclopedia of Ecotourism*, Wallingford: CAB International, pp. 155–72.

European Commission (2000a) *Sustainable tourism and Natura 2000, Guidelines, initiatives and good practices in Europe*, DG ENV, Brussels: European Commission.

European Commission (2000b) Natura 2000, European Commission DG ENV Nature Newsletter, Issue 13, December 2000.

FNNPE (1993) *Loving them to death? The Need for Sustainable Tourism in Europe's Nature and National Parks*. The Federation of Nature and National Parks of Europe: Grafenau, Germany.

Font, X. (2002) Environmental certification in tourism and hospitality: progress, process and prospects, *Tourism Management* 23(3), 197–205.

Font, X. and Tribe, J. (2000) Recreation, conservation and timber production: a sustainable relationship? In Font, X. and Tribe, J. (eds) *Forest tourism and recreation: case studies in environmental management*, Wallingford: CAB International, United Kingdom, pp. 1–22.

Font, X. and Tribe, J. (2001) The process of developing an ecolabel. In Font, X. and Buckley, R. (eds) *Tourism ecolabelling: certification and promotion of sustainable management*, Wallingford: CAB International, pp. 87–104.

Kun, Z. (2001) PAN Parks verification, draft 3.2, 11th September 2000, WWF: Budapest, Hungary.

PAN Parks Courier (2001) Summer 2001, Budapest: WWF Hungary.

PAN Parks Foundation (undated) *PAN Parks Accommodation BV*, Zwolle (Netherlands): PAN Parks Foundation.

PAN Parks Supervisory Board (2000) Resolutions meeting PAN Parks Supervisory Board (PPSB) on 29 September 2000.

Roerhorst, I. (2000) PAN Parks business partners: Quickscan of environmental assessment systems for the tourism industry, Zeist, Holland: WWF.

Synergy Ltd (2000) *Tourism certification: an analysis of Green Globe 21 and other certification programs*, Godalming: WWF UK.

Toth, R. (2000) Elements of success and failure in certification/accreditation. In *Ecotourism and Sustainable Tourism Certification Workshop*, 17–19 November 2000, Mohonk Mountain House, New Paltz, New York.

Van Ladesteijn, N. (2000) *Picture of PAN Parks anno 2000, Communication: evaluation of current practices and future possibilities*, Zeist, Holland: WWF.

WWF (1998) PAN Parks: investing in Europe's future, Zeist, Holland: WWF.

WWF (2000a) Squandering paradise? The importance and vulnerability of the world's protected areas, Gland, Switzerland: WWF International.

WWF (2000b) PAN Parks workshop on principles and criteria 4–6, Zeist (Holland) April 2000, minutes of meetings.

WWF (2000c) PAN Parks workshop on principles and criteria 1–3, Gland (Switzerland) April 2000, minutes of meetings.

Tourist Destination Areas

Part 3

Tourist Destination Areas

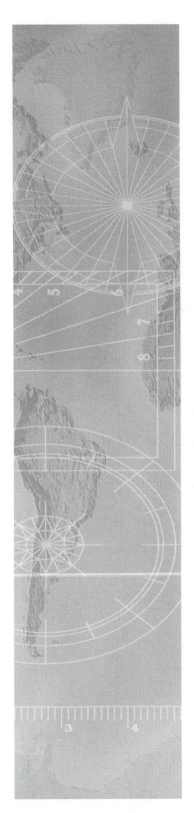

Perspectives on sustainable tourism in the South Pacific

David B. Weaver

Introduction

Any discussion of sustainable tourism, or tourism that respects and preferably enhances the environmental and sociocultural carrying capacity of a destination, must take into account the physical and cultural characteristics of the destinations that are being considered. Insularity is one such characteristic that can significantly influence the attainment of sustainable tourism outcomes. This chapter specifically considers the status of sustainable tourism in the South Pacific region as defined in Figure 8.1, a macro-region notable for its exaggerated insularity. The first of four major sections outlines the physical and human geographical characteristics of the study region, and this is followed by a generalized discussion of the regional tourism sector. The third section uses level of intensity as a basis for examining a variety of South Pacific destinations in order to assess the evidence for and against the existence of sustainable tourism practices. The fourth and final section considers the options for tourism in the study region in light of the preceding material. The chapter does not purport to be inclusive or all-encompassing in terms of the South Pacific destinations which

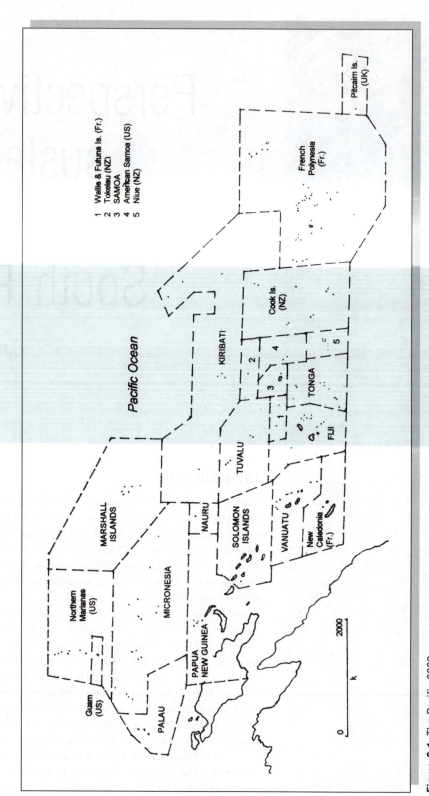

Figure 8.1 The Pacific 2002

are described or discussed. Furthermore, it does not attempt to draw any definitive conclusions about the presence or absence of sustainable tourism, but rather is intended to raise important issues for further investigation.

The geographical context

Any meaningful discussion of tourism in the South Pacific must be preceded by a consideration of the region's broader geographic, historic, economic and sociocultural characteristics. These constitute an 'external environment' to tourism that effectively determines whether sustainable tourism can be achieved and even if so, whether such a mode of tourism has any relevance if this broader context does not adhere to the precepts of sustainability (Weaver, 2001). In other words, the opportunities and constraints inherent in this external environment profoundly influence the likelihood of achieving a meaningful state of 'sustainable tourism', even after recognizing all the ambiguities and difficulties that are inherent in the latter term. Another purpose of this review is to emphasize the status of the South Pacific as a highly complex region in which the sub-regions (and destinations within those sub-regions) display considerable internal diversity.

Physically, the South Pacific study region can be divided into Polynesia and Micronesia on the one hand, and Melanesia on the other (Figure 8.1). The first two sub-regions are characterized by extreme insularity, consisting of small island entities separated by enormous expanses of ocean. In contrast, Melanesia comprises large islands clustered within relatively compressed archipelagos that account for 97.9 per cent (542 230 square kilometres) of all land in the study region (Table 8.1). Melanesia is also distinguished within the South Pacific for its variety of landforms, relatively undisturbed habitat, and high levels of biodiversity and endemism (Weaver, 1998). The entire study region is susceptible to cyclones, while seismic and volcanic activity are characteristic of plate boundary areas such as Papua New Guinea, the Solomon Islands, Vanuatu and Tonga.

The differences between Melanesia and the other sub-regions extend to human geography. Only 16 per cent of the regional population is located within Polynesia (8639 square kilometres) and Micronesia (3097 square kilometres) (Table 8.1). However, the lack of land in these sub-regions results in population densities higher by an order of magnitude than those of Melanesia (Table 8.1), and a higher degree of human-induced environmental degradation both on land and sea. Ethnically, each of the sub-regions is associated with a separate indigenous racial group after which each region is named, allowing for a significant degree of intermixture and acculturation as a result of ongoing historical contact, particularly in transitional border islands. Pre-European elements of these cultures remain robust, given that the South Pacific was one of the last regions to be formally incorporated into the global capitalist economy. This is especially true with regard to language and communal land tenure systems, while other attributes, such as religion, and

By state and region	Land area (km²)	Population 1998 (000s)	Population/ km²
Papua New Guinea	461 690	4599.8	10.0
Fiji	18 270	802.6	43.9
Solomon Islands	28 450	441.0	15.5
New Caledonia (Fr)	19 060	194.2	10.2
Vanuatu	14 760	185.2	12.5
Melanesia (Total)	**542 230**	**6222.8**	**11.5**
Guam (US)	541	148.1	273.8
Fed. States Micronesia	702	129.7	184.8
Kiribati	717	84.0	117.2
Northern Marianas (US)	477	66.6	139.6
Marshall Is.	181	63.0	348.1
Palau	458	18.1	39.5
Nauru	21	10.5	500.0
Micronesia (Total)	**3097**	**520.0**	**167.9**
French Polynesia (Fr)	3941	237.8	60.3
Samoa	2860	224.7	78.6
Tonga	748	108.2	144.7
Wallis and Futuna Is. (Fr)	274	15.0	54.7
Niue (NZ)	260	1.6	6.2
Cook Islands (NZ)	240	20.0	83.3
American Samoa (US)	199	62.1	312.1
Pitcairn Is. (UK)	47	<1.0	1.0
Norfolk I. (Aus)	34	2.2	64.7
Tuvalu	26	10.4	400.0
Tokelau (NZ)	10	1.4	140.0
Polynesia (Total)	**8639**	**683.4**	**79.1**
South Pacific (Total)	**553 966**	**7426.2**	**13.4**

Table 8.1
Land area and population in the South Pacific

economics, have been profoundly changed during the past 150 years of intensive European contact and subsequent acculturation. Fiji and New Caledonia are the only two entities where non-indigenous groups are roughly comparable in population to indigenous people. As a region, the South Pacific is characterized by high fertility rates and, despite high rates of out-migration, steady population increase and resultant added pressure on natural resources (McKnight, 1995). Politically, the South Pacific shares with the Caribbean the distinction of having the highest concentration of dependent political units (i.e., ten remaining dependencies), indicating that this region is also the last to be experiencing the formal de-colonization process. Melanesia has no remaining dependencies, but is characterized by a high level of political instability, as evidenced by recent upheavals in the Solomon Islands and Fiji.

In the South Pacific elements of physical geography, human geography and history have conspired to produce fragile environments and weak economic structures that are not indicative of, or conducive to, sustainable economic development in the 'western' sense. Bertram and Watters (1985) characterize the South Pacific as a region where the MIRAB syndrome (i.e., *mi*gration, *r*emittances, *ai*d and *b*ureaucracy) is prevalent, reflecting a reliance upon a narrow range of economic activities, and subsequently severe trade deficits and dramatic fluctuations in economic performance (Craig-Smith and Fagence, 1994). The MIRAB syndrome is most apparent on small outlying atolls, where insularity and isolation are exaggerated (Krausse, 1995), but is also evident in Melanesia despite that sub-region's much greater endowment of natural resources. In terms of per capita GNP, many South Pacific states rank among the world's poorest, with Papua New Guinea, the Solomon Islands, Vanuatu, Kiribati, Samoa, the Marshall Islands and Micronesia all being below US$2600 following adjustments for purchasing power parity (Weaver, 1998).

The tourism context

At a regional scale, the South Pacific is over-represented as an inbound tourist destination, with 0.13 per cent of the world's population, but 0.5 per cent of all international stayovers. This observation, however, is rendered all but meaningless by the highly skewed internal distribution of the sector, which is overwhelmingly dominated by inbound as opposed to domestic tourists. Just two small destinations, Guam and the Northern Marianas (the island of Saipan, specifically), account for almost 60 per cent of all stayovers, and this figure increases to over 80 per cent with the addition of Fiji and French Polynesia (Table 8.2). Tourist arrivals in the remaining eighteen destinations, and indeed in the numerous peripheral islands of the last three named destinations, indicate a more incipient level of tourism development, and a much higher level of return visits by former residents who tend to stay in local residences and spend less money. Interrelated factors that have contributed to this situation include isolation, the lack of infrastructure and accommodation, the scarcity of freehold land, and a lack of interest among potential investors, due in part to the presence of intervening opportunities in more accessible and established regional destinations such as Hawaii and Okinawa. In this context, Guam and Saipan can be seen as anomalies that have benefited from their proximity to Japan, the provision of infrastructure and other services as an outcome of World War II and their status as US dependencies.

Given the economic context, it is not surprising that South Pacific states and dependencies have been paying increased attention to tourism as a vehicle for helping to overcome the MIRAB syndrome and bringing into effect sustained economic development. This attention is not new. Tourism was already included as a component of development strategies in the late colonial and early post-independence period, when it was standard practice to uncritically endorse the sector as a panacea for underdeveloped countries in general. Jafari (1989), accordingly, refers to this as the era of the *advocacy platform*. By the 1970s, however, the negative impacts of poorly regulated tourism became more obvious, prompting

By state and region	1991 (000s)	1998 (000s) (A)	Percentage of region: 1998	Tourist/ resident ratio 1998 (B)	Intensity category (AB)	Tourism as estimated percentage of GDP
Fiji	259	371.4	13.7	0.46	HL	17
New Caledonia	81	103.8	3.8	0.53	LL	3
PNG	37	67.5	2.5	0.01	LL	<1
Vanuatu	40	52.1	1.9	0.28	LL	15
Solomon Is.	11	13.2	0.5	0.03	LL	2
Melanesia (Total)	**428**	**608.0**	**22.4**	**0.10**		
Guam	737	1137.0	41.8	7.68	HH	na
Northern Marianas	422	490.2	18.0	7.36	HH	50
Palau	33	64.2	2.4	3.55	LH	10
Micronesia	8	11.0*	0.4	0.08	LL	na
Marshall Is.	7	6.4	0.2	0.10	LL	5
Kiribati	3	5.4	0.2	0.06	LL	1
Nauru	1	1.0	<0.1	0.10	LL	na
Micronesia (Total)	**1210**	**1715.2**	**63.1**	**3.30**		
French Polynesia	121	188.3	6.9	0.79	HH	23
Samoa	35	77.9	2.9	0.35	LL	13
Cook Islands	40	48.6	1.8	2.43	LH	23
Norfolk I.	na	29.0	1.1	13.18	LH	na
Tonga	22	27.1	1.0	0.25	LL	6
American Samoa	18	21.3†	0.8	0.34	LL	5
Niue	1	1.7	0.1	1.06	LH	18
Tuvalu	1	1.1	<0.1	0.11	LL	na
Pitcairn Is.	na	na	na	na	LL	na
Tokelau	na	na	na	na	LL	na
Wallis and Futuna Is.	na	na	na	na	LL	na
Polynesia (Total)	**238**	**395.0**	**14.5**	**0.58**		
South Pacific (Total)	**1876**	**2718.2**	**100.0**	**0.37**		

Sources: Europa World Year Book, 1997 (GDP stats); WTO, 1997; 1998 data for Nauru from Fagence, 1999.
*1997 data.
†1996 data.

Table 8.2 International stayover arrivals in the South Pacific

widespread criticism of the sector and the emergence of a *cautionary platform*. Along with the Caribbean, the South Pacific emerged as a focal point of this critique, with references to tourism as a 'new kind of sugar' and a 'pleasure plantation' (see, for example, Finney and Watson, 1975; Britton, 1980). The well-known and often-tested destination life cycle model of Butler (1980), which foresees stagnation and decline as the likely outcomes of unregulated tourism development, may be seen as the culmination of the cautionary platform.

Actual attempts to put forward more benign models of tourism development are associated with the era of the *adaptancy platform* in the 1980s, which gave rise to supposedly more appropriate options such as 'alternative tourism', 'ecotourism' and, of course, 'sustainable tourism'. Explicit within this platform was the view that mass tourism was inherently bad and smallscale alternative tourism (i.e., tourism that is deliberately structured to contrast with conventional mass tourism) inherently good for small underdeveloped Pacific and Caribbean islands in particular. Alternative tourism and ecotourism, therefore, were equated with sustainable tourism. This perspective is now being challenged by the *knowledge-based platform*, which espouses a less ideological and more scientific perspective toward tourism (though adoption of a scientific approach may itself be seen as an ideological decision). From this platform, mass tourism and alternative tourism can *both* be either sustainable or unsustainable, depending on the circumstances that pertain to any particular destination (Weaver, 2000).

Sustainable tourism in the South Pacific

Since the early 1990s, virtually all South Pacific destinations have declared their interest in, and commitment to, sustainable tourism. Many planners and academics still adhere to the pro-alternative tourism biases of the adaptancy platform and argue that this is the only means for attaining sustainable tourism development in the region. Yet, by disassociating scale from sustainability, the knowledge-based platform holds that the attainment of sustainability does not necessarily depend on adherence to alternative tourism. Moreover, it has been argued that conventional mass tourism, in theory, confers sustainability-related advantages of scale that are not possible in alternative tourism (see, for example, Clarke, 1997). Intensity is used in this section as a criterion for placing South Pacific countries and dependencies into categories for discussion purposes, but given the above debate, no assumptions are made as to the advantages of high or low intensity relative to the attainment of sustainable outcomes. Rather, the evidence from the destinations themselves will be used to make such assessments. For classification and discussion purposes, 'intensity' is construed as a variable that arises from different combinations of absolute and relative criteria. The total number of inbound stayover arrivals represents the former while the latter is represented by the stayover/resident ratio. Of course, these are not perfect criteria since, amongst other reasons, returning former residents (who comprise a high proportion of stayover arrivals in destinations such as Tonga and Niue) are likely to stay in 'local' areas and blend into the local community, thereby not contributing to an obvious intensification effect. Cruiseship excursionists are omitted since this subsector occupies a relatively minor role in the region. Rankings of the listed destinations for both variables revealed gaps in the data that provide a logical basis for separating 'high' from 'low' intensity destinations. In both cases, the gap occurred between French Polynesia (188 300 arrivals and a ratio of 0.79) and New Caledonia (103 800 and 0.53) (Table 8.2).

Classified accordingly, the destinations fall into four possible categories: low traffic/low ratio (LL), low traffic/high ratio (LH), high traffic/low ratio (HL), and high traffic/high ratio (HH) (Table 8.2). Although all destinations, and especially the archipelagic states, have significant internal variations in the intensity of tourism, there are several reasons for basing classification on the entire state or dependency. Firstly, it is usually difficult to obtain even basic tourism data (except perhaps for accommodation) at the sub-national level. Secondly, it is not clear at what sub-national scale the classification should be made if this approach is adopted, since individual peripheral islands of a state may themselves display significant internal variations. Thirdly, whatever the internal differences, all regions and people within a single state or dependency are commonly affected in some ways by the national tourism industry, through the right to move internally in order to obtain employment, and through the dissemination of benefits resulting from tourism revenues. Though rejected as a basis for classification, internal variations nevertheless will still be recognized and taken into account, particularly in the section where options are discussed.

Low traffic/low ratio (LL) destinations

Low intensity destinations account for a clear majority of South Pacific states and dependencies, with several, such as the Pitcairn Islands and Tokelau, having virtually no tourist arrivals or facilities at all (Tokelau Apia Liaison Office, Samoa, personal communication, 1997). For those with at least some level of tourism development, the evidence does not always point toward sustainable practice or outcomes. The colonial heritage of most islands and the concomitant positioning of 'local' expatriates in positions of influence, for example, resulted in the marginalization of indigenous people during the 'involvement' phase of the tourism cycle throughout Melanesia (Douglas, 1997). This trend was, and still is, exacerbated by the lack of skilled locals in countries such as Tuvalu or Palau that have fewer people than a small English country town. A very similar situation pertained to other colonized small islands outside of the Pacific, such as the Caribbean island of Antigua (Weaver, 1988). The situation has improved somewhat in the post-independence era, though businesses owned by ni-Vanuatu (native people of Vanuatu) still accounted for less than 10 per cent of total expenditure within Vanuatu's accommodation sector during the mid-1990s (Milne, 1997).

The alleged dispersal of the tourism sector during the early stages of the cycle is often deemed to be congruent with sustainable tourism in that the resultant benefits are more accessible to a wider sector of the local population. Moreover, carrying capacities are not unduly stressed by over-concentrations of activity within specific tourism districts. Again, the evidence from the LL destinations is contrary, as urban areas are substantially over-represented as locations for tourist accommodation. On Pohnpei (a Federated State of Micronesia), virtually all hotels are located in the capital city of Kolonia (Dahl, 1993), while almost two-thirds of registered accommodation in Papua New Guinea is found in the three largest urban centres (PNG Tourism Promotion Authority, personal communication, 1997). This pattern owes to a combination of factors, including the prevalence of business-related tourism, the concentration of functions and services in urban areas, and the status of capital cities as international and internal gateways. Such concentrations, however, cannot automatically be considered unsustainable. Unlike beach environments, urban areas already accommodate a broad array of high-density activity within a highly modified and relatively cosmopolitan environment that usually has the infrastructural capacity to cope with this level of activity.

The Butler-type resort cycle implies that negative sociocultural outcomes are liable to occur as a function of increased tourism development. However, problems such as a pronounced demonstration effect, the commoditization of local culture and the entrenchment of the power and wealth of the local 'Big Men' are already apparent in incipient destinations such as the Solomon Islands (Lipscomb, 1998). The burning of the Anuha Resort in 1988 by customary Solomon Islands landowners, though cited as an isolated event, is indicative of the resident antagonism that might be expected to result in the later, not earlier, stages of tourism development (Douglas, 1997). Similar negative sociocultural developments occurred in Tonga as early as the 1970s (Urbanowicz, 1989), while inter-clan rivalries in the Tufi region of Papua New Guinea occurred because of tourism in the early 'involvement' stages of tourism development (Ranck, 1987). These examples are not meant to suggest that attitudes toward tourism in all LL destinations are antagonistic or that all of the affected cultures and societies are being undermined. Rather, they indicate that such destinations are not immune to negative outcomes just because tourism is relatively undeveloped and smallscale, or 'alternative'. The sustainability of tourism at this incipient stage can also be negatively affected by external factors such as logging, which in the Solomon Islands is estimated to be undertaken at a level three times in excess of a sustainable harvest (Lipscomb, 1998). In Nauru, environmental problems focus around the mining-related devastation that has affected almost the entire interior of the island (Fagence, 1999). An additional dissuasive factor for tourism development in the Solomon Islands was the outbreak of civil war in 2000 and the concomitant descent into political and social anarchy. Whether environmental or sociopolitical, such hostile external environments could ensure that the destination does not progress beyond tourism incipience within the foreseeable future.

Substantial fluctuations in the level of tourist arrivals are often seen as conflicting with sustainability, yet characterize many LL destinations simply because a small drop in arrivals can translate into a large relative decrease when the overall visitor base numbers are low. In Tonga, the lowest visitation month (1600 in February, as a five-year mean from 1991 to 1995) is just 45 per cent of the peak month of December (3579) (TVB, 1996). For Vanuatu, the same calculation revealed a figure of 54 per cent for 1996 (2639 in February, 4813 in September) (Statistics Office, 1997). Such variations are partly climate-related, but also reflect the large impacts exercised by specific events, such as a monopolistic airline's decision to reduce flight frequency, on small volumes of traffic. As a result, LL destinations tend to experience high levels of vulnerability and uncertainty in their visitor flows, for reasons other than seasonality. Exacerbating this vulnerability is a common dependency on a small number of tourist markets. For example, the two principal markets in Tonga accounted for 53 per cent of all stayover arrivals in 1995, while the equivalent statistic for Vanuatu was 70 per cent in 1996 (with Australia alone contributing 58 per cent).

Low traffic/high ratio (LH) destinations

Low traffic/high ratio destinations receive small absolute numbers of tourists in relation to the threshold established above, but still produce relatively large tourist/resident ratios because of the small local population. The Cook Islands, Niue, Norfolk Island and Palau are the four South Pacific destinations that fall into this category. In all four cases, the tourist/resident ratio exceeds 1.0, and at least 10 per cent of GDP is represented by tourism. The Cook Islands is one of the most tourism-dependent LH destinations and resembles a more intensively developed destination as well from the perspective of foreign participation. External interests control just over half (50.6 per cent) of accommodation rooms, with the proportion increasing to 58 per cent on the main island of Rarotonga. One surprising development, however, is the decline of market concentration as the destination has become more developed. Contrary to the expectations of the destination life cycle, the dependency of the Cook Islands on its primary market (New Zealand) has actually declined from 55.7 per cent to 21.8 per cent between 1979 and 1995, largely as a result of growth in Asian origin regions (Burridge and Milne, 1996). The tourism sector of Niue, in contrast, is marked by extremes in market dependency and fluctuation. In 1995, New Zealand supplied 83.5 per cent of all arrivals. The number of visitors during the lowest month of that year represented only 20 per cent of the traffic arriving in the busiest month (80 versus 410 visitors) (UNDP, 1997).

High traffic/low ratio (HL) destination

Fiji is the only South Pacific destination where a large absolute number of stayover arrivals is offset by a low tourist/resident ratio, owing to the country's relatively large resident population. Such generalizations, however, mask the actual complexity of the Fijian tourism sector, which ranges from mass resort tourism along some coastal areas of Viti Levu to exclusive resort island tourism, urban tourism (in Suva) and village-based ecotourism. Segmented in this way, all categories are represented in Fiji, and it is fair to characterize this destination as a microcosm of South Pacific tourism in general. Like the Cook Islands, inbound markets are becoming more rather than less diverse, with the two primary markets accounting for 57.2 per cent and 41.8 per cent of all stayovers in 1980 and 1993, respectively (Lockhart and Chandra, 1997). Another departure from the usual social impact assumptions is the finding by King et al. (1993)

that Fijians in the vicinity of Nadi, with its concentration of beach-based resorts, tended to express favourable attitudes about the tourism industry.

The small, exclusive resorts, usually located on small offshore islands, are also complex with respect to their relationship with sustainability. The Turtle Island Resort offers a case in point. On the one hand, this resort caters to a very wealthy elite (= a very strong wealth differential between host and guest), is owned by an expatriate American millionaire, and requires its employees to remain isolated from their families for extended periods of time. However, the Resort has also engaged in a major programme of vegetation rehabilitation on the island, provides almost 100 jobs, and has a strategy to encourage Fijian participation at the managerial level. It also uses solar power to provide much of its energy requirements, and has established an eye clinic and other medical services for the residents of the adjacent islands (Evanson, 1997; Harrison, 1997). At least in this case, the positive effects would seem to outweigh the negative impacts, although no generalizations about exclusive isolated resorts should follow. A more serious issue for Fijian tourism as a whole is chronic political instability, the latest crisis being the 2000 coup attempt by George Speight that resulted in a dramatic decline in visitor arrivals (Hing and Dimmock, 2001). Notably, Turtle Island was specifically targeted for takeover by indigenous Fijian coup supporters over issues of land rights, though the extent to which associated activism was legitimate or politically opportunistic is unclear (King and Berno, 2001).

High traffic/high ratio (HH) destinations

Only two South Pacific destinations, Guam and the Northern Marianas, have large absolute numbers of tourist visitors and high tourist/resident ratios arising from low resident populations. In several superficial respects, both destinations conform to the more mature phases of the resort cycle. Market concentration in Guam, for example, is indicated by Japan's 75 per cent share of stayovers, which increases to 89 per cent with the addition of Korea (GVB, 1997). The comparable statistic for the Northern Marianas is 85 per cent (62 per cent from Japan and 23 per cent from Korea) (MVB, 1997). Foreign participation in the tourism sector, another indicator of maturity according to Butler (1980), is also very high in both destinations, with fifteen of thirty hotels (with 50 per cent of all rooms) in Guam having Japanese general managers (GVB, 1997). The same situation pertains to seven of the ten largest hotels in the Northern Marianas (MVB, 1997).

Structurally, hotel size and room inventories are the largest within the study region. The average hotel size in Guam is 253 rooms, and the island provided 7601 rooms in 1997 (GVB, 1997). The Northern Marianas contained 3847 hotel rooms in 1997, virtually all located on Saipan (MVB, 1997). While these figures already raise concerns because of the small physical size of each destination, further increases are likely. As of 1995, the number of hotel rooms approved by the government of Guam was equivalent to the total amount in existence or under construction at that time. If announced or potential rooms are added, the inventory could increase to over 26 000 rooms (Table 8.3). Among the approved hotels are two that each provide over 1000 rooms (Marbo Cave Resort, at 1200, and Nansay Resort, at 1100) (GVB, 1997). The hotel sector in Guam, as in most intensive beach resorts, is highly concentrated, with 83 per cent of all rooms (and about one-half of all approved hotels) located along a short stretch of coastline at Tumon 'village' (GVB, 1997). However, an equally vigorous process of golf course expansion (Table 8.3) enhances the influence of tourism as a consumer of land. On Saipan, 69 per cent of all hotel rooms are located on a five-mile expanse of beach in the southwest of the island (MVB, 1997). While no statistics are available indicating the contribution of tourism to Guam's GDP, this can be inferred from employment data. Of 48 980 jobs in total as of March 1997, 11 892 (24 per cent) were directly related to tourism, and another 8766 (18 per cent) were indirectly related to tourism, for 20 657 in total (42 per cent) (GVB, 1997). The resultant figure is not inconsistent with the GDP statistic for tourism in the Northern Marianas.

Clearly, the current and potential intensity levels of tourism in the two HH destinations are impressive and of obvious concern to those wishing to develop a sustainable tourism industry, especially when other factors such as ownership and market concentration are taken into account. However, just as some of the characteristics of LL destinations do not appear coherent with sustainability, certain traits of the HH destinations appear compatible. With respect to seasonality, the lowest visitation month in Guam, calculated as a mean value from 1992 to 1996, is 78 per cent of the peak visitation month (April = 79 800; March = 101 900). The low/high month ratio for Saipan is a similar 84 per cent (GVB, 1997; MVB, 1997). Resident reactions to tourism on Guam, as well, do not indicate antagonism. Although solicited from only one segment of the market, an exit survey of US visitors in December 1996 revealed 'friendliness and courteousness of the people of Guam' as the local attribute given the highest rating on a Likert-type scale (6.1 of 7.0) (GVB, 1996). As for the physical carrying capacity of the island, high concentrations of tourism facilities and large hotel complexes may compensate in some degree for their obvious local stresses (high traffic, 'heat island' effect, induced housing development for hotel workers, etc.) in several ways. These include the provision of 'economies of scale' that allow for the effective management of waste, and the minimization of space required to house the tourist population (i.e., upward instead of outward, and in one small area instead of distributed throughout the island). A strong tourism industry may also in theory possess lobbying capabilities that prevent competing resource stakeholders (e.g., fishing and agriculture) from undertaking activities that undermine the attractiveness of tourism resources.

Tourism options

The South Pacific tourism industry can be summarized as highly skewed, with most destinations being characterized by low visitor numbers and low tourist/resident ratios. Only two destinations exhibit the opposite tendency. Intensity, however, is clearly no a priori indicator of sustainability. Low visitation levels are inherently vulnerable to extreme fluctuation, and tourism, even in its incipient stages, is inevitably influenced in a negative way by the MIRAB syndrome and by longstanding patterns of dependency with 'mother' countries. Islands with low levels of tourism development, moreover, tend to possess rudimentary infrastructure that equates with low carrying capacity and subsequent threats to environmental sustainability despite small visitor intakes. That low intensity tourism does not automatically equate with sustainable tourism, therefore, should come as no surprise. The question of sustainability will always be mediated by the realities of the small island syndrome of underdevelopment and by a longstanding regional history of acculturation, sociopolitical instability, and environmental degradation.

Sustainable mass tourism

If this impeding impact of the small island syndrome is granted, then the pursuit of higher intensity tourism may be a rational option for some South Pacific destinations or portions thereof, since there is often no 'unspoiled paradise' to be undermined by the development of mass tourism. To the contrary, it is the more tourism-intensive destinations that display higher prosperity levels on the basis of per capita GDP (allowing for anomalies such as the phosphate producing country of Nauru) (Europa World Year Book, 1997). This endorsement, however, is not unconditional, and supposes that intensive tourism is not appropriate in all locations and that its implementation be carefully regulated so as to minimize any further disruptions to the destination's economy, culture or physical environment. Preferably, the onus should also be placed on the various stakeholders, and on large corporations in particular, to contribute to the gradual amelioration of these disrupted sectors and spaces. Such could be a pre-condition for anyone, local or expatriate, for obtaining permission to establish tourism-related facilities.

Deliberate 'alternative tourism' (DAT)

Although tourism scenarios are continuous in nature with respect to their intensity, it is still useful for conceptual purposes to contrast 'mass tourism' with 'alternative tourism' as ideal types situated at either end of the tourism spectrum (Weaver, 2000). Alternative tourism, as described above, was conceived in the early 1980s as a mode of tourism deliberately structured to contrast with the supposedly unsustainable characteristics of conventional mass tourism. Accordingly, it was ideally characterized among other things by smallscale, local control, architecture that is congruent with the local culture and physical environment, and interactions with locals that are equitable and mutually supportive (Dernoi, 1981). A particular destination scenario can be said to gravitate, to a greater or lesser extent, toward one ideal type (i.e., alternative tourism) or the other (i.e., unsustainable mass tourism). At the less intensive end of the spectrum, most South Pacific destinations resemble 'alternative tourism' in at least some respects, though patterns of ownership, imports, market concentration and seasonality more typical of intensive destinations have already been identified. Clearly, the resemblance to alternative tourism in most of these destinations is superficial, as there is seldom any regulatory environment in place to ensure, as far as possible, that principles of local participation, environmental sustainability, etc., are followed. These places, essentially, are merely in the early stages of the (modified small island) destination life cycle, and accordingly can be described as circumstantial alternative tourism (CAT) destinations (Weaver, 1991, 2000). This would seem to apply, for example, to Papua New Guinea, where 85 per cent of the 14 000 short-term visitor arrivals in 1995 had visited nature-based attractions (PNG Tourism Promotion Authority, personal communication, 1997), but where little exists in the way of a formal ecotourism structure that adheres to core criteria of nature-focused attractions, learning outcomes, and sustainability (Blamey, 2001).

Several scenarios are possible for CAT destinations. In most instances, they will remain as such because there is no demand for any further tourism-related development, or such development is impractical due to inaccessibility or other factors. A second possibility sees these destinations following the S-curve trajectory that characterizes the Butler-type destination life cycle. A third scenario is the 'instant resort' phenomenon, wherein the area is earmarked for planned largescale resort development (e.g., Cancún in Mexico). In both cases, a very rapid transition from LL status to LH or HH status is possible because of the small resident population. A fourth scenario entails the establishment of a regulatory environment that steers the destination toward the principles of alternative (and hence smallscale sustainable) tourism. Places that adopt this approach can be described as *deliberate* alternative tourism (DAT) destinations. Such a strategy is implicit in the planning of many South Pacific destinations. Applied at the sub-national level, such as in mountainous interiors or peripheral islands, it may be designated as a *regional* DAT strategy (or R-DAT). Applied to an entire country or dependency, the term *comprehensive* DAT (C-DAT) may be employed, as discussed in the following sub-section.

Comprehensive DAT (C-DAT) destinations

C-DAT destinations are rare, although Dominica and Bhutan would probably qualify if a global survey were to be conducted (Weaver, 1998). In the study region, emergent C-DAT destinations include the Federated Micronesian State of Pohnpei, whose apparent pursuit of an environmentally sound, ecotourism-style policy (Office of Tourism & Parks, Pohnpei, personal communication, 1997), it should be noted, is motivated by the lack of beaches capable of supporting mass tourism. Nevertheless, pressure to pursue mass tourism is arising from concerns over the impending termination of special post-independence financial aid from the US government, and from calculations revealing that an annual visitor intake of 50 000 is necessary to compensate for the loss of those funding revenues (Dahl, 1993).

The Niue Strategic Development Plan identifies tourism as the sector with the greatest potential to facilitate sustainable development. A village-based strategy is being proposed as the centrepiece of a policy to 'develop a sustainable tourism sector whose activities are compatible with Niue's unique environment and culture, which are the country's principal tourist attractions' (UNDP, 1997). Tourism on Niue thus far is not seen as involving any substantial negative environmental or sociocultural impacts (De Haas and Cukier, 2000). Samoa is somewhat more evolved in the C-DAT direction, having already established such relevant mechanisms as the National Ecotourism Programme and the Samoan Ecotourism Network (Weaver, 1998; Zeppel, 1998).

Regional DAT (R-DAT) destinations

Several larger South Pacific destinations are initiating strategies that explicitly recognize a role for both mass tourism and deliberate alternative tourism. For example, Vanuatu's Tourist Development Master Plan emphasizes a hierarchical spatial structure of 'Primary' tourist destinations (international/regional gateway and port, larger volume of visitation) and 'Longer Term' tourist destinations. The latter are characterized by local or regional airports, limited infrastructure, smallscale tourist facilities, retained local customs and village lifestyles, and controlled visitation to environmentally and culturally sensitive areas. The latter tend to involve the smaller peripheral islands (McVey, 1995; UNDP, 1995).

In Fiji, the R-DAT concept has long been implicit in an 'islands policy' that discourages largescale tourism in peripheral island locations, a concept that has also been practised in the Bahamas with respect to the 'Family Islands' relative to Grand Bahama and Nassau, and in Trinidad relative to Tobago. While 'tourist resort islands' (such as Turtle Island Resort) are one option, most of these areas are designated as 'local subsistence islands' where 'only smallscale development will be permitted' (Lockhart and Chandra, 1997: 308–9). In contrast, largescale tourism is being fostered in certain districts of the main island, including the Coral Coast and Nadi. Other districts of this island, particularly in the interior, are focusing upon alternative tourism and smallscale ecotourism in particular. One example among several is occurring at Abaca village in the Koronayitu forest of western Viti Levu. Its establishment in the early 1990s coincided with the formation of a national park in the area. Abaca village initially constructed a traditional lodge to accommodate twelve visitors, and in 1993, the Abaca Ecotourism Co-operative Society Limited was registered to formalize the participation and ownership structure of the venture. Subsequently, another village was added to the scheme, and others have expressed an interest in joining. Each participating village is expected to dedicate a portion of their communal land to the national park, and is then entitled to hold shares in a company which promotes ecotourism in the area. In addition to the ecotourism revenues, tangible benefits to Abaca so far have included the formation of a medicinal plant arboretum, a tree seedling nursery, and the use of the tourism vehicle to transport children to school (Gilbert, 1997).

Part of the success of the Abaca venture is attributed to the village's proximity to the concentration of tourism activity at Nadi, and its subsequent linkages with the mass tourism sector of that area. According to Harrison and Brandt (1997), the cultivation of such opportunities as an 'add-on' to the mainstay resort product has long been a feature of the Fijian tourism sector. More recently, such relationships in Fiji and elsewhere are being formally recognized and promoted as a matter of mutual advantage to both types of tourism. Thus, the ideal outcome of the R-DAT strategy is the creation of synergies and symbioses between alternative and mass tourism, a possibility that is supported by Ayala (1996), Milne (1997) and Weaver (1998, 2001), amongst others.

Conclusion

Evidence from the diverse array of South Pacific tourist destinations suggests little or no correlation between scale of intensity and the presence of 'sustainable tourism'. Rather, the apparent presence or absence of sustainability, or indications of same, is dependent upon the unique circumstances that pertain to any given destination and the management responses that are made to these circumstances. Accordingly, there is no basis for supposing that tourism in intensively developed Saipan or Guam is any less sustainable than the incipient sector that characterizes Tuvalu or the Wallis and Futuna Islands, where government, infrastructure and society in general are ill-equipped to cope with even a small increase in arrivals. Complicating the issue of sustainability is the possibility that a destination may indicate this trait in some characteristics (e.g., is environmentally sound) but not others (e.g., is not locally controlled), thereby raising the question as to whether the destination is 'sustainable' in an overall sense. Moreover, a characteristic that appears unsustainable in itself may have sustainable consequences. For example, the transformation of land on Guam to golf courses is associated with environmental problems and the loss of agricultural self-sufficiency. However, these golf courses may generate enough revenue to allow the importation of diverse foodstuffs and to facilitate remedial environmental measures. Increased importation of food, in turn, might increase dependency, though the alternative to dependency may be abject poverty. Similarly, the concentration of tourism within a small area of Saipan (a characteristic of destination life cycle maturity that is usually regarded as negative) reduces the need for sprawling tourism facilities in other parts of the island. Concurrently, it offers conditions conducive to cost-effective and environmentally beneficial site hardening, such as the installation of tertiary sewage treatment that depends upon high volumes of waste production.

An equally important issue is whether the concept of sustainability, and concomitant planning options as described above, can be seriously considered from a single-sector perspective. Various external environ-ments over which tourism exercises little or no influence profoundly affect this sector in a direct or indirect way. The MIRAB syndrome is especially relevant to the South Pacific as is, unfortunately, the apparent increase in political instability and environmental degradation. Thus, for example, while deliberate alternative tourism appears to be emerging in the Solomon Islands, any judgements about its sustainability and longevity are rendered effectively meaningless by the fact that civil war and rapacious logging practices make most human activity in the Solomon Islands as a whole unsustainable. Adding to this uncertain environment, and especially relevant to South Pacific coastal areas and atoll-dominated countries such as Tuvalu and Kiribati, are the looming threats of rising sea levels and more numerous cyclones due to global warming. Whether sustainable mass tourism or deliberate alternative tourism is advocated for a particular South Pacific destination, the isolationist approach that typifies much planning and academic writing in the sector should therefore be rejected. The existing or potential impacts of these external environments must be taken into account when considering and implementing the options described above. Indeed, it can be argued that external environments are an omnipresent shadow theme that cannot be divorced from any considerations pertaining to sustainable tourism. In such a context, it is unlikely that any mode of tourism development, no matter how sustainable in itself, will serve on its own as a panacea for the persistent problems of South Pacific destinations.

References

Ayala, H. (1996) Resort ecotourism: a paradigm for the 21st century. *Cornell Hotel and Restaurant Administration Quarterly* **37**(5): 46–53.

Bertram, I. and Watters, R. (1985) The MIRAB economy in South Pacific microstates. *Pacific Viewpoint* **27**: 497–520.

Blamey, R. (2001) Principles of Ecotourism. In Weaver, D.B. (ed.) *Encyclopedia of Ecotourism*. Wallingford, UK: CAB International, pp. 5–22.

Britton, S.G. (1980) A Conceptual Model of Tourism in a Peripheral Economy. In Pearce, D.G. (ed.) Tourism in the South Pacific: The contribution of research to development and planning. Proceeding of UNESCO Tourism Workshop, Rarotonga, June 10–13, pp. 1–12.

Burridge, K. and Milne, S. (1996) Tourism, Development and the Travel Distribution System: The Case of the Cook Islands. Paper presented at Pacific Rim 2000, Rotorua, New Zealand, 4 November.

Butler, R. (1980) The concept of a tourist area cycle of evolution: implications for management of resources. *Canadian Geographer* **24**: 5–12.

Clarke, J. (1997) A Framework of Approaches to Sustainable Tourism. *Journal of Sustainable Tourism* **5**: 224–233.

Craig-Smith, S. and Fagence, M. (1994) A critique of tourism planning in the Pacific. In Cooper, C. and Lockwood, A. (eds) *Progress in Tourism,*

Recreation and Hospitality Management, Volume 6. Chichester, UK: Wiley, pp. 92–110.

Dahl, C. (1993) Tourism Development on the Island of Pohnpei (Federated States of Micronesia): Sacredness, Control and Autonomy. *Ocean & Coastal Management* **20**: 241–65.

De Haas, H. and Cukier, J. (2000) Smallscale tourism and sustainability in Niue. *Pacific Tourism Review* **4**: 1–6.

Dernoi, L.A. (1981) Alternative Tourism: Towards a New Style in North–South Relations. *International Journal of Tourism Management* **2**: 25–64.

Douglas, N. (1997) Applying the Life Cycle Model to Melanesia. *Annals of Tourism Research* **24**: 1–22.

Evanson, B. (1997) The Unique Turtle Island Experience. Paper presented at the Eighth Pacific Science Inter-Congress, July 17.

Fagence, M. (1999) Tourism as a Feasible Option for Sustainable Development in Small Island Developing States (SIDS): Nauru as a Case Study. *Pacific Tourism Review* **3**: 133–42.

Finney, B. and Watson, K. (1975) *A New Kind of Sugar: Tourism in the Pacific*. Honolulu: East–West Centre.

Gilbert, J. (1997) *Ecotourism means Business*. Wellington, New Zealand: GP Publications.

GVB (1995) *1995 Visitor Accommodations & Golf Course Plant Inventory*. Agana: Guam Visitors Bureau.

GVB (1996) *US Exit Survey December 1996: Summary of Principal Findings*. Agana: Guam Visitors Bureau, Research Department.

GVB (1997) Miscellaneous Tourism Statistics. Agana: Guam Visitors Bureau.

Harrison, D. (1997) Globalization and Tourism: Some Themes From Fiji. In Oppermann, M. (ed.) *Pacific Rim Tourism*. Wallingford, UK: CAB International, pp. 167–83.

Harrison, D. and Brandt, J. (1997) Ecotourism in Fiji: Making Sense of the Muddle? Paper presented at the Eighth Pacific Science Inter-Congress, July 13–19.

Hing, N. and Dimmock, K. (2001) A Fractured Paradise: Discussion of Issues Surrounding Fiji's 2000 Coup d'Etat and Their Impacts on Tourism. Paper presented at the 2001 CAUTHE National Research Conference, February 7–10.

Jafari, J. (1989) An English language literature review. In Bystrzanowski, J. (ed.) *Tourism as a Factor of Change: a Sociocultural Study*. Vienna: Centre for Research and Documentation in Social Sciences, pp. 17–60.

King, B. and Berno, T. (2001) Trouble in Paradise: Managing Tourism after the Coups in Fiji. Paper presented at the 2001 CAUTHE National Research Conference, February 7–10.

King, B., Pizam, A. and Milman, A. (1993) Social Impacts of Tourism: Host Perceptions. *Annals of Tourism Research* **20**: 650–5.

Krausse, G. (1995) Sustainable tourism for remote atolls in the Pacific. *International Journal of Sustainable Development and World Ecology* **2**: 166–81.

Lipscomb, A. (1998) Village-Based Tourism in the Solomon Islands: Impediments and Impacts. In Laws, E., Faulkner, B. and Moscardo, G.

(eds) *Embracing and Managing Change in Tourism: A Case Book*. London: Routledge, pp. 185–201.

Lockhart, D. and Chandra, R. (1997) Fiji: crossroads of the South Pacific. In Lockhart, D. and Drakakis-Smith, D. (eds) *Island Tourism: Trends and Prospects*. London: Pinter, pp. 302–1.

McKnight, T.L. (1995) Oceania: *The Geography of Australia, New Zealand and the Pacific Islands*. Englewood Cliffs, NJ, USA: Prentice Hall.

McVey, M. (1995) *Vanuatu: Tourism Sector Review*. Tourism Council of the South Pacific.

Milne, S. (1997) Tourism, dependency and South Pacific microstates: beyond the vicious cycle? In Lockhart, D. and Drakakis-Smith, D. (eds) *Island Tourism: Trends and Prospects*. London: Pinter, pp. 281–301.

MVB. (1997) *Hotels & Motels in the CNMI as of February 4, 1997*. Saipan: Marianas Visitors Bureau.

MVB (1998) Miscellaneous Statistics. Saipan: Marianas Visitors Bureau.

Ranck, S. (1987) An Attempt at Autonomous Development: The Case of the Tufi Guest Houses, Papua New Guinea. In Britton, S. and Clarke, W. (eds) *Ambiguous Alternative: Tourism in Small Developing Countries*. Suva, Fiji: University of the South Pacific, pp. 154–66.

Statistics Office (1997) Vanuatu. Miscellaneous Tourism Statistics. Port Vila.

TVB (1996). *Visitors Statistics 1995*. Nuku'alofa: Tonga Visitors Bureau, Research & Statistical Section.

UNDP (1995) *Tourism Development Master Plan* (Vanuatu). United Nations Development Programme and World Tourism Organization.

Urbanowicz, C. (1989) Tourism in Tonga Revisited: Continued Troubled Times? In: Smith, V. (ed.) *Hosts and Guests: The Anthropology of Tourism*. Second Edition. Philadelphia: University of Pennsylvania Press, pp. 105–17.

Urbanowicz, C. (1997) *Tourism and Private Sector Development Programme, Niue: Final Report*. United Nations Development Development Programme and World Tourism Organization.

Weaver, D. (1988) The Evolution of a 'Plantation' Tourism Landscape on the Caribbean Island of Antigua. *Tijdschrift voor Economische en Sociale Geografie* 79: 319–31.

Weaver, D. (1991) Alternative to Mass Tourism in Dominica. *Annals of Tourism Research* **18**: 414–32.

Weaver, D. (1998) *Ecotourism in the Less Developed World*. Wallingford, UK: CAB International.

Weaver, D. (2000) A Broad Context Model of Destination Development Scenarios. *Tourism Management* **21**: 217–24.

Weaver, D. (2001) *Ecotourism*. Brisbane: John Wiley & Sons.

WTO (1997) Yearbook of Tourism Statistics. Volume 1. 49th edn. Madrid: World Tourism Organization.

Zeppel, H. (1998) Land and Culture: Sustainable Tourism and Indigenous People. In Hall, M.C. and Lew, A. (eds) *Sustainable Tourism: A Geographical Perspective*. Harlow, UK: Longman, pp. 60–74.

CHAPTER 9

How sustainable is Mekong tourism?

Anita Pleumarom

Introduction

The Mekong River basin area with its peculiar history and great political, economic and social differences (the Mekong sub-region comprises Burma, Cambodia, Laos, Thailand, Vietnam and Yunnan in Southern China) is a region in which many of the issues and problems associated with tourism development can be observed. Until the 1980s, Thailand was the only country among the Mekong riparian states, which was fully integrated into the global capitalist system and had systematically developed a tourist industry to boost foreign exchange earnings and investment, as well as prestige in exchange for readily available cultural and natural resources. Over the last 20 years, tourist arrivals in Thailand have risen from one million to almost ten million annually.

Other Mekong countries remained more or less isolated from the rest of Southeast Asia after the Second World War because of post-colonial turmoil, the emergence of different political systems and American anti-communist warfare in Indochina. While Burma followed its own self-styled 'Burmese Path to Socialism', China – and later Laos, Cambodia and Vietnam – were part of the socialist block. Travel to, from and within these countries was restricted, and much of the poor tourism-related infrastructure dated back to colonial times.

With the collapse of the state socialist block in the late 1980s, all Mekong nations decided to reform their economies and boost tourism as an industry in the hope of quickly catching up with the Asian 'newly industrialized countries' (NICs). The growth of political and economic regionalism since the beginning of the 1990s has been vital for the emergence of several cooperation frameworks involving the Mekong Basin area, all of which prioritize the development of tourism and related infrastructure. Clearly, the recent tourism expansion into the Mekong sub-region has not happened incidentally or inevitably, but is the result of political will and substantial promotional efforts.

However, there is a clear tension in the Mekong Basin area between the requirement to meet the vast majority of the population who are poor and the prevailing policies of growth-driven economic development in the region. A central question is whether benefits from tourism can actually 'trickle down' and contribute to improve the living standard of disadvantaged social groups and indigenous peoples. Deprivation, uneven distribution of wealth, social inequalities and rapid depletion of natural resources, which set the stage for political, social, ethnic and ecological conflict, feature prominently in Mekong countries and make tourism a highly insecure industry.

Thailand has often been described as a negative tourism model because reckless development has resulted in the environmental degradation of many places, exacerbated economic inequalities and contributions to undesirable changes in society, such as the proliferation of the sex industry, AIDS, drug abuse, gambling, crime and cultural erosion[1]. Government official and industry leaders framing the Mekong tourism development have acknowledged that the industry causes a plethora of problems and responded by incorporating the notions of 'sustainable tourism' into their policies and plans. They maintain that with improved planning and management, past mistakes can be avoided in new destinations.

Has a new era in tourism development begun that can reverse the negative trends so that Mekong's neighbouring countries will be spared from a tourism onslaught as experienced in Thailand? To answer this question, this chapter begins by examining regional tourism plans with a focus on the Greater Mekong Subregion (GMS) scheme initiated by the Asian Development Bank (ADB). The next section presents case studies that suggest that destructive tourism projects persist and are spreading throughout the Mekong basin area despite the constant rhetoric of sustainable tourism or ecotourism. Finally, the last section discusses the question of sustainability by taking into account some broader issues such as the impact of globalization and lessons learned from the Asian economic crisis. It will be argued that the often ill-defined and reductionist sustainable tourism policies need to be replaced by holistic and people-centred development initiatives, if the goal is to work towards a sustainable future.

Tourism and regional development

Over the last decade all Mekong countries, except China, have become members of the Association of Southeast Asian Nations (ASEAN). This grouping has forged transborder economic cooperation programmes in the form of so-called 'growth triangles' with tourism development playing a prominent role. ASEAN even has its own Travel Association (ASEANTA) and declared 2002 as 'Visit ASEAN Year' under the theme 'ASEAN-Asia's Perfect 10 Paradise'[2]. In 1996, ASEAN also set up its own working group on Mekong Basin Development Cooperation, with the major proposal under this initiative being the creation of a regional rail network for freight and passenger traffic, linking Singapore with Yunnan via Kuala Lumpur, Bangkok, Phnom Penh, Ho Chi Minh City and Hanoi[3].

The Mekong River Commission (MRC), under the auspices of the United Nations Development Programme (UNDP), has presented plans for the Mekong subregion, providing for 'economic growth together with environmental protection and cultural enrichment', which includes tourism and related infrastructure development (MRC, 1995).

Another initiative is the Quadrangle for Economic Cooperation (QEC) which emphasizes the improvement of land, water and air transport to promote tourism and trade. Formed in 1993 by a group of Thai business people and backed by influential Thai and Chinese politicians, the investors promoting the QEC have been especially eager to win concessions and attract funds to build roads and to develop tourism projects in the border areas of Thailand, Laos, Burma and Yunnan. Their plans involve the establishment of hotels, resorts, casinos and shopping centres, as well as 'model cultural villages' catering to adventurous 'ecotourists'[4].

However, the most prominent framework and prime mover of Mekong tourism is the ADB's GMS scheme.

The GMS tourism programme

Since its formation in 1992, the GMS initiative has endorsed more than 100 development projects in the field of transport, energy, tourism, telecommunication, environment and human resource development. While seven priority projects are directly related to tourism, thirty-four projects pertain to road, railway, water and air transport, and more than fifty deal with hydro-electricity generation. The GMS tourism working group has successfully garnered support from governments, international development agencies, large industry associations, as well as corporations to promote the subregion as a single tourism market (ADB, 1996; PATA, 2001).

Apart from the ADB, representatives of the six Mekong countries' national tourism organizations (NTOs), international tourism associations such as the World Tourism Organization (WTO), the Pacific Asia Travel Association (PATA), ASEANTA, the UN Economic and Social Commission for Asia and the Pacific (ESCAP) and specialized UN agencies, have been involved in the GMS scheme. The Tourism Authority of Thailand (TAT), which has eagerly marketed Thailand as a 'gateway' to other Mekong countries, has also played a key role in the programme. Since 1996, TAT's office in Bangkok has accommodated the GMS tourism working group's secretariat known as the Agency for Coordinating Mekong Tourism Activities (AMTA)[5].

Thailand also hosted the first Mekong Tourism Forum (MTF) – an annual event initiated by the GMS tourism working group – on the occasion of PATA's annual conference in Pattaya in April 1996[6]. The MTF seeks possibilities to realize the 'Mekong Dream' – a concept designed by PATA to promote 'hassle-free' air and overland travel between Mekong countries since lack of accessibility, insufficient provisions for safety and difficult immigration regulations are seen by the industry as the main obstacles to regional tourism growth (Chandler, 1995). In addition, to raise market awareness of the subregion's tourism resources, a world-wide campaign was launched at the MTF 1996 event to promote thirty cultural and natural tourist sites as 'Jewels of the Mekong'[7].

While working towards the removal of all barriers to travel in the Mekong Basin area (including physical, economic, organizational and legal barriers) that have so far discouraged foreign visitors and investors, the GMS initiative has emphasized 'sustainable development' and 'ecotourism' as worthy goals.

The 'Concept Plan for tourism development in the Greater Mekong Subregion 1999–2018', outlines the GMS strategy for the next 20 years. The major goal is 'to consolidate a "Mekong" cultural tourism, ecotour-ism and adventure tourism network by linking destinations, circuits and routes' by the end of 2006. By 2018, it anticipates the GMS region will be 'one of the world's most important ecotourism and cultural tourism destinations' and 'a safe, accessible and "good value" (value for money) destination to experience the rich, natural, historical and cultural heritage of the peoples and places along and adjacent to the Mekong/Lancang River'[8] (AMTA, 1998).

Whereas ecotourism has nurtured notions of smallscale and controlled development, this plan aims at luring millions of additional international visitors to the Mekong subregion[9]. Moreover, the list of priority projects proposed in the study are in line with the ADB's GMS mega-infrastructure programme and reflect a heavy emphasis on improving transportation systems involving navigation, highway construction and air route expansion[10].

The study says 'In the long term, there will be emphasis on the creation of networks and gateways, transportation nodes and international standard facilities to accommodate all segments of the tourism market throughout the subregion' (AMTA, 1998). In other words, there will be a focus on ecotourism and other alternative tourism forms such as 'village tourism' as long as there are major bottlenecks in infrastructure, which restrict largescale tourism. Once all gates have been thrown open and the necessary facilities are in place, the plan is to tout for all shades of tourism, which ultimately means a shift to the development of main-stream mass tourism.

Meanwhile, it is widely acknowledged that the majority of the Bank's projects not only fail to meet their standards but are responsible for severe impacts on local communities and the environment[11].

For instance, the ADB put forward a proposal in 1996 for conservation management in watershed areas, which involves the gradual relocation of some 60 million mountain people in the subregion. This massive resettlement programme has been legitimated with the claim that the widespread practice of shifting cultivation is a major cause for environmental destruction[12]. In addition, a countless number of people are likely to be displaced and lose their traditional livelihoods by the Bank's more than fifty large dam projects.

According to ADB's belief, in the name of 'development' and 'poverty reduction'[13], local communities should abandon their traditional self-reliant lifestyles and economic activities and turn to ecotourism as an alternative source of income in new locations. At the 9th Ministerial Meeting of the GMS Economic Cooperation Programme held in Manila in January 2000, Warren Evans, manager of the ADB's Environment Division, said 'We need to persuade hill communities that it's in their best interest to conserve rather than exploit natural resources by encouraging community participation in ventures such as ecotourism. They can discourage poachers and illegal loggers and operate sound tourist facilities'[14].

To introduce a comprehensive conservation programme that involves unprecedented mass evictions and inevitably degrades indigenous societies and cultures and then to offer tourism as compensation is certainly one of the deepest ironies manifest in the GMS scheme[15]. Much more so as tourism studies reveal that only a tiny proportion of tourism income actually reaches villagers. For instance, Mingma Norbu Sherpa, a Nepalese representing the Worldwide Fund for Nature (WWF) argued at the ADB's first 'pro-poor tourism' seminar that in many cases, tourism's benefits do not make it to a country's outer reaches, even though those areas bear the impact of tourism. He cited Nepal's famous trekking areas as an example, where local people receive only 2 per cent of the tourism revenue[16].

Shivakumar, a development consultant based in Cambodia, concludes that the ADB and other donor agencies are primarily committed to creating a conducive environment for private corporations, rather than making a serious effort to lift weak and peripheral social groups out of poverty. 'In general, most projects developed by the donors, particularly the ADB and Japan, are capital-intensive while, at least in the short term, labour-intensive projects are needed in these nations to challenge poverty. They have not been able to propose a plan to combine simultaneously, in a balanced and mutually reinforcing manner, economic growth with welfare, empowerment, cultural renaissance, social transformation and sustainability. These observations lead one to conclude that reduction of poverty is not the priority of these projects . . .' (Shivakumar, 1997: 11).

The following examples will demonstrate how damaging tourism activities have proliferated throughout the Mekong subregion over the past decade and posed severe pressure on local people and the environment.

Real-life tourism tales

(1) Mass 'ecotourism' – Thai style

The rapid growth of tourism in Thailand during the 1970s and 1980s, particularly the upsurge of sex tourism, attracted severe criticism for its negative effects on Thai society.

The impact of mass tourism in Thailand on the local people, their culture, natural resources and built environment has been substantial. Two striking effects of over-zealous profit-oriented tourism development efforts have been: (1) the disproportionate shift of capital to mass tourism-related construction and real estate developments at the expense of other sectors such as agriculture and small industry which are locally oriented; and (2) the promotion of over-consumption and excessive local resources with attendant new social and environmental pressures on local people and environments. (Pholpoke 1998)

Coinciding with government and industry efforts to diversify Thailand's tourism products and to shed its worsening image as a 'spoilt' destination, has been the growing interest in 'ecotourism'[17]. Acknowledging that tourism in the past had caused severe damage, Seree Wangpaichitr, the former TAT Governor, said in an interview with the *Bangkok Post* in June 1998: 'Ecotourism is the heart of long-term tourism development.' He further argued that the mass tourism promotion by the TAT is not incompatible with ecotourism: 'The strategy is to distribute the mass of tourism to a great number of places so that resources will not be over-exploited while distributing the economic benefits to the wider public'[18].

Unfortunately, Thailand has longstanding experience with the mismanagement of forests, beaches, marine areas and other natural assets, and many hotels, resorts and other facilities have encroached on officially 'protected areas'[19]. Repeated attempts by the Tourism Authority of Thailand (TAT) and the Royal Forestry Department (RFD) to open up national parks to private tourism businesses have elicited great controversy. Since 1997, the RFD has worked on a proposal to grant leases to operators of illegal tourist facilities on resort islands – a highly disputed plan that is expected to be approved by the government in the near future[20].

Many observers were amazed by the strong opposition of local residents and environmentalists towards the filming in 1999 of 20th Century Fox's movie 'The Beach', starring Leonardo DiCaprio, in Phi Phi Island's National Park in Southern Thailand, which involved profound landscape changes at Maya Bay. But the protest actions and the related lawsuit filed by local government agencies and citizens against the film company and authorities, who gave permission to 're-design' a part of the park, need to be seen in the context of the fierce struggle for the protection and enforcement for Thailand's national park laws. Opponents repeatedly pointed out that 'The Beach' affair, which even led to an international boycott campaign against the Hollywood movie, was a precedence case, and the fight to save Maya Bay was not about just one island but about the fate of all parks in the country. The reason given by Thai officials for allowing the controversial film project to go ahead was to boost the country's tourism industry and income for local communities. But critics have warned that such incidents make a mockery of conservation efforts and the legal system, and set a bad example whereby commercialism can override any other issue in Thailand[21].

Indeed, the situation is worsening. Under the pretext of ecotourism promotion, the RFD has recently implemented massive tourism-related infrastructure projects – some involving logging operations – in parks countrywide, funded with loans from the World Bank and Japan. The frenzied construction of roads, parking lots, visitor centres, bungalows, camp sites and nature trails neatly coincided with the RFD's 'Visit National Park Year 2000' aimed at attracting more than 20 million domestic and international tourists to the parks during that year[22].

In Thailand, ecotourism development in nature reserves generally proceeds without the involvement of surrounding local communities in decision-making and without adequate discussion on who owns the land and natural resources, how land should be used, where and how tourist facilities should be built, visitor volume or regulations on tourist conduct; all of which has created and aggravated ecological problems and conflict between the government, private industry and communities. For instance, when the RFD proposed to increase the land area protected by national parks in northern Thailand a few years ago, some 10 000 people – primarily from ethnic minoritiy groups – rejected the RFD's plans to evict them from their lands and held street demonstrations in the city of Chiang Mai (Pleumarom, 1997/98).

The social injustice inherent in 'tourism-cum-conservation' projects is evident as they stop the access to land and natural resources of one social group – poor villagers who have often inhabited the area for generations – and open these areas for other groups – investors and paying ecotourists[23].

Whenever the Thai economy is in trouble, the government resorts to tourism as its saviour. With agriculture and industry staggering in the 1980s, it seized on services and declared 1987 'Visit Thailand Year'. Following the financial meltdown in 1997, the previous government of Chuan Leekpai responded with the 'Amazing Thailand' promotional campaign. Facing a new economic downturn, the present government, under Thaksin Shinawatra, vowed to boost foreign exchange earnings from tourism by 50 billion baht (US$1.1 billion) in 2001[24]. The target required that the country attracted an additional 1.9 million foreign visitors. Under the new plan, many thousands of hitherto undeveloped villages were earmarked for 'community-based ecotourism' projects. In the interim, a well-formulated conservation policy to counter the impact of increased visitor volume and spatial expansion of tourism was conspicuously absent[25]. This suggests that the country's natural resources will further be sacrificed for short-term economic gains.

(2) Golfers' dream – a farmer's nightmare

Since the late 1980s, golf has been aggressively promoted as a lucrative tourism business. Starting out from Thailand, the golf course boom spread into other Mekong countries causing immense environmental and social conflicts[26].

In the late 1980s and early 1990s, some 200 courses were built in Thailand. The construction of golf complexes – often involving other largescale developments such as hotels, residential houses, shopping centres, entertainment facilities, power plants, access roads and even airports – came under heavy attack for environmental reasons. Many of the projects were accused of encroaching on parkland and driving off farmers from their land (Pleumarom, 1994).

Golf courses require large stretches of land and replace biodiversity-rich wilderness areas and fertile agricultural lands. Another major concern is the enormous waste of water resources for such projects. According to the Mahidol University in Bangkok, the turf of an 18-hole international standard golf course consumes up to 6500 cubic metres of water per day which is equal to the daily household demand of 6000 city residents or 60 000 villagers[27]. While scarce water reserves are being diverted to keep the courses green, nearby communities are suffering due to the lack of drinking and irrigation water. In addition, the excessive application of chemical fertilizers and pesticides necessary to maintain the courses covered with foreign grass species threatens to pollute air, soil, and water, and create health risks for both wildlife and humans. Alarming reports were published in the Thai media about caddies and greenkeepers affected by acute chemical poisoning – e.g., headache, nausea, respiratory illnesses and skin diseases[28].

In the southern Lao province Champasak, Thai investors had plans to build a mega-resort project, including golf courses, hotels, casinos, a power station and an international airport, in a pristine area at the famous Lee Pee waterfalls on the Mekong River[29]. Although the developers promoted the resort as an 'ecotourism' venture, it was met with resistance by Lao and Thai environmentalists as well as local villagers because it would have involved deforestation, ecological disruption of the fragile Mekong river system, displacement of villagers, and probably undesirable social and cultural changes in nearby communities. Consequently, due to increasing public protests and financial difficulties the controversial project was halted[30].

Vietnam has also built a number golf courses to attract foreign tourists. Citizens protested when developers flattened a public forest in Thu Duc near Ho Chi Minh City for the construction of the Golf Vietnam Club[31]. The Thai developers of the King's Island Golf Resort at the Dong Mo dam reservoir near Hanoi built a golf course at the edge of the lake below the reservoir's spill way level without considering rising water levels during the rainy season. During devastating floods in 1994, provincial officials allowed the release of large amounts of water from the reservoir to save the golf resort, which resulted in the destruction of the rice crops in neighbouring farming areas[32]. Despite a 1995 governmental decree that prohibited converting more rice lands to other purposes, the South Korean conglomerate Daewoo received an investment licence to build a golf course on rice fields at Kim No village on the outskirts of Hanoi[33]. Violence broke out at the construction site, when angry farmers, who had not been properly informed about the project, tried to stop an army unit from plowing up the land for the golf course[34].

In Cambodia, several golf course projects surfaced around Phnom Penh, near the Angkor Wat temple complex, and in Sihanoukville as part of the huge Naga Island casino resort proposed by a Malaysian company[35]. For the construction of the Singapore-financed Cambodian Country Club at the Bang Ta Yab Lake outside of Phnom Penh, the developer wanted to drain a large stretch of marshland and remove more than 450 families who lived beside the lake (mostly fruit and vegetable growers). But the villagers refused to leave and protested to the authorities who, in turn, treated them as illegal squatters and refused to compensate them[36].

In military-ruled Burma as well, golf courses have sprung up at tourist sites, including luxury golf-plus-casino resorts such as the Golden Paradise Resort near Tachilek in the Golden Triangle and the Andaman Club on Thathay Kyun Island in the South[37]. For the development of the Myanmar Golf Club in Rangoon, the army blockaded the site to scare off the people who had been living there for decades. When this failed, the government arrested one member of each family and sent them to jail. The remaining families were then moved against their will to a 'new town' far outside of the city[38].

(3) Cultural heritage for sale – the case of Angkor Wat

In order to lure and entertain visitors, culture (as manifested in historical and religious sites, rituals, festivals, arts and crafts) has often been distorted beyond recognition in the process of being re-packaged as a tourist product. The famous twelfth century Angkor temple complex at Siem Reap – the most sacred site and national symbol of Cambodia – is a glaring example as to how cultural heritage is no longer for local people to celebrate, but increasingly commoditized to lure foreign visitors.

With the Cambodian government aiming for 1 million foreigners a year to visit Angkor Wat, grave concerns have been raised that the temple area and its surroundings could be destroyed within a few years. In 1995, UNESCO's World Heritage Committee even threatened to remove Angkor from the list of protected sites because Cambodian authorities had not met the necessary requirements such as adopting a cultural preservation law to deter the theft and smuggling of antiquities[39]. Thousands of invaluable artifacts have been stolen from the temple complex since it has opened to tourists. The government has vowed to take precautionary measures to ensure that protection zones at the historical and religious sites are respected. But this may not be enough to save Angkor due to inefficient bureaucracy, corruption and the absence of a functioning legislature and sufficient capacities to scrutinize, monitor and control projects.

Conservationists in and outside Cambodia were particularly appalled at the proposal for a US$20 million Angkor Wat high-tech sound-and-light show, saying it would turn the temples into a 'carnival-like attraction' or a 'Disney-like inane entertainment place'[40]. In 1995, the Malaysian YTL company claimed it would promote 'the biggest and best cultural event of its kind in the world'. The plan was to stage up to four performances per night, in which the temple as well as selected bas-relief carvings on its inner walls would be illuminated in colourful lights and voices in different languages be heard from loudspeakers. In Thailand, where tourist shows at historical monuments have become common-place, such activities have provoked debates regarding the extent to which old, fragile buildings are damaged.

The YTL company had also wanted to develop a 1095-hectare site near the northwestern temples into a tourism zone including several luxury hotels, golf courses, a commercial centre, a hospital and other facilities – a project which was expected to attract more than US$1 billion investment[41]. In January 1996, even King Norodom Sihanouk voiced strong concern about the 'commercialization' of Angkor and pressed for a review of YTL's plans for the light-and-sound show and hotel and the tourism complex in the area[42]. However, since Prime Minister Hun Sen's bloody coup against the co-prime minister Prince Norodom Ranariddh in July 1997, which resulted in a dramatic tourism slump in Cambodia, little has been heard regarding YTL's Angkor show and accompanying developments.

In an all-out effort to revive Cambodia's ruined tourism industry following the political turmoil, in 1999 the government adopted an 'open-skies' policy to increase international flights to Siem Reap, the gateway to the Angkor temples. Additionally, it organized an extravagant 'Angkor 2000' millennium show[43]. Tourism officials' hopes that the combination of direct flights from overseas and spectacular promotional events would make Angkor part of an international 'must-see' itinerary were being realized. In addition, the opening of new overland routes to Siem Reap from Thailand attracted more visitors and investors to the area and fuelled the construction of more tourism facilities around Angkor[44]. As a result, renewed warnings of threats to the temples were been voiced in public, and there were growing worries that local people would be increasingly exposed to the effects of uncontrolled tourism[45].

(4) 'A fascist Disneyland' – tourism and human rights in Burma

In 1996 the Burmese military government, which has been condemned by the international community because of its gross human rights violations, launched an ambitious tourism promotion campaign 'Visit Myanmar (Burma) Year'[46]. The junta hoped to attract more than 250 000 foreign visitors to the country during 1996–97 to increase currency earnings and gain recognition in the international community after decades of isolation and a bloody military crackdown on the pro-democracy movement in 1988. While Burmese tourism authorities and the industry stepped up promotion to sell the country as the 'Golden Land', critics increasingly delivered descriptions of Burma as a 'prison' for its citizens and a 'fascist Disneyland' for visitors (Lawrence, 2001).

Insisting that, in a country where people are denied basic rights, tourism cannot benefit that country, Burmese opposition groups and international human rights organizations have called for a tourism boycott to Burma. Democracy leader and Peace Nobel Prize laureate Aung San Suu Kyi has repeatedly urged foreign investors and tourists to stay away from the country until democratic reforms have been achieved[47]. The argument is that the income generated through tourism helps to sustain the oppressive regime and is spent on buying weapons and expanding military action against its citizens. Since every foreign visitor entering the country has to purchase foreign exchange certificates equivalent to US$200, and many tourist facilities are state-owned, a considerable proportion of tourist dollars goes directly into the junta's coffers. In addition, members of the military run their own tourism-related businesses or have formed joint ventures with private companies to increase their personal wealth and economic power (Lawrence, 2001).

The close links between the development of the tourist industry and human rights abuses have been well documented by official agencies such as the United Nations Human Rights Commission, the International Labour Organization (ILO) and Burmese and international civic groups[48].

Drawing on reports from Rangoon, Mandalay, Pagan, Taunggyi, Maymo and other places earmarked for tourism development, it is estimated that tens of thousands of families have been forcefully moved from their homes and land to pave the way for hotels, resorts and tourism-related infrastructure[49]. Most of the displaced people do not receive any compensation and have to resettle in areas which lack proper sanitation, electricity and water supply. Equally deplorable is the fact that ordinary people are forced into providing their labour to upgrade tourist sites and to build roads, railways and airports, in order to meet the increased transportation requirements for travel and tourism[50].

Burma's ethnic minorities, who have already suffered for decades under forced assimilation policies by the state, are now being lured away from their villages to serve as 'exotic' attractions in hotels or so-called 'model villages'[51]. In addition, thousands of Burmese women and girls, many of them from ethnic groups, have become victims of a burgeoning domestic sex trade and are being trafficked to Thailand to work as prostitutes[52].

That 'Visit Myanmar Year' turned out a failure can be partly attributed to the success of the strong global movement against Burma's tourism policies. Since 1997, tourist numbers have plummeted as a result of the Asian economic crisis and increasing international sanctions against the country. During the fiscal year 1998–99, Burma attracted only 120 000 foreign visitors, less than half as many that the junta had expected when it announced its 1996 tourism campaign[53]. Yet, Burmese officials remained optimistic and announced a new campaign aimed at increasing the number of tourists to Burma by ten times to 1 million in 2001[54]!

Discussion: the question of sustainability

The above investigation on tourism policies and practices in the Mekong region reveals the vast gaps between 'sustainable tourism' as a theoretical ideal: what has been planned, and what has been actually achieved. The grim realities, as described in the various case studies, leave serious doubts as to whether tourism development can be propelled towards more sustainability in the long term.

This is not to say that initiatives that have successfully managed to avoid major damage by fostering community based and environmentally sound tourist activities do not exist. It also should not be denied that some tourism companies have taken positive voluntary measures to mitigate impacts such as pollution. However, such 'success stories' are limited to a few micro-projects, and they have certainly not posed a real challenge to the status quo or considerably contributed to the redirection of the tourism industry as a whole.

A hard look at the overall situation leads us to the conclusion that the policies pursued by governments, national tourism authorities and supranational bodies, such as the Asian Development Bank, for the development of Mekong tourism have been those most suitable for promoting the industry rather than for the protection of the environment and the benefit of local communities. Put simply, in the words of Wall, tourism promotion in Asia over the recent years 'has consumed massive amounts of capital and has failed to create a sustainable product. It appears that there has been an implicit belief that tourism development is about the construction of high quality hotels and that, once these are in place, all else will follow' (Wall, 1998).

Indeed, little has been done to develop effective mechanisms to monitor and control developments aimed at curbing environmental degradation, social and cultural erosion and economic marginalization of the poor. Management plans, if there are any, are often ignored, and environmental, zoning and construction laws are not being properly enforced. Many critical tourism-related issues – such as corruption, social vices, encroachment of public lands and diversion of natural resources, displacement of local and indigenous communities, and political suppression and human rights abuses – are typically neglected by tourism policymakers and project managers. In the light of this, it is easy for critics to assert that 'sustainable tourism' in the Mekong region is little more than empty rhetoric and a public relations exercise to ward off public criticism[55].

What is it that makes it so difficult for tourism to deliver sustainable development, and why does there seem to be no prospect of significant positive change? Some explanations and aspects for further analysis will be provided in this last section.

Firstly, sustainability itself is not a fixed and agreed term, and thus is subject to interpretation. Associated with this are the various potential limitations of the concept that have been identified by various researchers. Wall (1997) notes that 'While [sustainable tourism] has drawn attention to the need to achieve a balance between business and environmental interests ..., as a single-sector concept, it fails to acknowledge the intersectoral competition for resources, the resolution of which is crucial for sustainable development'. Addressing the issues of power and vested interest, Mowforth and Munt (1998) state that 'the principles of sustainable tourism are open to manipulation in the service of operators and others in the industry. That is not to say that the principles are not worthy of attention by all those in the industry; but it does suggest that the motives of those who apply them should also be scrutinized'. Finally, Wheeller (1997) contends, 'there are continual exhortations on the need to adopt a holistic approach to the subject of tourism development, planning and sustainability ... A truly holistic approach would be one that embraces realism. Sustainable tourism unfortunately fails, at the practical level, even to acknowledge it.'

In fact, the planning for 'sustainable tourism' in the Mekong region has largely remained a theoretical exercise without sufficiently taking into account the milieu in which tourism is evolving. Therefore, Majone's argument is worth savouring: 'A practical problem is not solved by offering a theoretical solution that does not take into consideration the limitations upon which the context imposes. Thus, it is quite misleading to employ ideal standards in evaluating or comparing alternative policy instruments; the standards must relate to the particular context in which the instruments are used. And because the context in which public policy is made includes values, norms, perceptions, and ideologies, technical considerations are insufficient as a criteria of choice' (cited in Hall, 1994).

It is also important to note that the concept of 'sustainable tourism' is deeply rooted in Western environmentalism that often takes the form of 'enlightenment' and is dependent on achieving a certain level of prosperity and development. This, however, often appears to be at odds with the livelihood-based environmentalism in Southeast Asia and other parts of the Third World, where poor peasants and forest dwellers are struggling to defend and reclaim land and natural resources for economic and cultural survival (Hirsch and Warren, 1998). A better understanding of these contradictions may help to explain why so many ecotourism projects based on Western conservation ideals are resisted by local people and subsequently fail.

What is also often ignored is that globalization has induced its own particular political dynamics in the region, which are to the detriment of the commitment to achieve sustainable development. In this context, Parnwell's study on how Mekong tourism has become part of the global race-to-the-bottom is instructive (Parnwell, 1998). Highlighting examples of human rights violations in Burma, sex tourism and the HIV/AIDS crisis in Thailand, and the environmental impacts of golf tourism in the region, he argues 'the impact of tourism depends crucially upon the ownership of regulatory power' and explains how transnational agencies and corporations work through and with influential local actors and institutions – what he calls 'conduits of capitalism'. His conclusion is that regulation *for* the global tourism industry is taking precedence over the regulation *of* its development. As a result, local people, and especially the poor and marginalized, are exposed to greater political, social, economic and ecological insecurity (ibid.).

Since in poor countries, especially, tourism's economic viability is seen as a prime criterion for sustainability, the old question of who actually benefits from tourism needs to be raised anew in the face of globalization and liberalization. Third World tourism is mainly driven by foreign industry interests, and the economic gains for destination countries are often greatly overestimated.

A 1990 study on Thailand by the Bangkok-based National Institute and Development Administration, for example, came up with disillusioning results. At least 60 per cent of tourism revenue, amounting to US$4 billion in 1989, had been lost to 'leakages', being used for the import of goods and services and profits to foreign tourism corporations and other remittances (TDSC, 1991/92). A new study prepared by UNCTAD on the 'The Sustainability of International Tourism in Developing Countries' presents even more alarming findings (UNCTAD, 2001). It emphasizes that the economic, social and environmental sustainability of Third World countries' tourism industries is increasingly threatened by levels of financial 'leakages' that can easily reach 75 per cent, and escalating 'predatory practices and anti-competitive behaviour' of travel and tourism corporations based mainly in Europe and the United States. The UNCTAD report further points out that the combined impact of these factors undermines the economic viability of local enterprises and the ability of countries to allocate necessary resources for environmental protection and sustainable development (ibid.). Under these conditions, the proclaimed goals of sustainable tourism to enhance local economic benefits and the preservation of natural and cultural resources are extremely difficult to achieve.

Important lessons regarding the fragility of the tourism industry can be learned from the Asian economic crisis that began in June 1997 with the financial meltdown in Thailand (Pleumarom, 1998; Wall, 1998). It showed how much tourism is part of the fickle global economy, as well as being an industry that undergoes boom-and-bust cycles with serious consequences for the stability of national and regional economies.

There is little doubt that the inflationary tourism policies in the Mekong subregion in the early 1990s greatly contributed to the 1997 'crash'. During the era of the so-called 'bubble economy', indiscriminate and unsustainable investments led to the rapid conversion of lands into opulent tourism resort complexes. With progressive economic liberalization, the tourism, real estate and construction industries boomed in all Mekong countries, backed by local banks and global speculative capital[56].

In the immediate aftermath of the economic slump, Asian tourism markets almost collapsed[57]. In Thailand, the currency devalued and major corporations – many of whom had expanded into Mekong's neighbouring countries – were exposed for having mismanaged their way into massive indebtedness. Many tourism developers went bankrupt or were forced to downsize their projects. In particular, golf course and resort businesses, which had become a new symbol of globalized leisure enhancing the tourist lifestyle in Southeast Asian societies, experienced a dramatic downturn[58].

Many tourism-related infrastructure projects initiated by regional cooperation initiatives, including those of the ADB, were put on hold, as resources were needed to strengthen Asian countries' financial systems[59].

In Thailand, for example, the International Monetary Fund (IMF), the World Bank and the ADB granted a US$17 billion loan, which included a rigid Structural Adjustment Programme (SAP).

At that time, I had suggested that in environmental terms at least, the Asian crisis could be a blessing in disguise (Pleumarom, 1998). As a result of decreasing numbers of travellers, for example, airlines closed unprofitable routes, sold off aircrafts and cancelled orders for new aircrafts, and governments cut budgets for airport expansion and construction[60], which raised the prospect of less pollution and less damaging developments. Also, the malaise of rampant land grabs, park encroachments and environmental degradation in relation to tourism projects no longer seemed as threatening as before because Asian developers were cash-strapped (ibid.).

As it has turned out, however, Mekong tourism promoters not only returned to 'business as usual' but governments in the region have made all-out efforts to compensate for the heavy debts, declining growth and decreasing foreign exchange reserves through even more rapacious resource extraction policies[61]. A case in point is Thailand's present policy, aimed at turning every corner of the country into a tourist site and excessively boosting the number of tourists. Simultaneously, public and private investments in environmental programmes have significantly decreased because of the financial downturn.

Another question that should be asked is: Can tourism be sustainable in a region deeply affected by political instability, human rights problems and socio-economic crisis? In the context of the preparations for 'Visit ASEAN Year 2002', for example, tourism officials admitted that the event could be seriously hampered by political turmoil and social unrest in Southeast Asian nations but at the same time they tried to portray the problems as 'isolated incidents' to engender the notion of a 'carefree' holiday for consumers[62]. As Richter notes:

> Scarcity, deprivation, inequality, remnants of colonialism and the proxy wars of the superpowers set the stage for random violence, ethnic conflict, revolution, and even hostage-taking ... The very underdevelopment that exacerbates the resolution of political demands and frustrates economic aspirations is a potential asset in attracting tourism. Thus we have a paradox: nations, which are veritable hellholes for most of their citizens are sold as 'unspoilt paradises' to outsiders. (Richter 1995)

The concept of 'sustainable tourism' implies a high degree of public participation in the process, and public participation implies that local communities will have a degree of control over the tourism development process (Hall, 1994). However, the healthy-sounding words of 'local participation' and 'community control' often appear incredible and even bizarre, when applied to such destination countries as Burma, with no democracy or freedom for its own indigenous population. And 'Can a few corporate giants substitute for popular participation?' asks Shivakumar (1997). As regards tourism planning and management, regional initiatives such as the ADB-led GMS tourism scheme rely too much on foreign consultants[63], who often have little knowledge of local situations, whereas 'the type of subregional projects so far proposed defy the spirit of local participation and sustainable development to which most donors and multilateral institutions commit themselves . . .' (ibid.)[64].

The Mekong countries – particularly Burma, China, Vietnam and Laos – provide few opportunities for public participation in government decision-making. The exception to this generalization is Thailand, which has a relatively well-established civil rights and environmental movement, and a free press. Given the lack of individual freedom to speak out on development issues in the region, this task has by default fallen to a number of non-governmental organizations who, in turn, have sought to draw attention to the problems of tourism development, pressing for holistic and people-centred development policies that are not narrowly confined to tourism[65].

As outlined in the previous sections, major problems and conflicts have emerged because many rural and indigenous communities lost control of their land, natural and cultural resources and the political process as a result of 'top-down' tourism development. This being the case, one of the most urgent future tasks is to develop policies and tools to protect local people against uncontrolled and damaging tourism and to give them more power in development and conservation projects in general.

A number of grassroots-oriented organizations are already working in this direction and have put forward proposals aimed at tackling fundamental problems in development and natural resource management. For instance, an alliance of civil society organizations and local community networks in Thailand have developed a 'People's Agenda' that calls for a comprehensive reform of government policies and urges policy-makers to take the following actions:

- assert sovereignty over natural resources and not to relinquish control to transnational corporations;
- develop alternative economic systems based on the self-sufficiency of local communities, their use of natural resources and local knowledge systems;
- base its policies on natural resource management on a holistic view of nature and the diversity of natural ecosystems, cultures and knowledge systems;
- ensure local people's participation in drafting policies on the management of natural resources;
- guarantee, as well as strengthen, the rights of local communities to manage natural resources; and
- support the efforts of local community networks towards sustainable management of natural resources and local economic development (Rajesh 2001)

Importantly, the previously outlined agenda calls for just and equitable land reform that favours smallscale farming communities, and demands 'Foreign or Thai land-owners must be prevented from accumulating and controlling large areas of cultivable lands for speculative or non-farming purposes' (ibid.). This proposal aims to resolve the escalating land conflicts flowing from speculative investments in hotels, golf resorts and other land-consuming tourism-related developments that involve the expropriation of village commons, agricultural lands and natural areas, and, thus, increasing hardships for smallscale farming communities.

At the present time, there is little evidence that 'bottom-up' development alternatives such as the 'People's Agenda', based on the principles of economic equity, social justice, cultural integrity and ecological sustainability, are being heeded in tourism development planning, even though such grassroots-oriented proposals could be the key to root out the causes of problems. What are needed is more informed debate and public pressure to steer the tourism 'powers-that-be' towards a more holistic and people-centred approach and to persuade them to reorient their policies and practices accordingly. As Teo and Chang aptly note ' . . . one should not underestimate the salience of local players in the global game. It is by them that the success or failure of tourism development is ultimately decided' (Teo and Chang, 1998).

Endnotes

1 As for the impacts of tourism in Thailand in general see, for example, Meyer, 1988; TDSC, 1991/92; TEI, 1994; Cohen, 1996; various issues of *New Frontiers*, a bi-monthly news bulletin on tourism, development and environment in the Mekong Subregion.
2 *Bangkok Post*, 'Visit ASEAN Year to be a Joint Effort', 15.1.2001.
3 *New Frontiers*, 'ASEAN's Mekong Group Gets Off to a Tentative Start', 2(6), June 1996.
4 *The Nation*, 'Yunnan Conference: Cooperating on Growth', 5.12.1995; *New Frontiers*, 'Linking Laos to the World', 1(6) October 1995; *The Nation*, 'Four countries square off on the banks of the mighty Mekong', 27.5.1997; *The Nation*, 'Businessmen want access to new markets', 28.7.1997.
5 AMTA publishes a quarterly newsletter and has recently launched a GMS tourism website www.visit-mekong.com.
6 PATA is one of the world's most powerful business groupings dominated by the US private sector and has strongly influenced tourism policies in several South East Asian countries over the last four decades. It is comprised of around 2000 organizations involved in the travel and tourism industry worldwide, eighty-four of which are government promotion agencies, sixty-one airlines, 600 hotel businesses, 450 tour operators, 360 destination operators and corporations. In 1998, PATA relocated its headquarters from San Francisco to Bangkok to further underpin its interests in the region. For more information, see website www.pata.org.
7 As 'Jewels of the Mekong' are promoted in Burma: Rangoon (Shwedagon Pagoda), Kyaikhtiyo (Golden Rock), Mandalay (Mingun Pagoda), Taunggyi (Inle Lake), Pagan (Ananda Temple); in Cambodia: Angkor Wat, Phnom Penh and surroundings, Sihanoukville, Tonle

Sap Lake, Ratanakiri; in China's Yunnan province: Kunming, Stone Forest, Xishuangbanna, Dali, Lijiang; in Laos: Luang Prabang, Champasak, Vientiane, Xieng Khoung (Plain of Jars), Lak Sao; in Thailand: The Old Royal City (Rattanakosin Island-Bangkok, Ban Chiang, Prasat Hin Khao Phanom Rung Historical Park, Ubon Ratchathani Province, Chiang Rai Province; in Vietnam: Halong Bay, Hanoi City, Ninh Binh Province, Thua Thien Hue Quangnam-Danag Province (ADB, 1996).

8 Lancang is the Chinese name for the Mekong River.

9 According to official statistics, the GMS received 14.1 million visitors in 2000, with Thailand having the biggest share of 67.76 per cent; this was followed by Vietnam (15.14%), Yunnan (7.12%), Laos (5.22%), Cambodia (3.30%) and Burma (1.47%) (*AMTA Newsletter*, 'Visitor Arrivals to GMS Reach 14.1 Million in 2000', April 2001). The Concept Plans set a target of attracting an additional 2–2.5 million international tourists to the GMS by the end of 2006, and even higher growth rates are expected in the following years when more infrastructure projects will be completed (AMTA, 1998).

10 See also ADB (1996) and *The Nation*, 'Transport routes hold key to Mekong', 1.3.1996.

11 To some extent, the ADB admits the failure of projects they have funded, even though internal evaluations by the Bank are considered as conservative in their conclusions (TERRA, 2000). Walden Bello, Professor of Sociology and Public Administration at the University of the Philippines in Manila and Director of Focus on the Global South – a research programme based at Chulalongkorn University in Bangkok – refers to an assessment by ADB's Strategy and Policy Department, which says 'In most instances, operational performance was far short of projections.' This was due to 'weaknesses in project design, particularly where there was weak institutional capacity and there were inappropriate policies. Implementation of most projects tended to focus on completion of their physical infrastructure components rather than institutional development and support service components and policy reforms.' Bello further cites an internal source as saying that 'almost all forestry projects have failed', and only 36 per cent of projects in the Agriculture and Natural Resources Sector and 33 per cent in the Social Infrastructure Sector are rated 'generally successful' (Bello, 2000). At the ADB's 2001 annual meeting, Western donor countries and shareholders also stepped up pressure on the Bank to refine its development policies, avoid duplication of work and not to waste scarce resources, according to an *Agence France Press* report of 12.5.2001.

12 At a press conference in relation to ADB's second meeting of the GMS Working Group on the Environment in Bangkok in August 1996, Noritada Morita, then Director of the ADB's Programmes Department, defended the resettlement plan by saying 'We need to reduce the population of people in the mountainous areas and bring them back to normal life. They will have to settle in one place' (cit. in *The Nation*: 4.8.1996). Tourism industry representatives have also

expressed the view that poor communities constitute the main obstacle to sustainable development. A recent article on Mekong tourism in PATA's *Asian Hospitality Magazine* claims, for example, 'Due to extreme poverty in many parts of these emerging economies, local people neither understand nor really care about sustainable development. After having been left in the backwaters of the development process, their urge to get rich quick may clash with a long-term approach to the issue, with the destination paying the ultimate price' (PATA, 2001).

13 In accordance with the OECD's and World Bank's policies aimed at halving world poverty by the year 2015, the ADB has in recent years listed the alleviation of poverty as its 'over-arching' goal. In relation to its annual meeting in Honolulu in May 2001, it organized for the first time a seminar entitled 'Tourism and Poverty Reduction in Asia and the Pacific'. Statements by several Bank officials reveal that the ADB's 'new' pro-poor tourism strategy is actually based on the old 'trickle-down' concept; it proceeds on the assumption that tourism growth spurred by private-sector investment will boost job opportunities and the distribution of economic benefits, and will, thus, *eventually* bring about poverty alleviation and sustainable development. For more information on the ADB's pro-poor tourism seminar, see website http://www.adb.org, *New Frontiers*, 'ADB: Tourism as Tool in War Against Poverty', **7**(2), March–April 2001; *Honolulu Advertiser*, 'Poor Benefit Little from Tourism, Critics Contend', 9.5.2001.

14 Cit. in *New Frontiers*, 'GMS Projects set to roll again', **6**(1), January–February 2000.

15 For instance, Grainne Ryder, policy director of the Canadian organization Probe International said in an interview with *The Nation* 'For the ADB, the displacement of people means poverty reduction. The ADB first defines people as poor and as obstacles in their watershed and dam building plans, and so they must be moved; thereafter, jobs can be created as tourist guides, forest guards or even plantation workers' (cit. in *New Frontiers*, 'ADB's undemocratic structure and "poverty reduction" rhetoric exposed', **6**(3), May–June 2000).

16 Cit. in *Honolulu Advertiser*, 'Poor Benefit Little from Tourism, Critics Contend', 9.5.2001. Research conducted in Northern Thailand confirms Sherpa's findings. Canadian anthropologist Jean Michaud observed in Ban Suay, a Hmong community in Chiang Mai village, that by stepping into the tourist business, some villagers had been able to upgrade their financial position dramatically. In total, however, only about 3 per cent of the tourist money remained in the village, the rest went to urban-based tour agencies and outside businessmen such as pick-up drivers or those organizing elephant rides or bamboo-rafting. Michaud also found that 'In most villagers' opinions, from the moment tourism business was perceived to be a more risky one than anticipated, since some of the ingredients of traditional Hmong life inside households were becoming endangered by the increase both in tourist arrivals and further demand ... only those with nothing to lose would in such circumstances keep on' (Michaud, 1993). A study

by myself in a community of Dara-ang ethnic people in Chiang Mai came to very similar conclusions (Pleumarom, 1997/98).

17 The Thai government has been particularly sensitive to international media reports that portray Thailand as a centre of prostitution, drugs and AIDS and often countered such negative descriptions by arguing that the country has attractions other than nightlife to offer. For instance, in relation to a recent government campaign to restore 'social order' in Bangkok, Interior Minister Purachai Plumsombun claimed that foreigners visit Thailand because they want to see 'natural beauty' and do not come for prostitutes or to take drugs. Questioning that Bangkok would soon resume being a sex tourist's paradise. In response, Prime Minister Thaksin harshly criticized *Time* and urged the public not to read magazines whose articles were not 'constructive' to Thailand (*The Nation*, 'PM lashes out at Time', 10.9.2001).

18 Cit. in *Bangkok Post*, 'In Charge of Tapping the Tourists', 29.6.1998.

19 The Royal Forestry Department (RFD) which oversees 'protected areas' has been under constant attack by the Thai media, environmental organizations and academics for its incapability to properly manage ecosystems and natural resources; see, for example, the special issue of the *Thai Development Newsletter* on 'Natural Resource Management and the Poor in Thailand' (No. 24, 1994); *Watershed*, **1**(2) 1995/96, and Hirsch, 1998. According to Piyathip Pipithvanichtham of RFD's National Parks Division, major problems in parks are, for example: unclear boundaries, lack of management plans and guidelines, inadequate staff, lack of resources for research and education and too many development projects. She emphasizes that while the budget system 'allots very little money for conducting research projects of educational programmes within a park, most of the annual budget is for constructing buildings, paving roads, buying vehicles, hiring staff and paying administration costs'. In relation to forest encroachment and conflicts between park officials and local residents, she explains that difficulties are 'compounded by unscrupulous land developers such as resort and golf consortiums and politicians who use the issue to win votes ... With no support from politicians and local authorities, these problems have stymied the RFD's efforts' (Pipitvanichtham, 1997).

20 *New Frontiers*, 'Fight Against Park Encroachers Appears Lost', **6**(4), July–August 2000.

21 In a petition to the Minister of Agriculture and Cooperatives, dated 12 January 1999, forty-one Thai professors in law said: 'As professors of the law, we call on HE the Minister of Agriculture who is the person in charge according to the National Park Act ... to revoke the permission to film the motion picture named The Beach inside Nopparat Thara – Phi Phi Islands National Park as soon as possible and prosecute violators of the National Park Act, so that this case will set a standard and prevent similar events in other national parks, and to show the international community, which is following the news, that Thailand does not value money above righteousness; that

Thailand, Thai people, Thai civil servants and Thai politicians have dignity; that no foreign country or company, however much money it has, cannot buy Thai national parks, Thai righteousness and Thai law.' For more information on 'The Beach' affair, see various issues of *New Frontiers* (1999–2000) and the website of Justice for Maya Bay International Alliance (JUMBIA) at http://www.uq.edu.au/~pgredde.

22 *Asian Wall Street Journal*, 'Ecotourism Bulldozes Ahead', 30.6.2000; *The Nation*, 'National Parks Threatened by Tourist Tide', 14.5.2000; Tim-Team, 2000.

23 Krishna Ghimire of the United Nations Research Institute for Social Development (UNRISD) suggests that most official tourism-cum-conservation efforts in Thailand appear to have been concentrated primarily on 'driving away' local people from protected areas. 'The creation and management of protected areas has produced pro-longed discontent in many locations, although many of the protests have tended to be short-lived and sporadic due to the lack of outside political support ... Consequently, in Thailand today, many weaker social groups find themselves increasingly helpless and at the mercy of the RFD and the bureaucracy in Bangkok' (Ghimire, 1991).

24 *Bangkok Post*, 'Earnings Target Up Bt50 billion', 22.4.2001.

25 *The Nation*, 'A Quick Fix is Not the Answer,' 24.4.2001; *The Nation*, 'Tourism Plan Ignores Threats to the Environment', 25.5.2001.

26 In the face of the unprecedented golf boom in Thailand and other Southeast Asian countries in the early 1990s, the environmental and social impacts of golf courses became a major theme in scientific studies, NGO publications, newspapers and magazines; see, for example, MOSTE, 1993; *Asia Magazine*, 'Rough Justice', 15–17.4.1994; Pleumarom, 1994; GAG'M Updates (1993–1996); *The Economist*, 'Golfonomics: Asia in the Rough', 20.12.1997–2.1.1998.

27 Cit. in *Asia Magazine*, 15–17.4.1994.

28 *The Nation*, 'The Hazards of Golf Course Chemicals', 25.2.1995.

29 *Far Eastern Economic Review*, 'All this, Yours: Thai Developer Plans Controversial Resort in Laos', 16.6.1994; *The Nation*, 'Lao Resort Put to the Green Test', 3.2.1995; *Bangkok Post*, 'Work to Start This Month on $140-million Thai-Lao Resort', 4.4.1995.

30 *The Nation* 'World Bank Report Cast Shadow Over Resort Planned for Laos', 21.7.1995.

31 *Manager Magazine*, 'Eighteen Holes and a Public Protest', October 1994.

32 *The Nation*, 'VN Dabbles with a Huge Water Hazard', 10.2.1995.

33 *Bangkok Post*, 'Daeha Golf Course Exempt from Decree on Rice Fields', 9.5.1995.

34 *New Frontiers*, 'New Clashes Over Daewoo Golf Course', **3**(1), January 1997.

35 *The Business News*, 'Gambling Away Paradise Islands', 29.12.1994–11.1.1995; *The Nation*, 'Cambodia Gets into Swing of Golf Boom', 26.1.1996.

36 *Phnom Penh Post*, 'Locals Ponder the Price of a Game of Golf', 20.10.–2.11.1995.

37 *New Frontiers*, 'Golf Helps Swing Deals', **2**(6), June 1996.

38 *The Irrawaddy*, 'Going for the Green', **5**(4–5), 1997.

39 *New Frontiers*, 'Angkor Wat May Lose World Heritage Status', **1**(6), October 1995.

40 *Cambodia Daily*, 'Laser Spectacle to Beam Angkor to 21st Century, 10–12.11.1995; *Phnom Penh Post*, 'Angkor Secrets to be Lost in a Sound and Light Show Insult', 1–14.12.1995; *New Frontiers*, 'Development Plans for Angkor Wat 'Catastrophic'', **2**(3), March 1996.

41 *Cambodia Daily*, 'Siem Reap Development Zone: MOU Signed with Malaysians', 10–12.11.1995; *The Nation*, 'A Monumental Mistake', 6.3.1996.

42 *Bangkok Post*, 'Sihanouk Questions ANGKOR Wat Plans', 30.1.1996.

43 *New Frontiers*, 'Angkor in Focus', **6**(1), January–February 2000; *New Frontiers*, 'Tourism Industry Gaining Steam', 6 March–April 2000; *The Nation*, 'Open Skies Bring Flocks of Tourists to Cambodia', 13.12.2000.

44 *The Nation*, 'Siem Reap Hotel Boom', 28.3.00.

45 Such concerns were raised, for example, by delegates of a World Tourism Organization Conference in Siem Reap in December 2000. On this occasion, Prime Minister Hun Sen declared: 'The promotion of tourism without due consideration to the culture will lead to the culture being swallowed up by tourism' (cit. in *The Nation*, 'Striking a Balance', 16.12.2000).

46 As for the debate on tourism and human rights in Burma and campaigns against 'Visit Myanmar Year', see, for example, Sutcliffe, 1994, Tim-Team, 1994; NCGUB, 1995; Pilger 1996; Parnwell, 1998; various issues of *New Frontiers*, *Burma Issues* and *The Irrawaddy*; websites of the Free Burma Coalition http://www.freeburma.org and Tourism Concern http://www.tourismconcern.org.uk.

47 In an interview with the Singapore-based satellite network *Asia Business News* in July 1996, Suu Kyi said: 'We would like people to keep away during "Visit Myanmar Year" as a symbol of solidarity with the movement for democracy in Burma' (cit. in *New Frontiers* **2**(8), August 1996). Later, she told reporters: 'Yes, my mind has not changed in any way. Tourists should come back to Burma at a time when it is a democratic society where people are secure – where there is justice, where there is rule of law' (cit. in *Burma News*, Spring 1997).

48 In November 2000, the ILO decided to impose sanctions on Burma for its persistent use of forced labour. In addition, the UN General Assembly adopted a resolution in December 2000, condemning Burma for gross human rights violations, after the UN Human Rights Commission had released a report that deplored such abuses such as 'extra-judicial, summary or arbitrary executions, enforced disappearances, rape, torture, inhuman treatment, mass arrests, forced labour including the use of children, forced relocation and denial of freedom of assembly, association, expression and movement.' In July 2001, the

International Confederation of Free Trade Unions concluded at a conference in Bangkok that contrary to the military government's claims, Burma 'remains the world's biggest forced labour camp'. *The Nation*, 'Report Accuses Burma Government of Indiscriminate Violence', 18.10.2000; *The Nation*, 'UN Accuses Junta of Rights Abuse', 6.12.2000; *The Nation*, 'US and EU Back Tough Stance on Forced Labour', 22.3.2001; *The Nation*, 'Burma Under Scrutiny Again Over Forced Labour', 15.5.2001; *The Nation*, 'Burma Remains "World's Biggest Forced Labour Camp"', 26.7.2001.

49 See, for example, Sutcliffe, 1994; Smith, 1994; *Burma Issues*, 'Tourism Implosion', November 1996; Parnwell, 1998.

50 Sutcliffe, 1994; Burma Peace Foundation, 1995; Pilger, 1996.

51 *New Frontiers*, 'Welcome to Pine Country', 2(12), December 1996;

52 Human Rights Watch, 1994; various articles in *The Irrawaddys* special issue on 'Sex: The Forgotten Commodity', February 2001; *The Nation*, 'All Roads Leads to Misery', 9.4.2001.

53 *New Frontiers*, 'Visit Myanmar Year 1996: Dead on Arrival', 2(10), October 1996; *New Frontiers*, 'Hitting Back at Tourism Boycott Campaigns', 6(5), September–October 2000.

54 *The Nation*, 'Burma Vows One Million Tourists in 2001', 28.10.2000.

55 In relation to ADB's GMS tourism scheme, for example, Wangpattana's comments are thought-provoking: 'The power of the ADB's language of "development" is best illustrated by the fact that its language is often adopted by the very critics that demand "reform" of the Bank's policies and activities.' Conscious of the flak it is taking from public voices for funding controversial mega-projects 'the Bank has cleverly incorporated "poverty reduction" and "socially and environmentally sustainable growth" in the agenda' (Wangpattana, 2000).

56 The structural problems that ushered Thailand into the financial and economic crisis are, for example, analysed in Phongpaichit and Baker, 1998; Bello *et al.*, 1998; Laird, 2000.

57 *New Frontiers*, 'Grim Times for Asian Tourism', 4(1), January–February 1998.

58 An article in *The Economist* (20.12.1997) says: 'Many theories have been put forward to explain why the economic progress of Southeast Asia has so suddenly left the fairway: the forces of globalization; exclusive and unresponsive political systems; a pursuit of growth at the expense of everything else, including the environment and the livelihoods of the poor. The phenomenon of golf unites all these hypotheses . . . Golf courses, with their huge appetite for land and their dependence on ever-rising affluence, were among the most speculative investments. The bubble first burst in Japan, where more than 100 golf courses went bankrupt in the early 1990s and membership fees slumped to a fifth of their peak. In Thailand, three golf courses, once valued at the equivalent of US$200 million, were discreetly on the market in November [1997] for a mere US$18 million.'

59 *The Nation*, 'Bank Mulls Aid to Mekong Countries', 18.4.1999. Out of more than 100 approved projects, only ten of the ADB-financed sub-

regional infrastructure projects were completed or nearing completion by 2001 (PATA, 2001).

60 *New Frontiers*, 'Asian Air Travel Industry Fighting for Survival', **4**(4), July–August 1998.

61 Apart from giving tourism a new boost to bring more foreign exchange to Thailand, the government has also sought to promote other lucrative export products such as timber and prawns. Therefore, it has looked at reversing a logging ban imposed in the late eighties after parts of Thailand suffered devastating floods and mudslides, and there is also the plan to lift a 1998 ban on inland prawn farming, which was put in place after the practice destroyed 800 000 hectares of mangrove forests (Poonyarat, 2001).

62 *New Frontiers*, 'Visit ASEAN Campaign on the Roll', **7**(1), January–February 2001.

63 The original study for the tourism sector component of ADB's Regional Technical Assistance on Subregional Economic Cooperation (RETA 5535) was conducted by the American Lester Clark Tourism Resource Consultants in 1993 and 1994 (ADB, 1994). Later, ADB's Tourism Working Group commissioned a Japanese company, Pacific Consultants International Asia, to draft the Concept Plans for GMS tourism development (AMTA, 1998).

64 In an interview with Satoru Matsumo of the Japanese organization Mekong Watch, Touru Tatara, the Manager of the ADB Programme Department's GMS Unit, admitted the lack of people's participation in ADB's development projects. 'Although participation has been claimed for a long time, the ADB has not really implemented it . . . We should spend more time and commit more resources [to civil society participation]. For example, we should avoid the style, in which we construct a road based on only the consultant's report' (cit. in *Watershed* **5**(3), March–June 2000).

65 Koson Srisang, who was the Executive Secretary of the Ecumenical Coalition on Third World Tourism from 1986 to 1992 in Bangkok, proposed that the search for solutions in Third World tourism should include a discussion of alternatives to tourism. 'We should seek our own development rather than depending on tourism development . . . Where tourism is not yet there, forget about it. In fact, prevent it from coming in. And do something else as a way to develop our country, our communities and our people. Recognize the need for people's self-development. This is what I call an alternative *to* tourism; not alternative tourism' (Srisang, 1991/92).

References

ADB (1994) *Promoting Subregional Cooperation Among Cambodia, the People's Republic of China, Lao People's Democratic Republic, Myanmar, Thailand and Vietnam: Tourism*, Asian Development Bank (Interim Report).

ADB (1996) *Greater Mekong Subregion: Sixth Conference on Subregional Cooperation*, Kunming, Yunnan, People's Republic of China, 28–30 August.

AMTA (1998) *Concept Plans for Tourism Development in the Greater Mekong Sub-region 1999–2018*, Agency for Coordinating Mekong Tourism, Bangkok.

Bello, W. (2000) *ADB 2000: Senior Officials and Internal Documents Paint Institution in Confusion*, Focus on the Global South, Bangkok.

Bello, W., Cunningham, S. and Li Kheng Poh (1998) *A Siamese Tragedy: Development and Disintegration in Modern Thailand*, London/New York/Oakland, CA/Bangkok.

Burma Peace Foundation (1995) 'Forced labour on tourist projects', *Forced Labour in Burma – A Collection of Documents, 1987–1995*, No. 4, New York.

Chandler, N. (1995) 'River of dreams: the Mekong Alliance', *PATA Travel News*, March.

Cohen, E. (1996) *Thai Tourism: Hill Tribes, Islands and Open-Ended Prostitution*, Bangkok.

Economist, The (1997/98) 'Golfonomics: Asia in the Rough', 20 December–2 January.

GAG'M Updates (1993–1996) A documentation series published by the Global Anti-Golf Movement.

Ghimire, K.B. (1991) *Parks and People: Livelihood Issues in National Parks Management in Thailand and Madagaskar*, United Nations Research Institute for Social Development (UNRISD), DP 29, Geneva.

Hall, C.M. (1994) *Tourism and Politics: Policy, Power and Place*, Chichester.

Hirsch, P. (1998) *Seeing Forests for Trees: Environment and Environmentalism in Thailand*, Chiang Mai.

Hirsch, P. and Warren, C. (eds) (1998) *The Politics of Environment in Southeast Asia: Resources and Resistance*, London/New York.

Human Rights Watch (1994) *A Modern Form of Slavery: Trafficking of Burmese Women and Girls into Brothels in Thailand*, Asia Watch Women's Rights Project, New York.

Laird, J. (2000) *Money Politics, Globalization and Crisis: The Case of Thailand*, Bangkok.

Lawrence, N. (2001) 'Nice country – shame about the dictatorship', *The Irrawaddy*, January 2001.

Meyer, W. (1988) *Beyond the Mask: Transdisciplinary Approach of Selected Social Problems Related to the Evolution and Context of International Tourism in Thailand*, Saarbruecken/Fort Lauderdale.

Michaud, J. (1993) *The Social Anchoring of the Trekking Tourist Business in a Hmong Community of Northern Thailand*, Paper presented to the Fifth International Conference on Thai Studies, School of Oriental and African Studies, University of London, 5–10 July 1993.

Mowforth, M. and Munt, I. (1998) *Tourism and Sustainability: New Tourism in the Third World*, London/New York.

MRC (1995) *Preparation of the Mekong Basin Development Plan*, Bangkok Mekong River Commission Secretariat.

NCGUB (1995) 'Position on Visit Myanmar Year – 1996', National Coalition Government of the Union of Burma, Press Release by the exiled Burmese Government, Washington, 25 May.

Parnwell, M.J.G. (1998) 'Tourism, globalization and critical security in Myanmar and Thailand', *Singapore Journal of Tropical Geography* **19**(2).

PATA (2001) 'A river runs through it', Pacific Asia Travel Association, *Asian Hospitality*, 7 September.

Pholpoke, C. (1998) 'The Chiang Mai cable-car project: local controversy over cultural and eco-tourism', Hirsch, P. and Warren, C. (eds) (1998), *The Politics of Environment in Southeast Asia: Resources and Resistance*, London/New York.

Phongpaichit, P. and Baker, C. (1998) *Thailand's Boom and Bust*, Bangkok.

Pilger, J. (1996) 'In a land of fear', *The Guardian – Weekend*, 4 May.

Pipitvanichtham, P. (1997) 'Issues and challenges of ecotourism in the national parks of Thailand', Bornemeier, J., Victor, M. and Durst, P.B. (eds) (1997), *Ecotourism for Conservation and Communty Development*, Proceedings of an International Seminar held in Chiang Mai, Thailand, 28–31 January 1997, Bangkok.

Pleumarom, A. (1994) 'Sport and environment: Thailand's golf boom reviewed', *TEI Quarterly Environment Journal* **2**(4).

Pleumarom, A. (1997/98) 'Trekking tours: walking on the rights of local people', *Watershed* **3**(2).

Pleumarom, A. (1998) *Tourism, Globalization and the Politics of the Environmental Agenda*, Keynote to the 5th Congress of the World Leisure and Recreation Association (WLRA) on 'Leisure in a Globalized Society: Inclusion or Exclusion?', Sao Paolo, Brazil, 26–30 October.

Pleumarom, A. (1999) 'Mekong tourism brings disasters', *The Nation*, 2 February.

Poonyarat, C. (2001) 'Megaplans for tourism bring worries', *International Press Service*, 3 September.

Rajesh, N. (2001) 'A people's agenda for change', *Watershed* **6**(3).

Richter, L. (1995) Political instability and tourism in the Third World, Harrison, D. (ed.), *Tourism in Less Developed Countries*, Chichester/New York/Brisbane/Totonto/Singapore.

Sesser, S. (2000) 'Ecotourism bulldozes ahead', *Asian Wall Street Journal*, 30 June.

Shivakumar, M.S. (1997) *Sub-regional Economic Integration and the Poor: A Critique on the Development Initiatives in the Mekong River Basin*, Phnom Penh.

Smith, M. (1994) *The Impact of Tourism and Burma's Cultural Heritage*, Article 19, The International Centre Against Censorship, London.

Srisang, K. (1991/92) 'An alternative to tourism', *Thai Development Newsletter*, No. 20.

Sutcliffe, S. (1994) 'Burma: The Alternative Guide', Burma Action Group, London.

TDSC (1991/92) Regarding tourism development in Thailand, Thai Development Support Committee, *Thai Development Newsletter*, No. 20.

TEI (1994) 'Tourism, Ecology and Sustainable Development', Thailand Environment Institute. Special Issue of the *TEI Quarterly Environment*

Journal **2**(4).

Teo, P. and Chang, T.C. (1998) 'Critical issues in a critical era: tourism in Southeast Asia', *Singapore Journal of Tropical Geography* **19**(2).

Tim-Team (1994) 'The Forced Tourism Boom in Burma', Tourism Investigation and Monitoring Team, Bangkok.

Tim-Team (2000) *Tourism Projects in Thai National Parks Funded by the World Bank/Overseas Economic Cooperation Fund (OECF) Social Investment Programme*, http://www.twnside.org.sg/title/iye7.htm

Tourism Authority of Thailand (TAT) (1995) *Ecotourism in Thailand*, Papers presented at the ecotourism seminar organized by the TAT in cooperation with the Walden Mills Group in Bangkok, 7–8 December 1995.

Towards Ecological Recovery and Regional Alliance (TERRA) (2000) 'ADB: Development as if Corporations Matter', *Watershed* **5**(3).

UNCTAD (2001) *The Sustainability of International Tourism in Developing Countries*, Paper presented to the OECD Seminar on Tourism Policy and Economic Growth, Berlin, 6–7 March 2001, http://www.oecd.org/dsti/sti/transpor/tourism/news/UNCTAD.pdf

Wall, G. (1997) 'Is ecotourism sustainable?', *Environmental Management* **21**(4).

Wall, G. (1998) Reflections on the state of Asian tourism', *Singapore Journal of Tropical Geography* **19**(2).

Wangpattana, A. (2000) 'Deconstructing the ADB', *Watershed* **5**(3).

Wheeller, B. (1997) *Here We Go, Here We Go, Here We Go Eco*, Centre for Urban and Regional Studies, University of Birmingham.

Towards sustainability: examples from the UK coast

David Johnson

Introduction

The growth of tourism in the UK reflects the expansion of the industry worldwide. At the turn of the twentieth century the UK Government (DCMS, 1999) has calculated that British tourism:

- employs 1.75 million people in 125 000 businesses;
- has accounted for one in six of all new jobs created in the last ten years;
- is worth £53 billion a year; and
- brought 25.5 million overseas visitors to Britain in 1997.

This well-developed tourism economy is heavily dependent on the environment, heritage, culture and the diversity of local landscapes and local communities.

At the Earth Summit in 1992, the UK Government made a commitment to Agenda 21, the global environmental and development 'blueprint'. Whilst there is little explicit reference to tourism within Agenda 21, much is relevant; and local government is perceived to have an important role to play in its delivery. Local authorities were urged to develop and adopt a Local Agenda 21 – a sustainable development strategy at the local level – by 1996. Local Agenda 21 guidance favours establishing partnerships with other sectors including businesses, voluntary organizations and community groups.

A national UK strategy for sustainability (DETR, 1999) advocated inclusive social progress, effective environmental protection, prudent use of natural resources, and high and stable levels of economic development and employment. At the same time, consultation on how the UK might work towards sustainable tourism (as defined by Tourism Concern/WWF, 1992) stressed the positive potential contribution of a sustainable approach, and sought views on key issues associated with meeting the economic and social requirements of people within a framework of resource conservation (DCMS, 1998a). Issues examined included transport, community benefits and management of visitor flows. In terms of planning imperatives, the consultation stated that sustainable tourism should be accessible, particularly to public transport and those cycling or on foot, and it should be based wherever possible on an existing well-located infrastructure.

Key outcomes of this exercise have been the publication of a new UK Tourism Strategy (DCMS, 1999) and Sustainable Tourism Roundtable Guidance for local authorities (IDA, 1999). The former announced the formation of a new national body for tourism with sustainability at the heart of its mission. The latter translated sustainable tourism into six guidelines on the basis that tourism should:

- integrate activity, long term planning and partnership development;
- maintain and develop diversity;
- support local economies;
- use resources sustainably;
- involve local communities, stakeholders and the public; and
- research, share learning and experience.

Monitoring the delivery of sustainable tourism is, however, proving far more elusive than establishing guidelines. Miller (2001), in attempting to develop indicators for sustainable tourism, identified considerable expert disagreement over what constitutes sustainability and its conceptual boundaries.

This chapter focuses on coastal tourism. A series of case studies are presented as being reflective of the range of issues associated with the sustainable development of coastal tourism in the UK. The main contention of the chapter is that sustainable coastal tourism must focus on inherent strengths. For the rural coastline these relate to the physical environment, for the urban coastline a unique heritage. Neither should be compromised by tourist activity.

Coastal tourism

The EU Demonstration Programme on Integrated Coastal Zone Management (ICZM) defined the coastal zone as 'a strip of land and sea of varying width depending on the nature of the environment and management needs. It seldom corresponds to existing administrative or planning units. The natural coastal systems and the areas in which human activities involve the use of coastal resources may therefore extend well beyond the limit of territorial waters and many kilometres inland' (EC, 1997: 6). This is particularly applicable to coastal tourism given that tourists are usually confined to a relatively narrow area, but the infrastructure needed to support their activities including, for example, water and food supplies, transport access and accommodation for service staff, encompasses a much wider region.

ICZM has been defined as 'the process which brings all those involved in the development, management and use of the coast within a framework which facilitates the integration of their interests and responsibilities to achieve common objectives' (DoE, 1996: 1). The framework should highlight and account for the interrelationship between individual issues and the management of the coast as a whole, since decision-making within one locality or one sectoral area is likely to impact upon others. In practice ICZM is still in its infancy and the intensification of use in the marine and coastal environments has become a significant issue only relatively recently. Johnson and Seabrooke (1996) suggested that new approaches and institutional support are needed to manage the marine and coastal environment effectively, efficiently, and above all in a manner which does not permit these environments to become degraded.

To date, relatively little work on marine tourism as a subject area in its own right has been undertaken (Orams, 1999). However, it is well documented that tourism has the potential to have a major impact on coastal areas. French (1997) stated that it is the intensity of tourism in a small unit area that differentiates it from other forms of development. Particularly acute negative environmental impacts are:

- over-exploitation of natural resources to satisfy tourist demand;
- loss of natural habitat and biodiversity as a result of resort development; and
- increased pollution, arising particularly from sewage effluent treatment and disposal problems.

Authors such as Cooper *et al.* (1998) have also highlighted positive and negative sociocultural impacts, such as changes in local culture, congestion and crime, which affect both hosts and guests. These too are very evident on the coast, often changing the cultural heritage of traditional fishing communities, for example.

The 20 000 kilometre UK coastline has a long history of tourism. The physical variety of the UK coast has often determined the type of tourist activity. Tidally dominated coasts are popular for water-based recreation; wave and wind dominated coasts for beach activities; and built up urban coasts have historically engineered sea front environments to 'accommodate' tourist facilities (including piers, beaches protected by sea defences, and mass tourism attractions). Increasingly, however, the UK coastline is being valued for environmental conservation, including many areas of international environmental sensitivity. To date, for example, 100 coastal and marine Special Protection Areas have been classified under the EC Birds Directive (Directive 79/409/EEC (OJ L103, 25.4.79) on the conservation of wild birds) and thirty-five marine Special Areas of Conservation have been identified under the EC Habitats Directive (Directive 92/43/EEC (OJ L206, 22.7.92) on the conservation of natural habitats and wild fauna and flora).

Strategic approaches are required to integrate environmental considerations within coastal tourism policies and plans. Detailed tourism planning is needed to identify issues liable to have an adverse effect on sustainability. This should focus on both physical and socio-economic aspects. Minimizing the negative physical aspects of tourism can be achieved through the development of environmental risk assessments, determination of carrying capacities and identification of sustainabilty indicators. The latter include measurements of destination quality such as ecological impacts, energy efficiency and pollution control. Maximizing the local economic and social benefits of tourism requires support for local economies including sustainable tourism related employment. It should also pay attention to local community involvement, cultural impacts and health issues. Dumashie (1997) suggested that coastal tourism planning should involve the correct definition and balancing of location specific assets and liabilities. Examples, which she cited, are given below:

Assets	Liabilities
Good scuba diving	Sand storms
Brisk sailing	Jellyfish infestations
Good fishing	Strong currents
Attractive moorings	Endemic diseases
Cruising trips	Sea fog
Exotic hinterland	
Historic towns	

Management tools and techniques are also important, including environmental assessment of tourism projects, management plans for destinations, environmental auditing and life-cycle assessment of destinations, visitor surveys, environmental monitoring, and promoting the role of best practice, training and education.

Many sustainable tourism principles are not new. They reflect, for example, values enshrined in the UK Town and Country Planning system. Nevertheless, British coastal tourism decision-makers, and the communities involved, need to re-examine their tourism policies and practices. The following examples provide a 'snapshot' of work in hand.

Examples of sustainable coastal tourism thinking

Urban coastal regeneration – Redcar and Cleveland Borough Council

Many British seaside resorts, established in Victorian times, are suffering from a decaying infrastructure and outdated accommodation provision.

They have been slow to adapt to structural change in holiday trends. Additional reasons for resort decline include improved personal mobility, insensitive architectural designs of the 1960s, lack of investment and environmental degradation. The principal trend is for more British people to take their main annual holiday abroad, using domestic seaside resorts for shorter breaks. Over a period of twenty years market share has declined significantly. Trips taken to the seaside, nights spent at the seaside and money used at the seaside, as recorded by the UK National Tourist Boards, have all continued to decline in the period 1991–1997.

Recognizing the problem, reviews of resort issues by the English Tourist Board and Association of District Councils highlighted the need for a strategic approach, creation of an identifiable marketing image, partnership approaches and improved standards of visitor care.

Redcar and Cleveland Borough Council has been part of an EU-funded pilot study to demonstrate and evaluate the way forward in terms of developing successful resort regeneration action plans. This study comprised two European Network Projects that specifically examined the problems of resorts and the potential for achieving effective revitalization with minimal funding. Lane (1999) summarized the findings of both projects and, in particular, concluded that resorts are a key function and element of the coastal zone. He also concluded that the suggested regeneration action plan methodology parallels the framework suggested for the preparation of Local Agenda 21 Action Plans. Essential elements within a five-year regeneration action plan rolling programme are considered to be:

- establishing a vision, the political will and overall commitment to regenerate;
- research to create a better understanding of visitor needs and tourism infrastructure;
- generation of ideas including those of community groups and organizations and thus identifying the key issues such as zoning of development;
- formulation of policies, specific targetable actions and monitoring programmes; and
- provision of funding including attracting private sector investment.

The advantages of addressing this issue include reducing the potential for transformation and degradation of more natural sections of the coast. A central conclusion of the EU project was that 'existing resort areas provide a tremendous tourist resource and can handle, with minimum impact, substantial numbers of visitors' (Lane, 1999: 4).

The UK Government is currently encouraging resorts to collect relevant baseline data (DCMS, 1998b) and has tasked development agencies with raising the profile of resort regions to maximize chances of EU and other funding applications. The recently published strategy calls for 'imaginative, market led and sustainable regeneration programmes' and favours niche marketing, creating opportunities for all sectors of society, as one solution to reversing this economic decline (DCMS, 1999).

As a result, many UK resorts are now working to establish a new identity and focus, investing in upgraded well-designed modern facilities, and striving to manage visitor flows in order to minimize seasonality. Action orientated plans, based on visitor survey information and involving resort communities, have been adopted. Environmental issues are acknowledged as paramount to resort action planning and the creation of a high quality, vibrant and effectively managed beach area continues to be seen as a key feature.

This example illustrates at least some elements of sustainability. It represents a holistic and integrated coastal tourism management policy, within which attempts are being made to balance the environmental needs of the destination with the investment returns required by the private sector. However, a sustainable vision will not be enough. Public funding is needed to build new attractions, renovate accommodation and improve public transport links. To be sustainable, redevelopment of this kind has to respect the scale, nature and character of each coastal resort, as well as reflecting the importance of the hinterland environment behind the beach. It must also tackle social inequity and deprivation.

Pump priming – the Wales Tourist Board

Wales has a coastline of 1200 kilometres, which includes the only UK coastal national park and a unique coastal heritage. The Wales Tourist Board's (WTB) role is to provide pump-priming finance, ideas and advice for tourism operators. WTB has embraced sustainable tourism in four key aims. These are to:

1. develop and market tourism in suitable ways which bring social and economic benefit to Wales;
2. offer high standards of product, quality and service;
3. support and promote Welsh culture and the Welsh language; and
4. protect and improve the environment, the natural beauty of the country and its buildings.

In this context sustainable tourism has been interpreted as being about developing and marketing local products and produce, minimizing the environmental impacts of local visitor services and encouraging partnerships. Greenow (1999) highlighted the following examples of progressive steps, which illustrate how this is being achieved in Wales.

South Pembrokeshire Partnership for Action with Rural Communities (SPARC) • • •

This rural development initiative has involved the local community in all aspects of tourism development. Thirty-seven villages have been involved working in the region of outstanding natural beauty around the Pembrokeshire Coast National Park. SPARC has facilitated tourism planning based on initial assessments of communities. The result is a tourism programme that reflects shared community vision and therefore fosters local support. Green and heritage holiday packages using local cycle routes, public transport and luggage transfer services have been developed. This links with the efforts of 'greenways', an attempt to integrate an improved environmental transport network, which includes footpaths, cycle routes and an enhanced public transport service. Wales currently has two new National Cycle Routes, which take advantage of traffic-calmed roads and off-road byways. The Landsker Borderlands Trail, for example, is one of several trails successfully promoted to the Dutch, German and UK markets, for which some 60 per cent of incoming travel is by train. Alternative holidays, based on environmental and cultural interpretation, are generating significant income for the local economy. This last point, reducing the leakage of tourism generated spending, is an important element of sustainable tourism. The aim is also to achieve a balance between the needs of the visitor, the destination and the host community.

'Greening your Business' manual

The WTB have produced detailed guidelines for tourism operators, published in Welsh and English in the form of a manual. During 1998 manuals were sold commercially and issued to businesses securing WTB grants. As well as explaining the rationale for environmental action, the manual offers practical ideas for more environmentally friendly working practices whilst maintaining an attractive environment for tourists. Attention is given to:

- energy and water conservation (e.g., low energy light bulbs, insulation, thermostat settings, preference to showers over baths);
- purchasing (e.g., local supplies, organic food, minimum packaging);
- waste and recycling (e.g., materials management, composting, sewage disposal);
- visitor environment (e.g., access to gardens, home grown food, Welsh culture); and
- public transport opportunities.

In this instance encouraging the careful and efficient use of renewable and non-renewable resources and avoiding waste engenders sustainability.

Green Sea Partnership

The Green Sea Partnership is a public and private sector partnership, which includes WTB and the major public utility Dwr Cymru/Welsh Water, to co-ordinate and improve beach facilities and resources. Evidence of improvement in beach and coastal water quality has been the increase, from two in 1995 to thirteen in 1998, in the number of beaches gaining European Blue Flag awards. A Rural Beach Awards category has also been established for small, quiet beaches without recreation infrastructure. The Partnership aims to survey 120 of these smaller beaches annually. Public and private sector partnerships of this type can encourage sustainable tourism, not least by raising awareness of business benefits associated with good environmental practice and through the adoption of 'environmental management tools'. An informed public is more likely to visit and respect beaches demonstrating high environmental standards.

Managing visitor flows – the National Trust

The National Trust for Places of Historic Interest or Outstanding Natural Beauty is the UK's largest voluntary conservation organization, with a membership of 2.2 million and an annual income of over £83 million. Whilst the National Trust is a charity, and thus perhaps not strictly a tourist operator, the organization channels income from visitors into maintaining and enhancing landscapes and local culture. It is also an example of a voluntary organization whose core activity relates to sustainable development.

In 1965 the National Trust launched Enterprise Neptune, a campaign to save the coast both for and from the public, which aimed to:

- acquire unspoilt coastline for permanent preservation and public access;
- alert people to the increasing pressures and threats to the coast; and
- raise funds for the purchase of unspoilt coastline.

Over 35 years this initiative, now renamed the Neptune Coastline Campaign, has been spectacularly successful, raising over £33 million enabling the acquisition and management of 960 (or 1 in 6) kilometres of the coastline of England, Wales and Northern Ireland (Scotland has its own National Trust). This has included a wide diversity of coastal sites with different problems. Among them are a number of extremely popular sites where visitor management strategies and techniques have been implemented to promote sustainable tourism, at the same time respecting and integrating biodiversity conservation objectives. The National Trust encourages people to enjoy their coastal properties whilst at the same time promoting good stewardship. An educational programme entitled the 'Coastal Guardianship Scheme' involves local people with their coastal properties. Three of these coastal 'honey pot' sites are described below.

The Farne Islands

The Farne Islands off the north-east coast of England are home to large colonies of nesting seabirds. Yearly visitor numbers rose from around 3000 in the 1970s to over 50 000 in the mid-1980s, enthused by media wildlife coverage. The National Trust determined to limit visitor numbers and negotiated permits with local boat owners. The result is that now only eight boats have permits. They transport a maximum of 3000 visitors per day to one location for a one-hour visit; walkways are roped and boardwalks prescribed where needed; and nesting birds take little notice of the 'ecotourists'. Over time this approach has worked well, achieving improvements in both habitat conservation and the quality of the visitor experience. Visitors can observe seabirds at close quarters, they understand that their visit is not damaging the environment, and local boat owners benefit. In this case sustainable tourism is clearly about 'demand regulation', but it is also an example of tourist activity respecting the intrinsic value of the coastal environment and not prejudicing its long-term future.

Kynance Cove

The National Trust acquired Kynance Cove in Cornwall in 1935. The beauty spot attracts in excess of 100 000 visitors annually. In 1986 land adjacent to Kynance Cove was acquired. Prior to this the headland had been in private ownership and visitor facilities comprised a number of 'ad hoc' buildings, a large car park and eroding cliff top footpaths. The National Trust has demolished unsightly structures, incorporated a new car park within the landscape, restored and re-routed footpath access. Visitor income now funds environmental conservation.

Studland Bay

Studland Bay, at the western extremity of Poole Harbour in Dorset, is possibly the UK's most popular rural coastal destination, attracting up to 1 250 000 visitors each year. The National Trust owns a six-kilometre stretch of beach together with an immediate hinterland of dunes, marshland and lowland heathland of high nature conservation importance. Facilities, including a visitor centre, car parks and raised boardwalks, have been developed to accommodate large numbers at peak times. The visitor management strategy concentrates visitors in an area with high carrying capacity and protects fragile areas.

Heritage interpretation – Dorset County Council

Much of the county of Dorset's coastline is designated as Heritage Coast and much, including Studland Bay, is owned and managed by the National Trust. The Jurassic Coast Project is a three-year feasibility study that aims to address the fact that 80 per cent of the region's tourism income is derived from 20 per cent of visitors. The coastline, which is highly regarded for its landscapes, rural beaches and pretty villages, attracts large numbers of day visitors but these visits are restricted to a relatively short summer season.

A solution to improving the local standard of living, whilst simultaneously protecting the environment, is based on the region's outstanding geological heritage. The coastline reveals a complete Jurassic sequence from east to west (150 million years of geological history) and incorporates the largest coastal mudflow in Europe. Rapidly eroding cliffs are the source of world famous landforms such as Old Harry Rocks, Durdle Door and Lulworth Cove; spectacular fossils, including recent new dinosaur finds; and evidence of a fossil forest and dinosaur footprints. With the support of European Union funding, Dorset County Council is attempting to use this unique earth science legacy to generate 'out of season' tourist interest, extend visitor stay time and maximize economic benefit to the region. The initiative epitomizes sustainable tourism principles and reflects the dynamic nature of coastal conservation. In the past the conservation ethos has been preservationist. The Jurassic Coast Project will enhance opportunities for visitors to enjoy landscapes, ecology and local character and culture by maximizing the potential of information and communication technology to explain the dynamic nature of coastal processes. Niche tourism will feed on, rather than diminish, local distinctiveness and diversity. In this instance geology provides the linking theme and is the basis for a World Heritage Site bid for this stretch of coastline.

For Dorset County Council an investment in heritage interpretation provides the key to a more sustainable approach. Working papers have highlighted new educational initiatives, an interpretation strategy and a marketing approach. This supports the viewpoint that tourism can be a positive activity with the potential to benefit resident communities, visitors and the destination. It also complements the work of Purbeck Heritage, a partnership of councils, landowners and conservation bodies, together with Purbeck District Council's management plan to promote more sustainable forms of tourism in the region. Tourism planners in Dorset hope that special interest breaks, employing local experts, will benefit accommodation providers at times when tourist numbers are low. Geo-tourism potential (see Hose, 1996 and 1998) can be realized in the 'shoulder' months when coastal scenery is more dramatic and when fossils uncovered by winter storms are more likely to be found. Dorset Tourism Data Project statistics indicate that visitors drive around the coast to a series of short stay places of interest. The Jurassic Coast Project aims to provide these visitors and educational groups with sufficient interest in one place.

A site-specific focus for a more sustainable approach is Portland and the Isle of Purbeck. This 'island', linked to the coastline by a causeway, has been dominated by the quarrying industry and by its role as a strategic military base. Quarrying for Portland stone continues but the Royal Navy is relocating its operation. A Quarry Park, incorporating both working and abandoned quarries, is proposed as a tourist and educational alternative. A combination of unique geographic position, wildlife interest, spectacular views, cultural interest associated with buildings, structures and artefacts (including a sculpture park) made from Portland stone provide a 'one stop shop'. The focus on cultural heritage will create opportunities for local people to share their knowledge and enthusiasm with visitors. Increasing the participation of local people and communities in this way is indicative of an emphasis on social responsibility, another key element of sustainability.

Conclusions

Sustainable tourism acknowledges the fundamental link between long-term planning, conserving the environment, economic gain and profitability from tourism operations, and social equity. Appropriate tourism policy and planning on a holistic and integrated basis is required by all stakeholders. Success is based upon:

- maintaining and improving levels of natural capital stock through accurate and objective assessment of resources;
- controls to observe carrying capacities;
- an adequate investment in resource efficient ancillary services;
- opportunities for all parties to contribute, particularly local involvement;
- raising public understanding and promoting intergenerational equity;
- effective environmental policies, tourism management plans, and equitable economic and employment benefits; and
- long-term monitoring, assessment and feedback.

In a review for Tourism Concern, Leslie and Muir (1996) argued that take up of Local Agenda 21 within local authority tourism strategies in the UK was poorly funded and left significant room for improvement. Like so much of the hype generated by the sustainable development concept, much remains on paper rather than in practice. Since then the UK Government has at least attempted to raise the profile of sustainable tourism but politicians are still searching for easily measurable ways to ensure that tourism practice does not contravene sustainable development principles.

The UK coastline is an example of a natural resource that has been used and abused for many years. The case studies selected suggest that increased voluntary efforts to deliver sustainable tourism are currently being made. In these cases the management of tourist activities has the potential to re-shape the industry. A number of urban coastal resorts, such as Redcar and Cleveland, are planning positive regeneration projects. In hitherto unspoilt rural areas a sustainable approach is being developed on a partnership basis, by government agencies, voluntary organizations and local groups.

However, the case studies chosen also illustrate the absence of a coherent and comprehensive approach to the sustainable management of the UK coastal zone. Local government is leading much of the drive towards sustainable tourism at the coast and sustainability is not yet a mainstream concern for most private sector providers. Consequently, sustainable development ideals and actions have little prominence in the most popular coastal destinations such as Blackpool, Skegness or Newquay.

It could also be argued that the majority of UK tourists themselves give little thought to sustainability. Mass tourism along parts of the southern Spanish coast represents the antithesis of sustainability. However, some

1.5 million UK tourists holiday each year in the Spanish resort of Benidorm on the Costa Blanca, and on the Catalan coast, which includes the Costa Brava. Some environmentalists consider that pollution and over-development, much associated with tourism in these areas, have pushed their coastal ecology to a 'critical point'.

All the examples cited are attempting to combine protection or enhancement of the coastal environment, economic wellbeing of coastal communities, a healthy distinctive local culture, and maximum visitor satisfaction. Nevertheless, it also clear that better networks are needed to both apply the results of research and to promote and share good practice. Sustainability must be fully recognized as part of coastal tourism policy and decision-making, and its success or otherwise needs to be measured, judged and broadcast. Ultimately, in order to realize quantifiable gains, a proactive approach from the tourist industry will be required, along with a more responsible approach by tourists to their interactions with the natural and built environment.

Acknowledgements

The author would like to thank Mike Greenow, Wales Tourist Board; Richard Offen, National Trust; Peter Lane, Redcar and Cleveland Borough Council; and Richard Edmonds, Dorset County Council for providing detailed information on selected case studies.

References

Cooper, C., Fletcher, J., Wanhill, S., Gilbert, D. and Shepherd, R. (1998) *Tourism: Principles and Practice*. Second edition. Longman, Harlow.

DCMS (1998a) *Tourism – Towards Sustainability*. Consultation document. Department for Culture, Media & Sport, London.

DCMS (1998b) Measuring *the Local Impact of Tourism* (A guidance pack for Local Authorities). Department for Culture, Media & Sport, London.

DCMS (1999) *Tomorrow's Tourism – A growth industry for the new Millennium*. Department for Culture, Media & Sport, London.

DETR (1999) *A better quality of life: A strategy for sustainable development for the United Kingdom*. Cm 4345. Department of the Environment, Transport and the Regions, London.

DoE (1996) *Coastal Zone Management – Towards Best Practice*. Department of Environment, London.

Dumashie, D. (1997) The benefits and risks of coastal tourism. *Exclusive Economic Zone Catalogue*, 3rd Edition, pp. 84–9. Combined Service Publications, UK.

EC (1997) *Better management of coastal resources – A European Programme for Integrated Coastal Zone Management*. Official publication of the European Communities, Luxembourg.

French, P.W. (1997) *Coastal and Estuarine Management*. Routledge, London.

Greenow, M. (1999) Practical Balance. The Leisure Manager August 1999, pp. 25–27. *Journal of the Institute of Leisure and Amenity Management, UK.*

Hall, C.M and Page, S.J. (1999) *The Geography of Tourism and Recreation.* Routledge, London.

Hose, T.A. (1996) Geotourism, or can tourists become casual rockhounds? In Bennet, M.R., Doyle, P., Larwood, J.G. and Prosser, C. (eds) *Geology On Your Doorstep.* Geological Society, London, pp. 207–28.

Hose, T.A. (1998) Selling Coastal Geology to Visitors. In Hooke, J. (ed.) *Coastal Defence and Earth Science Conservation.* Geological Society, London, pp. 178–95.

IDA (1999) *Local Agenda 21 Roundtable Guidance: Sustainable Tourism.* Sustainable Development Unit, Improvement and Development Agency, London.

Johnson, D.E. and Seabrooke, W. (1996) Sustainable enjoyment: the need for leisure management at the coast. In Goodhead, T.J. and Johnson, D.E. (eds) *Coastal Recreation Management.* E&FN Spon, London, pp. 23–42.

Lane, P. (1999) *Tourism and Resort Action Plans – Identifying a Methodology.* Fact sheet 99/7, Institute of Leisure and Amenity Management, Reading.

Leslie, D. and Muir, F. (1996) *Local Agenda 21, Local Authorities and Tourism – a UK Perspective.* A report prepared for Tourism Concern by Glasgow Caledonian University.

Miller, G. (2001) The development of indicators for sustainable tourism: results of a Delphi survey of tourism researchers. *Tourism Management* **22**: 351–62.

Orams, M. (1999) *Marine Tourism: Development, Impacts and Management.* Routledge, London.

Tourism Concern/WWF (1992) *Beyond the Green Horizon.* Tourism Concern, London.

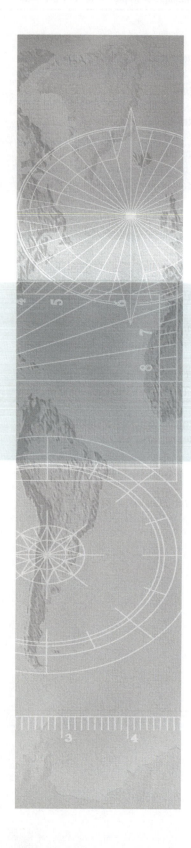

CHAPTER 11

Steps towards sustainability monitoring: the case of the Resort Municipality of Whistler

David Waldron and Peter W. Williams

Introduction

In response to more than a decade of unrestrained growth, British Columbia's tourism industry is under intense scrutiny as regards its impact on the community and environment. As a consequence several of the province's industry and community leaders have begun developing strategies that are designed to focus tourism development in more sustainable directions. A critical component of such strategies involves developing and implementing monitoring processes that provide credible measures of how well tourism is doing in achieving sustainability goals. In this regard, one of the province's most significant tourism destination communities has taken the lead in the development and use of a comprehensive monitoring programme. Over the past six years, the Resort Municipality of Whistler has been systematically monitoring its progress towards its identified growth management goals. This case study examines this monitoring programme with a view to determining its performance against recommended sustainability assessment processes.

The role of indicators

To assess progress towards more sustainable forms of tourism, there is a need for relevant monitoring systems. Ideally, these systems should focus on assessing the extent to which existing best practices in tourism are aligned with, and help to achieve, core sustainability goals. In this regard, sustainability monitoring should be focused on examining progress towards reaching a combination of ecological, social and economic imperatives (Arrow and Bolin, 1995; El Serafy, 1991; Goodland and Daly, 1996; International Council for Local Environmental Initiatives and International Development Research Centre, 1996; Maclaren, 1996a; Robinson and Van Bers, 1996; and Bossel, 1999).

Indicators can be used to measure progress towards sustainability goals, and when tracked over time, can also help identify trends in the condition of a phenomenon that has significance beyond that of the measurement itself (Dilks, 1995). For example, an indicator of transportation modes into a resort area could help to measure progress towards the achievement of non-renewable resource consumption and air-pollution goals. Ideally indicators used for assessing progress in the sustainability area should:

- be selected on the basis of input received from a broad base of stakeholders;
- be designed to meet the varying informational needs of these different audiences;
- include objective measurements (e.g., biophysical measurements such as water quality parameters);
- include subjective measurements (e.g., stakeholder perceptions and attitudes); and
- signal where necessary the need for comprehensive studies of more complex relationships (Maclaren, 1996a).

Developing indicators

Researchers and practitioners have identified several processes for developing sustainability indicators (Campbell and Maclaren, 1995; Fraser Basin Management Program *et al.*, 1995; Dilks, 1995; Maclaren, 1996a, 1996b; Manning, 1999). Many of these processes have commonalties that appear to be applicable in the context of tourism communities. These include visioning, scoping, determining indicator selection criteria, selecting indicators, analyzing and reporting findings, and soliciting feedback.

Visioning

A variety of methods have been suggested for collecting the information needed to create a truly community based vision of an area's sustainability goals. These methods include using a combination of town hall meetings; workshop brainstorming sessions; livingroom focus groups; questionnaire surveys; key informant or expert consultations; open house meetings and displays; and public meeting panel discussions to identify the set of goals to be achieved through tourism development activities (Stettner, 1993; Gill, 1996; Jamal and Getz, 1997).

Scoping

This second step involves establishing the scope of the monitoring programme. By creating an understanding of the role and benefits that a credible monitoring programme can create for existing tourism organizations and other community stakeholder groups, practical decisions need to be made with regard to:

- scope (politically, spatially, temporally); what development issues should be addressed; and
- how to determine what relevant data might be collected and by which methods within a monitoring programme.

By collaborating with tourism operators, local businesses, community and environmental groups (as well as neighbouring communities), and regional and provincial governments, a priority set of issues can be identified for monitoring. A balance must be found between providing an all-encompassing set of indicators and the fiscal realities of collecting, assimilating and interpreting the information (Dilks, 1995). This scoping exercise should address not only the range of issues and indicators to be measured, but also the spatial scale and range of audience to whom the findings of the monitoring programme's activities should be targeted. For instance, depending on the situation, the target audience might range from primarily community decision-makers, to business operators, to provincial government policymakers. All of these stakeholders may play distinct but important roles in influencing the way in which development unfolds in tourism areas. In each of these cases, it may be necessary to establish different levels of indicator reporting sophistication (e.g., range and number of indicators) in order to ensure relevance to each group (Brugman, 1997).

Choosing an indicator framework

Indicator frameworks provide systematic means of structuring the identification and selection of relevant subjects/issues to be monitored. A variety of different frameworks have been developed for application in varying sustainability monitoring contexts. Generally they fall into five broad categories.

Domain-based frameworks • • •

Domain-based frameworks can address a variety of tourism performance issues. These include not only economic performance indicators commonly associated with tourism industry activity, but also critical social and ecological concerns, which often provide the underlying foundation for much of tourism's potential sustainability. Depending on the circumstances, specific domain-based indicators can be selected or accentuated in order to emphasize critical linkages between environment, economy and society (Daly and Cobb, 1994; Maclaren, 1996a; Robinson and Van Bers, 1996). However, domain-based frameworks do not necessarily link indicators directly with specific management goals, thereby reducing their overall utility for monitoring progress towards sustainability.

Goal-based frameworks • • •

Goal-based frameworks focus on identifying indicators that can respond directly to sustainability goals (Manning and Clifford, 1995; Maclaren, 1996a). In a tourism community context, these goals may include such concerns as: achieving specified resident satisfaction levels; maintaining targeted visitor traffic levels; providing a specified supply of affordable employee housing; and protecting a specified amount of sensitive habitat for conservation purposes. Such frameworks are particularly useful in systematically reducing the number of indicators required for monitoring purposes. This makes monitoring and assessment processes more manageable in many cases. The overriding weakness with goal-based frameworks is that the separateness of each indicator reduces opportunities for identifying important inter-relationships between various factors affecting tourism's sustainability. For example, goals such as resident housing and environmental conservation can be pursued in isolation and may ultimately conflict with one another, but would not necessarily be considered within a goal-based indicator framework.

Sectoral frameworks • • •

Sectoral indicator frameworks respond to the needs and structures of existing institutional organizations. Typically, they focus on issues linked to the functions and focus of specific management groups. From a tourism community perspective, sectoral frameworks might describe indicators of existing land use, housing, transportation, recreation, and social infrastructure service conditions. Over time, the indicators measured in such frameworks can be useful in assessing the impact of specific management responses to particular development issues. However, this type of compartmentalized approach to monitoring tends to reduce the range of ecological, economic and social influences on specific issues.

Issue-based frameworks • • •

Issue-based frameworks address specific 'hot' topics such as traffic congestion, resident housing, and wildlife conservation. While valuable in short-term management contexts, these issue-based frameworks often lack the systematic rationale needed to provide a comprehensive perspective on issues having longer-term sustainability implications.

Causal frameworks • • •

Causal frameworks provide indicators that are useful in systematically measuring existing conditions, stresses, and responses related to sustainability issues (Hardi, 1995; Maclaren, 1996b). The strength of these frameworks lies in their ability to determine potential causal relationships between economic, social and environmental factors. Causal frameworks provide indicators that normally address issues concerning what is actually happening (i.e., state or condition indicators); why is it happening (i.e., pressure or stress indicators); and how management is addressing the pressure (i.e., response indicators).

Within causal frameworks, performance can be evaluated by comparing indicator trends with set management goals. For example, in the case of a mountain stream within a tourism community, an indicator of its condition (state) might be the water flow during low tourism visitation periods compared to its flow during peak visitor traffic periods. Per capita water consumption rates (pressure) might be used as an indicator of what current stresses are placed on the stream by visitors. Finally, a set of water conservation practices (response) might be used to assess the extent to which various water restriction targets are feasible under varying management regimes. While a very systematic approach to monitoring, past applications of causal frameworks have typically failed to address the within-domain interactions of essential components and structures within ecosystems (Rennings and Wiggering, 1997).

An integrated pressure–state–response indicator option • • •

Combining the strengths of the previously described indicator frameworks can provide more comprehensive alternatives for sustainability monitoring (Hammond and Adriaanse, 1995; Hardi, 1995). For instance, a domain-based approach combined with a pressure–state–response (PSR) system can offer a valuable integrated approach to systematically assessing tourism's progress towards a variety of interrelated goals (Manning, 1993; Manning and Clifford, 1995). Most importantly, this approach facilitates the integration of policy initiatives across sustainability imperative domains. In essence, this means that the relationship between various management response indicators within one domain can be examined in the context of a state and pressure measure in another domain. For example, an economic response indicator of increased resort promotion can be compared with environmental pressure indicators such as habitat area lost.

Identifying potential indicators

Numerous indicators are available to tourism and community planners. These include lists of 'core indicators' derived from general community and regional planning contexts (Dilks, 1995), as well as those designed specifically for tourism (Manning and Clifford, 1995). Many of these lists can be obtained on the World Wide Web. For example, the Sustainable Communities Network (http://www.sustainable.org) and Hart Environmental Data (http://www.subjectmatters.com/indicators) offer extensive indicator lists. Additional potential indicators can also be developed which respond to unique local sustainability goals. Community visioning may provide guidance concerning what these potential indicators might be.

Selecting indicators

Selecting a final set of key indicators from the long list of measurement options can occur in a number of different ways. For example, practical considerations such as data affordability and availability issues, as well as the perceived relevance to potential users, may help determine the overall appropriateness of specific indicators. Each indicator must be judged according to its appropriateness on a predetermined scale (Gosselin and Belanger, 1993; Long and Perdue, 1994; Dilks, 1995). Since conflicts may arise amongst decision-makers concerning the relative importance of each selection criteria, there may be a need to weight the relative importance of each factor. Once a set of preferred indicators has been identified, a review determining the completeness and balance of the final set can be carried out to ensure that all the major dimensions of sustainability are represented. The final set should be modified as required. The PSR matrix, in particular, is a useful framework for making this final assessment of completeness.

Analysing and reporting progress towards sustainability

After indicator measures have been collected, the findings should be analysed. Ideally this entails not only reporting individual indicator values, but also establishing historical trends in specific indicator values, and identifying progress towards specific sustainability goals. Furthermore, where feasible, cause and effect relationships between pressure, state, and response indicators should be attempted. This analysis phase may prove difficult as different opinions may exist about the meaning of indicator trends relative to sustainability goals. For example, the number of building permits issued in a tourism community may indicate economic prosperity to some, while it may indicate an unacceptably high rate of natural land conversion to those more interested in environmental preservation.

The reporting of the findings emanating from the collection process should be tailored to the target audience. For instance, a brief summary report with key indicators should be appropriate for the general public who may not be concerned with a lot of complex information. In contrast, a more detailed report can be prepared for technical staff. This information can also be made available to interested stakeholder groups upon request. Ideally, these reports should include:

- explanations of the significance of each indicator itself and an explanation of the types of value judgements incorporated into its selection;
- assessments of past trends and anticipated future trends in indicator values relative to established target levels;
- graphical representation of indicator trends; and
- where feasible, a discussion of linkages between indicators.

Soliciting feedback

Soliciting feedback to indicator reports should also be actively pursued. This can be encouraged in a variety of ways. For example, it might be useful to seek feedback via television, radio and print media, as well as public meetings, public surveys and focus groups. All of these techniques can help to refine indicator selection, measurement, and interpretation processes. In any reporting process, an acceptable level of relevant indicator information must be displayed in order to maintain stakeholder interest and at the same time the effort expended must not unduly tax personnel and financial resources of paid and volunteer data collectors in the community (McCool *et al.*, 2001). Responses to requests for indicator refinement by the lead agency must also be evident or the process runs the risk of stakeholder alienation.

The Whistler case study

Tourism development in general, and mountain community tourism in particular, are often characterized by a combination of conflicting demands placed on what are frequently limited and fragile natural resources (Stettner, 1993). Growth management is an approach to planning that seeks to capture the benefits of growth while mitigating its negative consequences. Typically, this involves implementing a range of management strategies including: protecting community sense of place; managing tourism related impacts; identifying community commercial and social priorities; securing stakeholder commitment to specific programme initiatives; and managing tourism demand towards specific community objectives (Gill and Williams, 1994). Such growth management strategies rely heavily on data in the form of indicators to chart progress towards more desirable and sustainable future conditions.

Since 1994, the Resort Municipality of Whistler has undertaken several initiatives to develop and implement a monitoring system that has several sustainability components. Originally enacted in 1976 to encourage compact development and discourage sprawl, Whistler's growth management strategy has expanded to become an integral part of the community's Comprehensive Development Plan and a focus for the municipality's monitoring programme. The growth management strategy addresses issues encountered in many mountain tourism communities (e.g., alpine environmental protection, land use sprawl control, affordable housing provision, community and tourism infrastructure development). In this respect, Whistler's growth management strategy is both innovative and exemplary. However, what distinguishes Whistler's growth management initiative programme from those of other tourism destinations is its monitoring programme. Initiated in 1994, the monitoring programme is intended to communicate information to the community on how the destination has been changing. This monitoring information is also used to encourage community discussion concerning the selection of appropriate strategies for managing future development and growth.

Many of the elements in Whistler's monitoring programme are consistent with the recommended steps for sustainability reporting described previously. The monitoring initiative addresses the influence of various growth pressures on: resident quality of life; natural environment quality; and affordable housing.

Whistler's visioning process

Whistler's Comprehensive Development Plan outlines several general goals that relate to an evolving 'vision' for the resort municipality. The vision is about the values, scope and priorities that should drive management activities in the resort municipality. The formal goals are to:

- enhance the Whistler experience, for those who live in Whistler and for those who visit and use the resort, by balancing the environmental, economic and social needs of the community and the resort;
- continue to move towards environmental sustainability, by fostering and participating in a wide range of environmental partnerships and management initiatives associated with maintaining the high quality of the area's natural and built environments;
- build a stronger resort community, recognizing that this is an important aspect of enhancing the resort; and
- achieve financial sustainability by implementing a range of public and private sector partnerships designed to support the community economy, as well as introducing a range of innovative and cost-effective methods of delivering municipal services (RMOW, 1993; RMOW, 2002).

The community's monitoring programme has been designed to measure change in the community as a result of growth. However, it should be noted that there has been no explicit consideration of the principles of 'sustainability' (except perhaps in an intuitive context related to 'sense of place' criteria) in establishing the appropriateness of the types and level of growth taking place in the community.

Scoping the Whistler monitoring programme

The target audience for the Whistler monitoring programme has been loosely defined as 'community stakeholders'. These stakeholders consist primarily of permanent residents and second homeowners. Stakeholder participation has, on the whole, occurred via annual 'town hall' meetings, community attitude surveys carried out in 1991 and 1995, livingroom focus groups in 1995, and a variety of community visioning processes since 1997 (e.g., community workshops, stakeholder group meetings, workbook surveys). The geographic scope of the monitoring programme was decided by the municipal planning department. It roughly matches the institutional boundaries of the municipality. Little explicit consideration has been given to temporal aspects of the data or indicator trends. Also, no limits have been placed on the amount of data, or number of indicators, reported. Reconsideration is currently being given to the scope of issues addressed by the monitoring programme.

The use of a sectoral/issue-based indicator framework

The data and indicators reported in Whistler's monitoring report have been presented in sectorally based categories related to: development; social characteristics; environment; community facilities and infrastructure; economic benefits; transportation; and resident and visitor satisfaction. This framework was selected by municipal planners in response to the institutional structures that existed at the time of the first monitoring programme. In 1995, the indicator framework was modified to incorporate both sectoral and issue-based indicators. While using the same basic framework, some of its content since then has been modified by the community's municipal planners in response to issues raised by stakeholders in the annual town hall meetings. For example, monitoring information dealing with the state of undeveloped valley lands, natural habitat conditions in protected areas, as well as air and water quality have been added in response to resident requests.

Indicator selection criteria

No explicitly defined criteria were used in selecting the indicators employed in the monitoring programme. However, municipal planning department representatives did use indicators that were: readily available (i.e., existing data or easily measured); displayed historical or trend information; were comparable with existing data and information; and responded to stakeholder issues expressed at town hall meetings.

Indicators selected

The Whistler monitoring programme reports information concerning all the indicators it selects. While no overriding 'key indicators' are highlighted, the most recent monitoring report (RMOW, 2000) includes over eighty indicators organized within a predominantly sectoral framework. Perhaps half of these indicators address some aspect of the concept of sustainability's environmental and economic imperatives.

Monitoring programme reporting

The resort municipality publishes its annual community and resort monitoring report for public distribution and reading. Typically, the report includes measurements associated with all of the selected indicators identified. In addition, an annual bulletin with summary indicator information is published. This document is intended to inform a wide audience and stimulate informed stakeholder debate about growth management issues.

Each year these reports, and an additional display of information, are viewed and discussed at an annual open house and town hall meeting. At the 1996 meeting, for example, formal discussion was encouraged around issues related to the most beneficial types of future land development, key growth management concerns, environmental programme issues, and future monitoring programme refinements. Similarly, in 1997, the focus of the town hall meeting was on seeking input to the municipality's vision statement that was in the initial phases of development at that time (Whistler, 2002). It was expected that this vision statement would eventually drive the focus of future monitoring efforts. Subsequent public meetings (1998–2001) have focused on specific sustainability issues, such as housing, transportation and watershed management.

The perspectives presented at these town hall meetings are considered by the municipal officials and staff when creating new policies and selecting new indicators for subsequent years. For example, transportation and affordable housing issues identified at previous town hall meetings have become municipal programme and monitoring priorities in subsequent years.

Notwithstanding these initiatives, gaining an appropriate level and representation of attendance at these reporting sessions is a continuing challenge. Efforts are under way to solicit feedback from younger people, as well as social and environmental stakeholder groups in the community, in order to create a more inclusive perspective concerning the impact of growth on Whistler.

Assessment of indicator performance

To date, Whistler has not placed a strong emphasis on linking each of its reported indicators to specific community sustainability goals. As a result it is difficult to assess whether or not the indicators have been effective in measuring progress towards these goals. Consequently, the municipality has not conducted a formal assessment of the effectiveness of the data or its indicators. However, there is some informal recognition that there is a need to create a more systematic linkage between the goals and the reported indicators. This recognition has emerged as the monitoring programme has matured, and as the demand for the inclusion of additional performance indicators has expanded.

Conclusions

In many ways, the Whistler Community and Resort Monitoring Programme represents an exemplary initiative. However, its full potential is not being achieved because the focus of the programme has been primarily to monitor various dimensions of growth impact as opposed to measuring progress towards the development of a more sustainable tourism community. As a consequence, there has been no clearly articulated vision, goals or process for the development of sustainability indicators (Table 11.1).

However, the Whistler monitoring programme is still valuable for a number of reasons. First, it was implemented with the clear objective of maximizing the involvement of a broad group of community stakeholders concerned about a wide range of tourism growth issues. In this context, stakeholders were invited to participate in community decision-making associated with such issues as community size, housing options, and environmental management. Second, the monitoring programme has also assembled a considerable amount of valuable information that is important for enlightened discussion by community stakeholders concerned about these and other growth related matters.

Despite the programme's best intent there is a growing sense that much of the monitoring information collected is not generating the type of discussion on pressing and emerging issues that it was intended to create. Possible explanations for this perceived apathy might include the lack of any well-accepted indicators of progress towards the resort community vision or goals, as well as the lack of a resort community vision that reflects the principles and objectives of sustainability. Only in recent times has a comprehensive programme been implemented to develop a vision of Whistler that clearly identifies a set of consensus-based community priorities and directions (Whistler, 2002). The community's local government believes that this visioning process and its subsequent vision statement will help to refocus, refine and improve the community's monitoring programme. In addition, the municipality has been developing a comprehensive Whistler Environmental Strategy (1999 to the present) along with a complementary community-wide sustainability awareness and engagement process called 'Whistler. It's our Nature'. Early observations indicate that these initiatives will stimulate the creation of a more focused monitoring process in the community.

Beyond the need for more explicit sustainability goal-indicator linkages, there are also lessons to be learned with respect to the development

Model sustainability reporting process criteria		Whistler growth management monitoring process
1. Identification of Community Sustainability Goals	Use a multi-method visioning process (e.g., town hall meetings, workshops, focus groups, open houses, surveys) to establish broad-based stakeholder defined sustainability goals.	Used goals established in Comprehensive Development Plan as proxy for community vision; input for CDP goals derived from limited number of open houses, information meetings and public hearings. No distinct focus on sustainability goals were identified.
2. Scoping	Determine target audience Consider spatial and temporal bounds Include institutional partners Establish relevant number of indicators.	Community stakeholders were target audience Spatial boundaries were lands within municipal jurisdiction Number of indicators and institutional partners were not established prior to implementation.
3. Choose Indicator Framework	Select combinational framework which maximizes ability of indicators to assess progress towards sustainability (e.g., PSR matrix/domain).	Used a combination of sectoral/issue-based frameworks Framework evolved in response to departmental organization and issues raised by stakeholders.
4. Define Selection Criteria	Select indicator criteria based on community values and sustainability goals determined through stakeholder involvement.	Formal selection criteria not explicitly defined; informal criteria were related to data availability, affordability and relationship to growth management.
5. Identify Potential Indicators	Use existing listings of indicators as base; use stakeholder input to refine listings to potentially viable sustainability indicators.	Used existing local and regional data which appeared to match best with stakeholder issues.
6. Select Final Indicators	Apply indicator framework and selection criteria to 'long list' and select a final set of indicators.	No formal process was used to select indicator list. No formal attempt was made to refine indicator listings based on sustainability or growth management goals.
7. Analyse Indicator Results	Compare indicator values and trends to specific indicator target levels based on community sustainability goals.	No analysis with the exception of 'bed unit ceiling' and a few other indicators such as air quality was undertaken. Few established targets were used to assess indicator values against goals.
8. Report Indicator Results	Report a relevant number of indicators to the target audience and solicit feedback.	Annual monitoring reports and discussions at town hall meeting were used to present findings and solicit feedback.
9. Assess Indicator Performance	Assess indicator measurement relevance to identifying progress toward established sustainability goals.	No specific goals for most indicators were established; therefore, no assessment of indicator performance was conducted.

Source: Adapted from Campbell and Maclaren, 1995; Maclaren, 1996a, 1996b.

Table 11.1 Comparison of sustainability reporting and Whistler growth management monitoring programme processes

process for assessing tourism monitoring programmes. In particular, emphasis should be placed on:

- involving a broad and inclusive group of stakeholders in the scoping exercise, as well as the selection of relevant indicators tailored to the target audience;
- developing partnerships with other local and regional institutions affected by tourism so as to increase cost efficiency and comprehensiveness in the collection of relevant data;
- using less compartmentalized indicator frameworks (e.g., pressure–state–response) which facilitate the reporting of tourism's growth on various dimensions of ecosystem integrity and natural resource consumption;
- using comprehensive indicator lists developed elsewhere to help guide the selection of relevant indicators which cover critical sustainability issues; and
- reporting the monitored indicator data to community stakeholders via a variety of communication mediums (e.g., monitoring reports, summary bulletins, newspaper articles) prior to and after public meeting presentations and workshops.

Whistler's monitoring programme was designed to disseminate relevant information to community stakeholders and stimulate enlightened discussion on future growth management decisions. However, it has only been partially successful in achieving this goal. Whistler and other resort communities considering the implementation of such programmes can enhance the appropriateness and relevance of their activities by taking a more sustainable community oriented approach to their monitoring programme. When taken together, Whistler's recent efforts, specifically: the generation of a vision statement for the area; the creation of a comprehensive environmental strategy; and the development of a sustainability awareness communication programme, point to the area being in a much better position in the near future to implement a truly focused and effective monitoring programme.

References

Arrow, K. and Bolin, B. (1995) Economic growth, carrying capacity, and the environment, *Ecological Economics* 15, 91–5.

Bossel, H. (1999) *Indicators for Sustainable Development: Theory, Methods, Applications*. Winnipeg, Manitoba, Canada: International Institute for Sustainable Development.

Brugman, J. (1997) Is there a method in our measurement? The use of indicators in local sustainable development planning. *Local Environment* **2**(1), 59–72.

Campbell, M. and Maclaren, V. (1995) *Municipal State of the Environment Reporting in Canada: Current Status and Future Needs*. Ottawa: Environment Canada.

Daly, H.E. and Cobb, J.B. Jr. (1994) *For the Common Good: Redirecting the Economy Toward Community, Environment, and a Sustainable Future.* Boston: Beacon Press.

Dilks, D. (1995) *Workshop Proceedings. Measuring Urban Sustainability: Canadian Indicators Workshop.* Ottawa: Environment Canada.

El Serafy, S. (1991) The environment as capital. In R. Costanza (ed.), Ecological Economics (pp. 168–75). New York: Columbia University Press.

Fraser Basin Management Program, Georgia Basin Initiative/Ministry of Municipal Affairs (1995) *Navigating for Sustainability. A Guide for Local Government Decision Makers.* Vancouver: BC Ministry of Municipal Affairs.

Gill, A. and Williams, P. (1994) Managing growth in mountain tourism communities. *Tourism Management,* **15**(3), 212–20.

Gill, A.M. (1996) Rooms with a view: informal settings for public dialogue. *Society and Natural Resources* **9**, 633–43.

Goodland, R. and Daly, J. (1996) Environmental sustainability: universal and non-negotiable, *Ecological Applications* **6**(4), 1002–17.

Gosselin, P. and Belanger, D. (1993) Indicators for a sustainable society. *Canadian Journal of Public Health* **84**(3), 197–200.

Hammond, A. and Adriaanse, A. (1995) *Environmental Indicators: A Systematic Approach to Measuring and Reporting on Policy Performance in the Context of Sustainable Development.* Washington, DC: World Resources Institute.

Hardi, P. (1995) *Models and Methods of Measuring Sustainable Development Performance.* Winnipeg, Canada: International Institute for Sustainable Development.

International Council for Local Environmental Initiatives and International Development Research Centre (1996) *The Local Agenda 21 Planning Guide.* Toronto, Canada: International Council for Local Environmental Initiatives.

Jamal, T.B. and Getz, D. (1997) 'Visioning' for sustainable tourism development: community-based collaborations, In P.E. Murphy (ed.), *Quality Management in Urban Tourism* (pp. 199–220). New York: John Wiley & Sons.

Long, P.T. and Perdue, R. (1994) Rural resident tourism perceptions and attitudes by community level of tourism. *Journal of Travel Research* **11**(3), 3–9.

Maclaren, V.W. (1996a) *Developing Indicators of Urban Sustainability: A Focus on the Canadian Experience.* Toronto: Intergovernmental Committee on Urban and Regional Research (ICURR).

Maclaren, V. (1996b) Urban sustainability reporting. *Journal of the American Planning Association* **62**(2), 184–202.

Manning, E. (1993) Managing sustainable tourism: indicators for better decisions. In S. Hawkes and P.W. Williams (eds), *The Greening of Tourism: From Principles to Practice.* Vancouver, BC, Centre for Tourism Policy and Research.

Manning, E. (1999) Indicators of tourism sustainability. *Tourism Management* **20**: 179–81.

Manning, E. and Clifford, G. (1995) What tourism managers need to know. A practical guide to the development and use of indicators of sustainable tourism. Unpublished paper. Madrid, Spain: World Tourism Organization.

McCool, S.F., Moissey, R.N. and Nickerson, N.P. (2001) What should tourism sustain? The disconnect with industry perceptions of useful indicators *Journal of Travel Research* **40**(2), 124–31.

Rennings, K. and Wiggering, H. (1997) Steps towards indicators of sustainable development: linking economic and ecological concepts, *Ecological Economics* **20**, 25–36.

RMOW (1993) *Whistler Comprehensive Development Plan*. Whistler: Resort Municipality of Whistler.

RMOW (2002) *Whistler 2002: Charting a Course for the Future*. Whistler: Resort Municipality of Whistler.

Robinson, J. and Van Bers, C. (1996) *Living Within our Means: The Foundations of Sustainability*. Vancouver, BC, The David Suzuki Foundation.

Stettner, A.C. (1993) Community or commodity? Sustainable development in mountain resorts. *Tourism Recreation Research* **18**(1), 3–10.

Farm tourism – its contribution to the economic sustainability of Europe's countryside

Lesley Roberts

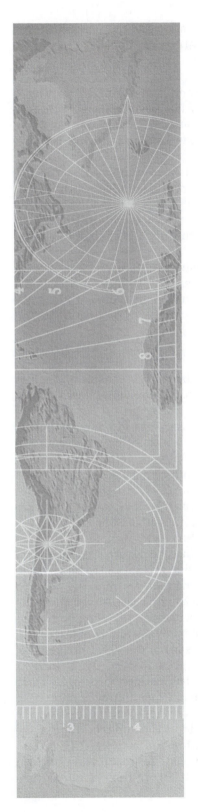

Introduction

Throughout Europe, the second half of the twentieth century witnessed numerous fundamental changes in agriculture. Collectively, a number of influences stimulated change, including:

- agricultural intensification, with farming technologies decreasing some factors of production, notably land and labour, whilst increasing output;
- the relative decline of agriculture's importance to rural economies;
- demographic changes involving a reducing dependency of rural residents on farming activities, ageing populations and counter-urbanization; and

- the emerging importance of leisure, recreation and tourism, transforming traditional spheres of agricultural production into places of countryside consumption (Baldock *et al.*, 2001).

In the interests of sustainable development, these changes required a move from *agricultural* development to *rural* development, with agriculture no longer considered in isolation from wider environmental and social issues. The evolution of the European Union (EU) rural policy is reflected in such an understanding.

This chapter explores the emergence of farm tourism as a coactive economic driver in rural areas. Within the context of the European Union funding framework, it focuses on the county of Devon in the Southwest of England, and investigates the extent to which farm tourism offers a sustainable economic complement to agriculture. The chapter aims to:

1. analyse the development of farm tourism in Europe and the UK;
2. explore the emerging relationship between farming and tourism; and
3. evaluate the significance of a growing interdependence for the economic sustainability of rural areas.

The development of farm tourism

The origin of farm tourism in Europe dates back to the nineteenth century when the only form of accommodation in rural areas was offered mainly by farmhouses. The mountainous rural landscape of the Alps, for example, attracted visitors from within and outside host countries (Taguchi and Iwai, 1998). In the UK, the antidote to unpleasant and unsanitary urban living conditions was to seek refreshment in the countryside, and by the end of the nineteenth century a marked interest in rural visiting was evident (Cherry and Sheail, 1993). Farm tourism was largely a form of 'social tourism', characterized by its low cost as well as the contact it allowed between different cultures (Nilsson, 1998).

In the second half of the twentieth century, with a more widespread availability of private transport, raised income levels, and generally greater amounts of leisure time, tourism grew to be one of the biggest and most significant global industries. Evidence shows that the marked increase in tourism activity of the 1960s was not a short-lived phenomenon (Patmore, 1983). Rural tourism and recreation (including both stays in, and day visits to, the countryside) have matched, and even exceeded, tourism growth generally. In the UK at the start of the 1990s, the value of rural tourism in England was estimated at £8 billion (RDC, 1992). In 2000, this estimate had risen to £12 billion (Sharpley, 2001; Robertson, 2001). To this latter figure may be added £278 million of expenditure resulting from day trips to England's countryside for recreational purposes (English Tourism Council, ETC, 2001). Overall, rural tourism and recreation in the UK is now estimated as a quarter of all tourism activity (ETC, 2001). Recent figures for Scotland (VisitScotland, 2001) estimate rural tourism (excluding recreation) to constitute almost 30 per cent of all tourism activity in the country.

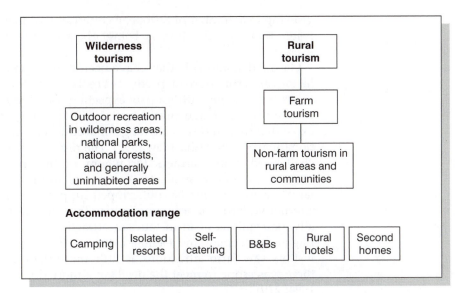

Figure 12.1
Model of non-urban
tourism (Source:
Opperman, 1997)

Farm tourism and rural tourism are not synonymous, yet difficulties in defining both terms render simple distinction complex. In an attempt to clarify distinctions between rural, other non-urban, and farm tourism, Opperman (1997) proposed a model of non-urban tourism (see Figure 12.1).

In defining farm tourism as a sub-sector of rural tourism, Opperman's distinction accords with that of Dernoi (1991) and Clarke (1999), with human activity, primarily agriculture, forming part of the experience. It is not necessary for tourists to participate in the work of the farm for the agricultural working environment to be a tourist attraction. Its contribution to the farm tourism experience may be as passive as appreciation of agrarian life (Clarke, 1999). The extension of farm tourism to attractions as well as accommodation can blur the distinction between farm and rural tourism (Roberts and Hall, 2001: 150). Traditionally, however, rural tourism is accepted to be a multi-faceted activity that has a range of different forms (Lane, 1994). Farm tourism, more specifically, refers to rural tourism conducted on working farms where the farming environment forms part of the product from the perspective of the consumer. In this sense it is a discrete form of rural tourism (Clarke, 1999).

The more recent development (in the latter part of the twentieth century) of farm tourism in Europe has been influenced by both supply and demand factors. On the supply side, agricultural production quotas, reduced commodity prices, extensification (low stocking densities), and set-aside (land taken out of agricultural crop production) have resulted in a reduction in farm revenues and the need for farm households to establish alternative means of income either on or beyond farm holdings for the long term (RDC, 1993). The changing emphases of European policies and funding mechanisms require farmers to review their roles as food producers and expand them to that of custodians of the countryside. Sectoral positions are no longer tenable. Integration across sectors is growing in a number of European countries (Baldock *et al.*, 2001) with the result that consideration is being given to alternative rural resource uses.

On the demand side there have been two fundamental changes in the historical farm tourism product. Firstly, farm tourism has undergone structural change with tourists expecting a high quality of accommodation and service (Taguchi and Iwai, 1998). Secondly, farm attractions have expanded to include a wide range of products in addition to accommodation (Sharpley and Sharpley, 1997). The resulting need for investment has challenged many farmers for whom profits from both farming and tourism have been small. In Austria, for example, demand for quality farm accommodation has outstripped supply, and visitors have turned to alternative forms of accommodation (Taguchi and Iwai, 1998). Additionally, perceptions of farm tourism attractions are changing. Research in England (Denman and Denman, 1990, 1993) suggested that many rural visitors saw farm attractions as little more than 'cuddly zoos' and that there was scope to meet the needs of a more diverse audience (Denman, 1994: 219).

Given the need for farms to broaden their economic bases and the availability of public funds to assist them in the process, there may be concern that, in the absence of an understanding of demand, supply-side influences will dominate development. This may result in an inefficient application of resources and/or over-supply of services. Is there a demand for farm tourism accommodation and attractions? Does farm tourism exist as a separate phenomenon from rural tourism? Do farms simply offer what visitors view as rural tourism products? Existing data may provide some indication of the fact that farm tourism does appear to be a discrete 'product'. A report commissioned by Southwest Tourism in the UK identified that consumers clearly recognize a farm holiday as something different: 'Importantly, they do not think about staying on a farm simply as a convenient form of accommodation in the countryside' (ADAS, *The Farm Tourism Market*, 2000, unpublished). If customer loyalty may be taken as an indicator of, and satisfaction with, a farm tourism product then research suggests that farm tourism is a discrete product. In her study of the Farm Holiday Bureau, Clarke (1999) identified three levels of customer loyalty to farm tourism: (1) 'traditional' loyalty reflects rebooking of the same farm accommodation (twenty per cent of farm-loyal customers fall into this category); (2) 'variety-seeking' loyals book different farm accommodation but within the same region; and (3) 'generic product repeat booking' represents 30 per cent of repeat buyers (see Clarke in Roberts and Hall, 2001: 211). Therefore, as farm tourism exists as an economic reality, its relationship with the farm and its contribution to the sustainability of farm businesses need to be explored.

The relationship between tourism and farming

There is widespread recognition of the social and economic roles of farm tourism (see Clarke, 1999). It supports both farm families and, more widely, rural communities; it helps diversify the economic base; maintains local employment; provides an incentive for custodianship; and establishes meaningful links between rural and urban residents (Denman, 1994). Farm tourism has been primarily developed because of the economic benefits it brings to restructuring farms. It is now considered to represent a symbiotic relationship for areas where neither farming nor tourism could be independently justified (see Busby and Rendle, 2000).

In the UK, the 2001 outbreak of foot and mouth disease raised the profile of farm tourism, and of rural tourism in general, and the slow shift of EU and government emphasis from agricultural policy to rural development policy is being accelerated. Annually, all tourism in the UK accounts for 4 per cent of GDP, approximately four times as much as farming, and it employs 7 per cent of the workforce compared with 1.5 per cent now employed in agriculture (Sharpley, 2001; Lawrence, 2001). Competent data does not exist to enable an evaluation of the economic value of farm tourism; however, visits to farms constitute 4 per cent of visits to attractions in the UK (ETC, 2001), and data at local levels suggests that tourism income is now vital in enabling families to continue farming (Denman, 1994; Southwest Tourism, 2001). In addition to its value in maintaining the social fabric of farming communities, therefore, farm tourism has an increasingly recognized economic function.

The policy environment

The current EU approach to rural policy has its roots in the European Commission's 1988 policy document entitled *The Future of Rural Society*, which has influenced more recent policies by combining Common Agricultural Policy (CAP) issues with those addressed by Structural Funds. Structural Funds exist to help European areas experiencing difficulties. Traditionally divided into Objective Areas, funds are targeted at, for example, areas whose development is: lagging behind an average (Objective 1), or areas facing particular structural difficulties (Objective 2). Many rural areas of Europe qualify for Objective 2 status because rural decline is resulting in above-average levels of unemployment. Together with community initiatives such as the LEADER (*Liaisons Entre Actions pour la Developpement des Economies Rurales,* an EU rural community initiative characterized by its emphasis on grassroots development) programme and the more recent Agenda 2000 reforms of the CAP, Structural Funds aim to guide progression towards rural development that meets the demands of Europe's changing countryside.

The need for reform of the CAP has been argued for more than a decade at transnational, European, and national levels. The World Trade Organization does not favour the CAP as it stands (WWF, 2001). As set out in the Cork Declaration, European commissioners are seeking to move the CAP further towards a holistic approach by redirecting agricultural funds to a wider range of rural development spending (Baldock *et al.,* 2001). National administrations are already jointly funding a range of rural development measures. In England, the Rural

Development Programme (ERDP) has been established to oversee funding of Objective 2 Areas. As pressure mounts to develop policies that give greater recognition to the countryside's multidimensionality, programmes such as ERDP measures, including a Rural Enterprise Scheme (RES), fund 'basic services for the rural economy and population' including the renovation and development of villages and conservation of the rural heritage, and tourist and craft activities (DEFRA, 2001).

However, the ways in which such policies may be developed in practice depend upon the values placed on the broad range of rural activities. Agriculture may represent a diminishing proportion of the UK's GDP but it is still the major contender for land use in the countryside. Whilst its centrality to rural policy-making may decline, it can still be expected to be of considerable influence in new policy measures. For example, the extent to which non-commodity farm outputs are jointly produced with agricultural goods provides one focus for a policy alignment (OECD, 2001). 'Jointness' exists if the production of two or more goods is interlinked in such a way that a change in the supply of one also affects the supply of the other. Provision of the non-commodity output (landscape, for example) may only be possible if carried out in conjunction with the production of the agricultural commodity (crops or livestock). There are then said to be economies of scope (OECD, 2001). Although not included in the OECD analysis, farm tourism would appear to represent an example of 'jointness' with agricultural production because of farming's centrality to the visitor experience. The question of 'jointness' or interdependence appears to be critical for the future policy importance of farm tourism, and thus its contribution to the economic and social sustainability of rural areas.

Case study – farm tourism in England's Southwest counties

The rural counties of Devon, Cornwall and Somerset comprise the southwest areas of England (see Figure 12.2). Farmhouses form 12 per cent of the region's tourist accommodation stock, while self-catering on-farm accommodation makes up 23 per cent of the self-catering supply in the region (Southwest Tourism, 2001). As is characteristic of farms in the region, most farm tourism establishments are relatively smallscale, almost two thirds having fewer than six bed spaces. In the early 1990s, 23 per cent of farms provided some form of tourism enterprise (Denman, 1994). Falls in the supply of serviced farmhouse accommodation have been noted in the last 10 years with comparative research data suggesting that these were predominantly lower quality establishments (Southwest Tourism, 2001). Currently, although no farm tourism units offer accommodation in the highest quality categories (4 and 5 'crowns'), around 65 per cent have two or three 'crowns' (indicating a reasonably high standard of accommodation) compared with only 50 per cent of general bed and breakfast establishments in the region. Average tariffs are rising, especially for accommodation in peak season where there appears to be a premium for quality farm-based self-catering over and above non-farm

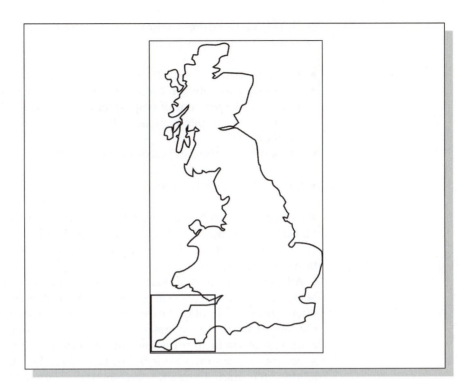

Figure 12.2
Locating England's
Southwest country

accommodation. The range of facilities available reflects the greater availability of space; most commonly provided are pony-trekking, games rooms and play areas, stabling and fishing. Prior to changes in the Structural Funds framework and eligibility criteria, the Southwest had been an EU Objective 5b region, eligible for funds as a result of agricultural decline. However, Structural Funds reform in 1999 merged Objectives 2 and 5b to support areas facing the need for economic diversification. Some parts of the Southwest, no longer eligible for such funding (because rural unemployment no longer falls beneath the EU thresholds), are currently benefiting from transitional arrangements, but rural enterprises must seek future funding through the Rural Enterprise Scheme administered by regional development agencies. However, businesses in Cornwall, for instance, have become eligible for Objective 1 funding.

Farm tourism partnership

Clarke (1998, 1999) has pointed out the lack of investment in marketing by rural tourism operators generally, and farm tourism operators in particular. She emphasizes the benefits to individual providers of moving beyond stand-alone marketing, towards collaborative marketing at both local and national levels. In 1996, a group of farmers in the Southwest region, operating under the banner of 'Farm Tourism 2000', formed a co-operative to address what they saw as the growing problems of the region's farm tourism industry. These were identified as being:

- a rapidly growing supply with insufficient regard to markets;
- an inability to convert latent into effective demand – research showed that while 45 per cent of respondents expressed a desire to take a farm holiday, only 5 per cent actually did so (Denman, 1994; Southwest Tourism, 2001);
- a lack of marketing information for both farmers and potential visitors; and
- the need for collaboration.

Three years on, in November 1999, following extensive research into the market, the group launched its farm tourism brand *"Cartwheel"* (Figure 12.3), the first of its kind in the country. *Cartwheel* is an independent, farmer-led company.

All *Cartwheel* accommodation is inspected, with the safety of visitors being a high priority. Where food is offered, it is locally grown, and often organic. Member farms offer a range of experiences. Some offer the opportunity for contact with animals, others for exploring the countryside via farm trails and interpretation centres. Some simply offer a natural environment for relaxation. Member farms pay an initial joining fee and thereafter an annual membership fee that varies according to business size and advertising space required in promotional materials. In return for their fees, businesses receive market information, advertising in a brochure and on the website, training (for example in IT skills) photographic services, and web-page design,

Figure 12.3
The *Cartwheel* logo (reproduced with permission from Cartwheel)

membership of the network, access to other providers, and encouragement to work collaboratively to increase the critical mass of activities and accommodation in the region. Clarke (1999) illustrates the importance of both the value of a broader understanding of marketing by individual small businesses and the collaborative nature of marketing decisions and actions. Recognition of both is reflected in the membership of *Cartwheel*, which has grown in two years to over 200 farms, about 5 per cent of all farm attractions in the region, and includes visitor attractions, camping and caravan sites, restaurants, and shops as well as accommodation. The EU Structural Funds reform complicates the organization's future. *Cartwheel* is eligible for funding because of its roles in strengthening farm diversification and rural integration, but must now seek Objective 2 funding through the ERDP programme.

'Damage Barton' – the story of a member farm

Damage Barton Farm is owned by one of *Cartwheel's* founding members. The farm comprises 500 acres on the coast of North Devon (see Figure 12.1), and is a stock-rearing beef and sheep farm. Primarily a grass pasture farm, some rough grazing of gorse and bracken typifies the coastal strip. Half of the land is National Trust tenanted and the remainder is owned by the operating family. The farm grows 35 acres of cereals for its own consumption, almost enough to provide all of the farm's straw needs, and the basis of its cereal feed. Twenty acres of swedes are used for fattening lambs. The farm produces 600 tons of silage and some hay. Damage Barton manages its coastal land strip according to management prescriptions of the EU Countryside Stewardship Scheme and uses funds to repair banks, put fencing and walls in place, and replant hedges.

The owners, a husband and wife team, bought Damage Barton in 1962 and were first generation farmers. When they bought the farm nearly 40 years ago, it already had a tourism component in the form of a field used by the Caravan Club and the Caravan and Camping Club. Access to the land was the only service provided, and the arrival of two caravans was cause for excitement. Little attention was paid to the tourism business in early years because of the investment required by the agricultural side of the business, then the mainstay of the farm. Today, 155 pitches (hired parking spaces for touring caravans) are provided for members of the two clubs. Over 30 per cent of custom comes from repeat bookings. Each pitch is serviced with electricity. There are two washing and toilet blocks with amenities including hot showers, washing machines and dryers, open 24 hours a day. There is also a small visitor centre. In order to achieve this level of growth and service improvement, the owners have had to reinvest farming income into the tourism business. Initially this was done in anticipation rather than expectation of demand, but a staged development programme through the late 1980s and 1990s, necessitated by the limited availability of investment funds, enabled the farm to respond gradually to market growth without the need to use external capital. Falling agricultural income necessitated the renewed interest in diversification in tourism. Margins on stock rearing had always been fairly small and, as production support fell, so too did farm income. Recreational access offered an alternative commercial land use.

By 2001, Damage Barton was a trading partnership shared between two generations, the owners' son and daughter-in-law now also being partners, and continuity of management and ownership is thus ensured. The tourism enterprise is considered to be an integral part of the farm business. Indeed, since 1996, it has provided the greater part of the farm's income thus rendering the two businesses interdependent. Without the attraction of the farm, many visitors would not come. Without the tourism enterprise, the farm could not continue to trade. Neither business is sufficient to support the family on its own. Could Damage Barton expand its tourism enterprise further? The owners believe there is evidence of demand to support such expansion, but it would mean the employment of a number of new staff, which, they believe, would change the nature of the business. Farm tourism is an intensely personal business (Nilsson, 1998), much of which is repeat, and the owners feel that personal contact with the host farmers is one of the business's main attractions for visitors. A key feature of farm tourism is the opportunity it provides for cultural exchange through personal contact. Not only does this present urban visitors with an opportunity to learn about farming practices, it also helps to reduce the isolation of many farming families. At Damage Barton, in recognition of the importance of personal interaction with guests, the family welcomes all visitors personally. Visitors are involved with, and notified of, daily farming activities by way of notes recorded on a blackboard in the visitor centre which provides a means of farm interpretation.

The owners' choice has been to maintain the size of the tourism element and retain the business as a family one. Nevertheless, Damage Barton is increasing its tourist appeal. One of the senior partners, now in semi-retirement, is developing a valley walk on farmland, by creating a wildflower and woodland area, incorporating a footpath of about 750 metres leading to the sea. Under present funding arrangements, no financial assistance is available for such schemes. New rural development measures may well fund initiatives like these where the existence of a trail supports conservation and adds to a farm's tourism capital. It is interesting to note, however, that although tourism provides the greater portion of farm income, the owners strongly associate themselves with farming rather than with tourism. Although they recognize the pleasures and benefits of the tourism business, they want it primarily to allow them to continue to farm.

Foot and mouth disease – an agricultural or a rural crisis?

Throughout the UK, the symbiotic relationship between farming and farm tourism was put to the test by the recent outbreak of foot and mouth disease. Some farms and much farmland were closed to visitors as farmers and the government worked to contain the spread of the disease.

Government departments, local authorities, and other public sector bodies found that they were working in a policy vacuum with regard to rural tourism. Advice and guidance were thus both patchy and confusing, and the mixed messages received by the general public had the effect of reducing rural visiting almost completely for some weeks (and in places, some months). In fact, in the Southwest region, although access to farmland was restricted, and farm visitors were required to follow rigorous disinfection procedures, 80 per cent of farms were still technically 'open'. North Devon, however, was one of the centres of the disease, and public perception, shaped by media coverage, resulted in a 65 per cent downturn in business, characterized by cancellations and a lack of forward bookings. Attractions fared worse than accommodation, many experiencing no visitations at all. Being within an infected area, the site at Damage Barton was closed from normal opening in mid-March 2001 until Easter 2001, and until late May it experienced a 64 per cent fall in tourism business. The hegemony of agriculture in rural space was maintained. Politicians, it seems, were unprepared for the effects that countryside 'closure' would have on rural communities. Despite the theoretical rhetoric, therefore, practice revealed a continued lack of understanding that, although rural landscapes are still dominated by agriculture, economies are not. As a result, an agricultural crisis became a rural one and farm tourism was unable to support farming in the manner of a diversified business.

Conclusions

As this chapter has highlighted, future changes in the CAP that reduce financial support for agricultural production are widely anticipated. As a result, Europe's farmers expect to undergo one of the most decisive reductions in focused agricultural support for 40 years (Potter, 1999). The implications for rural land use are profound and alternatives to agriculture will continue to be developed by farmers who will be paid, instead, for sound environmental management and the provision of a range of diversified services.

In order to contribute to the sustainability of rural areas, farm tourism should represent a sustainable product. Questions of rural tourism's overall sustainability have been frequently raised (Bouquet and Winter, 1987; Bramwell and Lane, 1994; Sharpley and Sharpley, 1997; Butler *et al.*, 1998; Roberts and Hall, 2001) and it is not the purpose of this chapter to recount the various debates. More specifically, Denman (1994) selects a number of criteria identified for 'sustainable tourism' against which he evaluates farm tourism as a sustainable 'industry'. However, in order to contribute more widely to the economic sustainability of rural areas, farm tourism enterprises must recognize the benefits of collaboration. Farm tourism consists of a large number of small, independent providers, and its diversity, dispersion and fragmentation render efficiencies of scope through co-operation difficult if not impossible (Roberts and Hall, 2001: 204). Better use of marketing processes may also help to create more economically sustainable forms of provision by reducing provider isolation (Clarke, 1999). The nature of family-owned firms, predominating in farm tourism, often results in an under-optimization of resources and low returns on capital. Damage Barton's decision to resist expansion in order to remain a family business is a good example of this in practice.

This chapter has illustrated the extent to which farm tourism businesses are becoming embedded within rural economies. In this respect, practice is running ahead of principle. Agricultural policy should no longer be considered in isolation from wider policy concerns, and the failure to address this issue has been one of the most serious problems for rural policy in Europe to date (Baldock *et al.*, 2001). Despite the earlier assertion that it is difficult to distinguish between rural and farm tourism, the case study supports the view that it is the symbiosis of farm tourism and agricultural production that distinguishes farm tourism from other forms of rural tourism (Nilsson, 1998). The jointness of production that links commodity and non-commodity outputs in the creation of a range of farm tourism goods and services is a key concept, and renders farm tourism an appropriate target for policy and public sector support in the future. Recognition of this favours *farm* development rather than *agricultural* development as a more sustainable approach for such businesses.

However, in arguing for farm tourism's place in the rural policy agenda, it is critical to note that a redirection of EU subsidies from agricultural production to other forms of farm activity may not be economically sustainable. It has been argued that much agri-environmental expenditure, for example, is not strictly for environmental purposes, and is little more than disguised income support for farmers (Potter, 1998: 103). It is important, therefore, that the shift from agricultural to rural policy results in an associated development shift. A transfer of subsidy of itself does little to improve the economic sustainability of rural areas unless the subsidies are permanent features. Through the General Agreement on Tariffs and Trade (GATT), however, there will be pressure for their eventual elimination (Potter, 1998: 103). The achievement of sustainable development requires the creation of well-functioning markets that maximize welfare via an efficient allocation of resources. Thus, to contribute meaningfully to economic sustainability, the supply of farm tourism must respond to demand. Subsidies should therefore focus on processes of development as well as outcomes in order to achieve this. Undoubtedly, to support such a development process, a greater understanding of the farm tourism sector is required.

References

Baldock, D., Dwyer, J., Lowe, P., Eriksen, J.-E. and Ward, N. (2001) The Nature of Rural Development: Towards a Sustainable Integrated Rural Policy in Europe. A scoping study for the World Wildlife Fund European Policy Office. http://panda.org/resources/programmes/epo/publications/agpub/cfm.

Bouquet, M. and Winter, M. (eds) (1987) *Who from their Labours Rest: Conflict and Practice in Rural Tourism*. Gower, Aldershot, UK.

Bramwell, B. and Lane, B. (1994) *Rural Tourism and Sustainable Rural Development*. Channel View Publications, Bristol, UK.

Busby, G. and Rendle, S. (2000) The Transition from Tourism on Farms to Farm Tourism. *Tourism Management* **21**, 635–42.

Butler, R., Hall, C.M. and Jenkins, J.M. (1998) Introduction. In Butler, R., Hall, C.M. and Jenkins, J.M. (eds) *Tourism and Recreation in Rural Areas*. John Wiley and Sons, Chichester, UK, pp. 3–16.

Cherry, G. and Sheail, J. (1993) *The Urban Impact on the Countryside*. Cambridge University Press, Cambridge.

Clarke, J. (1998) Marketing Rural Tourism: problems, practice and branding in the context of sustainability. In Hall, D. and O'Hanlon, L. (eds) *Rural Tourism Management: Sustainable Options*. The Scottish Agricultural College, Auchincruive, pp. 130–46.

Clarke, J. (1999) Marketing structures for farm tourism: beyond the individual provider of rural tourism. *Journal of Sustainable Tourism* **7**(1), 26–47.

DEFRA (2001) *EU Structural Funds: Objective 2*. Department for Environment, Food and Rural Affairs, London.

Denman, R. (1994) Green Tourism and Farming. In Fladmark, J.M. (ed.) *Cultural Tourism*. Donhead Publishing, London.

Denman, R. and Denman, J. (1990) *A study of Farm Tourism in the West Country*. West Country Tourist Board.

Denman, R. and Denman, J. (1993) *The Farm Tourism Market*. Report for the English Tourist Board.

Dernoi, L. (1991) About Rural and Farm Tourism. *Tourism Recreation Research* **16**(1), 3–6.

ETC (2001) *Working for the Countryside. A Strategy for Rural Tourism in England 2001–2005*. English Tourism Council.

Lane, B. (1994) What is rural tourism? *Journal of Sustainable Tourism* **2**(1/2), 7–21.

Lawrence, F. (2001) Green Unpleasant Land: Reports of the costs of the foot and mouth outbreak have concentrated on agriculture, but the tourist industry faces devastating losses. *The Guardian*, 19 March, London.

Nilsson, P.A. (1998) Stay on a farm – a study of the ideological background to farm tourism. In Hall, D. and O'Hanlon, L. (eds) *Rural Tourism Management: Sustainable Options*. The Scottish Agricultural College, Auchincruive, pp. 374–90.

OECD (2001) *Multifunctionality: Towards an Analytical Framework*. OECD, Paris.

Opperman, M. (1997) Rural tourism in Germany; farm and rural tourism operators. In Page, S. and Getz, D. (eds) *The Business of Rural Tourism, International Perspectives*. International Thomson Business Press, London, pp. 108–19.

Patmore, J.A. (1983) *Recreation and Resources: Leisure Patterns and Leisure Places*. Blackwell, Oxford.

Potter, C. (1998) Conserving Nature: agri-environmental policy, development and change. In Ilbery, B. (ed.) *The Geography of Rural Change*. Addison Wesley Longman, London, pp. 85–105.

Potter, C. (1999) Defining the rural policy context. In Grenville, J. (ed.) *Managing the Historic Rural landscape*, Routledge, London, pp. 10–17.

RDC (1992) *Tourism in the Countryside*. Rural Development Commission, London.

RDC (1993) *European Experience of Rural Development*. Rural Development Commission, London.

Roberts, L. and Hall, D. (2001) *Rural Tourism and Recreation. Principles to Practice*. CAB International, Wallingford, UK.

Robertson, V. (2001) Tips on Cultivating a Crop of Tourists. *The Glasgow Herald*, Glasgow, 9 April.

Sharpley, R. (2001) Rural Tourism and Sustainable Development: a governance perspective. In Mitchell, M. and Kirkpatrick, I. (eds) *New Directions in Managing Rural Tourism and Leisure: Local Impacts, Global Trends*. The Scottish Agricultural College, Auchincruive.

Sharpley, R. and Sharpley, J. (1997) *Rural Tourism. An Introduction.* International Thomson Business Press, London.

Southwest Tourism (2001) *The Farm Tourism Industry in the West Country – A Summary Report*. http://www/southwesttourism.co.uk/rnd/farmtour.htm

Taguchi, K. and Iwai, Y. (1998) Agri-tourism in Austria and its implications for Japanese rural tourism. In Hall, D. and O'Hanlon, L. (eds) *Rural Tourism Management: Sustainable Options*. The Scottish Agricultural College, Auchincruive, pp. 527–38.

VisitScotland (2001) *Tourism in Scotland*, forthcoming statistics, Scottish Tourist Board, Edinburgh.

Worldwide Fund for Nature (2001) *Conserving Nature while Farming*. www.panda.org/resources/programmes/epo/ag_r_dev/agrimission.cfm

Part 4

Tourism Enterprises and Attractions

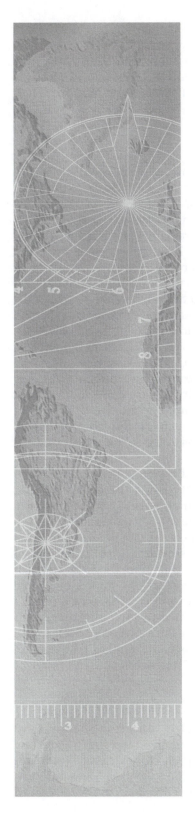

13

Uganda's Bwindi Impenetrable National Park: meeting the challenges of conservation and community development through sustainable tourism

Andrew Lepp

Introduction

In Sub-Saharan Africa, a human population in need of development is increasing the pressure on the region's natural resources. This pressure is particularly strong around national parks and preserves where people have been denied access to the resources viewed as necessary for development. As a result, park managers often find themselves in competition with local people (Mugisha, 2001, personal communication, 12 June). The traditional response to this competition has been the strict enforcement of park boundaries and the adoption of an 'us versus them' mentality. However, alternative responses are now proving more successful. Innovative and creative approaches to park management are resolving this conflict by simultaneously conserving park resources while stimulating local development. This case study explores how one national park in Uganda has been able to meet the challenge of conservation and development through the introduction of sustainable tourism.

Historical background

Uganda is an equatorial nation of 241 139 km^2 (the size of Great Britain) located in East Africa. It shares its eastern border with Kenya, to the south are Lake Victoria and Tanzania, to the west Rwanda and the Democratic Republic of the Congo (DRC), and to the north Sudan. Located within these borders is an amazing diversity of flora, fauna and human cultures. This diversity is reflected in the land itself. The glacier-capped Rwenzori Mountains crown the western horizon and rise from lush tropical forests. The western Rift Valley and its dry savannah contrast with the papyrus swamps and wetlands in the Lake Victoria basin where the source of the Nile River can be found. And finally, in the east, the sun rises from behind the 4321 metre Mount Elgon, an extinct volcano. Owing to this diversity, by the late 1960s Uganda was home to a prosperous tourism industry. At that time, roughly 100 000 tourists visited Uganda each year and made tourism the country's fourth largest earner of foreign exchange (BINPTDP, 1992). Unfortunately, the young industry came to an abrupt end in the early 1970s due to political unrest marked by the rule of dictator Idi Amin. Also at this time, much of the wildlife which contributed to the country's popularity was killed for food and trade.

It was not until the mid-1980s that the political climate in Uganda improved and the rule of law was restored. By 1986, a stable government was in place and free elections were forthcoming. By the late 1980s, conditions in the country allowed for re-investment in Uganda's once lucrative tourism industry. However, the loss of charismatic wildlife in previously popular safari parks such as Queen Elizabeth and Murchison Falls precluded them from competing with similar tourism attractions in neighbouring Tanzania and Kenya. This called for a redirection of Uganda's tourism industry away from East Africa's famed big game safaris. By capitalizing on a global interest in tropical forests, Uganda's new tourism development strategy highlighted its own forest resources as tourist attractions, and by so doing, created a niche for itself in the competitive East African market. The keystone of Uganda's new tourism industry became the Bwindi Impenetrable National Park.

Bwindi Impenetrable National Park

Bwindi Impenetrable National Park (BINP) is located in southwestern Uganda. It is situated in three separate counties and surrounded by eighteen parishes. To the south of the park, the Virunga volcanoes dominate the landscape while to the north the Rwenzori Mountains can be seen. BINP also shares a border with the DRC and covers 330 km^2 of extremely rugged topography ranging from 1160 metres to 2607 metres in elevation. As such, it is one of only a few forests in Africa with lowland, medium altitude and montane ecosystems in continuum. This makes BINP the most biologically diverse forest in East Africa (MBIFCT, 1993). It is from this dense, often impassable forest, that Bwindi takes its name. In fact, Bwindi means 'a difficult place to pass through' in the local Rukiga language. Within the park are more than 220 species of trees, 100 species of ferns, 340 species of birds, 200 species of butterflies, and 120 species of mammals, including half of the world's population of the highly endangered mountain gorilla (approximately 310). In order to ensure the preservation of this ecologically important area, the forest was gazetted a national park in 1991 and a World Heritage site in 1994.

Despite its global significance, the creation of BINP was not well received among the local people (Mugisha, 2001, personal communication, 12 June). BINP is situated within three districts in Uganda: Kisoro, Kabale and Rukungeri. At the time of the park's creation in 1991, Uganda's average rural population density was 85 people/km^2. However, Kisoro district averaged 302 people/km^2 and Kabale district 246 people/km^2 making them the first and third most densely populated districts in the country, respectively (MBIFCT, 1993). There was, and still is, tremendous human pressure on the land around BINP. Therefore, the creation of the park meant that valuable resources would be taken from a needy local population. Historically, the forest was an important source of revenue. Local people used it for timber, gold mining, hunting, and the harvesting of fruits, medicinal herbs and a variety of other forest products. Removing these resources from the local economy created hostility towards the park and its staff. Indicative of this hostility was the penchant for referring to the early park staff as baboons, an animal loathed for its destructive crop-raiding tendencies.

As this brief history of the park shows, the creation of BINP was accompanied by two major challenges: the conservation of a globally significant ecosystem that includes one of the world's most endangered mammals (the mountain gorilla), and creating development opportunities for local people who lost access to valuable resources. These challenges are typical of many parks throughout Sub-Saharan Africa.

BINP's Tourism Development Plan

The park's inception in 1991 was accompanied by hundreds of thousands of US dollars of loans and grants targeting conservation. In addition, technical assistance from a variety of non-governmental organizations (NGOs) was provided. However, it was recognized that the long-term ability of BINP to meet the dual challenge of conservation and development depended on its own revenue-generating capacity. More importantly, local people needed justification for the park's conservation, justification in the form of direct economic benefits. Towards this end, tourism was seen as the best option. Prior experience with mountain gorilla tourism in Rwanda and the DRC proved that it could be a profitable enterprise; in 1989, gorilla tourism in Rwanda was the nation's third largest earner of foreign exchange (BINPTDP, 1992). Unfortunately, both Rwanda's and the DRC's success with gorilla tourism was short-lived due to political turmoil and war. As a result, Uganda was positioned to become the world's premier mountain gorilla tourism destination. To capitalize on this opportunity, a tourism management plan was developed for BINP in 1992 and implementation began soon after.

BINP's tourism development plan was guided by five principles (BINPTDP, 1992):

1. tourism activity must support conservation, not be an end in itself, and be sustainable in the sense that it does not act to disturb or destroy the very attractions it is based upon;
2. local participation in tourism activities will be encouraged wherever possible and relevant, including policy matters and practical economic involvement;
3. tourism development will take place in a context of environmental awareness, through guidance on appropriate ways to develop accommodation and other tourist facilities;
4. policy and planning will leave room for adaptation and experiment under the guidance of a steering committee; and
5. private sector activity will be encouraged under appropriate supervision and monopoly interests avoided (p. 24).

It was believed that by following these guidelines, the objective of encouraging tourism focused on viewing mountain gorillas and other natural attractions in BINP could be tailored to meet the park's dual objectives of conservation and development. Specifically, the plan intended tourism to be sustainable, conservation oriented, beneficial and empowering for local people, environmentally aware and economically viable.

From the viewpoint of environmental sustainability and conservation, the health of the mountain gorillas was the highest priority. Because gorilla tourism throughout Africa was relatively new, its long-term effects on the animals had not been thoroughly studied. Therefore, it had to be approached cautiously. The underlying concern was the genetic similarity between gorillas and humans (BINPTDP, 1992). Because of this similarity, it was believed that gorillas might be susceptible to diseases brought into the park by tourists. In order to reduce these risks, the tourism development plan allowed only two groups of gorillas to be habituated to the presence of humans. This represented less than 10 per cent of BINP's gorilla population. The two groups would be monitored daily and their health compared to a control group which was not habituated. Furthermore, the plan devised strict guidelines to regulate tourist/gorilla interaction. Specifically, each habituated group would be visited by only six tourists a day for a period of only 1 hour, visitors had to maintain a distance of at least 5 metres from the gorillas at all times, and children under fifteen as well as sick adults would not be permitted to participate. These controls would be rigorously enforced. In addition, educating the tourists and increasing their environmental awareness prior to viewing the gorillas was made a fundamental component of the tourism operation.

With regard to the spread of tourism's benefits into the local community, the creation of economic activity was the most obvious route. Local people would be hired as guides, trackers and porters. Park infrastructure development would use local materials and labour. Tourist accommodation would provide employment opportunities and linkages to the local economy through the sale of food and handicrafts. However, considering the large number of people living around the park, such avenues would provide a relatively small number of benefits. Therefore, more innovative approaches were needed, approaches which would spread benefits throughout the distant communities and reach large numbers of people. Revenue sharing and community extension work were two such ideas. Revenue from gorilla tourism was expected to be high and the plan called for 10 per cent of this revenue to remain in local communities for development projects. Furthermore, local people would be given the power to determine which projects would be funded from the shared money. BINP would also employ 'community conservation rangers' whose job would be to provide expertise in community development and conservation projects. Education was proposed to link all such development activities to tourism revenue generated by the park. In this way, the plan proposed tourism as the means to produce community-wide benefits and improve local attitudes about the park.

Evaluating BINP's Tourism Development Plan

It has been almost 10 years since the development of BINP's tourism plan and during this time well over 20 000 visitors have trekked to the gorillas. The cost of visiting the gorillas more than tripled from 80 US dollars in 1993 to 250 US dollars in 2001, yet the park continued to operate near capacity. BINP has become the largest source of revenue for the Uganda Wildlife Authority (the parastatal body which manages Uganda's national parks and reserves) (Mugisha, 2001, personal communication, 12 June). Profits from BINP fund protected area management throughout the country. From an economic standpoint, gorilla tourism at BINP is clearly a success for the Uganda Wildlife Authority (UWA). This, however, was never really in doubt. Instead, the necessary question to evaluate is whether gorilla tourism is a sustainable approach to conservation and community development around BINP.

Before BINP was gazetted a national park in 1991, the largest threat to the mountain gorilla's survival was destruction of habitat due to logging and mining (BINPTDP, 1992). Without a doubt, creation of the park has ended these activities and the gorilla's habitat is secure (Mugisha, 2001, personal communication, 12 June). In addition, the daily presence of rangers, guides and tourists in the forest has been credited with curbing these and other illegal activities such as the hunting and trapping of wildlife (BINPMPR, 1997). The gorilla population is now increasing, with exact numbers to be obtained in a census planned for 2002. The two habituated groups of gorillas experiencing tourism are living normally and reproducing at regular rates, suggesting that tourism is low impact and unobtrusive. Based on this success, and coupled with the demand for gorilla tourism, BINP began habituating a third group of gorillas with the intention of having them ready for tourism by late 2001. However, unexpected events with these newly habituated gorillas have challenged the sustainability of gorilla tourism in BINP. It is these challenges to which this case study now turns.

This third group of habituated gorillas, called Nkuringo group, has become so accustomed to the presence of humans that they now spend the majority of their time outside the park near the village of Ntungamo located in Nteko parish. They often feed and sleep on people's farms. Among the problems that this has created is a health risk to both gorilla and human populations due to prolonged and close contact with each other. As if to confirm these fears, the gorillas recently contracted scabies and it is believed that the infection was spread through human contact. A subsequent survey conducted in Ntungamo village found that four of the 182 households were infected with scabies as well (Ajarova, 2001, personal communication, 23 May). It was also found that this village has very low latrine coverage and no rubbish pits. The habituated gorillas frequenting this village have most likely been exposed to human waste and rubbish. On the bright side, UWA was very quick to act on behalf of both gorilla and community health. The gorillas were immediately treated for scabies and a full recovery is expected. In the village, educational sessions were organized focusing on health and hygiene, and a village clean-up day was organized during which over 200 kg of garbage was collected. Fortunately, the daily monitoring of the habituated gorillas diagnosed the problem early, and before it could become more serious. In hindsight, the Nkuringo gorilla experience may be for the best. In addition to raising awareness about disease transmission, it has taught park managers that communities living around the park can have as much of an impact on the gorilla's health as the tourists who visit the gorillas on a daily basis. This lesson emphasizes the importance of community education and cooperation for the sustainability of gorilla tourism.

In addition to these conservation lessons, events currently taking place in Ntungamo village reveal how tourism can improve community attitudes about BINP. Before the advent of tourism, gorillas entering onto community land would be chased deep into the forest or worse (Mugisha, 2001, personal communication, 12 June). The situation in Ntungamo is quite different. The community is not only tolerating gorillas in the farms but is actually excited to have them there. The reason for the change of attitude is clear. The community has already started clearing a spot for the construction of a tourist campground and hostel. They are anxious for tourism to begin as they see economic benefits flowing from visitation. This situation also provides BINP with a unique opportunity to expand its partnership with local people. This will be necessary if tourists are to view gorillas when they cross from the park onto community land (Ajarova, 2001, personal communication, 23 May). In Ntungamo, innova-tive approaches are needed in order to keep tourism sustainable and under the control of BINP's professional managers.

That a community would equate gorillas with economic opportunity is not unprecedented at BINP. Until the habituation of the Nkuringo group, all gorilla trekking originated in the village of Buhoma in Mkono parish at the park's main entrance. From Buhoma, tourists would trek to one of the two habituated groups of gorillas. Community members from Buhoma and the surrounding parish, with the assistance of a US Peace Corps Volunteer, formed a co-operative and secured a grant from the United States Agency for International Development (USAID) enabling them to construct simple tourist accommodation. The result was the Buhoma Community Campground. This co-operative is governed by a committee composed of a representative from each village in the parish. The committee decides how profits will be spent. All profits go towards local development in the parish and completed projects include the construction of three schools and two medical clinics. The organizational success of the Buhoma campground was offered as a model for the village of Ntungamo which was planning tourism with the Nkuringo gorillas (Ajarova, 2001, personal communication, 23 May). A potential problem with the Buhoma site is that outside interests have bought land in the area and are now competing for the tourist dollar. As a result, some tourism revenue is leaking out of the community.

Clearly, tourism has had an impact on the parishes surrounding the park which receive tourists, but even with the addition of the Nkuringo gorillas, tourism directly benefited only two parishes. This left sixteen parishes in need of tourism's benefits. Spreading tourism's benefits to these other parishes has been the task of BINP's revenue sharing and community conservation programmes. To date, tourism revenue sharing has generated nearly half a million US dollars and funded over twenty community-based projects including road construction, schools and medical clinics. Although change has been slow, it seems these developments may be improving local attitudes towards the park (CARE International Uganda, 2000).

CARE (an international conservation oriented NGO) conducted a longitudinal study from 1997 to 1999 to measure changes in community attitudes towards the park. The survey was based on two random samples of adults living around the park. The sample was stratified to ensure that every parish was represented. The 1997 survey included baseline socio-economic data. Three different indicators were found to be significant in characterizing the wealth of the respondents: ownership of a house roofed with iron sheets (versus grass thatching); ownership of a radio; and land ownership versus land needs. It was found that 65 per cent of the respondents had iron sheets for roofing; 34 per cent owned a radio; and 7 per cent believed that they had more than enough land (32 per cent just enough, 41 per cent not enough, 20 per cent had no land at all). Comparison with a follow-up survey completed in 1999 shows only slight changes, where it was found that 71 per cent of respondents had iron sheets for roofing; 57 per cent owned a radio; and 3 per cent believed they had more than enough land (22 per cent just enough, 53 per cent not enough, 21 per cent had no land at all). Thus, some indicators of wealth had slightly increased but so had the apparent need for more land. The significance of this information is that it shows that the majority of individuals around the park, despite the hundreds of thousands of dollars tourists spend there annually, have not experienced a significant economic windfall. Considering this, the investigation focused on whether attitudes about the park were remaining negative.

In 1997, people were first asked to state the costs and benefits of living near the park, and which was greater. Overall, 68 per cent felt the costs were greater. Secondly, the people were asked if they felt better off or worse off than other people with the same quantity and quality of farmland who happened to live further from the park. Overall, 77 per cent said they were worse off. Finally, people were asked about the distribution of park benefits between local people and potential outside beneficiaries (tourists, other Ugandans, UWA staff, the international community, etc.). Overall, 51 per cent of respondents felt that outsiders received more benefits, 39 per cent felt local people received more benefits, and 10 per cent felt it was an equal split. These same questions were again asked in 1999 and revealed a positive change. By 1999, the percentage of people surveyed who felt that the costs of living near the park outweighed the benefits dropped to 46 per cent; those who felt that they were worse off than other people with the same quantity and quality of farmland who happened to live further from the park dropped to 49 per cent; and, finally, those who felt that outsiders received more benefits dropped to 44 per cent, while the percentage who felt that local people received more benefits rose to 45 per cent, and only 6 per cent felt it was an equal split (CARE, 2000). This suggests that an improvement in attitude towards the park is taking place. Because socio-economic data does not indicate a clear increase in individual wealth, it may be that this change in attitude is correlated with the park's many community-based development projects. The success of tourism revenues in funding these projects and improving livelihoods may be responsible for the improving attitudes towards the park. This is an area for future research. However, this much is clear, judging by the competition for resources in Africa, community support is essential if natural resource-based tourism is to be sustainable.

At this point in BINP's history, nearly 10 years after the development of its first tourism plan, the park can claim success. The dual objectives of conservation and development are slowly but surely being met. The mountain gorilla is now safely protected and tourism has contributed to its conservation. Likewise, tourism has provided community-wide benefits such as improved roads, education and health care, which will hopefully lay the groundwork for greater future development. However, 10 years is not a true test of a project's sustainability. Many challenges still exist as human populations around the park continue to increase. An interesting finding in the CARE survey of local people is that they are beginning to want more individual benefits from the park and tourism (CARE, 2000). Additional future challenges to the park's success may come from across its international border with the DRC, where instability has already proven disruptive to BINP's tourism.

In early March, 1999, a small force of rebels operating out of the war torn DRC crossed into BINP and murdered eight tourists and one park warden.

During the ensuing mêlée, much of the parks infrastructure, including the community campground, was pillaged, burnt and otherwise destroyed. It was a horrible human tragedy and seemed likely to cripple Uganda's growing tourism industry and scar the country's favourable international image. In fact, this was the rebels' stated goal. However, what actually followed was quite to the contrary. The people around the park mobilized themselves to improve security in the area. The military formed a new partnership with the park staff and deployed troops along the border. The Ugandan President guaranteed the future security of all tourists. The community campground was rebuilt and there are plans to expand it, and most importantly, the tourists returned. The park is once again operating at near full capacity and has had no further incidents (Mugisha, 2001, personal communication, 12 June). The resilience of the park to this tragedy would not have been possible without the full co-operation of local people, park staff, the Ugandan government and the international community. This may be the strongest indication yet of the sustainability of BINP's tourism development plan.

Concluding remarks

Despite its ecological uniqueness, Bwindi Impenetrable National Park is typical of parks throughout Sub-Saharan Africa. The challenge that these parks face is the conservation of valuable and sometimes endangered natural resources in the face of a growing human population. The lesson that must be learned is that the continued existence of these parks depends on their ability to extend the benefits of conservation to local people. In the case of BINP, tourism has proven to be a sustainable method of achieving this goal. However, the model that BINP presents should be studied carefully before it is implemented at other parks and protected areas. Firstly, BINP still relies heavily on donor support despite the lucrative tourism there. This is because BINP is not independent of the UWA and its profits must fund protected area management throughout the country. Therefore, the national context within which a tourism development plan is proposed should not be overlooked, as it can affect its sustainability. Secondly, revenue sharing may not be feasible in parks without a high dollar attraction, such as that derived from mountain gorillas. If not planned wisely, revenue sharing can quickly raise the hopes of rural people and leave them unfulfilled. Thirdly, the expert and regular monitoring of natural resources is essential if tourism is to be sustained. The importance of this was demonstrated by BINP's quick and effective response to a scabies outbreak among the Nkuringo gorilla group. Having said this, the most critical point remains. Regardless of the circumstances, innovative and creative ideas are necessary for spreading tourism's benefits throughout rural communities. Traditional economic channels employ only a small portion of local people. Furthermore, local enterprise can sometimes be out-competed by more capital laden external investors. As this case study of BINP demonstrates, keeping tourism's benefits local is the key to sustainability.

Acknowledgements

I wish to thank Ajarova Lilly, Tourism Development Manager, Uganda Wildlife Authority, and Mugisha Arthur, Director of Field Operations, Uganda Wildlife Authority.

References

BINPTDP (1992) *Tourism Development Plan*. Bwindi Impenetrable National Park.

BINPTDP (1997) *Management Plan Revision*. Bwindi Impenetrable National Park.

CARE International Uganda (2000) *Report of the Participatory Mid-Term Review of CARE's Development Through Conservation Project*.

MBIFCT (1993) *Research and Monitoring in Bwindi Impenetrable National Park and Mgahinga Gorilla National Park*. Mgahinga Bwindi Impenetrable Forest Conservation Trust.

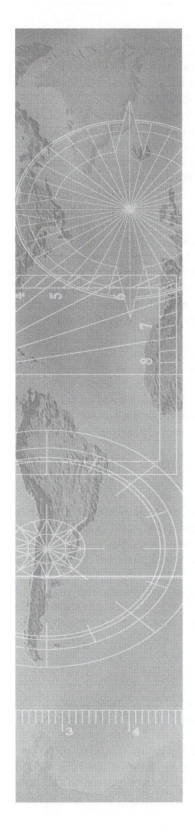

Convicts and conservation: Con Dao National Park, Vietnam

Greg Ringer

Introduction

The phenomenal growth of tourism experienced by the East Asia-Pacific region in the 1990s, almost double the world average, has played a formative role in reuniting and empowering countries long fragmented by conflict and genocide. Stimulated by an increase in disposable income and leisure time, greater political stability and openness, and aggressive promotional campaigns, tourism is further credited by proponents with discouraging unsustainable practices in environmentally sensitive areas, while simultaneously creating greater opportunities for women and ethnic minorities to participate in the development process. As a result, governments throughout the region are now busy (re)positioning their countries as 'authentic' destinations for visitors interested in local culture and nature (Ringer, 1998; WTO, 2000).

However, not every country or community in Asia will succeed as a tourist attraction, and those that do may discover that the economic benefits are less consequential than the social costs, as residents find their governments more intrusive and traditional practices rendered inauthentic for tourists' consumption. Further obstacles include the tarnished image associated with the sex tourism industry in Bangkok; continued land-ownership and use conflicts; ill-defined jurisdictional roles and boundaries; ethnic and gender disparities; a lack of coordination between participating agencies; and a preference for largescale development projects financed by international donors (Bank of Hawai'i, 2000; Cohen, 1996; Cook, *et al.*, 1996; Houston, 1999; Howe *et al.*, 1997; *New Zealand Herald*, 2000; Phongpaichit *et al.*, 1998; Rigg, 1997; Seabrook, 1996; Sittirak, 1998; *The Daily Post (Rotorua)*, 2000a).

The challenges of balancing such development with environmental conservation – and the possibilities offered by tourism in reconnecting an area long defined by its history of conflict, through expanded networks of travel and communication – are the topic of this case study on Con Dao National Park (CDNP) in southern Vietnam. Both strategy and process, the practices initiated on Con Dao, establish a framework for community and government leaders who truly wish to:

- successfully market *and maintain* protected areas as destinations for both foreign and domestic visitors;
- create long-term funding support for environmental conservation and education projects that unite both parks and communities;
- generate and support economically and socially sustainable employment opportunities; and
- develop meaningful, collaborative partnerships among the diverse stakeholders.

In achieving these goals, initiatives on Con Dao seek to balance tourism's promised benefits with the ecological significance and fragility of the park's marine and terrestrial environments. They also seek to affirm conservation as the primary function of a national park, yet acknowledge the economic needs of the destination community. In a landscape where resources are finite and political conditions uncertain, the proposed pathways additionally serve to reinforce the belief that sustainable tourism requires a sustainable community.

Background

Hoping to capitalize on the boom experienced by its neighbours in the Greater Mekong Subregion (Cambodia, the Lao PDR, Myanmar, Thailand, and China's Yunnan Province), Vietnam has recently taken significant steps to attract more international visitors. Plans to introduce single pricing at twenty-one tourist sites to remove the distinction between local Vietnamese and foreign travellers are expected to facilitate visitation and investment, as are simplified visa regulations and greater access by foreign airlines. In addition, sixteen cities and provinces have established local tourism promotion boards, and, in 1999, the Vietnam National Administration of Tourism opened an overseas information bureau in France. Added to these efforts, the Vietnam State Steering Board, spent approximately 14.5 billion Vietnamese dong (US$1.05 million) in 1999–2000 on marketing the country's tourist attractions through a website and electronic newspaper.

Not unexpectedly, given the pro-tourism stance of the Vietnamese government, there are now many innovative developments taking place in the tourism area, amongst which is the Asian Development Bank's (ADB) funded ecotourism 'demonstration project' administered by the World Wide Fund (WWF) for Nature-Indochina Programme in Con Dao National Park. The site of an infamous prison complex originally constructed by the French in the late 1800s, and subsequently used by the US-backed Saigon government during the 1960s to intern political prisoners, the island supports a diversity of flora and fauna that are increasingly prized for both their ecologic and their economic value (Ringer and Robinson, 1999; Ross and Andriani, 1998).

Con Dao

Located in the South China Sea, approximately 160 km offshore from the 'Nine Dragons' of the Mekong Delta, the Con Dao archipelago consists of Con Dao island and thirteen smaller islets (Figure 14.1). Con Dao town, with a population of approximately 4200 persons – 75 per cent of whom are military – is the district capital and headquarters for the national park. Considered both a political and an ecological 'hot spot', CDNP is the second largest marine park in Vietnam with 14 000 ha of marine habitats and 5998 ha of protected terrestrial forest land (Figure 14.2).

The park's waters are famed for their ecological diversity, including endangered green sea turtles and dugongs, and reputedly, the highest collection of giant clams in the world. The island's forests are equally noteworthy, including nearly 300 species of trees, of which forty-four are found nowhere else in Vietnam. Because of this high level of biodiversity and the presumed potential for ecotourism, Con Dao is designated an 'Area of Highest Regional Priority' in the World Bank's Global System of Marine Protected Areas (FIPI, 1999; Ross and Andriani, 1998).

The ADB-funded demonstration project in CDNP joins other similar experimental programmes in southern Cambodia and central Vietnam. The intent of these 'ecotourism demonstration' projects is to showcase practical options for sustainably managing tourism in protected areas throughout Asia, by identifying processes and methodologies that prove effective in conserving resources and stimulating greater public participation. Based on input received from the participating agencies, marine ecotourism was made a central component of CDNP's *Five-Year Management and Investment Plans (1998–2004)*, as was the need to encourage and subsidize local tourism enterprises owned by community members, women, and ethnic minorities (Hulse, 1999; Ringer, 1997).

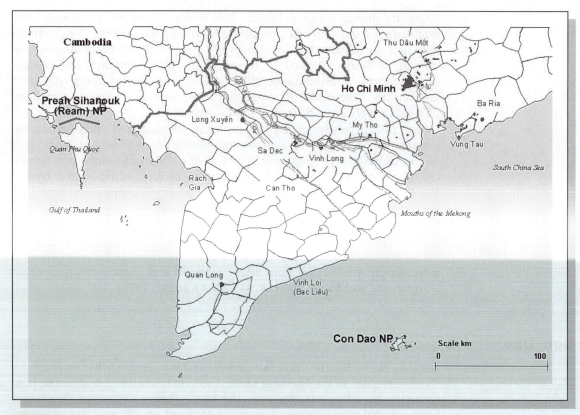

Figure 14.1
The Mekong Delta

Destination analysis

As a prelude to discussing in detail sustainable tourism initiatives on Con Dao it is useful to examine in more detail its attractions and infrastructure base along with the challenges it currently faces. It is essential to keep in mind, however, that tourism development on Con Dao is still at the incubation stage, and both preferences and practices continue to evolve as managers and residents assess the impacts and changing dynamics of travel to the island.

Attractions • • •

The islands of CDNP have remained relatively undisturbed until recently, due largely to their use as a prison, distance from the Vietnamese mainland, and their mountainous interiors. As a result, forestry researchers from the government-planning institute in Ho Chi Minh City have discovered a diverse range of mammals and marine life throughout the archipelago, including deer mice, the rare black squirrel,

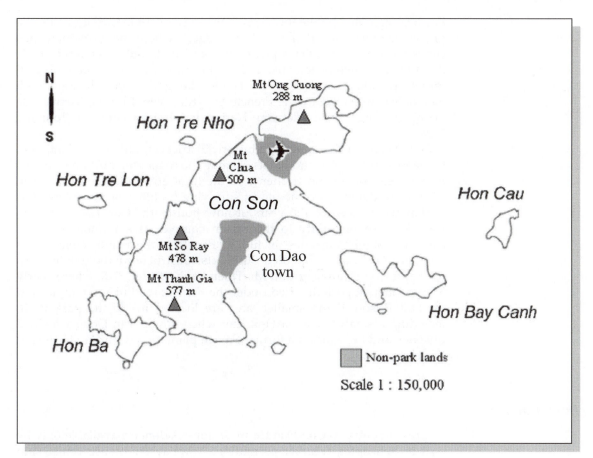

Figure 14.2
Con Dao National
Park

macaque monkeys, the giant water monitor lizard, butterfly and parrot fish, giant clams, and the endangered green sea turtle and dugong. Seasonal migrations of dolphins and 'black whales' (*Prodelphinus malayensis*) have also been recorded in the coastal waters of the park by staff from the Institute of Oceanography in Nha Trang and the Institute for Environment and Sustainable Development at Hong Kong University of Science and Technology. Indeed, studies conducted between 1997 and 1999 suggest that the islands may offer the highest species diversity of corals found in Vietnam – and the most attractive in all of Vietnam in terms of ecotourism (Ringer and Robinson, 1999; Ross and Andriani, 1999).

Though the natural environment is certainly the primary attraction – and concern – of park managers, it is difficult to discuss development options for CDNP without consideration of the cultural attractions that exist on park and district land. Among the most significant is the prison complex initially constructed by the French colonial government in 1862.

Further expanded by the former Saigon government in the late 1950s, the prison includes the infamous 'Tiger Cages', where many of Vietnam's current leaders were held captive until the fall of South Vietnam in 1975. A national cemetery situated nearby includes the grave sites of 2000 former prisoners, including Le Hong Phong and Vo Thi Sau, both nationalists executed by the French, yet still revered by the Vietnamese people (Giang, 1996; Vietnam National Administration of Tourism, 1998).

Con Dao town also contains a historic district centrally located adjacent to the prison complex and hotels. Among the remaining buildings are the former head office and residence of the local governors, constructed in 1873. Considered to be the oldest surviving building on the island and unchanged for nearly 126 years, it now houses the Con Dao Museum. Also in close proximity to the prison complex is a number of other culturally significant sites, including Pier 914 (the name refers to the number of prisoners who died during its construction); the remains of a road and stone wall near Cau Ma Thien Lanh (Bridge 350), where nearly 350 prisoners reportedly died under the French; the Phi Yen temple; and the Salt Prison. Some smaller sites are located inside the park itself, including a small house on Hon Cau where Pham Van Dong was held prisoner, and the ruins of a former French plantation (Con Dao Historical Museum, 2000).

Infrastructure • • •

At present, entry to Con Dao for most non-residents is available only by boat or helicopter, weather permitting. A Malaysian-owned cruise ship from Star Cruise Lines used to stop at Con Dao each week while en route to Thailand. However, the port calls (which began in October 1999) ceased in September 2000, reportedly because the passenger load averaged only 200 persons per sailing, or less than a third of the ship's total capacity. Consequently, visits to Con Dao remain relatively small in number, totalling less than 3000 annually, based on admission records maintained by the park office and the Con Dao Historical Museum (2000). However, ADB (2000) and Phuong (2000) reported that the airstrip was to be upgraded to accommodate 70-passenger prop jets operated by Vietnam Airlines, and that there were plans to launch an inter-island ferry from Singapore.

Additional data provided by the two largest government tour operators, Saigontourist and Vietnam Tourism, indicated that 46 per cent of the international ecotourists who visited southern Vietnam – and by extension, Con Dao – were from East Asia, followed by Europe (7 per cent), North America (3 per cent), and Australia/New Zealand (1 per cent). Most arrived during the brief dry season (April–July) when travel by boat was more reliable and less expensive for Vietnamese nationals, and as a result some overuse of certain sites was occurring during this period (Dảo, 2000). Nonetheless, the Ba Ria-Vung Tau provincial government, in whose domain CDNP lies, was still very much concerned with expanding visitation (CDNP, 1999). Indeed, with this goal in mind it announced plans to launch a high-speed boat in early 2002, capable of carrying 200 passengers from the provincial capital of Vung Tau to Con Dao island in only 7 hours. A similar boat would transport guests to a South Korean planned, 500-room hotel complex located near the park entrance. The provincial government was also planning to extend the 27-km paved road connecting the airport, Con Dao town, and Ben Dam port to eventually encircle the entire island. This construction project was designed to facilitate access to the west coast for day visits and for security patrols by the military (Con Dao District, 2000).

Challenges

While efforts at growing visitation may benefit the local economy, they might also cause extensive environmental degradation. Soil erosion and the dumping of hazardous waste now threaten sensitive marine environments along the route of the road construction, as do the harvesting of coral, and turtles for sale and consumption. The runway expansion and a proposed casino on the island's north will result in the elimination of significant bird-nesting sites and possible contamination of nearby beaches. The potential shortage of drinking water in the future (particularly during the dry season) is also an environmental challenge that must be addressed.

On Hon Bay Canh, where the park maintains a guard station, fresh water must be supplied by boat – though the Vice-Minister of the Ministry of Agriculture and Rural Development (2000) had voiced his intention to construct water cisterns on each of the islands where ranger stations exist. In Con Dao district, the local government is already constructing additional storage facilities, prompted by the accelerated loss of the island's fresh water and mangrove systems to development. It is therefore not surprising that it is worried about the consequences should the island's population total 15 000 inhabitants by the year 2010, as projected in the district's Master Plan (1992). Given the limited amount of land available outside the park, such growth would also place tremendous pressure on the island's other resources and likely necessitate further importation of food and supplies by helicopter or ship.

Limited electrical capacity on Con Dao is also a major issue and inconvenience, since the system is shut down completely between midnight and 0600 hours except for hotels and private homes with generators. Waste disposal presents an additional challenge. Although garbage is collected by the district, most residences rely on poorly-maintained septic systems for human waste, and solid waste is frequently abandoned on parklands contiguous to inhabited areas.

Additional stopovers by cruise ships, as some tour operators desire, and the completion of a proposed hotel where the island's only source of fresh water now lies, will only generate further conflict between businesses who favour 'high-end' tourism and proponents of smaller scale attractions and facilities. In addition to the total number of visitors, the current mix of Asian and Western tourists has other implications for the nature and level of development on Con Dao in terms of facilities, attractions, and activities. Interviews with self-labelled Asian and Western ecotourists in 1999–2000, for example, established that many Asian visitors to Con Dao prefer to travel in large groups and to stay in local hotels or other comfortable accommodations. The majority of Western ecotourists, however, opt to travel independently and seek more direct, cross-cultural experiences and a simpler standard of accommodation. Information concerning such experiences and services, nonetheless, is not easily obtained as the island lacks a formal information centre, and interpretative materials are only available in Vietnamese. While the Historical Museum does offer informal referrals, neither staff nor the displays provide information on the park or tourism-related facilities nearby, and the guides who lead tours of the prisons speak only Vietnamese (Ringer and Robinson, 1999; Sage, 2000).

At present, almost all of the money and operating equipment for CDNP comes from international donors, lending institutions or visitor fees, with very little contributed by the government of Vietnam itself. This dependence on foreign aid, while certainly necessary because of the lack of adequate funding from the national government, has impeded some innovative park efforts because staff feel hindered by the stipulations that accompany this assistance. The lack of adequate finances has also forced the park director to selectively manage certain natural and historical resources, while ignoring the conservation and protection of others (CDNP, 1999; Ringer and Robinson, 1999).

Political challenges also exist. As many of Vietnam's current and recent leaders were incarcerated on Con Dao, the national government must formally approve all development related to CDNP (the current *1993–2010 Master Plan* was finalized at the Prime Minister Level, an event unique for a district level plan in Vietnam). In addition, consent from the military and Border Army is often required before entrance into certain areas is permitted, and visitors must surrender their passports when travelling between islands within the park.

Sustainable tourism Initiatives

To respond effectively to the socio-economic, political, and environmental challenges it faces, a number of critical steps have been undertaken by park officials since 1999. Some of the actions are institutional, while others are more personal in scope but equally constructive. Each effort, however incremental, is designed to foster greater co-operation between government agencies at the district and national level, and to broaden decision-makers' appreciation of the crucial role played by the park's ecosystem both ecologically and economically.

Among the more wide-reaching measures undertaken are those by the Asian Development Bank (ADB), in collaboration with WWF-Indochina, to build more decision-making capacity at the local level, and to promote the sustainable use of coastal and marine resources in the western portion of the South China Sea (or 'East Sea' in Vietnam). An ecotourism planner and a marine biologist hired by WWF assisted local staff in preparing an environmental and educational assessment of the park's biology and tourism resources in 1999–2000, and additional staff training in ecotourism practices, interpretation, and guiding is planned or already under way. Meanwhile, capital investments are being solicited for conservation, interpretation, and the construction of ecotourism-related facilities on Con Dao, Hon Bay Canh, and Hon Cau islands (CDNP, 1999; Ringer and Robinson, 1999).

Aware that conservation also depends upon the cooperation and support of the local population, officials from the park and district government now support greater community awareness and use of its resources. On Con Dao, the Minister of Agriculture & Rural Development has plans to develop a small agricultural site within the park to provide fruits and vegetables for residents, and local schoolteachers are encouraged to participate in conservation activities that enable students to appreciate the park's biodiversity and the challenges facing protected areas in Southeast Asia. In Ho Chi Minh City, the Faculty of Tourism at Van Lang University has implemented an internship program on the island for Vietnamese students and residents interested in acquiring practical experience in ecotourism and natural resource management (Huong, 2001).

A second training program jointly developed by CDNP and the Provincial Tourism Department, with the co-operation of the Border Army, is also now under way to license local boat operators to ferry ecotourists to islands for camping, wildlife viewing, swimming, and snorkelling. This will provide economic and educational benefits for local residents, and hopefully, encourage them to support conservation efforts in the park. The combined steps will also enable the director of CDNP and district officials to identify and manage the issues of highest priority (Ringer and Robinson, 1999).

To further minimize any unintended ecological impacts, the environmental management plan recently prepared for the park by WWF staff (Robinson, 2000) designated specific restricted-use zones to protect Con Dao's coral reefs, sea grasses, and mangrove forests. These areas are the primary habitats for most of the forty-four endangered plant and animal species listed in the *Vietnam Red Book* for CDNP (UNEP, 1999). As part of that zoning activity, seven functional areas for managing the marine and terrestrial areas according to use have been proposed:

1. strict protection, scientific research, and limited ecotourism;
2. turtle nesting beaches;
3. dugong/sea grasses;
4. rehabilitation of the natural environment;
5. marine ecotourism areas;
6. limited natural marine resource development; and
7. port/harbour development.

A zoning group has already been formed to collect relevant scientific and biological information to determine the specific functions and site locations of the designated zones. Upon completion of the analysis and boundary maps, the park managers will propose specific regulations to govern permissible activities in each area according to their intended function: resource protection, scientific research, or ecotourism and port development. Until such information has been obtained and approved, maximum daily limits on visits to sensitive sites have been established. These limits range from a high of thirty visitors (including eighteen overnight campers) for Hon Cau, to a total of only six hikers (subject to district and military approval) on the trail to Nui Thanh Gia. These restrictions are intended to assure a quality experience for ecotourists seeking to enjoy nature, while minimizing disturbances to wildlife and marine life. They also reflect the park staff's limited ability to manage tourists and to simultaneously perform their conservation and enforcement duties.

Further management recommendations

To support the park's efforts to conserve biodiversity, and the district's efforts to develop alternative sources of income and employment for local residents, the following activities and guidelines are suggested for consideration in Con Dao's final management plan. The suggestions acknowledge the financial constraints that currently impede the park director's efforts to provide more meaningful interpretation of Con Dao's history and resources. They also take advantage of the human and environmental resources currently available, and the attention and assistance available through international organizations, such as the ADB and WWF.

Funding

As it is difficult to distinguish between visitors who come to Con Dao as ecotourists and those who come for other purposes, all non-residents pay a single, multi-tiered entrance fee on arrival (students are exempt to encourage greater use of the park for educational purposes, while foreign residents pay more than Vietnamese nationals). Along with concession fees private operators within the park would be charged, and a proposed one-time Conservation Development Charge levied against all new construction on district land. All income would go into a Conservation Fund and the money then used only for environmental education and protection in the park or Con Dao district.

The Conservation Fund would be jointly administered by representatives of CDNP and the District, with earnings divided equally. This single fee would replace the separate admission fee charged by the Museum, as well as entrance fees to the national park. However, 'user fees' would continue to be charged for any activity within the park that requires a park ranger to provide a service beyond his/her normal duties (such as interpreting natural and cultural features, guiding along an unmarked trail, or leading a group of snorkellers). Other recreational programmes offered by CDNP or private businesses may also require the payment of additional user fees, including boat trips to the outer islands, overnight accommodation, bicycle rental, snorkelling, and diving. All tourism-related revenue, including the visitor entrance fees, concession fees, and Conservation Development Charges, would be deposited into the Fund. This money would be used *only* for the construction, maintenance, and operation of facilities related to ecotourism, biodiversity conservation, and environmental education. Permissible areas of expenditure might include:

- opening a park interpretation and environmental education centre;
- exhibits and operation of the Museum;
- training of guides for CDNP and the historic district;
- purchase of environmentally-sensitive natural areas, which may be privately owned;
- preservation of historical buildings; and
- the design and preparation of educational activities and displays for local schools.

To address any concerns that tourists might have with the fee structure, information given to them on arrival would describe specific projects financed with visitor revenue so that they know they are directly contributing to the protection of Con Dao's natural and historic resources. This process also helps assure residents that the costs and benefits of tourism development are fairly distributed.

Interpretation and conservation

Mechanisms for educating visitors to Con Dao about its history and marine environment are currently lacking. Perhaps the most important requirement in this regard is a visitor interpretation/environmental education centre. Such a centre would contain informative multilingual displays of Con Dao's natural and historic resources as well as maps and other visitor information needs. As regards maps, these would act to highlight scenic, cultural, and recreational attractions, as well as major walking trails, lookouts, etc.

For visitors and residents interested in participating more directly in conservation efforts, opportunities to actively assist park rangers in protecting sea turtles and mangroves in the park are needed, as is a system of trails for hiking, bicycling, and wildlife viewing. The park and district could also act to co-sponsor the development of a Youth Conservation Group in the form of a local non-governmental organiza-tion. The goals of such a group would include increasing environmental awareness amongst those of similar age, and to undertake specific conservation-related projects that would be of benefit to the park and the district. In addition, youth members could be enlisted to help post signs throughout the park, supplemented with self-guiding brochures in several foreign languages, identifying significant natural features and cultural artifacts.

Accommodation

At present, there are three hotels on Con Dao island; however, several traditional Vietnamese bungalows are planned for the smaller islands of Hon Cau and Hon Bay Canh. Utilizing renewable materials and authentic building practices wherever feasible, these accommodations will be simply constructed, elevated on stilts to minimize land disturbance, and built to blend into the natural environment. Self-composting toilets will be a feature of these properties and hirers will be responsible for removing non-compostable rubbish when they leave.

Camping facilities on each island could be constructed and operated by private concessions selected by the park manager. Capital for materials and construction would be provided by the concessionaire, with all specifications being first approved by a park-designated architect. Although the bungalows will be privately-funded, ownership would remain with the park. In exchange for providing the capital to construct the bungalows, the concessionaires would be granted an exclusive, long-term lease (not to exceed 10 years) to use the buildings for ecotourism-related purposes only. The concessionaires would also be entitled to 90 per cent of the gross revenue (10 per cent of the gross revenue would be contributed to the Conservation Fund described elsewhere). Upon satisfactory completion of the initial lease period, concessionaires would be required to submit a competitive bid to renew their leases but may – at the discretion of the park director – receive preference in the selection process. To ensure that visitors do not negatively affect vegetation, water quality, or turtle nesting areas on each island, park rangers would supervise all construction and tourism activities.

Conclusion

The central task for residents, tourists, local governments, and the tourism industry on Con Dao is to develop and market a model of tourism that supports continuing visitation, while at the same time maintaining and enhancing the natural and cultural resource base upon which such visitation is based. Anxious to take advantage of the opportunities – and fully cognizant of the challenges – park managers and local residents of Con Dao have taken the first steps. While the recent nature of many of the actions outlined in the preceding sections prevent any firm conclusions being drawn, the initial impressions of staff directly involved in the planning and design process (including those from WWF, CDNP, the Forestry Planning Institute, and the Ba Ria-Vung Tau Provincial government) are that meaningful progress is being made towards the creation of a community-based tourism programme that is:

- sensitive to community concerns to maintain the cultural and natural heritage by limiting the number and character of visitors;

- inclusive, by mandating local participation in the planning and management process;
- capable of providing a mix of simple, efficient services to international visitors and Vietnamese residents alike; and
- ecologically and socially sustainable, incorporating both behavioural and biological parameters (Ringer and Robinson, 1999; Robinson, 2000; Sage, 2000).

Indeed, so persuasive are the initial results and institutional support, the national government is now using Con Dao as the model for tourism development in the country's other national parks. Should Con Dao's experiment with alternative tourism prove successful over the long term, it may also help stimulate similar projects in the Mekong and thereby create the basis for ongoing 'interdependent subregional growth [and] a firm foundation for sustainable development' (Matoba, 1997:88).

Acknowledgements

I would like to thank Dr Lan Huong and Mai Ngoc Khuong of Van Lang University, Ho Chi Minh City, Nathan Sage, Aubrey Hord, and Alan Robinson, WWF-Indochina Programme Project Director, for their valued friendship and assistance in promoting sustainable tourism and communities in Vietnam. I also wish to express my appreciation to Teresa Weaver and Jennifer Lewis for their continued support and interest in sustainable tourism worldwide.

References

American Express International, Inc./PATA-Asia Division (1996) *Jewels of the Mekong*. Ismay Publications, Ltd, Hong Kong.

Anderson, K. and Gale, F. (eds) (1992) *Inventing Places: Studies in Cultural Geography*. Longman Cheshire, Melbourne.

Asian Business (1996) Thai tourism mirrors rapid economic growth. 1 October (http://web3.asia1.com.sg/timesnet/data/ab/docs/ab0480.html).

Asian Development Bank (1998) *Mekong Lancang River Tourism Planning Study: Concept Plans*. Regional Technical Assistance Project RETA No. 5743, ADB, Bangkok.

Asian Development Bank (2000) *TA: Mekong Tourism Project Preparation*. ADB, Bangkok.

Associated Press, The (2000) ASEAN to launch joint tourism campaign next year, 23 January (http://mycnn.com).

Bank of Hawai'i (2000) *Federated States of Micronesia Economic Report*. Honolulu: BOH.

Bishop, R. and Robinson, L.S. (1998) *Night Market: Sexual Cultures and the Thai Economic Miracle*. Routledge, New York and London.

CDNP (1999) Personal contact with staff of Con Dao National Park, 28 October.

Cohen, E. (1996) *Thai Tourism: Hill Tribes, Islands, and Open-Ended Prostitution.* Studies in Contemporary Thailand, No. 4, White Lotus, Ltd, Bangkok.

Con Dao District (1992) *1993–2010 Master Plan.* Con Dao District Office of Planning, Vung Tau, Vietnam.

Con Dao District (2000) Personal contact with staff in the Office of Planning, Con Dao, 18–26 May.

Con Dao Historical Museum (2000) Personal contact with admissions staff, February 8.

Con Dao National Park (1999) Personal contact with director, November 3–15.

Cook, I.G., Doel, M.A. and Li, R. (1996) *Fragmented Asia: Regional Integration and National Disintegration in Pacific Asia.* Ashgate, Aldershot, UK.

Corben, R. (1996) Optimistic outlook. *Asia Travel Trade.* March: 33–5.

Daily Post, The (Rotorua, NZ) (2000a) Joint Asian tourism deal signed in Thailand. 7 October: A5.

Daily Post, The (Rotorua, NZ) (2000b) South-east Asia in danger of continuing crisis. 31 July: A8.

Dảo, N. (2000) Conservation Science and Development Officer, WWF Indochina Programme, Hanoi. Personal contact, Con Dao, 4 May.

Engelhardt, R. (1997) Nam Ha ecotourism project proposal. Ref: 143.34 (CP-TUR) CA/1333/97, United Nations Educational, Scientific and Cultural Organization, Bangkok.

FIPI (1999) Personal correspondence, Ministry of Agriculture & Rural Development Sub-Institute of Forest Inventory and Planning No. 2, Ho Chi Minh City, Vietnam.

Fox, C. and Kohler, N. (1999) *Ecological and Social Sustainability in International River Basins: Local Participation in Natural Resource Planning in the Xe Kong and Se San River Basins of Laos, Cambodia, and Vietnam.* Sylff Working Papers No. 12, Global Foundation for Research and Scholarship, Tokyo.

Giang, H. (1996) *Nhang Boc Tranh Côn Dao: The Paintings from Con Son Prison Island.* Nha Xuat Ban Tre, Ho Chi Minh City, Vietnam.

Hall, C.M. (1997) *Tourism in the Pacific Rim.* Addison Wesley Longman, South Melbourne.

Hall, C.M. and O'Sullivan, V. (1996) Tourism, politics and political stability in the Pacific Rim: image, ethics and reality. Paper presented at *Pacific Rim Tourism 2000: Issues, Interrelationships, Inhibitors.* Centre for Tourism Studies, Wairiki Polytechnic University, Rotorua, New Zealand.

Hall, C.M. and Ringer, G. (2000) Tourism in Cambodia, Laos and Myanmar: from terrorism to tourism? In C.M. Hall and S.J. Page (eds) *Tourism in South and South East Asia: Issues and Cases* (pp. 178–94). Butterworth-Heinemann, New York, NY.

Herod, B. (2000) Cambodia PM urges Mekong nations to help save river. *CamNews* 1 November: 1.

Hitchcock, M., King, V. and Parnwell, M. (eds) (1993) *Tourism in South-East Asia.* Routledge, London and New York.

Houston, R. (1999) The future of ecotravel in Asia? *The Ecotourism Society Newsletter* **3**: 1–2 and 10.

Howe, J., McMahon, E. and Propst, L. (1997) *Balancing Nature and Commerce in Gateway Communities.* Island Press, Washington, D.C. and Covelo, CA.

Hulse, D. (1999) Programme director, World Wide Fund for Nature – Indochina Programme, Hanoi. Personal contact, 16 October.

Huong, P. (2001) Acting Director, Department of Science Research & International Relations, Van Lang University, Ho Chi Minh City. Personal contact, 2 July.

Inter Press Service (1999) Technology – St. Maarten: using the Internet to boost tourism. 15 July (http://customnews.cnn.com/cnews/pna.show_story?p_art_id=4057746&p_section_name=&p_art_type=1271778&p_subcat=Travel+%26+Leisure&p_category=Industries).

International Monetary Fund (1997) *International Financial Statistics.* Washington, D.C.: IMF.

Klyne, S. (1997) The paperless solution. *Asia Travel Trade* March: 15–47.

Mak, J. and White, K. (1992) Comparative tourism development in Asia and the Pacific. *Journal of Travel Research* Summer: 15–23.

Matoba, Y. (1997) The Mekong River Commission: planning for the future. In B. Stehsholt (ed.) *Developing the Mekong Subregion* (pp. 86–9), Monash Asia Institute, Monash University, Clayton, Victoria, Australia.

Matsui, Y. (1996) *Women in the New Asia: From Pain to Power.* White Lotus, Bangkok.

McCaskill, D. and Kampe, K. (eds) (1997) *Development or Domestication? Indigenous Peoples of Southeast Asia.* Silkworm Books, Chiang Mai.

Ministry of Agriculture and Rural Development (2000) Personal correspondence, Hanoi, 23 October.

Myre, G. (2000) Vietnam welcomes this U.S. invasion. *The Orlando (Florida) Sentinel* 21 May: L–14.

New Zealand Herald (2000) Red tape hindering Vietnam, says UN. 29 November: E12.

Orams, M.B. (2000) Towards a more desirable form of ecotourism. In C. Ryan and S. Page (eds) *Tourism Management: Towards the New Millennium* (pp. 315–23), Elsevier Science, Ltd, Oxford, UK.

Palasri, S., Huter, S. and Wenzel, Z. (1999) *The History of the Internet in Thailand.* University of Oregon Books, Eugene.

Palmer, A. and Bejou, D. (1995) Tourism destination marketing alliances. *Annals of Tourism Research* **22**(3): 616–29.

Pante, F. (1997) Investing in regional development: Asian Development Bank. In B. Stensholt (ed.) *Developing the Mekong Subregion* (pp. 16–21). Monash Asia Institute, Monash University, Clayton, Victoria, Australia.

PATA (1996) *Jewels of the Mekong: Cambodia, Yunnan, China, Lao PDR, Myanmar, Thailand, Vietnam.* Ismay Publications Ltd, and Pacific-Asia Travel Association, Hong Kong.

PATA (1999) Special report on ASEAN tourism. *Issues & Trends: Pacific Asia Travel* March.

Phongpaichit, P., Piriyarangsan, S. and Treerat, N. (1998) *Guns, Girls, Gambling, Ganja: Thailand's Illegal Economy and Public Policy*. Silkworm Books, Chiang Mai.

Phuong, L.H. (2000) Deputy General Manager, Saigontourist Travel Service. Personal contact, 3 May, Ho Chi Minh City.

Picard, M. and Wood, R. (eds) (1997) *Tourism, Ethnicity, and the State in Asian and Pacific Societies*. University of Hawai'i Press, Honolulu.

Register-Guard, The (Eugene) (2000) Tourism notes: Vietnam sets tourism goals. 5 August: 4H.

Rigg, J. (1997) *Southeast Asia: The Human Landscape of Modernization and Development*. Routledge, London.

Ringer, G. (1997) *Recommendations for Recreational Development at Kirirom and Ream National Parks, South Central Cambodia*. Ministry of Environment, Royal Government of Cambodia, Phnom Penh.

Ringer, G. (ed.) (1998) *Destinations: Cultural Landscapes of Tourism*. Routledge, London and New York.

Ringer, G. and Robinson, A. (1999) *Ecotourism and Environmental Education Proposal for Con Dao National Park, Vietnam*. World Wide Fund for Nature-Indochina (WWF) and Ministry of Agriculture and Rural Development, Ho Chi Minh City and Hanoi.

Robinson, A. (2000) Personal correspondence, WWF Project Director, Con Dao Ecotourism Demonstration Project, 11 November.

Ross, M. and Andriani, I.A.D. (1998) *Marine Biodiversity Conservation at Con Dao National Park, Vietnam*. Institute for Environment and Sustainable Development, Hong Kong University of Science and Technology, Institute of Oceanography in Nha Trang, and Con Dao National Park, Ha Noi.

Sage, N. (2000) Personal correspondence. US Fulbright Scholar, Ho Chi Minh City, 8 May.

Seabrook, J. (1996) *Travels in the Skin Trade: Tourism and the Sex Industry*. Photo Press, London and Chicago.

Singh, A. (1998) Asia Pacific tourism industry: current trends and future outlook. *Asia Pacific Journal of Tourism Research* **32**(2): 48–50.

Sittirak, S. (1998) *The Daughters of Development: Women in a Changing Environment*. Zed Books Ltd, London.

Stensholt, B. (ed.) (1997) *Developing the Mekong Subregion*. Monash Asia Institute, Monash University, Clayton, Victoria, Australia.

Taemsamran, J. (1997) Thailand needs Mekong links: regional tourism the next wave, TAT believes, *Bangkok Post* 30 January: 3.

Tan, P. (2000) Marketing the Mekong to a cost-conscious world, *PATA Compass: The Magazine of the Pacific Asia Travel Association* February–March: 8–9.

TAT (2001) Personal correspondence, Tourism Authority of Thailand, Bangkok, 4 April.

Taylor, K. (1998) Surface orientations in Vietnam: beyond histories of nation and region. *The Journal of Asian Studies* **57**(4): 949–78.

Theobald, W.F. (ed.) (1998) *Global Tourism*. 2nd edn, Butterworth-Heinemann, Oxford.

UNEP (1999) *Vietnam Redbook*. UN Environmental Programme, Geneva, Switzerland.

Vietnam National Administration of Tourism (1998) *Vietnam Tourist Guidebook*. Tourism Information Technology Center, Hanoi.

Wieman, E. (1996) Reaching new heights. *Asia Travel Trade* March: 11–13.

WTO (1997) *Tourism Market Trends: East Asia and the Pacific*. World Tourism Organization, Madrid.

WTO (2000) *WTO Tourism Statistics Database*, World Tourism Organization. (http://www.world-tourism.org/esta/statserv.htm).

Xinhua (1999) Vietnam strives to develop tourism. 16 August (http://my.cnn.com/jbcl/cnews/o?template=mycnn).

CHAPTER 15

The tale of the Little Penguins and the tourists – making tourism sustainable at Phillip Island Nature Park

Rob Harris

Introduction

Much of Australia's natural heritage now lies inside national parks and reserves dotted island-like around the continent. Phillip Island Nature Park (PINP) located near the entrance to Port Phillip Bay in the Australian state of Victoria is no exception. The park is surrounded by land long ago cleared for agricultural and pastoral pursuits as well as, in more recent times, for housing and recreational activities. This loss of habitat, combined with a range of other related factors, has seen the number of Penguin colonies on the island decrease dramatically to the point where today only one remains. The future of this colony, now protected within the PINP, has until relatively recent times also been in doubt. Tourism, it is argued in this case study, has been central in generating the resources and necessary political will to ensure the effective long-term management of this last remaining colony.

This case study begins by overviewing the history of environmental management at, and visitation to, PINP. The significance of the economic benefits that flow to state and local economies from the Park's operations are then discussed, along with the role these have played in the site's preservation. The physical environmental impacts that have resulted from visitation, along with other threats to the Park's environment, are then reviewed before examining the various approaches that have been employed to ameliorate these. The nature of current visitor experiences will then be addressed, before going on to examine how effective the present management regime has been in delivering these experiences in a sustainable way. Finally, selected issues regarding the role of tourism in the sustainable development of the Park will be discussed.

Background

Phillip Island is located at the Southern end of Western Port Bay, some 140 kilometres by road south of Melbourne. Europeans first settled Phillip Island in the 1850s at which time there were ten Little Penguin colonies located along the island's shoreline. Clearing for agricultural and pastoral pursuits from the mid-1850s, and in more recent times, for housing and recreational purposes, was the primary causal agent in reducing this number to one by the beginning of the 1980s (Dann, 1992). Other factors identified as impacting upon penguin numbers include: the introduction to the island of predators (dogs, cats and foxes); the spread of exotic weeds that have acted to exclude penguins from their traditional breeding areas; and the introduction of rabbits with their similar habitat requirements, and whose feeding and burrowing activities caused significant erosion within traditional penguin breeding areas (Harris and Bode, 1981).

The last remaining penguin colony is located on a part of the island known as Summerland Peninsula, an area of approximately 340 hectares (see Figure 15.1) (Phillip Island Nature Park Board of Management, 1999). This area had also been the subject of a variety of land uses since human settlement, with the most significant, from the viewpoint of maintaining penguin numbers in the area, being a large housing subdivision. In 1927 a significant area of the peninsula was subdivided into residential blocks. This area was prime penguin habitat (Newman, 1992). Of the remaining land most was held by the local council; however, some was in private hands, specifically the Spencer-Jackson family. This family began the process of reserving land for the use of Little Penguins when, in the early 1930s it donated four hectares to the local shire to be used as a penguin reserve. Shortly afterwards the Shire of Phillip Island reserved additional

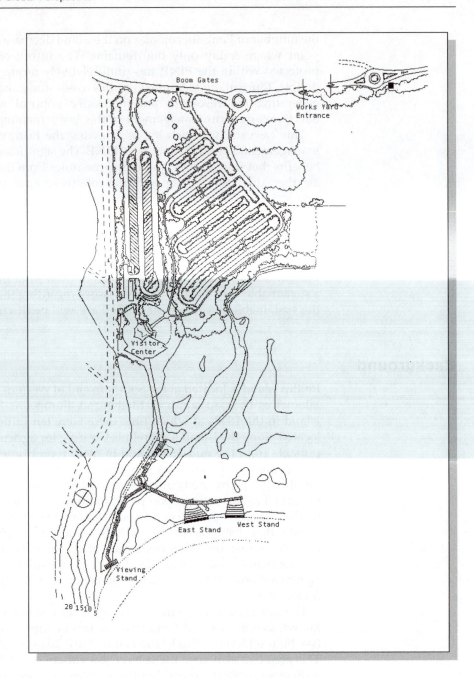

Figure 15.1
Summerland
Peninsula Penguin
Parade Site

land to which it later added in 1955 (Newman, 1992). Partly fuelling the desire to protect the Little Penguin on the Summerland Peninsula was the nightly 'Penguin Parade', which first began attracting visitors in the 1920s (Dann, 1992).

From the mid-1950s up until 1981 the local Shire controlled the reserve and managed the nightly 'Penguin Parade' which, by the end of this period, had become a significant tourist attraction. In 1981, the Victorian state government, concerned by the way the site was being managed, and by statistics showing a significant decline in penguin numbers, sought control of the area through an amendment to the Crown Land Reserves Act. This amendment was passed and a committee to oversee the Park's management was established (Newman, 1992). The responsibilities of this committee were later (1996) expanded to include all other crown land and reserves on Phillip Island. At this time the committee of management was reconstituted as the Phillip Island Nature Park Board of Management (PINPBM) (Scrase, 1997, personal communication, 8 July). The goals of this new body were to:

- have the park recognized as a centre for excellence in wildlife conservation, research and education;
- conserve and enhance the wildlife and its habitat and other natural and cultural values of the park;
- provide opportunities for high quality ecotourism experiences and facilitate wildlife viewing and scenic viewing;
- provide outstanding and safe recreational opportunities for people with different needs and abilities;
- value staff and community input to park development and programmes;
- participate in regional, state and national tourism forums;
- train and develop staff to deliver high quality customer service and assist staff to reach their potential;
- maintain profitability and increase profit within the park in order to fund research, visitor facilities, conservation and management;
- provide leadership in co-operation with other bodies to access external funds for the economic development of the park, island and region; and
- ensure the park is managed as an efficient business (PINPBM, 2000).

With an eye to ensuring all key stakeholders are represented, the state government selects members of the PINPBM. The current committee totals twelve, with members being drawn from the following organizations and government departments (PINPBM, 2000):

- state government nominee (2);
- local tourism industry (1);
- local council (1);
- local community (2);
- Conservation Society (1);
- tertiary institution engaged in penguin research (1);
- tertiary institution engaged in koala research (1);
- financial adviser (1);
- friends of PINP (1); and
- park management (1).

A core responsibility of this Board is the development and implementation of a management plan for the area. The most current of these was finalized in 2000 and involved taking into account some 173 submissions from the public and other interested organizations.

Economic impact

It is doubtless, as Scrase (1995) notes, that the significant economic benefits at both a local and state level flowing from visitation to the 'Penguin Parade', were instrumental in the decision by the Victorian Government to bring PINP under its control. The nightly 'Parade' of penguins returning to their burrows after a day's fishing at sea had become a significant component of Victoria's tourism product by the early 1980s. By 1993 Tourism Victoria estimated the annual net expenditure in the state arising directly and indirectly from the penguin parade at AU$50 million (Scrase, 1995). A more recent estimate by the consulting firm KPMG (1995) has revised this figure upward to AU$96 million. Another study of economic impacts is due to be conducted in 2002 (Scrase, 2002, personal communication, 15 February).

Within the confines of Phillip Island itself, the Park had become the island's largest employer by the mid-1990s, with a total of 100 full-time and part-time staff, a figure that rises to 130 during the peak Christmas holiday season (Scrase, 2002, personal communication, 15 February). The Park also injects over AU$2.2 million into the local economy in salaries as well as purchasing a significant percentage of its business inputs from island businesses or from nearby areas (Scrase, 2002, personal communication, 15 February). It is also the case that many tourism and non-tourism businesses on the island benefit directly from tourist expenditure as a result of the stimulus provided by PINP.

In terms of direct income generated through PINP's own activities, admission fees raised approximately AU$4.6 million in 2000/2001, while other operating activities, essentially the sale of souvenirs and the provision of food and beverages, raised a further AU$3.5 million. In 2000/2001 these revenues resulted in an operating profit of approximately AU$1.1 million (Scrase, 2002, personal communication, 15 February). This level of income has allowed PINP to be self-funding, with the exception of larger capital works programmes for which it must apply for government grants.

Visitation

While it is likely that some visitation to the area now encompassed by the Park took place prior to the late 1920s, it was not until that time that organized penguin viewing trips began to be run by some entrepreneurial island residents (Newman, 1992; Dann, 1992). These residents would meet visitors at the island's ferry and punt landings and escort them to Summerland Beach to watch the penguins arrive back at their nesting sites after feeding in the sea in the early evening. With the construction of a vehicular suspension bridge that linked the island to the mainland, visitation began to grow markedly. Over the next 40 years the popularity of the 'Penguin Parade' saw increasing numbers of intrastate and interstate visitors, as well as visitors from overseas, make the trip to Phillip Island. By the mid-1980s the 'Parade' attracted some 250 000 (PINPBM, 1985). This number has since doubled, with visitor numbers reaching 520 000 in 2001, approximately 60 per cent of whom were from overseas (Scrase, 2002, personal communication, 15 February).

A significant aspect of visitation to the Park is that it has now become highly industrialized from a tourism industry perspective, with 50 per cent or more of visitors arriving on packaged tours. This is particularly the case with overseas visitors where it is estimated more than 80 per cent purchase pre-packaged day tours to PINP (Scrase, 2002, personal communication, 15 February).

Physical environmental impacts and management responses

From the time of the first organized tours to Phillip Island Nature Park (PINP) in the 1920s until the first efforts to control visitor access to the site in the mid-1960s, some degradation of the area's physical environment occurred (Scrase, 1995). Specifically these impacts resulted from a desire by visitors to ensure a close 'first hand' experience of the penguin 'Parade'. To achieve this goal it was common for visitors to trample (and collapse) penguin burrows as they made their way to and from the beach, and to create their own tracks in doing so. This latter impact saw some destabilization of dunes adjacent to the beach occur, reducing their value as a penguin habitat. It was also common for visitors to try to handle the penguins and to further stress them through the use of close range flash photography. Additional problems evident during this time were deaths resulting when penguins crossed the main access road and losses sustained from introduced predators, primarily foxes (Dann, 1992).

In the late 1960s it became evident to the local shire that the penguin colony under its care was to some extent in danger of being 'loved to death'. The first step taken to ameliorate problems flowing from visitation was the construction of fences and viewing platforms with the intent of discouraging visitors from entering penguin nesting areas (Scrase, 1995). Few additional efforts were made at managing visitation to the site through until the beginning of the 1980s. An incident in 1980 in which 136 penguins were killed deliberately by the driver of a motor vehicle, did result in all roads, other than the main access roads, being closed to visitors from dusk until dawn (Scrase, 1997, personal communication, 8 July).

By the early 1980s researchers were concerned that a significant decrease in the number of breeding Little Penguins within the Park was occurring (Dann, 1992). Although it must be noted that visitation to the site was not seen as a major contributing factor to the declining penguin numbers (Norman et al., 1992). This situation was conveyed to the then state government, who, concerned for the welfare of the penguins and the maintenance of the significant economy that had built up around them, placed the Park under its control in 1981 (Scrase, 1995). As part of this process a new Committee of Management was formed that was required to:

protect the Little Penguin population and its environment, make them available for viewing by the public, generate a store of knowledge to educate the public and have the on-going means to attract visitors and funds to support management of the Park.

(Newman, 1992)

Over the next 4 years the Committee of Management set about developing a Penguin Protection Plan (PPP). This plan was completed in July 1985, and involved the:

- allocation of funds for scientific research into the Little Penguin;
- purchase of a nearby housing development, Summerland Estate, and the staged rehabilitation of this land as penguin habitat; and
- development of a comprehensive site management plan (Newman, 1992).

It is particularly noteworthy in the context of this plan that the Victorian state government agreed to fund the purchase of an entire housing estate comprising 780 allotments, 180 of which contained houses, over a 15-year period (Newman, 1992). At the time of writing, this process is not yet complete; however, the government continues to honour its obligation, purchasing a further two houses and seventeen vacant allotments in 2000, by which time 84 per cent of the estate had been returned to public ownership (PINPBM, 2000). This is perhaps the first, and only, example in the Australian context of an instance where a (human) community has been essentially displaced for the good of a particular animal species. Arguably such action would not have been taken without the presence of the significant tourism economy that had built up around the Little Penguin.

The site management plan component of the PPP acknowledged the need to more effectively deal with rising levels of visitation. While noted previously, the effect of tourism on the Little Penguin colony had been slight, visitation was nonetheless rising, and the potential for a significant increase in visitor related impacts was therefore a very real one. To deal with this issue steps were taken to more effectively isolate visitors from penguins, while at the same time trying to ensure the maintenance of quality visitor experiences. To achieve these dual outcomes a substantial redevelopment of a section of the Park's beachfront area took place. This redevelopment, at a cost of some AU$3.6 million, was funded largely by the Park itself with some contributions from the Federal and state governments, and involved the construction of:

- beach viewing stands capable of seating approximately 4000 people, which are designed for optimum penguin viewing (see Figure 15.2);
- elevated boardwalks that facilitate visitor access to the beach without disturbing the sensitive coastal dune systems – the penguins' home. These boardwalks also provide a viewing platform overlooking the penguin colony, and allow unrestricted access for penguins to their burrows; and

Figure 15.2
Beach viewing
stands – Penguin
Parade

- a visitor centre, containing interpretive displays, printed material and audio-visual facilities (Scrase, 1995).

Since these developments have occurred a further AU$3 million has been spent on improving on-site displays, enhancing commercial facilities (notably the restaurant and shop), expanding the sealed parking area and improving the lighting in this area, and building a penguin rehabilitation facility. This latter facility treated 346 penguins in 2000, the majority of these for oil contamination (Scrase, 2002, personal communication, 15 February).

Financial resources generated by visitation have also been used to develop programmes and practices designed to: eradicate feral animals (sixty-nine foxes and sixty-eight cats were trapped/killed inside the Park in 2000); educate local community members re the responsible care of domestic pets (see Figure 15.3); control introduced plant species; relocate penguins to rehabilitated areas; and replant degraded areas. As regards this last point, some tens of thousands of trees, shrubs and other native plants have been planted on the Summerland Estate in an effort to restore it to its pre-European state (PINPBM, 2000).

PINP's Board, it should be noted, is aided by volunteers in its efforts to manage the park environment and penguin colony. These individuals are involved in a variety of programmes including: providing interpretation services to visitors; weed eradication; rescuing wildlife and seed collection and propagation (PINPBM, 2000).

Research is also a core aspect of PINP activity, with its latest research strategy having been approved by its Board in February 2000. This strategy embraces such actions as: providing assistance to post-graduate students engaged in penguin research; seeking research grants;

Figure 15.3
Brochure on responsible cat ownership distributed to Phillip Island Residents by PINP (reproduced with permission from Phillip Island Nature Park, Australia)

Cats make great pets for responsible owners.

But remember cats are hunters. Even well fed cats hunt, stalking up to one kilometre from their home – day or night.

On Phillip Island, uncontrolled cats can do as much damage during the day as at night. They kill our native birds, lizards, mammals and frogs. Roaming cats are also in danger from other cats, cars and diseases such as Feline AIDS and cat flu.

Phillip Island Nature Park has a responsibility to protect wildlife. Any unidentified cat on Nature Park land is considered feral (wild) and may be destroyed.

Being responsible – it's up to you...

- Keep your cats inside – day & night.
- When outside, put your cat in a run or cattery.
- Register & desex your cat.
- Ensure your cat has a collar with address tag and two bells.
- Report feral or roaming cats to the Nature Park.

Looking after Phillip Island Nature Park – together.

Phillip Island Nature Park PO Box 97 COWES 3922
Ph: 03 5956 8300 Fax: 03 5956 8394
www.penguins.org.au

Phillip Island
NATURE PARK Australia

WINNER
1999 VICTORIAN
TOURISM AWARDS

commissioning studies; and participating in collaborative research/ activities with universities and other bodies (e.g., in 1999 PINP joined with the International Union for the Conservation of Nature, and other interested organizations, in the preparation of a conservation and management plan for world penguins) (PINPBM, 1999).

The visitor experience

Providing quality experiences for what can be up to 4000 paying visitors on a single night is a major challenge. To achieve this goal access to the Park is only provided via the interpretive Centre where visitors can interact with a large range of displays detailing such matters as the life cycle of penguins, the dangers they face, and their habitat requirements (see Figure 15.4). This Centre also contains a small theatrette, a cafeteria and a large shop where items ranging from toy penguins, film and items of clothing can be purchased. Additionally rangers are available to answer any questions.

Access to the beach is via raised boardwalks, along which a number of interpretive displays are located. In addition to these, signs stating that cameras are not be used to photograph penguins appear at regular intervals. Once at the beach visitors view from two large purpose built viewing stands (see Figure 15.2). Alongside these stands is a series of lighting towers used to illuminate the beach area just after dark when the penguins arrive. Between the stands a tower has been constructed upon which sits a small commentary box. From this box a ranger provides information to visitors concerning the 'parade'. In addition to the

Figure 15.4
Interpretive
displays at the
Visitor Centre

commentary, instructions are provided concerning such matters as the importance of staying on fenced paths. It is noteworthy that the continued non-observance of an instruction not to use flash photography by a small percentage of visitors ultimately led to the PINPBM banning cameras from being used altogether in October 1999. Instead, good quality and moderately priced photographs were made available for purchase in the Visitor Centre. Interestingly, Penguin Parade staff observed that this decision has had the effect of encouraging visitors to relax and enjoy the experience more. Rangers have also found that they are able to provide more information, and pay more attention to the needs of visitors, as they are not constantly having to remind them of the importance of not using flash photography (PINPBM, 2000).

In the period immediately leading up to the parade, and immediately after it, rangers are strategically positioned at the beach front, at viewing platforms, and along walkways, to act as both an interpretive resource and to ensure that visitors act in accordance with the guidelines provided to them. Once the parade is finished, visitors return via the Interpretive Centre where they can again access the various displays before leaving. Departing visitors are also asked to be careful when leaving the Park as approximately fifteen penguins a year are killed by cars (Scrase, 2002, personal communication, 15 February).

As noted earlier, the majority of visitors are from overseas. In response to this, PINP has: employed a mandarin speaking ranger to liaise with tour groups; translated its Interpretive Centre audio visual programme into Mandarin and Japanese; and produced a taped commentary and visitor's guide in a number of languages. Prerecorded instructions given at the parade itself regarding appropriate behaviour have also been prepared in several languages (PINPBM, 1995).

In addition to servicing the needs of parade visitors, a variety of education and interpretive services are provided to school and university groups. In 2001 PINP's rangers delivered education programmes to some 12350 students. Additionally, a further 2175 people participated in the activities programme which included snorkelling, presentations on penguins, and short interpretive walks dealing with seals and seabirds (PINPBM, 2000). Other information and interpretive services provided by PINP include a website (http://www.penguins.org.au), a newsletter (*Phillip Island Nature Watch*), and a column in the local newspaper designed to inform the local community of wildlife activity in the park (PINPBM, 2000).

To assist the Board of Management in meeting the needs of visitors, marketing research is conducted on a regular basis (the latest being 2000) to determine basic demographics as well as the degree to which visitor expectations are being met. The outcomes of these surveys are used to refine service delivery systems. Additionally, when large changes to the site and its services are planned, research is conducted with visitors to gain their perspectives on these changes. For example, in 1995, prior to the redevelopment of the Interpretive Centre, an extensive survey was conducted to identify the type and level of information required by visitors as well as the on-site services (e.g., food and beverage outlets and opportunities to purchase souvenirs) they required (PINPCM, 1995).

Assessing the outcomes

The various management plans that have been implemented since 1985 have played a significant role in turning around a situation that, if allowed to continue, would have likely seen the penguin colony cease to exist by the mid-1990s (Dann, 1992). Penguin numbers have now returned to their estimated post-World War II numbers (28 000–30 000). Additionally, the production of chicks, as estimated from six study sites, is now 1.11 per breeding pair. This figure is well above the average for the past 30 years (PINPBM, 2000). Moreover, the Park's plant life has been substantially restored with the result that erosion has been virtually eliminated and other species, particularly the Short-tailed Shearwater, now breed within the Park's perimeter (PINPBM, 1997). Significantly, from a tourism perspective, these results have been achieved in an environment that has seen visitor numbers grow by a factor of two over the 17-year period since 1985 when the first management plan was put into effect.

Other issues and concluding comments

The processes employed at PINP, and their success in conserving the threatened Little Penguin colony, raise some important issues as regards tourism and natural resource conservation. Firstly, in the presence of significant economies based around visitation, those engaged in conservation are likely to find their options constrained in the sense that there will be significant pressure to factor the maintenance and growth of visitation into their decision-making processes. Related to this point is the potential that such economies have to be used by individuals/organizations with a conservation agenda to 'push' governments and other stakeholders in that direction. In the case of PINP it is extremely questionable whether the state government would have acted to buy back an entire real estate subdivision on the basis of an argument built solely around the protection of the Little Penguin colony. Indeed, the Charter of the Board of Management established by the state government clearly reflects the significance of visitation and economic considerations in its operation.

Secondly, the PINP case demonstrates the capacity of highly structured 'experience' delivery systems underpinned by a 'hardened' environment, to meet the needs of visitors while at the same time minimizing environmental impacts. This system has been extremely successful in controlling visitor movement on site; the time they spend on site; the type of interaction that takes place between them and the penguins; and their general behaviour. Indicative of this success, as Dann (1992) notes, is the similar rate of breeding in areas affected by tourism to those of adjacent areas without public access, and the absence of any penguin movement away from the tourist area. The 'gated' nature of such systems also means that visitation can generate a significant revenue stream that can be used for conservation purposes. In this regard almost AU$500 000 was spent on research, education and interpretation and Park protection in 1999/2000 (PINPBM, 2000). The downside of such systems, however, has been the need to sacrifice some natural values in parts of the Park in order to construct the necessary infrastructure. In the case of PINP approximately 10 per cent of the penguin nesting area is open to public visitation, while an area of approximately four hectares is taken up by car parks and an Interpretive Centre (Scrase, 2002, personal communication, 15 February).

Thirdly, the capacity of humans to relate to a species, to see them as cute, 'touchable' or exotic, can be a significant factor in the conservation process. Without the 'bond' visitors to the Park feel with the Little Penguins, an industry would not have built up around them and arguably the forces acting for their conservation would have been far weaker. This observation is of relevance to natural area managers as it raises the issue of leveraging this bond not only to protect particular species but also other less 'appealing' animals that share the same habitat. In the case of PINP, the Board of Management has been able to use the income from the Little Penguin 'parade' to successfully manage the full range of species within the Park, including Short-tailed Shearwater, Western Water Rats, Little Forest Bats and Mutton-Bird (PINPBM, 2000). In the case of the Short-tailed Shearwater, funding for a programme designed to rescue and release birds that come into contact with power lines or other obstacles (a recurring problem with juvenile Shearwaters attempting their first migration) has been provided. This programme resulted in some 686 birds being rescued in 1999/2000 (PINPBM, 2000).

Lastly, this case study displays how effective conservation can take place in the context of rising visitor levels, providing a holistic management strategy is adopted. The key ingredients of such a strategy, as demonstrated here, are: a primary focus on resource conservation; generation/provision of adequate financial resources to perform the conservation task; research; and a highly industrialized visitor experience delivery system built around an understanding of their needs.

Acknowledgements

I wish to thank David Scrase, Acting General Manager, Phillip Island Nature Park.

References

Dann, P. (1992) Distribution, population trends and factors influencing the population size of the Little Penguins *Eudyptula minor* on Phillip Island, Victoria. *Emu* **91**(5): 263–72.

Dann, P., Norman, I. and Riley, P. (eds) (1994) *The Penguins: Ecology and Management*, Surrey, Beattey & Sons, Sydney.

KPMG (1995) *The Economic Impact of the Phillip Island Penguin Park.*

Harris, M. and Bode, K. (1981) Populations of Little Penguin, Short-tailed Shearwaters and other seabirds on Phillip Island, Victoria. *Emu*, **81**: 20–28.

Newman, G. (1992) Studies on the Little Penguin *Eudyptula minor* in Victoria. *Emu* **91**(5): 261–2.

Norman, F., Du Guesclin, P. and Dann, P. (1992) Little Penguin *Eudyptula minor* in Victoria: Past Present and Future. *Emu* **91**(5): 402–8.

PINPBM (1985) *Survey of Visitor Use, Expectations and Satisfaction*, Phillip Island Penguin Park Committee of Management.

PINPBM (1986) *Annual Report 1985–6*, Phillip Island Penguin Park Committee of Management.

PINPBM (1995) *Annual Report 1994–5*, Phillip Island Penguin Park Committee of Management.

PINPBM (1996) *Annual Report 1995–6*, Phillip Island Penguin Park Committee of Management.

PINPBM (1997) *Annual Report 1996–7*, Phillip Island Nature Park Board of Management.

PINPBM (1998) *Annual Report 1997–8*, Phillip Island Nature Park Board of Management.

PINPBM (1999) *Annual Report 1998–9*, Phillip Island Nature Park Board of Management.

PINPBM (2000) *Annual Report 1999–2000*, Phillip Island Nature Park Board of Management.

Scrase, D. (1995) Philip Island Penguin Park. In Harris, R. and Leiper, N. (eds) *Sustainable Tourism: An Australian Perspective*. Butterworth Heinemann, Sydney.

Making paradise last: Maho Bay Resorts

Christina Symko and Rob Harris

Introduction

Developing appropriate tourism facilities and accommodations in fragile environments requires inspiration, innovation and technical ingenuity. Ecolodge developers contend both with the challenge of finding ways to build in harmony with nature and the need to engage visitors in nature-based experiences so that they have an enhanced understanding of the environment around them (Ceballos-Lascurin, 2001). This case study details how one ecolodge developer, Maho Bay Resorts (MBR) in the US Virgin Islands, has sought to address these challenges. In so doing MBR has sought to encompass the philosophy of sustainability in its broadest sense, extending beyond the environmental dimension to embrace economic and social goals linked to surrounding communities.

Maho Bay resorts

Located on the island of St John in the US Virgin Islands' National Park, Maho Bay Resort operates four properties: Maho Bay Campground, Harmony Studios, Estate Concordia Studios and Concordia Eco-Tents. Maho Bay Campground (MBC) opened in 1974 with eighteen tent-cottages hidden among trees, and connected by elevated wooden walkways.

Figure 16.1
Concordia Eco-
Tents at Maho Bay
Resorts

The ecologically sensitive construction, land use and operations associated with this development stimulated significant media attention,
which in turn generated strong growth in market demand. Since 1974,
another ninety-six tent cottages have been constructed, resulting in the
campground covering some fourteen acres. Harmony studios (HS),
comprising twelve two-storey luxury units located on a 3-acre site on a
hillside above Maho Bay Campground, was the next 'product' to be
developed. Estate Concordia Studios (ECS), another luxury development comprising nine units, followed. The most recent 'product' to
come on line is the Concordia Eco-Tents (CET) (see Figure 16.1), a
more up-market version of the MBC tents. Both the CET and ECS
developments are on a 5-acre site on the southeastern shore of St John
Island.

As would be expected, significant differences exist between the
construction costs of these different forms of resort accommodation. The
original tent-cottages at the Maho Bay Resorts campground can be
constructed at a cost of about US$7000 each, while the luxury units at
Harmony Resort and Estate Concordia Studios cost in the vicinity of
US$80 000. The Concordia Eco-Tent, developed after guest feedback
indicated a preference for the same close-to-nature experience as offered
by the MBC, but with private baths, running water and kitchen facilities
(Hawkins *et al.*, 1995), cost in the vicinity of US$30 000 per unit, including
walkways and individual utility systems. These construction costs, even
those of the more expensive HS and ECS resorts, are significantly less
than those of the more traditional forms of tourism facility development
found in the region.

Market demand for the various MBR products has been strong with
occupancy levels approaching 100 per cent in the high season (mid-
December to mid-April), while off-season occupancy rates are significantly above the norm for the Caribbean as a whole.

Sustainability practices

The Maho Bay Resorts' Mission Statement reflects a commitment to sustainable tourism development:

> *To provide a positive and educational experience for our guests while continuing to pioneer the principles of profitable, environmentally sensitive tourism* (www.maho.org).

This mission is reflected in MBR's efforts to: reduce environmental impacts flowing from its operations; conserve the islands' natural environment; educate guests regarding environmental matters; and engage with the local community.

Minimizing environmental impact

The facilities at Maho Bay were built by hand and without largescale clearing or road construction. First, boardwalks were constructed above the ground with manually dug holes for the posts. In this way disturbance to existing animal and plant communities was minimized. Over these boardwalks 'green' construction materials were then carried in. These materials included a range of recycled items such as old automobiles, bottles and garbage bags; composite timber for framing; and a range of energy efficient building products[1]. The underside of these same boardwalks was later used to carry electrical and other services, thus avoiding the need to dig trenches. All site construction took place around existing vegetation, ensuring that the area remained as pristine and natural as possible, thereby eliminating the need for any extensive rehabilitation.

Steering MBR's operational philosophy are the three 'Rs' (reduce, reuse, recycle). A brief summary of the approaches in each of these areas follows.

Reduce • • •

MBR seeks to reduce its use of resource inputs in a variety of ways, including:

- using spring-loaded taps to reduce water wastage;
- employing low-flush toilets, that save up to three gallons per flush over regular toilets, and waterless urinals;
- using water storage tanks on nearly all buildings in order to minimize dependence on energy-intensive and ecologically damaging desalinated water [2], and to reduce energy costs associated with 'pumping' water;
- using unheated water in the bathrooms of most accommodation types;
- reducing guest energy usage by having all electrical devices (except the refrigerator in units that are so equipped) automatically turn off when a guest locks their doors behind them;
- serving draft soda and beer instead of bottled beverages;
- ordering restaurant and retail store supplies that require minimal packaging;

Figure 16.2
Solar panels on the roof of a Harmony studio unit

- purchasing bulk kitchen and housekeeping supplies;
- employing 100 per cent biodegradable laundry detergent and limiting the amount of bleach used to a minimum, allowing resultant wastewater to become a viable water source for secondary usage; and
- using photovoltaics (see Figure 16.2) as the main power source for the resort (MBR is not connected to the island's electricity grid), and additionally employing in the Concordia Eco-Tents, wind generators and passive solar water heaters.

Reuse

Examples of MBR's reuse practices include:

- the 2000–7000 gallons of nutrient rich effluent water generated by MBR's wastewater treatment plant each day is used to water an organic orchard that provides food for the resort;
- all houseware items supplied in the tent-cottages and restaurant are reusable;
- packing and shipping boxes are returned to suppliers, who refill them with the resort's next order; and
- a 'Help Yourself Centre' allows guests to leave items they no longer require so that these products can be used by other visitors.

Recycle

A range of innovative actions are in evidence as regards recycling practices, including:

- composting food, paper and cardboard waste to nourish an organic garden and orchard (see Figure 16.3);

Figure 16.3
Compost bins at
Maho Bay Camp

- melting down aluminium on site and using it to create functional and decorative items for sale through the resort's shop;
- using the residue from composting toilets in the planting of indigenous trees and scrubs; and
- crushing glass to use as aggregate in cement, or to recycle into new glassware using the resort's kiln.

In addition to practising the three 'Rs' MBR has a policy of purchasing recycled products wherever possible. Many of the items used in the construction of the resort were composed of recycled, or largely recycled, material. For example, the wood used in construction of the walkways and railings of the Harmony suites is a wood polymer composite lumber, made from recycled plastic and sawdust. Additionally, all nails used were made from recycled steel, as were some furnishings (e.g., recycled rubber tyre rugs, and the tiles used for counter and table-tops).

Conservation of natural resources

Associated with MBR's concern regarding minimizing its environmental impacts is its commitment to ensuring the long-term protection and conservation of the natural resource base on which its future depends. In this regard, it has sought to maintain and enhance the natural environment in and around its developments by using a variety of means. These include: employing only indigenous vegetation in the landscaping process; establishing unobtrusive sites from which visitors can view the island's wildlife (e.g., birds, mongooses, lizards and other animals); and educating guests regarding the need to refrain from feeding animals so that they may remain wild and independent from human influence. The elevated walkways MBR has constructed also reflect the extent to which it has gone to maintain the quality of its environment. There are three miles of these wooden walkways, laid out in such a way that they avoid site features such as trees and rocks, or accommodate them (as is the case with some trees) by cutting a hole through walkway timbers. The elevated nature of these structures also allows for the free movement of animals around the site. Other, less direct means of conserving the natural environment employed by MBR include a policy that prohibits the purchase of products known to originate from endangered plants or animals.

Education

The very structure and design of MBR's facilities provides its guests with numerous opportunities to learn about such matters as alternative energy use, waste reduction and resource conservation methods. Indeed, in 1998 Stanley Selengut, the owner of MBR, made this point clear when he noted that 'there's a secondary purpose to these dwellings. It's not just to have them work well, it's also to have them function as a teaching machine.' Perhaps the most obvious example of this is the computer system that has been installed in the Harmony Resort units that allows guests to monitor their own energy and water consumption, thereby helping them to understand the relationship between their consumption patterns and available resources.

MBR also seeks to encourage its guests to learn and interact with the island's physical environment. With this goal in mind, an interpretive trail has been constructed through the resort area that provides insights into local plants and wildlife. In addition, nightly presentations on the ecological and cultural history of the area are provided to give the guests a greater appreciation of the resort's ecological context. Resort staff are also encouraged to explain to guests aspects of the resort's design and operations that are acting to reduce impacts or generally enhance the environment. This kind of dialogue and interaction can serve to transform a holiday into a memorable learning experience. As a further means of fuelling guest interest in environmental matters, MBR has decided to encourage its guests to become members of the International Ecotourism Society (IES) during the United Nations International Year of Ecotourism in 2002. Such encouragement takes the form of deducting the price of membership for IES, a part of the worldwide movement towards less environmentally damaging tourism, from the cost of a stay at any of its properties.

In a broader context, MBR's design and operational practices can be said to have provided a model for low impact sustainable tourism ventures (Hawkins *et al.*, 1995). In 1991, for example, the United States National Park Service conducted a workshop on sustainable design at Maho Bay Campground. Attendees included participants from the American Institute of Architects; American Society of Landscape Architects; the Ecotourism Society; National Parks and Conservation Association; National Oceanic and Atmospheric Administration; Greenpeace; local representatives from the Virgin Islands; private architectural and engineering firms; and ecotourism resort operators. As a result of this workshop the National Park Service and MBR formed a partnership to produce the first prototype design guidelines for sustainable camp-ground design (see Appendix). In 1994, MBR was also the host of the First International Ecolodge Development Forum and Field Seminar. At this meeting scientists and practitioners were provided with a rare opportunity to share creative ideas and methods for operating economically viable and ecologically sensitive ecolodges, while at the same time experiencing an example of such. Following on from its involvement in such events, MBR will in 2002 host a five-day workshop on photovoltaic technology run by Solar Energy International. MBR is also the subject of a video by Clean Islands International Inc. that is shown to school students and various other groups in the Caribbean region.

Community involvement

While initially focusing on dimensions of sustainability, MBR has more recently sought to stress the development of more socially and culturally sustainable practices. Evidence for this can be found in: the employment of local residents whenever possible; the purchasing of most services and supplies from local sources; and the engagement of local artists to entertain guests (Selengut, 2002, personal communication, 29 March). Additionally, MBR strives to work in a spirit of mutual co-operation with its local community.

An innovative means by which MBR is seeking to contribute to the cultural life of St John Island is its Recycled Art Centre. This centre seeks to explore any and all forms of art that can be made out of recycled materials (e.g., pottery, mosaics, painting, photography, paper-making, fibre art, glass blowing, jewellery, bead-making, woodworking and metal work) and invites interested artists to visit, dividing their time on an equal basis between working at the resort and being artist in residence at the centre.

Conclusion

Maho Bay Resorts has been, and remains, very much a pioneer in the creation and development of sustainable resort development practices. At MBR these practices are reflected in its commitment to protecting the physical environment and in its efforts to ensure the resort provides benefits to the community in which it is located. MBR has demonstrated that it is indeed possible to provide for the comfort and enjoyment of guests, preserve the natural resource base on which the future delivery of such benefits are based, and operate a sustainable business. The extent of MBR's success is evident in its use as an 'experimental' model by the US National Parks Service, and its hosting of various events concerning ecolodge design and operations. The guiding approach to MBR's efforts to date is perhaps best summed up by its owner, Stanley Selengut, who noted: 'I am not a philosopher, but if I have learned anything about sustainable design over the past twenty years, it is that it is ego-less. It is about what works and listening to both nature and your customers.'

Acknowledgements

We would like to thank Mr R. McCormick, Director of Media Relations, Maho Bay Resort and Stanley Selengut, Owner, Maho Bay Resort.

Endnotes

1 Maho Bay Resorts has a key list of suppliers and manufacturers of recycled building materials and alternative energy and waste management systems that it uses. This list appears on its web site – www.maho.org.
2 For every four gallons of water pumped from the sea for desalinization, three gallons are pumped back with a 33 per cent higher saline content. The resulting increase in salt content in the adjacent bays damages the fragile offshore marine environment.

References

Cebellos-Lascurain, H. (2001) *Integrating Biodiversity into the Tourism Sector: Best Practice Guidelines.* Report to United Nations Environment Programme. Mexico City: Program of International Consultancy on Ecotourism.

Curwood, S. (1998) Eco-Resorts in the Virgin Islands. *Living on Earth,* August 21, National Public Radio.

Hawkins, D., Epler Wood, M. and Bittman, S. (1995) *The Ecolodge Sourcebook for Planners and Developers.* Vermont, The Ecotourism Society.

Appendix

Design guidelines for the Maho Bay/National Park Service Agreement to Develop Prototype Sustainable Campgrounds

This document and the prototype guidelines were developed to provide prospective architects with design specifications for our future projects. It addresses three main topics: the Structure and Design of Prototype Eco-tent Dwellings; Eco-tent Conservation; and Additional Site Uses. Each section covers specific structural elements that should be included in sustainable design, as well as examples from the Maho Bay eco-tents and suggestions for education and interpretation in units.

Prototype eco-tent dwelling – structure and design

Sustainable design balances human needs (rather than human wants) with the carrying capacity of the natural and cultural environments. It minimizes environmental impacts, importation of goods and energy, as well as generation of waste. The ideal situation would be that if development was necessary, it would be constructed from natural sustainable materials collected on site, generate its own energy from renewable sources such as solar or wind, and manage its own waste.

Eco-tent designs must be:

Affordable – building costs should be under US$30 000 per unit, including walkways and individual utility systems.

Vernacular and site specific – incorporating the natural landscape as well as some local character.

Location

- Place the site-adaptive eco-tents on the more pristine and fragile settings of the site.
- Build solid support buildings on the worst, or previously damaged sections.
- Avoid visual pollution of the landscape.

Background: At Maho, sensitive siting combined with ecological restoration has actually repaired some of the local environment. If it is necessary to build a swimming pool, it should be located on sloping terrain to accommodate the slope of the bottom of the pool, perimeter footings can be hand dug if necessary. Tennis courts, etc., should be built on flat terrain, etc.

Size

- The units should be as small as possible to fit within existing trees and topography.

Background: Two optimum unit dimensions have worked well at Maho:

Choice A = 16′ × 16′ footprint with a 2′ × 8′ extension for the open porch (the toilet and shower are outside the unit connected by the walkway).

Choice B = 16′ × 16′ footprint with a porch area outside the unit connected by the walkway (in this version the toilet and shower are inside the units).

Interior design

- The units should sleep a family of four with privacy and comfort, and up to six people if necessary.

Background: A 16 × 16′ square floor plan can be divided into four 8′ × 8′ sections: a bedroom, kitchen area, living room with a queen-size sleep sofa, and either an open porch or a toilet shower area. The bedroom should be a bit larger to accommodate two twin beds with some space in between, a sleeping loft can hold an additional two children. Extending the porch 2′ would allow for a larger bedroom.

Materials

The complete life-cycle energy, environmental, and waste implications of each building material must be examined. This cradle-to-grave analysis is the tracing of a material or product, and its by-products, from its initial source availability and extraction through refinement, fabrication, treatment and additives, transportation, use, and eventual reuse or disposal. This tracing includes the tabulation of energy consumed and the environmental impacts of each action and material.

- Units should use recycled and local building materials where possible (see Harmony Supplier list).
- Materials should be light and portable.
- Structural members should have minimum standard dimensions.
- Materials should be used so that there is very little waste, for example if fabric is 64″ and only 54″ is needed, the additional material used for another purpose.

Background: Maho has been successful with a light wood framed structure, supported on 4″ × 4″ posts and covered with heat reflective fabric for the roof and nylon-reinforced, laminated fabric for the walls. Other ideas might be considered for different climates or situations, for example metal framing instead of wood, straw bale, rammed earth, or hemp for walls, etc.

Walkways

- The units should be connected by elevated walkways to minimize site disturbance.
- The walkways should allow easy access to difficult terrain at the campground.
- The walkways should be built first so that workmen and building materials can traverse the walks during construction.
- Electrical wiring and water pipes should be fastened to the underside of the decking.

Background: Using an elevated walkway system has allowed the Maho Bay resorts a minimum of site erosion over their twenty year history, even on a steep sloping site.

Construction

- The site is to be left as undisturbed as possible.
- Prefabrication should take preference to site building.

- The dwellings should be easy to build by low skilled labour, and sit on hand-dug footings or anchored to boulders.
- Heavy construction equipment should be avoided.

The construction process is an integral part of the building plans. Where conflict exists, the decision should always be for the environment.

Background: Maho Bay uses only specialized heavy equipment which can work from roads to avoid site disturbance (e.g., concrete pump, back hoe, 4-in-1 bucket on our bulldozer, etc.)

Orientation

Units should be elevated to accommodate space for composting toilets and cisterns underneath the platform. Consideration should also be given to wind directions and sun angles:

- Units must support passive solar heating/cooling and energy production.
- Composting toilets should be located down wind.

Background: The tents at Maho Bay are built on sloping terrain to provide room under the platform for the toilet and cistern. On flat land the platform should be elevated to a height over the compost bin.

Roof

- Roof should be designed to catch rainwater with drainage to a cistern.
- Roof should be heat reflective with overhangs to protect dwellings from intense mid-day sun.

Background: Reflective coating and overhangs help to prevent heat from penetrating the dwelling, this is integral for passive cooling techniques. Water collected from the roof is filtered to be potable.

Storage space

- The tents should have plenty of pegs for hanging guests' clothes, as well as shelves/storage for luggage. It is important to use every inch of space.

Background: Storage space within the units has been an issue in the Maho eco-tents.

Climate · · ·

- Units should be designed to protect the guests from changes in climate (wind, rain, temperature, etc.).

Background: The Maho Bay tents use screening, roll down shades, pulleys, bungee cords, etc., to allow for opening and closing the dwelling as necessary (Estate Concordia is a very hot and windy site).

Natural disasters · · ·

- The units must deal with local natural trauma (hurricane, rock slide, fire, earthquake, etc.).

Background: In the Virgin Islands the major problems are termites and hurricanes. We use termite-proof building materials and furnishings which are weather resistant. We also use outdoor furniture, waterproof couch and bed coverings, stainless steel and marine fittings, Monel staples, etc. Fabric is connected to the structure by Monel staples so that the fabric blows loose in a hurricane and there remains little wind resistance on the structure. Screens are removable so they can be taken down before the hurricane. Tarp and ropes can be stored under units to cover the furnishings.
For California – consider solutions for fires, earthquakes, and rock slides (e.g., controlled burning, etc.).

Atmosphere · · ·

- The units should provide a sense of privacy while maximizing views and interesting natural 'assets'.
- The structures, however, should be subordinate to the ecosystem.

Background: Adequate space and vegetation between the units, and careful and creative siting in the field can provide a sense of privacy and interest within the campground. Positive sensory experiences are also important for the guest: sight, sound, touch, smell.

Landscape · · ·

- The campground should heighten the sense of intimacy that the guest has with the surrounding natural environment.

Background: Choose sites in interesting areas with a good view. The dwellings should be light, open, and oriented toward views. Planting of aromatic and colourful native trees and plants will attract wildlife like hummingbirds. Planting is also used for privacy screening. This flora is supported by the compost from the toilet and grey water from the shower.

Restoration • • •

- Sustainable site design requires holistic, ecologically based strategies to create projects that do not alter or impair but instead help repair and restore existing site systems.
- Development should address ecological restoration of the site.

Background: At Maho Bay it is necessary to control feral animals and exotic imported plants and trees. Initiation of a native plant landscaping programme has helped to attract indigenous wildlife. In the Virgin Islands the birds, bats, lizards, and tree frogs in turn help control the biting insects.

Eco-tent conservation • • •

ENERGY: Responsible energy use is fundamental to sustainable development and a sustainable future. Energy management must balance the justifiable demand with the appropriate supply. The process couples energy awareness, conservation, and efficiency with the use of primary renewable energy resources. To sustain its own wise use of energy, the sustainable development must demonstrate benefits rather than sacrifices to its users (which includes visitors and operators).

Renewable electric power • • •

- The units should be energy self-sufficient using renewable electric power and maximizing passive solar design.

Background: The eco-tents at Maho Bay successfully use photovoltaics and wind for electric power. Hydro and big-gas for energy might be appropriate in some cases.
Education: This is an interesting educational opportunity for the customer. When the batteries are full the guest is actually wasting by not using energy. It is important to encourage consumption when power is available and conservation when it is not.

- A gauge is necessary to monitor available energy in the battery, and indicate when batteries are full.
- A voltmeter allows guests to adjust solar panels to the optimum angle to the sun.
- A barometer helps with weather forecasting.
- An occupancy sensor should be used to minimize energy use when unit is not occupied.
- Timers on appliances to avoid overuse.

Ventilation and cooling • • •

- Passive and natural techniques should be used.

Background: At Maho, the tents use solar design such as roof overhangs, heat reflective glass and fabric, and planting for shade, in conjunction with wind scoop ventilation, Venturi principle, and evaporative cooling. Other alternatives might be thermal chimneys, earth sheltering, etc.

Education: The best strategy for keeping a dwelling cool is to keep it from getting hot in the first place. That means shading to block the hot mid-day sun but not the cooling breezes. Cooling techniques can be more elusive than other aspects of the eco-tents, so it is important to post signs about:

- Evaporative cooling principles.
- Ventilation by wind scoops and Venturi principle.
- Heat reflection by reflective fabric and glass.
- Shading – use of planting and trees, awnings and roof overhangs to protect from the sun.

Heating

- Guests should be able to secure units to hold heat, as well as to open up units to maximize ventilation for cooling.

Background: There is no need for heating on St John, although the eco-tents can be closed to trap in heat on cool nights. In colder climates the units should maximize solar design: mass for insulation, techniques such as circulated air heated by hot water storage inside the unit, or a back-up propane heater.

Education: Heating should be customer interactive; for example, a simple way to keep people warm is to layer more clothing.

Water supply and collection

- Units should have cistern-holding capacity which stores rain water collected from the roof.

Background: Since there is not always enough rain to accommodate guests, the cistern provides storage for rain water as well as water that is trucked in. Rain is collected off the roof and stored in a cistern (cisterns can be interconnected with overflows for alternate filling). The guest hand pumps water from the cistern into a black container over the shower which provides water pressure and functions as a hot water heater. This container feeds both the shower and sink and has gauges showing water level and temperature. If the water is too hot, the guest can pump more cold water from the cistern into the black solar heater. The gauge at the sink and the shower shows water use versus supply in the cistern, and total water use during the guest's stay (use low flow fixtures).

Education: User education and awareness is vital to a successful water conservation programme. Positive reinforcement should be provided to visitors by informing them of their actual water savings as well as their responsibility in achieving the goal of water conservation.

Fixtures • • •

• The units should use energy efficient fixtures compatible with solar design.

Background: The Maho Bay camps use Sun Frost refrigerators, DC fans, microwave ovens, solar efficient lighting, compact fluorescent bulbs, solar pumps, a two burner stove run by propane, etc. Natural daylight should be used wherever possible.

For Hawaii – beach frontlighting should be designed not to disorient turtle hatchlings.

Lighting should be low intensity and directed downward or reflected with cut off angles, or set back from the beach so not directly visible.

Education: Use meters to show electric consumption by appliances. Timers on fans, appliances, and lights help to make guests aware of their energy use.

Waste • • •

The only way to avoid environmental harm from waste is to prevent its generation. Pollution prevention means changing the way activities are conducted and eliminating the source of the problem. This does not mean doing without, but doing differently.

Composting toilets • • •

• Human waste should be treated with a composting toilet.

Background: Several models of composting toilets have been experimented with at Maho Bay – a toilet with minimum water flush seems to work the best.

Education: The toilet must be designed with gauges showing heat and moisture content so the guest can monitor the health of bacteria in the compost. If the temperature drops in the bin, the guest adds organic material (i.e., sawdust or food scraps) to the mass and stirs with a lever. If the compost pile gets too dry, the guest pumps water from the bottom over the mass. A sign placed near the toilet can provide interpretive information that explains to the guest how a composting toilet works.

Compost from toilets should be used for local planting.

Food waste • • •

• Appropriate food waste should be disposed of in a composting bin, and the balance used for animal feed.

Education: The campground should be designed to promote food waste composting: provide an area for collecting scraps and install a programme for sensible use of compost.

Waste water

- Water conservation includes using water of lower quality such as reclaimed wastewater effluent, grey water, or runoff from ground surfaces, for irrigation of vegetative landscape or food crops.
- Where applicable, separate grey water (showers, sinks, etc.) from black water (toilet waste).
- Grey water should be filtered through a one-foot-wide stone trough filled with soil and then used for drip irrigation.

Background: At Maho Bay, grey water is used to support vegetative growth, and rejuvenate indigenous plant and animal life in the area (natural drainage patterns should be taken into consideration). Nutrient rich grey water can be used to grow small gardens near or around units and also for producing food.

Back-up systems

- Units should have back-up support systems in case guests run out of power or water.

Background: At Maho Bay, there is propane back-up for cooking, candles for light, and public watering stations when necessary. The units are also equipped with a five gallon water container and an ice chest (ice is available at the commissary).

Additional site uses

Restaurant and eating pavilion
Performing arts pavilion
Dormitory housing for students
Teaching (classroom) facilities
Separate pavilion for conference/workshops, etc.
Swimming pool
Tennis courts
Other sports activities
Maintenance facilities (workshop/storage)
Food storage (freezer, refrigerator)
Commissary
Office space

Food production area

Located adjacent to the restaurant, possibly using a fish pond, planting shed, orchard, etc., to use wastewater and compost from the resort. The food will then be featured in the restaurant.

Workshop • • •

Repairs, woodworking, crafts, prototype development, and product testing.

Nature centre • • •

Trail development, bird watching, plant identification, wildlife sanctuary.

Research development and testing centre (outside funding needed) • • •

- Development of sustainable electric power sources.
- Development of natural waste treatment systems.
- Development of smallscale manufacturing processes to convert local trash into building materials.
- Development of a solar kiln backed by propane to support local manufacturing of trash into building products.

> I am not a philosopher, but if I have learned anything about sustainable design over the past twenty years, it is that it is ego-less. It is about what works and listening to both nature and your customers. (Stanley Selengut)

References

Australian Commonwealth Department of Tourism, National Ecotourism Strategy, 1994.

Barnett, D.L. and Browning, W.D. (1995) *A Primer on Sustainable Building*. Rocky Mountain Institute, Snowmass, CO.

Heede, R. (1995) *Homemade Money: How to save energy and dollars in your home*. Rocky Mountain Institute, Brick House Publishing, Amherst, NH.

Raymond, P.W. (1984) Sea Turtle Hatchling Disorientation and Artificial Beachfront Lighting. The Center for Environmental Education Sea Turtle Rescue Fund, Washington, DC.

St John, The (1995) Virgin Islands, Concordia Sustainability Demonstration Prototype, Synopsis of the July 1995 Planning Workshop.

US Department of the Interior (1993) National Park Service, *Guiding Principles of Sustainable Design*. Denver Service Center.

William McDonough Architects (1992) Architects, *The Hanover Principles: Design for Sustainability*. New York.

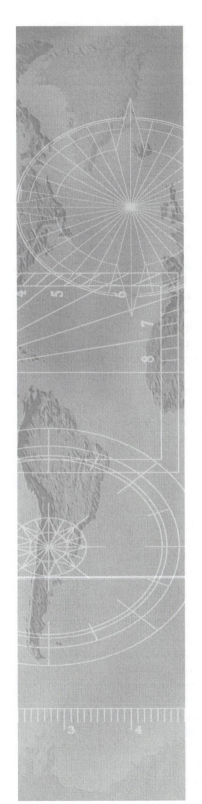

CHAPTER 17

The Fairmont Chateau Whistler Resort: moving towards sustainability

Esther Speck

We all have the power of one. Each one of us can begin to make a difference, and collectively, a lot of individuals can move mountains (or save them) . . . and corporations can make single decisions to shift policy that in time will produce major cultural and behavioural change. (David Roberts, General Manager of the Fairmont Chateau Whistler Resort)

Introduction

This case study of the Fairmont Chateau Whistler Resort (FCW) illustrates how a hotel resort is actively contributing to sustainable tourism development by striving to operate within an environmentally, socially and economically responsible framework. The case sets the FCW apart from many other resort hotels for several reasons. It illustrates how a sustainability programme can be developed from a foundation of spontaneous environmental initiatives. Specifically, it describes how the FCW has developed a strategic programme from sustainability principles, outlines how this agenda has been implemented, and highlights some of the key environmental and social practices that have been undertaken.

However, before moving to discuss these matters, some background is provided on FCW itself and its parent company, Fairmont Hotels and Resorts.

Fairmont Hotels and Resorts

The FCW is part of Fairmont Hotels and Resorts, a Canadian company that manages national and international luxury hotels. Over the past decade, this company has become a North American tourism industry leader and catalyst in 'greening' hotel operations. In 1990 the company's corporate office surveyed all employees to find out whether or not they would be supportive of an environmental programme. The survey determined that 91 per cent of employees strongly supported more environmentally responsible practices within the hotels where they worked. In response, a corporate greening programme called 'the Green Partnership' was launched across the company's hotel chain. Over the years, this programme has evolved from an environmental guidebook to a more comprehensive incentive and monitoring programme that is administered by a corporate environmental office. From the inception of the Green Partnership programme, the FCW has actively participated in a range of environmental management pursuits.

Fairmont Chateau Whistler Resort

The FCW is an all-season hotel resort that opened in 1989. This chateau-style hotel is located in Whistler, British Columbia, approximately 120 km north of Vancouver. Whistler is a community that has evolved from the site of a few remote fishing lodges in the early 1960s into a world-class destination. The FCW resort is situated at the base of Blackcomb and Whistler mountains, overlooking the core of the village. FCW has 560 hotel rooms and employs over 600 staff. Its guest rooms are complemented with administrative space, six independent meeting rooms, three major ballrooms, a number of hospitality suites and a rooftop garden terrace. FCW's facilities also include two restaurants, a bar, a health club, spa, staff housing and an 18-hole golf course.

The Whistler area's beautiful mountain environment attracts not only visitors, but is also home to some 9500 year-round residents. Largescale residential and commercial developments over the past two decades have placed extensive pressure on the natural ecology of the area, as well as on the social fabric of the community. The FCW recognizes these stressors, and has made it a priority to minimize the negative impacts of its operations by undertaking programmes to enhance both the community and the area's natural environment.

The sustainability journey

As part of its involvement with its parent companies 'Green Partnership Programme', FCW established a Green Team with representatives from all hotel departments. This group was responsible for implementing many of the environmental initiatives suggested by the corporate programme. The success of this group's efforts have twice been acknowledged over the past ten years with FCW being awarded the title of 'Fairmont Environmental Property of the Year'. In addition, such efforts have seen FCW establish itself as a leader in environmental management in the Whistler community.

Building on its previous environmental management successes, in 2000 FCW embarked on a more ambitious set of initiatives. The first of these initiatives was the development of a vision of social responsibility for its staff, guests, the community, environment and other constituents. To enact this vision David Roberts, the General Manager of the FCW, who has a special appreciation of the natural beauty of Whistler, recognized that sustainability initiatives in the operations of FCW had to be taken to a more strategic level. While FCW was seeking answers as to how this might be done, the founder of The Natural Step (TNS) framework[1] for sustainability was visiting Whistler and held several compelling presentations on this particular subject. As a result of these presentations FCW decided to join with five other organizations including private businesses, local government and a resident environmental group[2] to collectively use TNS to create a shared vision for sustainable practices, not only for their own individual organizations, but for the entire Whistler community.

While FCW had long been dedicated to both environmental and social practices, there was no overall strategy that acted to guide and prioritize actions in these areas. Using TNS as its base, FCW began for the first time in 2001 to work towards the achievement of its vision of social responsibility in a strategic way.

Developing a sustainability programme

Systems

A successful sustainability programme requires awareness, understanding and commitment to sustainability goals from management and staff. In order to engage the leadership team, all FCW managers participated in a Whistler Sustainability Symposium that was organized by the local TNS group. To train staff, a group of in-house trainers underwent a 2-day TNS 'train-the-trainer' session. These individuals developed a sustainability awareness programme and delivered training for each department. To create a common language and awareness throughout the entire hotel operation, TNS training was also integrated into new employees' orientation programmes.

The FCW Sustainability Programme began with a preliminary environmental review to gain a better understanding of current resource flows and practices. From this review, four priority areas for improvement were chosen as an immediate focus for action. These were waste management, energy management, developing sustainable products and services, and community philanthropy. In addition, supply chain management was identified as an important strategic means for reducing environmental impacts.

Within FCW, Solution Teams were formed to identify and prioritize problems and actions in each of these areas. Team members were those individuals in the hotel resort who had the knowledge and position to implement change, such as the chief engineer, as well as other enthusiastic staff. To ensure resources and accountability, each of the Solution Teams was led by a member of the resort hotel's executive management group. Once the teams were formed, they participated in 'Ideas to Action' workshops, where they reviewed the current reality of FCW operations and envisioned an ideal, sustainable future for the hotel resort's operations. Based on the difference between this vision and the current reality, each team set its own measurable objectives for 2001. Projects to reach these objectives were then brainstormed, prioritized and selected. These projects continue to gain momentum and have been successful for several reasons. Firstly, member commitment was established because the teams defined their own objectives. Secondly, project goals were grounded in reality because the members were the experts within their own areas of operation. The members of the teams were also from different departments, so they learned to consider the challenges across all divisions rather than just in their own.

In order to monitor progress and demonstrate economic, environmental and social benefits, efforts are made to make team objectives measurable, and are designed to be tracked regularly. For example, the Waste Solution Team identified a 12 per cent reduction in waste to landfill as one of their objectives for 2001. In order to assure reliable measurements, the FCW installed a compactor where waste is accurately measured with each tipping. This is a change from previous volume-based weight estimates. Twenty-four hour waste audits have also been organized to biannually determine the composition of waste and to identify areas for improvement.

The teams review their progress on an ongoing basis, and the measurements are communicated to the rest of the Green Team members. Since the success of many of these initiatives depends directly on the participation of all employees, it is important that staff be constantly updated on progress. The executive management team reviews the process and outcomes of the programme annually at strategic retreat sessions.

Practices

Practices that contribute to environmental sustainability can also provide significant short- and long-term business benefits. Potential business benefits include cost savings, innovation, avoidance of future liability, improved staff morale and motivation, enhanced public reputation, increased market share and strengthened stakeholder relationships. This section highlights FCW practices that have been successful in realizing both ecological and business benefits.

Communicating and training • • •

Management and staff understanding is central to the success of FCW's environmental programmes. Staff need to understand the reasons for, and goals of, each programme in order to actively contribute. Programme leaders at the FCW understand this and facilitate the sharing of information in various ways. For example, the FCW has an internal Communications Committee that includes at least one representative from each department. The committee's monthly meeting is one means for receiving feedback to and from individual departments regarding environmental initiatives. Another highly effective means of communication is a mandatory weekly operations meeting among all managers. At these meetings sustainability activities are discussed on a regular basis. The FCW also has environmental bulletin boards in all departments and publishes a bi-weekly staff newsletter, called 'Tell Me a Story'. This well-read newsletter contains an environmental column called *'On the Green Front'*. Another effective way in which FCW communicates environmental information is through 'green' theme days in the staff cafeteria. These are held at least three times per year.

Staff capacity with respect to participating in sustainable practices is also developed in many other ways. For example, each employee participates in TNS Awareness Training, and has a half-day of specific waste, energy and safety training as part of their official employee orientation programme. Other seasonal and departmental training activities supplement this programme. These include 'Black Bear Awareness Training' that is delivered every spring. FCW also has an ever-expanding library of literature dealing with sustainability issues, where interested staff can sign out books, videos and a newspaper scrapbook.

Staff training, however, is not simply about acquiring skills in order to undertake an immediate task at hand. It is also about building capacity and skills that enable employees to respond to changing demands and opportunities for new activities. Through the ongoing environmental education that the Chateau Whistler provides, employees are introduced to key elements of environmental responsibility as well as to techniques for implementing these stewardship ideals.

Reaching out and building awareness and capacity among external groups, such as guests, the community and business partners, is also very important. The FCW undertakes a growing number of initiatives in this regard. For example, both the hotel and the golf course are proactive in offering tours of their facilities to guests, schools and other interested groups. Over the past year, the FCW has hosted six groups from elementary school to university, who are interested in tourism and sustainable development practices. FCW representatives have also spoken at conferences and actively participated in community and social responsibility events, such as Clean Air Day and the British Columbia

Ethics in Action Award Programme. The hotel resort also sponsors educational talks and events by local individuals. These include a popular monthly slide-show series by a local bear researcher. Recognizing the value of dialogue and group commitment, the FCW also hosted a community sustainability symposium as well as a corporate environmental conference in 2000.

Another method of communication with guests and residents is through interpretive signs at the golf course. These signs along the course's walking trails identify features such as native plants and their traditional uses, bird species frequenting the area, interesting historical occurrences, and information about local stream and fish ecology. Both residents and tourists appreciate this unique opportunity to learn and experience the natural environment and wildlife of the area.

Reducing, reusing and recycling

The FCW works to increase the efficiency of its resource use by reducing, reusing and recycling. Examples of resourceful ways of decreasing the resort hotel's material flows include: administration's decreased use of paper via extensive use of computer communication technology; the landscapers' efforts to hand-pull weeds rather than use toxic herbicides; the development of an organic herb garden on the roof-top patio in order not only to reduce reliance on pesticide, but also increase the property's ambience for guests. Different hotel departments are also using alternative products that are more environmentally benign. For example, the hotel kitchen is currently testing a new product to keep banquet food dishes warm. This product is made of renewable sugar cane, contains no toxic materials and is purchased in a recyclable container.

The hotel resort views all waste as an inherent inefficiency and is creative in reusing products wherever possible. For example, empty plastic pails from the kitchen are used by other hotel departments for maintenance purposes, or are taken by staff for personal use. Paper is recycled and bound into notepads or used for draft photocopying. Unused guest room amenities, such as soaps and shampoos, as well as larger items like furniture, are all donated to local charities. Some waste output has also been used as an input to make a completely new product. For instance, FCW has developed a partnership with a progressive regional company called International Bio-Recovery that makes high-quality fertilizer out of food and organic waste. FCW provides the company with organic waste that is normally difficult to dispose of locally due to its attractiveness to the area's bears. The relationship with International Bio-Recovery serves to assist a local company, while diverting approximately 500 kilograms of waste from the community's local landfill on a daily basis.

If waste cannot be used, it is recycled whenever possible. The FCW has developed a comprehensive recycling programme in which efforts are made to ensure that as much sorting as possible occurs at the source. To make this process easier for employees, recycling stations are labelled and colour coordinated throughout the hotel resort. Even guests are engaged in the recycling efforts. FCW programmes demonstrate that many recycling initiatives can be implemented while meeting high guest standards. For example, recycling in guest rooms is encouraged with attractive wicker baskets that have four labelled compartments for different recyclable materials. These were custom designed and are found in every FCW guest room. Since the implementation of this programme, housekeeping waste going to landfill has dropped by over 30 per cent – from over 2 lbs (1 kg) to 1.4 lbs (0.6 kg) per guest per day. Guest rooms also have toilet paper, tissues and stationery which are made from recycled materials.

Working with the supply chain ● ● ●

While reducing, reusing and recycling activities have contributed significantly to FCW waste reduction, many material flow problems are actually 'purchased' as packaging and products. Service industries such as hotels can make significant impacts by managing their supply chain relationships. The FCW illustrates efforts to influence supplier initiatives with respect to material flows. The resort hotel's kitchen, for example, has worked with a major supplier to replace the traditional waxed cardboard boxes in which meat is transported with reusable plastic totes. This diverts at least half of a ton of bulky waste from the landfill annually. The FCW's golf course has negotiated with suppliers to purchase bulk fertilizer, which is then directly filled into machines as needed. This system saves over 1500 plastic bags that would otherwise go to landfill.

Products with recycled and low-impact content are purchased when possible. Most of the hotel resort's cleaning products, for example, are bought from a national supplier specializing in industrial cleaning products that are produced to meet high ecological standards. Furthermore, the FCW is working with its corporate purchasing department on several projects designed to reduce waste production. For example, the purchasing department surveyed all major FCW suppliers to identify opportunities for partnership and improvement in environmental practices. It was found that approximately half of the respondents did have environmental policies and programmes in place. Additionally, over 80 per cent of suppliers contributed ideas for improving their environmental practices as regards their dealings with FCW.

Conserving energy and water ● ● ●

Hotel resort operations are particularly resource intensive in terms of energy and water consumption. Energy and water use can place significant stress of natural environments and the financial bottom lines of hotel operations. In order to monitor its energy and water consumption FCW has contracted an outside company (Energuard). This company provides data on these matters to the hotel's Energy Solution group thus allowing it to determine the extent of its progress towards its stated goals of reduced energy and water usage. The Energy Solution group, amongst other things, have been responsible for undertaking a full lighting audit, and are working on a three-phase retrofit to convert from incandescent to fluorescent lamps. Fluorescent lamps last longer and save energy (reducing consumption from 100 to approximately 28 watts per light). The financial advantages to be gained from this project are significant. It is expected that the payback period for various components of this project will range from 6 months to 2 years, depending on the project programme. Furthermore, the hotel also offers fluorescent lamps to employees at cost so as to increase staff awareness of energy savings.

Infrastructure initiatives to reduce water consumption include installing low-flow showers and toilets in all guest rooms. To reduce water on the golf course, FCW has also devised a stringent monitoring programme for its irrigation system. All water use is recorded and audited regularly. Additionally, maintenance staff irrigate only the dry areas that need attention, rather than watering the entire course on a regular basis.

Guests are also involved with conservation through FCW's sheet and towel change programme. Rather than changing guest sheets daily, longer-term guests are informed that their sheets will be changed every three days, unless they request otherwise. This programme resulted in CA$125 000 in energy savings in the first year. Furthermore, towels are only laundered when guests indicate that they would like to have them changed. The hotel resort estimates that 30 per cent of guests choose not to have towels washed everyday. These policies not only save water, energy, detergent, and transportation emissions, but also extend the life of the sheets and towels.

Conserving natural areas

To facilitate the implementation of sound environmental practices, it is advantageous to incorporate environmental objectives into the physical design and programming of tourism facilities. Design and operations at the FCW golf course illustrate this principle. The course's original design helped the facility to retain animal habitat and reduce maintenance costs. Of the eighty-five acre golf course expanse, thirty acres receive no maintenance at all; fifty acres are mowed regularly and are only fertilized once annually with a 70 per cent organic slow release formula. Less than 1 per cent of the course's turf is ever treated with chemical pesticides and fungicides. This only occurs when necessary to control weed or pest outbreaks. The development design ensured that healthy riparian zones were left bordering the three trout-breeding streams that flow through the golf course. Furthermore, many of the maintenance staff have been trained and certified as streamkeepers by the Pacific Streamkeepers Federation. They are responsible for the weekly monitoring of the number and species of fish that migrate through the creek, and pass this information along to the local municipality for their ongoing Monitoring Programme. Other conservation efforts supported by the hotel resort include educational talks and training about local bear populations, bird and tree species, as well as interpretive signage and pamphlets used to communicate with guests and visitors.

Providing sustainable products · · ·

The FCW has been innovative in developing services that support sustainability principles. One manner in which sustainable services can be promoted is to obtain and communicate the importance of environmental certification to visitors and employees. The golf course, for example, has achieved and maintains 'Audubon Cooperative Sanctuary System' certification. This indicates that its operations meet high industry standards, as evaluated by an independent third party.

The FCW has also developed other unique services that are based on sound environmental principles. For instance, it has implemented a green meeting product called 'EcoMeet'. This package of environmental products is available to meeting and convention planners and their clients. It offers four optional components: eco-service, eco-cuisine, eco-accommodation and eco-programming. Each of these components meets between twelve to twenty specific criteria. For example, criteria for 'eco-cuisine' include using organic ingredients for meals. Other criteria include a mini-audit on meeting waste, biodegradable pens, environmental rooms, and activities with environmentally and socially responsible tour providers.

Social sustainability practices · · ·

The ideals of sustainable tourism extend beyond the protection and conservation of the ecological environment to ensuring the sustainability of the surrounding cultural and social environments. Ventures should be undertaken to maintain respectful, inclusive and capacity building relationships between residents, visitors, employees and other groups. The FCW engages in various partnerships of this kind. It has implemented and continues to develop both community and employee programmes to strengthen the social fabric upon which its operations depend. An overview of these programmes follows:

- *Forming partnerships*

  Active engagement in community life is a critical tool for strengthening relations among businesses and residents in tourism dependent regions. Involvement with local groups is an important step in achieving both environmental goals and the ethos of social sustainability. Partners working together towards attaining common goals may be more effective in achieving important objectives than might otherwise be possible. Such partnerships highlight the many interdependencies that exist between the resort hotel and the broader social, environmental and economic issues confronting the Whistler community. They also illustrate examples where members are dedicated to working together in defining and achieving a common vision.

The TNS partnership between the FCW and five other Whistler community groups is a good example of collaboration among local business, government and residents in support of community values. This strategic alliance has been critical in supporting the community's efforts at developing a more sustainable future. Similarly, FCW's participation in the Whistler Fisheries Stewardship Group programme has strengthened the ability of that organization to mitigate local stream degradation resulting from increased development at Whistler. A collective of the three local golf courses (including the FCW golf facility) called the 'Whistler Golf Sustainability Consortium' provides another example of how groups can operate more effectively as a team. The three organizations have crafted a common vision of what golf courses in Whistler might look like in an ideal future. They share resources, learning and purchasing power in order to reach their goals and vision.

- *Engaging volunteers*

Small communities tend to rely on a familiar circle of hard-working volunteers. To support such efforts, the FCW encourages wider involvement through grants to local volunteer groups. Five of these grants were awarded in 2000. The hotel also hosts an annual 'Volunteer Fair', where local groups are invited to set up booths and promote their programmes in order to engage new supporters. This fun event engages staff, schools, community members and even guests!

- *'Room with a View' programme*

In 1995, the Chateau Whistler formed an alliance with the British Columbia Children's Hospital in an effort to help sick children and demonstrate community support. The FCW provides opportunities for some of these patients to visit Whistler with their families or caregivers and stay for up to five free nights at the resort hotel. Through this FCW programme, thirty to forty families are accommodated at the resort hotel every year.

- *'Adopt a Shelter' programme*

The FCW has paired up with a nearby community women's shelter and offers support for this programme. At least one van-load of used furniture, drapery, bedding, kitchenware and other goods are donated on a weekly basis to the shelter. This initiative is helping the shelter to continue to support women in need and assist them in establishing new homes after leaving the shelter. FCW's maintenance staff also visit the shelter frequently and perform odd repair jobs free of charge to help keep the building in good condition.

- *Supporting local products*

Initiatives that support local talent and products contribute to both economic and social community sustainability. The FCW believes in recognizing and building local capacity, and demonstrates this commitment in many ways. Much of the artwork found in the hotel resort has been produced by regional artists. The menus in the hotel resort's main restaurant are decorated with local wildflowers painted by a long-time Whistler resident. Many of the paintings found on the hotel's walls are images of local landscapes painted by a nearby Squamish First Nations artist. Also, many of the materials used in the construction of the hotel were locally manufactured or purchased. For example, the stone surrounding the hotel fireplaces came from a nearby quarry, and a local stonemason created the mantles. The FCW also purchases many of its seasonal food products from local suppliers, supporting local growers both socially and financially. In addition, the hotel resort supports a weekly farmers' market in front of the hotel where local produce, crafts and other items are sold. This market supports the local economy and assists in creating a sense of community for both Whistler visitors and residents.

- *FCW Charity Foundation*
A recent initiative which is fully volunteer-driven is the establishment of an official FCW Charity Foundation. The hotel resort's employees organize events and use other opportunities to raise funds that are then redistributed to local non-profit benefactors through the Foundation. For example, when a school group from the Vancouver Native Education Center was hosted for a field trip, the cost of the entire day including lunch was sponsored by the Foundation. Additionally, several annual fund-raising events are organized, including a golf tournament and an evening concert. External donations to the Foundation are also encouraged.

- *Supporting employee living expenses*
Housing and general living costs in resort communities are often high. The cost of living in Whistler is no exception. Finding affordable accommodation is a significant problem for both seasonal workers and more permanent residents, even though the Whistler municipality has taken various steps to help alleviate these pressures. In light of this problem, the FCW helps its employees by providing 240 staff with housing at rates that are significantly below market rates (at least 25 per cent less). The hotel continually seeks new opportunities to provide for more staff. It acquired another house in 2001, thus offering studio and one-bedroom apartments to an additional twenty-four employees. Generally, the younger and more transient staff tend to live in these accommodations. However, to support those who live in nearby towns which are more affordable, the hotel resort offers a travel subsidy.

- *Building employee capacity*
Employees are the heart of hotel operations, and the FCW sets high standards in providing a safe and meaningful workplace. An employee's personal and professional growth is a priority at FCW. All new staff are greeted with a two and half day orientation. This emphasis on development continues. Training investments in 2000 totalled about CA$3 million dollars, with 615 employees undertaking programmes. The hotel resort also has a progressive career development programme with a policy of internal promotion where possible. It also provides full funding for part-time external studies. These training programmes help to remove the traditional 'glass ceilings' often confronting local people wanting to advance in the tourism industry. They also help to build an empathetic and co-operative culture within the organization.

Future developments

Although the FCW's efforts towards more sustainable forms of tourism practice qualify them as a leading industry example, the organization is continuing to strive for improvement. FCW plans to increase its efforts to create more sustainable operations by addressing challenges in the following areas.

Management systems

FCW needs to ensure that environmental and social objectives are prioritized and integrated into daily activities. Management and staff operate in a fast-paced, ever-changing environment, one in which employment turnover is endemic. Therefore, it is important that sustainability objectives are reflected in cultural values as well as operational and management systems. FCW intends to address these challenges by tying its environmental and social objectives to existing employee evaluation practices. FCW also intends to expand its measurement and reporting system to include environmental and social indicators. The importance of these additional metrics is highlighted by the Director of Operations' comment that 'we would do things quite differently if environmental and social objectives were measured as closely as financial objectives' (McGowan 2000, personal communication, 10 July).

Supply chain management

Through purchasing practices, the FCW has enormous opportunity to influence the sustainability of its own organization along with those of its suppliers and service providers. By phasing out products, packaging and services that generate negative environmental impacts, the hotel reduces its need for internal programmes to deal with their consequences. In its efforts to address 'upstream' material flow problems, the FCW is focusing on supplier relationships. However, one of the many purchasing challenges it faces is that many of its products are purchased through corporate nation-wide contracts. In response to this, FCW plans to work very closely with its parent companies' regional and national purchasing departments in setting and achieving procurement goals that reflect FCW material flow reduction philosophies.

Community and other partnerships

As has been discussed previously, partnerships and collaboration allow groups to pool resources and attain goals that they might not be able to achieve individually. The FCW and other community businesses could further broaden community sustainability practices through the development of additional strategic partnerships. FCW could, for example, build on existing relationships with other organizations that promote and support sustainable practices. For example, the hotel resort might explore collaboration opportunities with regional non-profit organizations that promote environmentally responsible tourism. The FCW might also benefit from greater stakeholder input in its decision-making processes. Although many managers live in Whistler and are members of local groups, the hotel currently lacks programmes that involve wider stakeholders in planning, policy review or decision processes.

Lessons learned

As FCW has sought to progress its efforts in the area of sustainable tourism development, its management have learned a number of important lessons. Of these, perhaps five stand out as major 'signposts' for other tourism business seeking to travel this path.

(1) Take small, focused steps

The FCW has found that the best way to overcome the daunting nature of achieving sustainability ideals is to simply focus on principles and long-term goals, begin with small steps, and learn from these. A step-by-step approach builds the motivation, credibility and capacity that are needed to set and achieve new and future successes. Furthermore, early initiatives are also often those that have higher financial returns, which can then be invested into programmes that may be more challenging or have lower immediate returns.

(2) Measure outcomes

The FCW recognizes the value of baselines, benchmarks and measurement. It is important to document material and energy flows in order to gauge levels of improvement over time. If there are no initial baselines or inaccurate benchmark measurements, it is not possible to track the benefits of initiatives. Without such measures, it is difficult to justify future action and resource allocations. Such monitoring is critical in gaining support for further projects and encouraging others to undertake similar initiatives.

(3) Staff involvement

The FCW has grown to appreciate the value of building staff understanding and ownership of programmes. The process by which an initiative is implemented, or a plan is designed, can be just as important as the actual initiative or the plan itself. Environmental and social sustainability ideals are operationalized differently throughout the organization. As employees are the experts within their own operational areas, all staff must be involved for success. FCW strives to be clear in its communication and inclusive in its programme design so that affected staff understand the reasons behind initiatives and can be motivated to implement change.

(4) Communicate the organization's 'story'

The FCW has learned that it is important to create a vision and a story that everybody understands, talks about and contributes to. Such a story-line about events and successes builds excitement and momentum. It also allows individuals to communicate these events to other groups. FCW has recently begun to be more purposeful in sharing its story with staff in presentations and daily conversation. Furthermore, the hotel resort has also found that it is helpful to initiate projects that are highly visible and affect many employees, as these clearly communicate cultural values and management commitment.

(5) Leadership

The FCW is committed to a leadership role in achieving sustainability concepts and goals. Their approach to achieving more sustainable operations presents a useful learning tool for others in the Resort Municipality of Whistler and in the tourism industry. The hotel resort has set the stage for a new operational model. It now faces the challenge of broadening its circle of influence and support, and further entrenching sustainability values into its organizational culture and systems. If it is to be successful in this regard it needs to foster creativity and learning as regards sustainable development, and continue to push beyond the boundaries of its existing activities.

Conclusion

FCW has sought to engage with the principles and concepts associated with sustainable tourism development in a strategic fashion. In doing so it has sought to integrate its various dimensions into its own organizational fabric, as well as that of the businesses and community with which it interacts. Also, it has embraced a broad view of sustainable development, extending beyond protection and conservation of the ecological environment to also include its surrounding cultural and social environments.

As FCW has engaged with the concept of sustainable development over the past 10 years, it has learned a number of key lessons, central amongst which are: the need to adopt a step-by-step approach guided by defined principles and long-term goals; the importance of measuring outcomes; the significance of staff involvement in programmes and activities; the value of creating a vision and a story around the organization's sustainable development activities; and the significance of leadership in both the successful introduction of a sustainability programme, and in its broader acceptance by other businesses and the community.

Acknowledgements

This case study is based on existing literature, and personal interviews with a variety of key informants. Gratefully acknowledged are discussions with FCW personnel including David Roberts (General Manager); Sonya Hwang (Director of Public Relations); Dan McGowan (Director of Operations); Bert McFadden (Golf Course Supervisor); Christine Monopoli (Executive Housekeeper); Rui Pereira (Chief Engineer); and Charmaine Tener (Learning Coach). In addition, informative insights for this case were provided by Christina Symko, Executive Director, Association of Whistler Area Residents for the Environment.

Endnotes

1 The Natural Step framework for sustainability consists of four System Conditions that define sustainability. The framework is used by organizations to develop a shared view of business reality that integrates sustainability considerations into strategic decisions and day-to-day operations. It provides participants with a common sustainability language and a planning tool.

2 Adopters of the TNS framework in Whistler were the Fairmont Chateau Whistler Resort, AWARE (Association of Whistler Area Residents for the Environment), Whistler-Blackcomb Mountain, the Resort Municipality of Whistler, Tourism Whistler and One-Hour Photo.

References

Baum, T. (1995) Sustainable tourism development: The human resource dimension. *Tourism and Sustainable Community Development*, TTRA Canada Conference Proceedings. 1995.

Fairmont Hotels and Resorts (2001) URL: www.fairmont.com.

Hassan, Salah (2000) Determinants of market competitiveness in an environmentally sustainable travel industry. *Journal of Travel Research* **38**(3): 239–45.

Hawkes, S. and Williams, P.W. (1992) *The Greening of Tourism: From Principles to Practice*. Burnaby, BC: Simon Fraser University: Centre For Tourism Policy and Research, and Industry Science and Technology Canada-Tourism, Globe '92.

Natrass, B. and Altomare, M. (1999) *The Natural Step for Business*. New Society Publishers, Gabriola Island, Canada.

Sims, Susan (1994) Giving Guests a Choice. *Successful Meetings* **43**(8): 31.

Wildlife conservation, tourism and the private sector: the case of Earth Sanctuaries Limited

Rob Harris

Introduction

The Australian environment has changed markedly since the arrival of the early European settlements, due mostly to land clearance for agriculture, pasture creation, housing and industry. Additionally, feral animals and introduced plants have invaded vast areas, significantly degrading ecosystems as they have spread across the country. The outcome of these developments has been to place Australia's rich biodiversity under threat. In the first '*State of the Environment*' report commissioned by the Federal government, large numbers of mammal (29 per cent), bird (20 per cent), reptile (7 per cent), fish (13 per cent), and amphibian (15 per cent) species were identified as being either extinct, endangered or vulnerable (State of the Environment Advisory Council, 1996). As regards plant species, 16 per cent of Australia's wild plant species are now estimated to have originated from overseas (Low, 1999). Additionally, 5 per cent of native plants have been identified as being endangered or vulnerable (State of the Environment Advisory Council, 1996). These worrying trends have been in evidence in Australia for many years, and served to provide Dr John Wamsley with the rationale for the establishment of Earth Sanctuaries Propriety Limited in 1988, and later (1993) Earth Sanctuaries Limited (Harris and Leiper, 1995).

This case study seeks to examine the central role of tourism in the business strategy of Earth Sanctuaries Limited (ESL), Australia's first publicly listed company with the stated primary goal of conserving wildlife, and the reasons why the future of this organization is now in doubt. The case study begins by giving a brief overview of the development of ESL from a single sanctuary to the present; ESL currently operates ten such areas. It then examines ESL's mission, objectives and business strategy and overviews its conservation outcomes to date. The final part of this case study discusses key causal factors that have led to the present situation where ESL's future, at least in its current form, is under immediate threat. Central amongst these factors, it is argued here, is the balance the organization has struck between its business mission of conservation and its need as a publicly listed company to generate a return to its shareholders, primarily from tourism related services.

Origins and development

In 1969 Dr John Wamsley purchased a 14-hectare property in the Adelaide Hills, South Australia, that he named Warrawong. This property had previously been used as a dairy farm and was devoid of native vegetation. Wishing to repair the damage from 100 years of intensive farming and restore the area's flora and fauna, Dr Wamsley embarked on an extensive re-vegetation programme. By 1980 he had been successful in establishing over 50 000 native plants on the property, but found that native birds and animals attracted back by maturing vegetation were falling prey to cats and foxes. To overcome this problem he built a vermin-proof fence around his land, with the result that the bird and animal population within the compound rose sharply. At this time, he also began to introduce into Warrawong rare and endangered mammal species which, in the absence of predators, also thrived. These animals included the Short-nosed Bandicoot, Rufus Bettong and Red Necked Wallaby (Harris and Leiper, 1995).

The success Wamsley experienced at Warrawong caused him to think in terms of creating similar fenced environments at other locations, and of how he could fund a network of such reserves. He opened Warrawong to the public in 1985, seeking to determine if tourism could be used to underpin his efforts. At this property he: conducted morning and afternoon guided walks; built a number of self-contained tents; developed

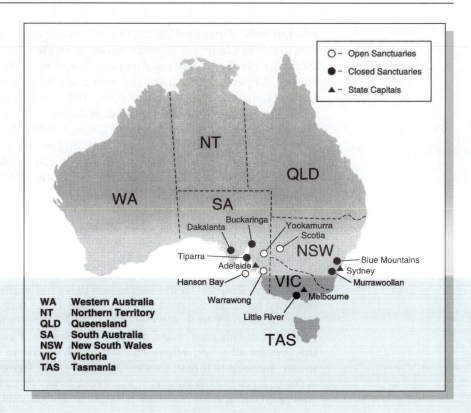

Figure 18.1
Sanctuaries
operated by Earth
Sanctuaries
Limited. Source:
Arentino *et al.*, 2001

a restaurant and souvenir store; and catered for smallscale conferences and weddings. He was sufficiently satisfied with the Warrawong experiment to form the view that tourism could play a significant role in supporting an expanded organization, the core business of which was conservation (Harris and Leiper, 1995).

With the intention of pursuing this objective, Wamsley established Earth Sanctuaries Propriety Limited in 1988. Through this company he began developing a number of sanctuaries, employing a staged development process based in large measure on the one he had used at Warrawong. This process, in essence, involved: selecting a habitat zone in which to establish a sanctuary; identifying the least degraded, most representative area within the identified zone; constructing a fenced compound around all, or part of, the site; eradicating feral animals; reintroducing (as required) animals that once lived in the area; commencing a programme of habitat re-vegetation (as required); developing an interpretation plan in order to protect the site from the impact of visitors and to facilitate their understanding of it; and the development of tourism infrastructure and supporting visitor management systems (Harris and Leiper, 1995). By the end of 2001 ESL was operating ten sanctuaries, four of which had moved through these stages to the point where they had been opened to the public (see Figure 18.1).

Over a 12-year period from 1988, ESL raised AU$21.1 million to support its mission (Harris, 2001). ESL's capital-raising efforts were assisted in large measure by its founder's decision to change the structure of the business from a private company to that of a public company (Earth Sanctuaries Limited) in 1993, and the later listing of this company in 2000 on the Australian Stock Exchange. By the end of 2001 ESL's capital base had allowed it to establish nine sanctuaries. Additionally, it was acting on behalf of a US based company to manage a tenth sanctuary (see Figure 18.1). These areas in total covered approximately 90 000 hectares of which some 9500 were feral fenced (Arentino *et al.*, 2001).

ESL's growth from a single to a multi-site business is reflected in its overall operational and business practices. ESL's business structure had evolved from essentially that of a 'sole trader' to that of a public company, whose board, at the end of 2001, possessed a strong business, as opposed to conservation, background. Board members at this time included three chartered accountants, two solicitors and one business economist (ESL, 2001). Also in place at this time was a professional management team comprising a CEO, five sanctuary managers, and one Wildlife Officer (ESL, 2001). Additionally, ESL had developed substantial expertise in raising funds from capital markets to fuel its growth. Indeed, ESL had seemingly addressed many of the weaknesses identified by McKercher (1998) of small nature based tourism enterprises. These included: reliance on a small management team; strong owner influence; few specialist staff; performance of a variety of roles by management; and a limited ability to attract finance.

Mission, objectives and business strategy

ESL's stated mission is to conserve Australia's unique biodiversity by creating at least one sanctuary in each of its eighty major habitat zones. Whilst some of ESL's corporate objectives reflect its concern to operate successfully as a business, most reflect this mission, specifically:

- conserving Australia's flora and fauna within a commercial environment;
- developing sanctuaries within the major habitat zones in Australia;
- providing a programme of interpretation and education at each sanctuary;
- operating each sanctuary in a sustainable way; and
- providing assistance, by way of a consultancy service, to landholders seeking to conserve biodiversity on their land (ESL, 2000a).

Tourism has been a significant factor in ESL's strategic thinking since the company's formation. Reflective of this has been the more than doubling of tourism specific revenue from approximately AU$600 000 in 1994 to AU$1.4 million in 2000 (or approximately 75 per cent of ESL's total revenue) (ESL, 2000a). Other revenue sources include: a consultancy service providing advice on feral animal eradication, native animal management and feral proof fencing; feral animal proof fence construction; and management services for private sanctuaries (ESL, 2000a). However, ESL has not been able to fund its growth from these activities. Instead it has relied largely on its capital raising activities for this purpose. In this regard recent years have seen ESL operate at a cash deficit of AU$2.5 million per annum, a situation which ESL acknowledges cannot be sustained (ESL, 2000b).

Recognizing the need to refocus ESL's business strategy in order to address its major cash flow problem, the ESL board, under the leadership of its newly appointed chairman Dr Don Stammer (a business economist), made the decision in 1999 to limit land purchases and most of its property development activities to areas in close proximity to selected major population centres on Australia's east coast (i.e., Melbourne, Sydney and Canberra) for a five-year period. This decision was made for the express purpose of significantly growing tourism revenue to the point where a cash surplus would result, allowing ESL to fund future growth from this source (ESL, 1999). To progress this strategy ESL listed on the Australian Stock Exchange in 2000. This listing was successful in raising AU$12.3 million (Milne, 2000).

Money raised from ESL's float was largely allocated to the development of an area fifty minutes driving time from the centre of Melbourne which ESL had previously purchased for AU$5.5 million (ESL, 2000b). This site is known as Little River Sanctuary. According to a feasibility study conducted by the consulting firm KPMG the site was projected to generate a cash surplus after three years, and by 2006, a profit of AU$3.049 million per annum based on an estimated 100 000 visitors (Milne, 2000). Such projections were not unrealistic given the performance of similar reserves in the state of Victoria that provide opportunities to view rare Australian wildlife. For example, a Penguin reserve (Phillip Island Nature Reserve), located 1.5 hours driving time from Melbourne, attracts over 500 000 visitors annually (Harris, 1999). It should also be noted that the business climate in which Little River would have opened was predicted to have been a favourable one from a tourism perspective. The Tourism Forecasting Council of Australia (2001) anticipated average growth rates of 7.8 per cent per annum in inbound tourism, and 1.9 per cent per annum in domestic tourism, for the ensuing ten years.

Profit from the Little River Sanctuary was to be directed by ESL into the development of two recently purchased east-coast sanctuary sites, specifically Blue Mountains (approximately 2.75 hours driving time from Sydney) and Mullawollen (1.5 hours drive north of the nations capital, Canberra). Towards the end of ESL's first five-year east-coast development plan it also intended, depending on profit performance, to establish further sanctuaries, this time in Queensland, near the large population centres of Brisbane and the Gold Coast (ESL, 2000a).

Conservation outcomes

According to ESL's 2001 Annual Report, its land holdings contain populations of fifteen species of endangered, threatened or rare animals that collectively total 2285 individuals. These animals include: Southern Brown Bandicoot, Brush Tailed Bettong, Rufous Bettong, Yellow Footed Rock Wallaby, Bilby, Platypus, Eastern Quoll, Bridled Nailtail Wallaby, Stick Nest Rats, Hairy-nosed Wombats and Numbats (ESL, 2001a).

Additionally, significant regeneration of native plant species has occurred, particularly inside fenced areas, at some sanctuary sites. For example, Wamsley estimates that after fencing a large area of Yookamurra, and removing rabbits and goats, an additional six million plants have germinated and survived (Harris and Leiper, 1995).

Regular translocation of small numbers of animals between sanctuaries has been occurring for some years in order to minimize problems of inbreeding and to reintroduce species to areas where they have long since vanished. Additionally, animals are regularly exchanged with Australian zoos and National Parks and Wildlife Services in order to manage genetic diversity (ESL, 2001). ESL has also been successful in obtaining breeding stock of several rare, endangered or threatened animals from national park agencies, such as the Rufous Hare Wallaby (Queensland National Parks and Wildlife Service) and the Western Bilby (Northern Territory Parks and Wildlife Commission) (ESL, 2001).

ESL can be said to have played a significant role in educating not only visitors to its sanctuaries on aspects of Australia's native fauna and flora and the difficulties they face, but the broader community as well. As regards the latter, ESL has attracted significant media coverage in Australia and overseas (e.g., *Life Magazine*), assisted by the many (20) tourism-related awards it has won since 1988, including a prestigious Conde Nast Traveler's Choice Award in the category of Ecotourism (ESL, 2002a). Wamsley's personal efforts, such as the wearing of a cat skin hat to public functions, have also been particularly successful in drawing public attention to ESL and its mission (Harris and Leiper, 1995).

Causal factors threatening ESL's future

Investor perspectives and financial performance

The financial market's view of ESL, and its current strategic direction, has been somewhat contradictory up until very recently. A number of stockbroking firms, such as Falkiners Stockbroking Limited and Findlay and Co. Limited, viewed ESL as a sound long-term investment, with the latter recently stating:

> *Earth Sanctuaries Limited is an excellent investment for those wishing to make a contribution to the conservation of Australia's wildlife, while also investing in the longer term. A more ethical investment would be difficult to find, and as shown in the following cash flow analysis, the wilderness sanctuaries should be self-sustaining within a five year period. The share price is likely to be driven by a continuing strong appetite for 'feel good' ethical investments that also provide the real prospect for commercial returns.* (Falkiners Stockbroking Limited, 2001)

Other stockbroking firms viewed ESL in a less positive light. The stock broking firm Ethical Investment Services, for example, advised its clients not to invest in Earth Sanctuaries, and suggested to those that did to 'assume your investment is more of a donation for the next few years' (Manning, 2002). Another firm, AMP Henderson Global Investors, did not include ESL shares as part of its Sustainable Future Fund, as it did not achieve the fund's financial objectives (Manning, 2002). Given that ESL's dividends were of a nominal nature, and that no dividends at all were paid in 2001 (ESL, 2001), such views are understandable. Indeed, ESL's lack of short- to medium-term returns is likely to have been central in its share price falling from AU$2.50 when it first listed in 2000 to AU$1.60 a few months later (ESL, 2000a).

Before resigning in January 2002, ESL's then chairman noted that it was likely to be the case that many of ESL's investors were more concerned with the idea embodied in the Earth Sanctuary concept than with profit (Stammer, cited in Cameron, 2002). Supporting this view is the fact that a significant percentage of investors (10 per cent in 2000) donated their dividends back to ESL, while still others indicated their intent to bequeath their shares to the company (Cameron, 2002). The 'well' of such investors is, however, not fathomless as ESL has discovered. Requiring a further AU$7 million to complete its Little River Sanctuary, ESL has been unable to raise any additional funds via the share market (Cameron, 2002). Without this additional equity, and the cash flow that a completed Little River Sanctuary would generate, ESL's future, at least in its current form, is now very much in doubt.

Unable to raise additional equity, and with the real potential of facing future cash flow difficulties, ESL made its situation known to the stock market in January 2002 resulting in its share price falling rapidly to 16 cents per share, down from a listing price of AU$2.50 eighteen months earlier (Cameron, 2002). At the time of writing ESL had appointed a consultancy firm, Challenger Corporate Finance, to assist it in restructuring its operations (ESL, 2002b). As part of this process expressions of interest have been sought for the purchase of all ESL assets. The immediate past chairman of ESL summed up the situation that led to the difficult financial position ESL now faces by noting that 'had the 7000 shareholders got a good feeling in both their heart and their pocket, it would have been easier... to raise money on the stock exchange' (Stammer, cited in Cameron, 2002).

Nature of core assets

A key factor influencing ESL's poor share price performance is the nature of its core assets. Unlike, for example, traditional wildlife parks, which tend to showcase animals for profit, ESL's conservation focus meant that it spent considerable money, time and energy seeking to develop assets in the form of rare, endangered or threatened species, which presently cannot be sold and, as such, have no market value. This situation was compounded, until recently, by Australian Accounting Standard AASB 1010 that stated that '...the revaluation of a class of non-current assets shall be its recoverable amount' (ESL, 1997). This approach to valuing assets meant that ESL was precluded from valuing its natural resources in any way other than that which would be able to be obtained from their sale on the open market. As both the commonwealth and state governments in Australia have extensive legislation dealing with the protection of native fauna and flora and associated trade in, and property rights to, native species, ESL's ability to do this, and therefore benefit financially from its core activity of conservation, was extremely limited (Arentino *et al.*, 2001). This situation changed, to some extent, on the 1st of July 1998 when Accounting Standard AASB 1037, which covers self-generating and regenerating assets, was introduced. This standard applied to all companies from the financial year ended 30th June 2001 (Booth, 1999). Essentially, this changed ruling allowed ESL to place a value on its fauna and record this value on its balance sheet.

The approach which ESL decided to employ to value its fauna assets under AASB 1037 was to value them using the cost of re-establishing species' populations and associated translocation costs. Using this approach, the following valuations were made in 2001:

- Threatened species – species requires some form of conservation due to its vulnerability – AU$1500 per animal;
- Rare species – species numbers have declined to the point where it is likely to move into the endangered category in the near future if causal factors continue – AU$3000 per animal; and
- Endangered species – the species is in danger of extinction – AU$6000 per animal.

Based on these values, the net market value of animals on ESL land in 2001 was calculated to be AU$5 412 000 (ESL, 2001a). This calculation was made based on a species census, the validity of which was determined by an external consultant from the University of Adelaide (ESL, 2000a). While such figures better reflect the company's value, they do not enhance borrowing power, nor do they influence dividend growth significantly, as ESL cannot, as noted previously, sell its animal assets under present government regulations (Greg, cited in Booth, 1999).

Business strategy

Unlike public sector conservation organizations, such as national park agencies, ESL's future, given its private sector nature, is not underwritten by the public purse. Indeed, as Gray (2002) points out, the reason why most protected areas are public goods in the first place is that the private sector cannot extract a profit from their operation after paying for maintenance and general upkeep. Compounding this problem is the observation that a similar product to that offered by ESL to consumers is available free or at a low cost from national parks.

Another difficulty faced by ESL is the cost of moving an area of land through the stages noted previously before it could be opened to the public. In the case of the Little River Sanctuary, for example, AU$6 million had been spent on land purchase, fencing, water and power infrastructure, architect fees and habitat restoration before development was suspended (ESL, 2001a).

Given restrictions on the trade in wildlife, ESL's decision to use tourism as its main cash flow vehicle could reasonably be seen as a sound business strategy. It's early decisions, however, to purchase land in locations remote from major population centres (i.e., Yookamurra, Scotia, Tiparra, Dakalanta, and Buckaringa sanctuaries), and therefore potential tourist markets, appears to have been guided more by conservation than tourism considerations. This observation has been made by several observers of ESL's current situation, including Barry Cohen, a former Federal Environment Minister, and himself a wildlife sanctuary operator. Cohen believes that most of ESL's sanctuaries were simply too far from major tourist markets to generate adequate revenue from visitation (Cohen, cited in Cameron, 2002). Hamilton (cited in Reuters, 2002) of the think-tank The Australia Institute, also makes this point adding that such location decisions appear to be the outcome of confusing environmental goals with commercial goals.

ESL's east-coast strategy arguably held out significant potential for generating the revenue necessary to improve its cash flow situation and hence its stock exchange performance, but it was not without risk. ESL through this strategy was moving into a market place where it was likely to confront significant competition from established wildlife park operators with long standing links with the tourism industry, particularly tour operators. Little River Sanctuary, for example, would have been one of five private wildlife parks/reserves within 1.5 hours by road from Melbourne, although it would have been amongst the closest of these. In the case of Sydney, there are six established wildlife parks/reserves, all significantly closer (by 1 hour or more by road) to the Central Business District (CBD) than the two sanctuary sites (Blue Mountains and Mullawollen) ESL had purchased for later development. The issue of location is particularly significant when the time and budgetary constraints that many tourists operate under are taken into account. Related to this are the restrictions that location (and associated travelling time) can place on the capacity of day tour operators based in, or near, CBD locations to package product such as that of ESL's (Harris, 2001).

While competition was likely to have been a factor in ESL's successful entry into east-coast markets, the uniqueness of the ESL product, with visitors being able to experience rare, threatened and endangered wildlife in a natural setting, may well have provided it with a significant marketing edge. This 'edge', however, was unlikely to go unchallenged in the medium to long term. Already one sanctuary, Calga Springs, 1 hours drive north of Sydney, had employed a similar sanctuary development model to that used by ESL. This fully fenced feral free reserve opened to the public in March 2001 (Cohen, personal communication, 28 May 2001).

The success of ESL's east-coast strategy is also likely to have been affected by the need to 'bleed' off some of the profits it might have generated to maintain its existing sanctuaries, most of which were not open to the public. While ESL had begun to address this issue by placing some 'non-performing' sanctuaries up for sale in 2000 and 2001 (ESL, 2001a), such efforts may have been perceived by the market as too little and too late.

ESL's business strategy essentially involved the ownership of all its sanctuary sites, the exception being Hansen Bay on Kangaroo Island that it managed under contract (Arentino *et al.*, 2001). This being the case its growth was limited by its ability to attract new capital through the sale of shares, or its capacity to generate a profit from its operations, some of which could then be used for reinvestment purposes. A possible way around this limitation which was not explored by ESL is the business strategy of franchising. There would have been a number of potential benefits available to ESL through the employment of such an approach, including the ability to expand the number of its sites at a significantly faster rate than that which otherwise would be the case, and at minimum business risk. However, to engage in franchising, ESL would have needed to refine its business, animal management and visitor servicing systems to the point where they could easily be duplicated, with appropriate assistance from ESL, at new locations. Given that in New South Wales alone, an area one-third the size of the national park estate (approximately 500 000 hectares) is gazetted as private wildlife refuges (Cameron, 2002), the alternative of franchising may still be worth considering by a restructured ESL.

Conclusion

The conservation process is generally viewed as one that produces public rather than private benefits. ESL has sought to challenge this assumption with a business model that is dependent largely on tourism and that seeks to produce both conservation outcomes and financial returns to shareholders. The idea embodied in ESL has inspired investors to support its growth from a single 'outlet' operation in 1988 to an AU$20 million dollar-plus enterprise with ten locations some twelve years later. The 'well' of investors willing to support ESL in the absence of short- to medium-term financial returns would appear, however, to have been exhausted. ESL now finds itself in the position of not being able to implement its current five-year strategy of developing sanctuaries near east-coast population centres in order to grow its tourism revenue base, and of needing to restructure its operations dramatically simply to survive. This restructuring could well see ESL revert to a one or two sanctuary operation in the absence of a 'white knight' with a willingness to provide the AU$7 million or more required to allow it to continue its present strategy.

The central problem in ESL's case appears to have been the balance which it originally struck between its conservation and revenue generation goals and which were finally judged by the market place to be unacceptable. While ESL's assertion that tourism would eventually develop to the point where meaningful returns would be paid to shareholders might well have proven true in the longer term, the market was not willing to wait. ESL's initial strategy of locating sanctuaries in areas of high conservation value, but removed from major population centres, compounded the problem of generating acceptable returns from tourism. Its revised east-coast strategy, from the market's perspective, might also have been seen as having some level of risk associated with it given that meaningful levels of competition were present on the east coast from both private sector wildlife parks and national park services.

As ESL seeks to chart a revised course in order to shore up its short-term future, certain key lessons would appear evident. Given the severely constrained capacity of ESL to engage in the sale of endangered, rare or threatened wildlife, ESL's conservation agenda needed to be circum-scribed by its capacity to generate revenue, primarily from tourism. This being the case, ESL's ultimate goal of developing sanctuaries in all major habitat zones in Australia, while highly commendable, was unlikely to be achievable through a reliance on tourism. The visitation levels required to support the ESL sanctuary development process are realistically available only at certain locations. Acknowledgement of this can be found in ESL's somewhat belated decision to focus its attention on the development of east-coast sites from 1999, a decision which might reflect the change in its board at this time.

Whatever view is taken on ESL's current plight, it still must be acknowledged that this enterprise was the first with the stated goal of conservation to list on the Australian Stock Exchange, and to raise substantial funds by so doing. If ESL is successful in its restructuring efforts, the lessons it has learnt to date will likely see it strike a more pragmatic balance between conservation and the need for revenue, particularly from tourism. Such a balance will probably result in a revised, and less grand mission for the organization, particularly if it again seeks to own and operate its sanctuaries. As regards this last point, the possibility of franchising sanctuaries, a common business growth strategy in many sectors of the tourism industry, may offer ESL some prospect for longer-term growth. Given the large amount of private land already gazetted as wildlife refuges in states such as NSW, there may indeed be many John Wamleys ready and willing to take up the conservation challenge under ESL's leadership, and in a commercially responsible way.

Acknowledgements

I would like to thank Barry Cohen, Owner/Operator, Calga Sanctuary.

References

Arentino, B., Holland, P., Peterson, D. and Schuele M. (2001) *Creating Markets for Biodiversity: A Case Study of Earth Sanctuaries Ltd.* Productivity Commission.

Booth, M. (1999) Book Entry of 'a Living Asset', *The Advertiser*, Wednesday, October 20, p. 43.

Cameron, D. (2002) It was a wild idea, http://www.smh.com.au/news/0201/19/review/review12.html.

Cooke, G. (2001) Aussie Leader in Green Profits. *The Canberra Times*, Thursday, February 8, p. 10.

Earth Sanctuaries Limited (2002a) http://www.esl.com.au/awards.htm, accessed 28 January.

Earth Sanctuaries Limited (1997) *Prospectus*, 1 April–31 March.

Earth Sanctuaries Limited (1999) *Annual Report*.

Earth Sanctuaries Limited (2000a) *Annual Report*.

Earth Sanctuaries Limited (2000b) *There is a Way* (pamphlet).

Earth Sanctuaries Limited (2001) *Earth Sanctuaries News*, February.

Earth Sanctuaries Limited (2001a) *Annual Report*.

Earth Sanctuaries Limited (2002b) http://www.esl.com.au/media_restructure.htm, accessed January 28.

Earth Sanctuaries (no date) *Saving Australian Wildlife with Earth Sanctuaries* (Flyer).

Falkiners Stockbroking Ltd (2001) *Investment Report*, February.

Gray, F. (2002) Earth Sanctuaries Limited Selling It's Sanctuaries, www.abc.net.au/worldtoday/TWTChronoidx_Tuesday15January2002.htm.

Harris, R. (1999) Phillip Island Penguin Reserve: an example of industrialised sustainable tourism. *The Environment Paper Series* **2**(2), 33–8.

Harris, R. (2001) Tourism and Conservation: The Case of Earth Sanctuaries Limited. *The Environment Papers Series* **4**(2), 59–64.

Harris, R. and Leiper, N. (1995) *Sustainable Tourism: An Australian Perspective*. Butterworth-Heinemann, Sydney, pp. 3–10.

Hirshberg, C. (2000) A Kangaroo in Your Portfolio. *Life Magazine*, April, pp. 64–6.

Lowe, T. (1999) *Feral Future*. Viking, Ringwood, Victoria.

Manning, P. (2002) Ethical funds unscathed by Earth Sanctuaries failure. *Ethical Investor*, Jan. 16, www.ethicalinvestor.com.au.

McKercher, B. (1998) *The Business of Nature Based Tourism*, Hospitality Press, Melbourne.

Milne, C. (2000) Float Success Brings Growth. *The Adelaide Advertiser*, Saturday, April 15, p. 60.

Painter, J. (1998) How one man's mission turned ecology to profit. *The Age*, Thursday 3 September, p. 8 (Business section).

Reuters (2002) Australian Species in Peril as Savior Flounders http://asia.cnn.com/2002/WORLD/asiapcf/auspac/01/18/australia.savior/.

State of the Environment Advisory Council, Australia (1996) *State of the Environment*. CSIRO Publishing, Collingwood, Victoria.

Tourism Forecasting Council (Feb. 2001), *Forecast*.

Wamsley, J. (1996) Wildlife Management: The Work of Earth Sanctuaries, in Charters, T., Gabriel, M. and Prasser, S. (eds) *National Parks: Private Sectors Role*. USQ Press, Brisbane, pp. 156–64.

Selected organizations/programmes

Introduction

This section lists selected organizations and programmes which are acting to progress the goal of sustainable tourism development in one or more ways.

Business Enterprises for Sustainable Tourism (http://www.sustainabletravel.org/)

Business Enterprises for Sustainable Tourism (BEST) has a strong belief that 'tourism can benefit destinations by providing better livelihoods for residents, preserving the natural environment and celebrating local culture, and that tourism can even restore cherished cultural traditions and landscapes and enhance the quality of life in economically disadvantaged communities'. BEST was conceived as a way of making this 'vision' a reality. BEST's website outlines its programmes and activities (including think-tanks it has conducted on sustainable tourism); provides case studies; and describes (in general terms) sustainable practices for different types of tourism businesses.

Centre for Environmentally Responsible Tourism (http://www.c-e-r-t.org/)

The Centre for Environmentally Responsible Tourism (CERT) was established in 1994 as an independent membership organization with the goal of demonstrating how responsible tourism can protect the environment, wildlife and cultural aspects of holiday destinations. CERT seeks to show how travellers can play an important part in protecting the world's natural resources and in developing a sustainable future not only for destinations, but also for the travel industry. CERT involves the traveller, the travel industry, and conservationists in the achievement of its aims.

It's website contains information regarding its membership and award schemes, as well as its destination information packs (of which there are currently 189) that have been designed to educate travellers concerning how they can minimize their impact on destinations.

Centre for Tourism Policy and Research, Simon Fraser University, Vancouver (http://www.sfu.ca/~dossa/index.htm)

This Centre seeks to:

- provide a focal point for graduate level studies and professional development education with a distinctly integrated resource and business management orientation;
- encourage and conduct policy, planning and management research designed to enhance the effective and sustained use of the tourism resource base;
- facilitate the distribution of leading edge policy, planning and management information through the development and delivery of tourism seminars, workshops, conferences and publications; and
- provides access to a wide range of high quality tourism and recreation market databases.

The Centre's website acts as an on-line research tool for those interested in developing, sharing and disseminating knowledge concerning the creation of more sustainable forms of tourism development.

Cooperative Research Centre for Sustainable Tourism (http://www.crctourism.com.au)

The Cooperative Research Centre for Sustainable Tourism is an initiative of the Commonwealth Government of Australia in association with the Australian tourism industry, and selected Australian universities. Its mission is to: develop and manage intellectual property (IP) generated by cooperative research activities between universities, government and industry; deliver innovation to business, community and government; and to enhance the environmental, economic and social sustainability of tourism. Its website includes: brief summaries of its past and current research projects; links to related sites; a bookshop; and an on-line magazine.

ECoNETT (http://www.greenglobe.org/econett.htm)

In December 1995, the World Travel & Tourism Council and the European Commission undertook a joint project to develop an information network for tourism and the environment – ECoNETT – the European Community Network for Environmental Travel & Tourism. ECoNETT's goal is to increase overall awareness of sustainable travel and tourism, and in turn, stimulate changes in management practices in destinations and corporations to achieve sustainable travel and tourism development. This is being achieved by making information on good practice, codes of conduct (e.g., European Charter for Sustainable Tourism in Protected Areas, Africa Travel Association – Responsible Traveler Guidelines), activities of experts and organizations, etc., available through its website. Supporting this service is a regular newsletter, which is available on the net and by post.

Eco-Tip (http://www.eco-tip.org/)

Eco-Tip is a database run by ECOTRANS, the European network for sustainable tourism development. Eco-Tip provides examples of environmentally sustainable practices by tourism businesses and eco-labelling systems for tourism, as well as useful links and other services.

Ecotourism Association of Australia (http://www.ecotourism.org.au/)

The Ecotourism Association of Australia (EAA) was formed in 1991 as an incorporated non-profit organization, and is the peak national body for the ecotourism industry. The Association has approximately 500 members including ecotourism accommodation, tour and attraction operators; tourism planners; protected area managers; academics and students; tourism, environmental, interpretation and training consultants; and local and regional tourism associations. EAA's website contains details of its nature and ecotourism accreditation, and guide certification programmes.

Ecotourism Society (http://www.ecotourism.org/)

Individual membership-based organization. Services include listings of research studies conducted, a quarterly newsletter and an on-line bookshop.

ECOTRANS (http://www.ecotrans.org/)

ECOTRANS is a European network of experts and organizations in tourism, environment and regional development, which is seeking to promote good practice in the field of sustainable tourism. It was established in 1993 at the International Tourism Exchange ITB in Berlin. The name ECOTRANS embodies two basic principles: the link between ecology and economy, and the transfer and publication of know-how. Membership is drawn from non-governmental organizations and consultancies from nine European countries. ECOTRANS produces various publications, all of which are listed on its website.

End Child Prostitution in Asian Tourism (http://www.ecpat.net/)

ECPAT is a network of organizations and individuals working together for the elimination of child prostitution, child pornography and trafficking of children for sexual purposes. It seeks to encourage the world community to ensure that children everywhere enjoy their fundamental rights free from all forms of commercial sexual exploitation. A significant programme area for this organization is that of child sex tourism. The ECPAT website contains a number of downloadable reports/studies on this topic.

EQUATIONS (http://www.equitabletourism.org)

EQUATIONS is a non-profit organization based in India which was established to research and promote holistic tourism. It seeks to 'transform the inherently exploitative nature of mass commercial tourism', and 'question the real benefits of tourism to host communities'. EQUATION's website includes discussion papers on selected issues, and offers publications for sale.

European Environment Agency (http://themes.eea.eu.int/Sectors_and_activities/tourism)

The European Environment Agency (EEA) aims to support sustainable development and to help achieve significant and measurable improvements in Europe's environment through the provision of timely, targeted, relevant and reliable information to policy making agents and the public. Amongst the material on EEA's website is an indicator system for assessing tourism pressure on the environment. Various EEA reports on tourism are also available through its website.

Green Globe 21 (http://www.greenglobe.org)

Green Globe 21 was established by the World Travel and Tourism Council as a vehicle for developing environmental management and awareness in the Travel and Tourism industry, and to provide a practical means through which companies could act to improve their environmental performance. Its website contains an overview of its activities, along with case studies and membership criteria.

Indonesian Ecotourism Network (http://indecon.i2.co.id/)

The Indonesian Ecotourism Network (INDECON) was established in 1995 with the intent of promoting, developing and researching ecotourism in Indonesia. INDECON was an initiative of the Institute for Indonesia Tourism Studies (IITS) in association with the Bina Swadaya Foundation (BST) and Conservation International Indonesia Programme (CI-IP). The INDECON website contains details of selected tourism related conservation projects in Indonesia and discussion of the organization's achievements to date.

International Council for Local Environmental Initiatives (http://www.iclei.org/)

ICLEI is the international environmental agency for local governments. Its mission is to build and serve a worldwide movement of local governments to achieve tangible improvements in global environmental and sustainable development conditions through cumulative local actions. More than 350 cities, towns, counties, and their associations from around the world are full Members of the Council, with hundreds of additional local governments participating in specific ICLEI campaigns and projects. By performing a keyword search on 'tourism' it is possible to gain access to a comprehensive list of case studies, programmes and projects on local initiatives for sustainable tourism.

International Hotels Environment Initiative (http://www.ihei.org/csr/csrwebassist.nsf/content/f1c2a3b4.html#1)

The International Hotels Environment Initiative (IHEI) was established in 1992 by chief executives of the world's leading hotel groups, all aiming to bring about continuous improvement in the environmental performance of the global hotel industry. CEOs and senior executives from eleven international hotel chains form the Council of the IHEI, and provide leadership and funding. With the cooperation and active participation of hotels and related organizations around the world, the Initiative provides practical guidance for the industry on how to improve environmental performance, and how this contributes to successful business operations. The IHEI website overviews the Initiative and provides details of its various publications and programmes.

International Scientific Council for Island Development (http://www.insula.org/tourism/)

International Scientific Council for Island Development (INSULA) is an independent body that seeks to contribute to the economic, social and cultural progress of islands throughout the world, as well as to the protection of island environments and the development of their resources. Within such a context, INSULA aims to collaborate with any organization at the national, regional or international level sharing the same goals and interests. The INSULA website features a comprehensive summary of publications, conferences and initiatives contributing to the sustainability of tourism on islands.

Pacific Asia Travel Association (http://www.pata.org/)

The Pacific Asia Travel Association (PATA) provides marketing, research and educational opportunities to a membership of government tourist offices, airlines, hotels, travel agencies, tour operators and related companies. PATA's mission is to enhance the growth, value and quality of Pacific Asia travel and tourism for the benefit of its membership. This organization's website contains summaries of various conferences and reports it has held/commissioned regarding sustainable tourism. Additionally, it provides details regarding the activities (e.g., conferences, publications) of the PATA Office of the Environment and Culture that was established to continue PATA's role in progressing a sustainable tourism future. The APEC/PATA Code for sustainable tourism can also be found on this site.

Partners in Responsible Tourism (http://www.pirt.org/)

Partners in Responsible Tourism (PIRT) is a network of individuals and representatives of tourism companies who have a strong interest in adventure travel and ecotourism, and who are concerned about the impact of tourism and tourism development on local environments and cultures, particularly those of indigenous peoples. The PIRT website contains information on its various activities as well as a *Traveler's Code for Traveling Responsibly*.

Small Island Developing States Network (http://www.sidsnet.org/1d.html)

The Small Island Developing States Network (SIDSnet) was initiated in 1997 as a follow-up to the Barbados Programme of Action, the blueprint for the sustainable development of small islands. In addition to the specific web pages on tourism and small islands, SIDnet features, in concert with the United Nations International Year of Ecotourism, a series of successful examples of ecotourism practices in SIDS countries.

Tour Operators' Initiative for Sustainable Tourism Development (http://www.toinitiative.org)

Most tour operators recognize that a clean and safe environment is critical to their success. Fewer have the management tools or experience to design and conduct tours that minimize their negative environmental, social and economic impacts while optimizing their benefits. To develop and implement these tools in their own operations, and encourage other tour operators to do the same, a group of tour operators from different parts of the world joined forces to create the Tour Operators' Initiative for Sustainable Tourism Development (TOISTD). The Initiative is voluntary, non-profit, and open to all tour operators, regardless of their size and geographical location. The Initiative has been developed by tour operators for tour operators with the support of the United Nations Environment Programme (UNEP), the United Nations Educational, Scientific and Cultural Organization (UNESCO) and the World Tourism Organization (WTO/OMT), who are also full members of the Initiative. The TOISTD website includes case studies, tour operator sustainability indicators, and membership details.

Tourism Concern (http://www.tourismconcern.org.uk/frame.htm)

A UK-based charity set up in 1989 to bring together people concerned about tourism's impact on communities and the environment, both in the UK and worldwide. It seeks to raise awareness of tourism's impact for the general public, government decision-makers, and the tourist industry itself via such means as the various campaigns it conducts. Tourism Concern (TC) produces a number of publications including books, a magazine and a Community Tourism Directory, descriptions of which appear on its website. This site also provides TS's *Travelers Code*.

Tourism Watch (http://www.tourism-watch.de/)

The Church Development Service of the Protestant Church in Germany established Tourism Watch (TW) in 1975 as a worldwide Special Desk for Tourism. It is involved in training programmes and in solidarity initiatives surrounding the issue of 'Third-World' tourism, and it promotes socially and environmentally responsible developments in tourism. The website for TW contains a list of publications relating to socially/environmentally responsible tourism development, and an on-line newsletter.

United Nations Commission on Sustainable Development (http://www.un.org/esa/sustdev/report99/csd7report_en.htm)

United Nations Commission on Sustainable Development (CSD) was created in December 1992 to ensure effective follow-up of the United Nations Commission on the Environment; to monitor and report on implementation of the Earth Summit agreements at the local, national, regional and international levels. The CSD is a functional commission of the UN Economic and Social Council (ECOSOC), with fifty-three members. Decision 7/3 of the Seventh Session for the CSD (which can be accessed on-line) addresses the issue of the development and imple-mentation of strategies and policies for sustainable tourism based on Agenda 21.

United Nations Environment Programme – Tourism (http://www.uneptie.org/pc/tourism)

The United Nations Environment Programme (UNEP), established in 1972, works to encourage sustainable development through sound environmental practices everywhere. Its activities cover a wide range of issues, including sustainable tourism development. UNEP's goals in the tourism area are to: increase the benefits tourism can bring to sustainable use of natural resources, including biodiversity; reduce tourism-related degradation and pollution of natural resources, including biodiversity; facilitate cross-cultural learning and environmental education; and increase the quality of life of the people who live in tourism destinations through poverty alleviation, employment, and distribution of economic benefits, particularly in developing countries. Details of UNEP's tourism-related programmes, publications, conferences and initiatives can be found on its website.

World Tourism Organization (http://www.world-tourism.org/)

The World Tourism Organization (WTO) is the peak international tourism body in the field of travel and tourism. It serves as a global forum for tourism policy issues and a practical source of tourism know-how. The WTO's membership includes 139 countries and territories and more than 350 Affiliate Members representing local government, tourism associations and private sector companies, including airlines, hotel groups and tour operators.

The WTO has a significant involvement in, and commitment to, sustainable tourism development as is reflected in its many activities, programmes, initiatives and publications relating to the sustainability of the tourism industry. As regards the latter, its publications include: *Sustainable Tourism Development: Guide for Local Planners; What Tourism Managers Need to Know: Indicators of Sustainable Tourism;* and *Agenda 21 for the Travel and Tourism Industry.* Its website details its activities and programmes, and includes an on-line publication purchase facility. Also included on this site is the WTO's *Global Code of Ethics for Tourism.*

Index